IT'S TWELVE INCHES HIGH...

Compiled by

Tony Matthews
Perry Dyball
Brian Spurrell
Sue Melkman

Football Supporters Association

AND IT'S MADE OF SOLID GOLD

ISBN No : 0 9518587 0 X

Football Supporters Association (FSA), PO Box 11, Liverpool, L26 1XP
First Published by FSA 1991

Cover picture - Colorsport

In buying this book you have contributed to a struggle in which, for once, the whole of football is on the same side...
The fight against one of the least understood of diseases, Multiple Sclerosis.

Contents

Introduction

In April 1991, the London Branch of the FSA was approached by Bromley Clarke of ARMS (Action and Research for Multiple Sclerosis) with a request to participate in a large-scale football related charity project.

The concept of Football Against MS (FAMS) had been born, and Bromley was busy telling about his plans for the project.

"I know, we'll do a book!" was our reply. Oh yeah, only a book! We did have some expertise, if that's the right word, in writing fanzines. But a book - no.

Anyway, since we were planning a charity event of our own and looking for a suitable cause, we joined forces with ARMS.

Another of our ideas was to organise matches between fanzine teams. We had done that before...

Eagle Eye keeper Mathews puts on the style

NMTD and Eagle Eye captains exchange fanzines before the match

... On 30 December 1989, teams from "Eagle Eye" (Crystal Palace fanzine) and "Never Mind The Danger" (Norwich City fanzine) locked horns at the National Sports Centre a few hours before the Palace-Norwich match.

In a tense and hotly-contested match, the NMTD team, in fancy dress, opened strongly but their costumes proved to be quite a hindrance, and they spent most of the game in their own half defending resolutely against a strong Eagle Eye side playing in 1890s strip - well, rugby shirts and Bermuda shorts sprayed with black car paint! Long shorts were a shrewd move on the artificial surface...

The game ended 0-0 after NMTD's goalkeeper - or ghoulkeeper, as he was dressed as the Ghost of Christmas Past - pulled off two saves of Gordon Banks proportions. A penalty shoot-out followed. Best of three. Eagle Eye went first and after their 3 penalties the score was 1-1 leaving NMTD with a chance to grab the spoils with the final spot kick. They missed! So a final scoreline of 1-1. The prospect of a few pints was now more alluring than that of prolonging the agony.

We adjourned to The Goathouse, a fine hostelry, still in our rather unusual atire, where we quenched our thirst and collected cash from the rather bemused customers.

The NMTD team - Mark Forrester, Stephen Collins, Chris Dade, Perry Dyball, Jon Southgate, Simon Barker, Darren Keeble, Alan Thomas, Paul Read, Keith, Aidie and Max

An honourable draw, and - more to the point - the match and subsequent street collections at Selhurst and Carrow Road raised some £1400 for the two charities concerned, the Jenny Lind Children's Unit at the Norfolk & Norwich Hospital, and Capital Radio's Help a London Child appeal.

If anybody reading this fancies organising a similar game for FAMS, go ahead and do it - it's a good cause, and anything that brings rival fans together is both very worthwhile and great fun.

Anyway, back to the book. As we were more than familiar with fanzines we decided that a compilation of them would be the best bet. As part of the work the Football Supporters Association is doing for FAMS we polled every fanzine we could. Well, the list from "When Saturday Comes" to be precise, asking for a contribution.

For those of you that are still unaware of what fanzines are, here is a short explanation.

Fanzines are magazines written and produced by football supporters, which aim to provide a forum for discussion of issues affecting their club or football in general, and of course to entertain. The essential thing about them is that they are independent of the club whose fans they represent, and are thus free to criticise where necessary. This does not mean they are trying to harm the club's interests; rather, it shows they care for their club, for as the saying goes, "the opposite of love is not hate, but indifference".

Fanzines of various kinds have existed for decades, but perhaps the closest comparison to the football fanzine culture was the growth of "punk" fanzines in the late 70s. The link does not end there: many fanzine writers were inspired by this period, and one likened the first three issues of "When Saturday Comes" to the first three Sex Pistols singles in their effect on their generation. There were a handful of club-based fanzines before "WSC" and "Off The Ball" appeared in the spring of 1986, but these magazines' influence and the growth of the Football Supporters Association struck a chord with large numbers of supporters whom the traumatic events of the previous year had convinced of the need for an alternative voice. "Reclaim the Game" was the FSA's slogan, and within two years over 100 fanzines were doing just that.

The articles started to come in, slowly at first, but by mid October we had articles and cartoons from over 90 football fanzines written by and for supporters of clubs in all four divisions of the Football League, the Scottish League, Wales, and non-league clubs from all over Great Britain. As well as these we have guest appearances from the two most famous football cartoon strip characters ever, namely Roy of the Rovers and Billy the Fish.

Together they illustrate the ups and downs, highs and lows, laughs, frustration and joy of being a football supporter. People who have experienced life on the terraces and in the stands will find that these articles ring many a familiar note; for people who haven't, this is as good an introduction to the trials of being a football supporter as any.

We hope you enjoy this book, and remember, next time you take in a match, hunt out the fanzine - it's written by people who really care about football, and it should give you a laugh as well.

Tony, Perry, Brian and Sue

On The Ball In Westminster !

By Tom Pendry MP
Chairman : All-Party Parliamentary Football Committee

Where were you last year when you heard the result of the first Conservative leadership ballot between Margaret Thatcher and Michael Heseltine? It's a question to which most people can still give an exact answer, despite the passage of time. But a teasing addition to sports pub quizzes up and down the country might be "Where was Gary Lineker when he heard the result?"

Hard at work at Tottenham Hotspur's training ground? In discussion with Graham Taylor about England's prospects? Making a charity appearance? No, Gary was actually in Parliament itself, addressing a meeting of the All-Party Football Committee on the subject of "Football's Return to Europe, the Players' View"!

Indeed, it was Gary who first read out the ballot result to the numerous MPs who were assembled in the Commons Committee room to hear his entertaining talk. "Well, it looks like it's gone to extra time" he quipped. "If it's still level after the next round, don't ask me to take the penalty shoot-out!"

Gary was one of numerous football personalities and administrators invited last year to address the All-Party Parliamentary Football Committee, which was formed over a decade ago by myself and Jim Lester MP to bring together Members of Parliament to argue the case for football within the corridors of power in Whitehall and Westminster. Since then it has grown to be one of Parliament's largest backbench committees.

As an all-party group, the work that the Football Committee does within Parliament seldom makes the headlines, relying as we do on behind-the-scenes, consensual methods to achieve results rather than adopting the confrontational approach that all too often provides the sole fodder for newspaper journalists and editors.

Nevertheless, the outcome of our efforts through, for example, sending delegations to Government Ministers, submitting evidence to official Inquiries and marshalling arguments in Parliamentary debates, is there for all to see.

The most high profile victory was the defeat of the proposal for compulsory football Identity Cards. The Football Committee Officers met with Lord Justice Taylor during the course of his Inquiry and submitted evidence to him arguing strongly against the idea of ID cards.

HOUSE OF COMMONS
LONDON, SW1A 0AA

And although some might think that it was solely the contents of the Taylor Report that convinced the Government to abandon its scheme, the truth is that a major factor in their defeat was the reports coming to the Prime Minister from the Government whips who attended our meetings throughout the passage of the Football Spectators Bill that they could not deliver the votes of the Conservative members on the football committee for the cards.

Nevertheless, the ID card campaign, coming on top of the events at Heysel and Hillsborough, can now be seen as having played a very positive role in acting as a catalyst for good in football — not least of course in the rise of the Football Supporters Association itself and the continuing expansion of the alternative fanzine scene.

That positive role was never more conclusively demonstrated than in the coherent and impressive manner with which supporters' representatives gave evidence late last year to the Home Affairs Select Committee inquiry into 'Policing Football Hooliganism'. It will come as no surprise, I am sure, to those familiar with the Select Committee's welcome report that no less than three officers of the All-Party Football Committee were involved in writing it.

It is a shame that the Government's response to that report hasn't been as encouraging, refusing to back down from its threat to impose on clubs huge increases in policing costs, who have already seen these costs double since 1987-88. There can be little justification for this since football has shown itself willing and able to make its grounds safer places. Indeed figures recently released to me by the Home Office revealed that last season arrests at football matches fell by a remarkable 31% and ejections by 27%.

This provides an example of the positive work that is being carried out within football itself. Of course the launch of football against MS is another example. The use of football to provide backing for research into Multiple Sclerosis, shows clearly the potential benefits that can flow to both the game and the community when they work in harmony.

Supporters have demonstrated that they possess an as yet underdeveloped source of ideas and commitment within the game. It is high time they were brought into the higher echelons of football to make their contribution and develop the role that they have mapped out thus far. Football Supporters Against MS can only help their cause.

TOM PENDRY MP
CHAIRMAN: PARLIAMENTARY ALL-PARTY FOOTBALL COMMITTEE

SPOT THE BALL

Chelsea Vs Arsenal at Stamford Bridge
Saturday 2nd February 1991

Pitch: Firm. Arsenal playing right to left in light sleeves and shorts.
Weather: An area of high pressure, (1030 MB), over the North Sea giving generally fine, but cold conditions over much of southern England. A cold front moving into the south-west hints at possible wintery showers later. Temperature: max. +4 degrees centigrade, falling to nearer +2 by full-time.
Using your skill, judgement and a sound understanding of the new off-side laws place an 'X' (with a ball-point pen), where you believe the ball to be.

BRIAN MOORE'S HEAD

LOOKS UNCANNILY LIKE
LONDON PLANETARIUM

The main aim of Brian Moore's Head has always been to attempt to make people laugh. Not for us the serious line adopted by some other fanzines. You can't support a club like Gillingham and take it too seriously, not if you don't want to walk around in a permanent state of depression. That is not to say that we don't have a deep feeling for the club, it does hurt when the team fails. But, you've got to laugh haven't you.....

POLICE 5

HAVE YOU SEEN THIS MOUSTACHE?

THE SCENE OF THE CRIME

Gillingham's season was in tatters last night following the shock theft of manager Damien Richardson's moustache. Police are appealing for witnesses to the crime, which it is believed took place in Richardson's bathroom in the early hours of the morning. So far no clues have been found, and the police believe that the moustache may have been taken out of the country. However, they stress that if anyone has seen anything suspicious, or if you are offered a cheap moustache in the pub, please get in touch with your local police station. They are also appealing for members of the public to be on their guard against unscrupulous moustache thieves. Richardson's moustache is described as about one inch tall, and dark brown in colour. A reward has been offered for it's safe return.

PRINT CRAZY

* THE TALL ORIENTAL LOOKING PEOPLE WITH LONG HAIR XI

1/ HARVEY LIM

2/ ..erm..

3/ ..can't think of anyone else - sorry...

Claim to Fame:

A BMH editor has got an auntie who bought a house off the bloke who invented the flavours for 'Spangles'. Bloomin' impressive or what?

We had the police round just before Christmas investigating a theft from my Dad's car. When they'd finished and got up to leave I sensed a chance to get some revenge for the way football fans have been treated over the last few years. Sadly, just as I was about to ask the two officers to remain in their places in the living room for a couple of minutes whilst the front room was cleared of people, and then escorting them back to the station, I lost my bottle.

Mike Trusson re-lives his spectacular two-footed tackle seen in the game against Torquay United

SIGMA SQUARED

(and Lovell converted the tangent of the opposite over the hypotenuse)

- Or, British Party Politics and Gillingham F.C. since 1938, a statistical study.

It can have escaped few people's attention that, since Mrs Thatcher's resignation from office, Gills have not so much 'moved up a gear', as actually opened the garage doors and turned on the engine. So the questions on many people's lips are; do the John Major years hold the promise of better things to come? What lessons can be learnt from the past? And will Graham Garden ever stop smiling?

Firstly, to silence the critics who may already be thinking that this article is based on such flimsy evidence as that used in "Chariots of the Gods" by Eric Von Daniken, 'Flying saucers have landed' by George Adamski and 'Fly fishing' by J.R. Hartley, consider these facts. Gillingham have only ever won promotion in a year in which Labour has won a general election, and have been relegated under every Conservative administration since Stanley Baldwin (bar one). There, that has made you sit up and take notice hasn't it. Consider the facts in detail.

1938: The Conservatives are in government with Neville Chamberlain at number 10. There is a crisis in Munich and an even bigger one at Priestfield as Gillingham are booted out of the football league for being consistently crap (Rumours that their expulsion was part of the deal to appease Hitler which included the annexation of Sudatenland have never been proved).
1940: Churchill replaces Chamberlain. Gillingham languish in the Kent League. Hitler languishes in the bath with Eva Braun.
1945: General election at home and Labour win a shock victory. Clement Atlee moves into number 10 and Gillingham move up to the Southern League.
1950: Labour are wobbling, but hold onto power with a majority of 6. It is enough to secure Gillingham re-election to the Football League.
1951: Winnie is back (no, not Mandela, Churchill) and Gillingham are condemned to the doldrums for the rest of the decade, finishing 22nd no less than 4 times.
1955: In April Churchill retires, leaving the way clear for Gillingham to finish 4th, their best ever. Sir Anthony Eden succeeds him, and wins a snap election with an increased majority.
1956: Racked with remorse over Suez and Gills failure to win promotion to the second division in 1955-56 Eden resigns, MacMillan takes over.
1958: Gillingham are transferred to the fourth division, sowing the seeds of the Profumo scandal.

1963: Alec Douglas Home renounces his peerage and his season ticket to Leyton Orient to allow him to take over from MacMillan, retiring because of ill-health.
1964: Labour, under Harold Wilson, topple the Conservatives with a small overall majority, but it is enough to send Gillingham up to division three as champions by a similarly tight margin over Carlisle.
1966: Wilson increases his majority in Labour's second consecutive general election win and Gillingham go close to promotion to the second division.
1970: Contrary to all the opinion polls, the Conservatives under Edward Heath beat Labour. Ted the Teeth takes power, and Gills take a nose-dive back into the fourth division the following year.

1974: The miners are striking, and so are the Gills front-line, so frequently in fact that Brian Yeo is the Football League's top scorer. Heath is thrown into a panic and goes to the country on March 1st. Although securing no overall majority, Labour's lead over the Conservatives is enough to ensure that their leader Harold Wilson becomes Prime Minister and the following month Gillingham are promoted back to division three.

1979: April 28th - Gillingham are on the verge of promotion to division two for the first time. Rivals Shrewsbury are beaten by two late Ken Price goals at Priestfield. Surely nothing can stop them now? May 3rd - general election. Thatcher is in and so is the Gills luck. Two days later they are beaten at Swindon in slightly acrimonious circumstances (so much for harmony where there is discord). The following week they are held to a draw at Colchester after being 2-0 up. The dream is over.
1980's: Near misses in the middle of the decade, including a play-off replay against Swindon, but history is against them. Finally the inevitable, relegation under every Conservative administration since Stanley Baldwin (except one) and it happens in 1989. Spooky isn't it?

- John Cole

THE KELVIN MORTON PUZZLE PAGE

OKAY KIDS, PUT YOUR CONTACT LENSES IN AND GET OUT YOUR THINKING CAPS COS IT'S THE...

MIND STRANGLER 1: - DON'T PANIC! WE'RE STRAINING OFF OUR POWERS OF OBSER-VATION AND CAN YOU TELL WHICH OF THE FOLLOWING OBJECTS IS <u>NOT</u> A FOOTBALL?

A) CHEESE
B) ARCHBISHOP OF CANTERBURY
C) EINSTEIN'S THEORY OF RELATIVITY $E=mc^2$
D) JUPITER
E) R. WELLS, LONDON

NO, I AM NOT A BLEEDIN' FOOTBALL!

MIND STRANGLER 2: - UH OH! SOMETHIN' MIGHTY UNFRIENDLY IS GOING ON MIDFIELD. BUT KELV HAS YET TO NOTICE! QUICK! HELP HIM FIND HIS WAY THROUGH THE MAZE...

WHERE AM I?

HUH! HUH! TACKLE THIS GOLDEN BOY

UH, DON'T FEEL TOO GOOD.

MIND STRANGLER 3: - OH DEAR! THE MATCH IS ABOUT TO START. CAN YOU SPOT THE POTENTIAL TROUBLEMAKER?

AHA! A HUGE GAP IN THEIR DEFENCE!

YOUR WEAPONS ARE USELESS, EARTH-SCUM

KILL! KILL! KILL!

HATE

I NEED TO TASTE HUMAN MEAT!

MIND STRANGLER 4: - THIS OBJECT HAS BEEN PUZZLING KELVIN FOR SOME TIME. CAN YOU HELP HIM BY JOINING THE DOTS TO LEARN WHAT IT IS. WE HAVE INCLUDED A GRID TO HELP:
CORRECT SEQUENCE 1,2,3.

MIND STRANGLER 5: - OUR TYPESETTER HAS CLEVERLY LEFT A CRUCIAL LETTER OUT OF THIS WORD AND KELVIN WILL NEED IT SOON! QUICK, TAKE A LETTER FROM THE BOX ON THE LEFT TO COMPLETE IT, BEFORE KELVIN NEEDS TO USE THE WORD.

E E E E E E E E

"FR_E KICK" WE'RE GO!

WOOF! WOOF!

FANS   CLUE

MIND STRANGLER 6: - "WHERE THE F*** IS MY LABRADOR GOT TO?" EXCLAIMS KELVIN. CAN YOU HELP HIM FIND IT? MARK A CROSS ON THE PITCH WHERE YOU THINK IT IS.

ANSWERS: 1- SHEFFIELD WEDNESDAY, 1967. 2- YES, IT WAS TWO MINUTES INTO INJURY TIME. 3- BECAUSE HE LOOKS FUNNY AND HIS EYES ARE TOO CLOSE TOGETHER. 4- NO, THE VIKING SPACE PROBE FOUND NO EVIDENCE OF LIFE ON MARS. 5- "BETTER UNDER THE TABLE THAN UNDER THE GROUND." - H.P. LOVECRAFT. 6- ZELDA FIRST APPEARED IN ISSUE #7 OF THE UNCANNY X-MEN, WHICH WAS PUBLISHED BY MARVEL COMICS IN SEPTEMBER 1711.

This week in 990 A.D. Innoff the Post, (the Heligoland inter-national), returning from a three week lay-off due to plague, was the inspiration behind New Brompton's 2-0 win at Wessex League champions Silbury Hill. Scoring the first with a volley from 60 cubits out and setting up the second for Edmund Heritage the Hairy, Innoff was also lucky enough to carry off the man of the match award, (a comely wench from nearby Glastonbury). The First teams mid-week league fixture was called off due to dysentry at Strood, (some things don't change). However, the reserves match at Sheppey United went ahead despite the team arriving late due to a chariot-jam on Watling Street and an attack by Vikings on the ferry from Sitting-bourne.

In fading light, Brompton came back from being twice behind to win 3-2. Returning supporters unfortunately clashed at Newington with a party of Jutes returning from a match at Reculver Athletic, the Away Travel club's cart was overturned and several geese escaped. The driver of the cart was also later charged with being two flagons of mead over the limit.

Brompton finished the week preparing for the visit of the Angles from Colchester Garrison, who were expected to be at full strength with the return of several players who had been on international duty during the week, including Canute the Sheep-worrier, star of Northumbria's 2-1 win in Lower Saxony. He had made it back home in time to be selected in spite of the Long-boat workers strike.

.Cecil Goat-Fancier goes close against Silbury Hill

IT'S A BOY MRS. MORTON!

KELVIN-THE EARLY DAYS

Follow the Gills

TO THE PLANET SATURN	Saturday 1st December	
Admission Prices:	Titan Gaseous Stand	6.83 Zargs
	Hyperion View Terrace	5.17 Zargs
	Matchday micro-wrist-computer satellite update	75 Zoati

Matchday Suggested Route: A2/M2 to the M25. Travel through the Dartford Tunnel and then accelerate into low Earth orbit. Once over China increase speed to escape velocity overcoming Earth's gravitational pull and swing round the Moon. Fly-past Mars, turning left at Phobos. Navigate the asteroid belt and cross Jupiter's orbit, passing the leading Trojan group to your right. On arriving at Saturn, pass under the ring-plane and the ground is on your left. Ample parking.
Mileage: 786 million miles. Travelling time: 4 years (approx).

GFC Away travel will be organising a coach, departing 8.30am, fare £12.00

ARTHUR VOLE ~ HE FEIGNS DISINTEREST WHEN HIS TEAM SCORE A GOAL! BY OSCAR WILDE

SID! YOU'RE!

THANKS JIM!

FLIP!

I NEVER REALISED THERE WERE SO MANY HARMFUL ADDITIVES!

CORN FLAKES

THE IBROX HAMILIATION

A Hamilton Accies fan recalls how eleven heroes in Red & White hoops conquered Rangers in the 1987 Scottish Cup, 3rd. Round. and made Greame Souness feel as sick as a dead parrot!

The Date: Sunday Feb. 1st. 1987

The Time: 9:00am

Archie awoke suddenly, bolt upright, his mind racing. He'd just had the most wonderful, pleasurable dream imaginable, and amazingly, Linda Lusardi hadn't been in it. "Hang on a minute?" he thought, "was it a dream?".

The images had seemed so vivid; crystal clear in fact. He went downstairs, still unsure. It had certainly seemed real enough. Then he saw the newspaper headlines: "Humiliation". "Shockers". "Gardener Marries Cabbage" (that stupid paper boy's delivered the Sunday Sport to the wrong house again!).

"Am I still dreaming?" Archie thought to himself. No! It was all flooding back to him - the greatest day of his life! He diligently read the reports. It seemed plastic surgery would be required to remove his smile. His Dad, a Rangers fan, was putting a brave face on it, trying to pretend he was glad for Accies, but his son knew differently. All over Scotland at that moment, thousands of bluenoses were waking up, feeling the complete reverse of how he had felt. "Naa, it never happened, it wiz jist a nightmare. Let's see ra paper - AAAARRRGGHHH!!!"

Archie cast his mind back to the previous day's events. He remembered squirming in his seat as "Fergie" (Hamilton's infamous terrace Mouth) shouted "Rangers are oot! Rangers are oot!" half an hour before the game even started. Also, the feeling of inferiority, looking around the vast arena that is Ibrox, embarassed that we could only bring a few hundred fans. He recalled the frightening sensation as the Rangers team was read out.

As the game got underway, Archie slumped back in his seat and waited for the inevitable first goal... and waited... and waited.

"Hey", he thought as the half time whistle blew, "we're doing OK!". Sure, it was all one way traffic, but Dave McKellar was gathering cross after cross, and putting the occassional great save into the bargain. In defence, McKee, Collins and Fulton were outstanding. Our luck seemed to be in. Maybe we'll just lose 1-0, or even scrape a draw. The gubbing that he'd expected certainly wasn't going to happen.

The second half started with more Rangers domination, but it was all to no avail. The natives were certainly getting restless, as chance after chance went abegging. McKellar pulled off a miraculous save from a Sally McCoist header, and a Fleck lob went past.

Then it happened. The goal that made 35,000 people soil their underwear.

Did it really go in? Archie, unsure of the answer to this question, rose from his seat like someone with cramp getting off the toilet. He looked around himself, expecting to see stunned, disbelieving faces. But no! Everyone was cheering and clapping and jumping up and down like Zebedees!

It was certainly happening alright. Archie realised he should just sit back and enjoy the final 20 minutes. He replayed Sprott's goal over and over in his head, trying frantically to remember the build up. All he could recollect was the stunned realisation that Aiders only had Woods to beat, and the way the ball nestled snugly into the net.

OHMYGODWHATASAVE!!! Archie was brought back into the land of the living by a majestic leap from McKellar, turning over a Colin West bullet header. How long could this man defy, almost single-handedly, the Rangers attack?

Suddenly, Accies went on another attack, (OK their second)! Amazingly, Gerry Collins found himself within gobbing distance of Chris Woods, but somehow failed to score.

Being a pessimistic sort, Archie expected Rangers would now waltz up the park and equalise. A cacophony of sound greeted Rangers' every attack, with legions of Teddy Bears staring coronaries in the face. The final few minutes seemed to last for ever, and Archie was sure somebody was tampering with the scoreboard clock.

At last, Mr. Jim McCluskey decided that was that, and 400 or so Accies fans went mad. Albert Craig had just mounted Dave McKellar, and Gerry Collins was punching big holes in the Govan air. Accies had done the impossible, the improbable and the implausible, AND they did it with Ally Brazil in the team.

Meanwhile, back to the Sunday morning, and Archie was re-reading the reports for the 5th time... just to be sure you understand.

Crying Time Again
A **Hamilton Academical** Fanzine

To settle all those pub arguments and bets: There is not (and never has been) a letter "s" at the end of the name "Academical"!

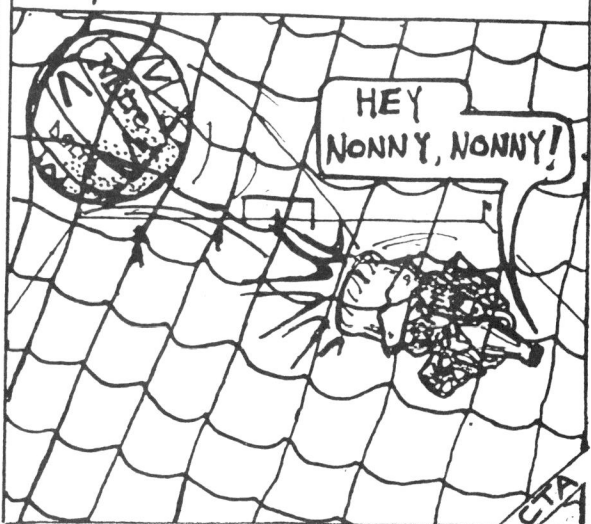

PoP GoEs FoOtY!

THE EXPRESSION SHE PULLED FANZINE TAKES A CRITICAL LOOK AT FOOTBALL AND IT'S EFFECTS ON THE BRITISH MUSIC SCENE...

Ever gazed around the terraces at half time to inspect what the bloke next to you is wearing, have you ever spent the tedious task of wading through all those over priced club tops (early Crimbo Pressies), those highly original, 'these colours don't run' (I think you'll find they do for five quid a go!), Those tacky 'I love Vinny' T-shirts to find out what other wonderful 'advertisements' are lamented all over the chests of your mysterious object of desire(?)

Here at Elland Road, you get a good cross section. There are the boys, who are sussed and wear the right T-shirts with the right kind of bands on display (except the EMF ones of course!).
There are the girls, not very sussed wearing yucky 'Wacko Jacko' T-shirts and only in the crowd to woe at Gary Speed's legs.
And then there are the Dire Straits fans! Life must be full of excitement for these people (especially if they support Charlton Athletic as well!), But do not fear they'll have that lovely (colourful?) Black T-shirt on everyday, with the tour dates splashed all over the joint, he sticks his chest out with unashamed pride (the bloke actually went to one of these gigs! Have you ever bothered to try and guess which one he actually went to?).

Here in Leeds, the footy/music crossover was at it's most fashionable in 1989, while the Vinny Jones T-shirts were becoming big business amongst the hard of thinking, lads in

Leeds wear found to be proudly wearing T-shirts from bands who had not yet, really made a huge impact elsewhere in the country such as the Stone Roses, James, Happy Mondays and The Farm.

Many of these bands have been tagged by the music press as "footy bands" especially the likes of Scousers The Farm, self confessed Liverpool supporters the music press has always heralded them as a band that came straight from the terraces.

Although they have tried to eagerly rid themselves of the tag, they have in the past played on this image, from the days when lead singer Peter Hooton used to be found wandering the streets on matchdays selling his now seminal fanzine "the End" and the band using "Kop" samples, as side affects, during songs in their old live set.

The early nineties shows there is a definite Happy Mondays influence on the terraces, even though the band hardly went to a match in their lives their popular 'seedy' attitudes and 'casual' dress sense has spread through the terraces on a huge scale, oh and drummer Gaz Whelan nearly became a footballer but dropped his balls and picked up the sticks instead (Oo-er!).

The football/music crossover has reached it's celebratory heights when Elland Road staged an event that attracted somebody from nearly every club in England and Scotland?, It wasn't a football match, it was a pop concert. The Happy Mondays brought everybody together to a venue that has fittingly nurtured the flavours and style of the band and the influence can be seen week in, week out on the terraces.

On a local level, the meteoric rise of Leeds United under the fresh guidance of Sergeant Wilko, has earned Leeds fans a varied reputation around the land and this may all prove a celebration on our home turf, but it hasn't been met with as much appreciation at other venues for obvious reasons. Six lads that have come from the terraces (and left them behind) are Leeds band the Bridewell Taxis, their success on the independent scene has closely matched the rise of their local football team. The fans they attract have proved to be very much 'football orientated' as many a song has been drowned out by the chants of "we are Leeds" and delirious stage invasions have occurred at many home town gigs.

But the band have found to their cost such a following does not improve your chances of getting bigger elsewhere, and the reputation they have elsewhere in the country has prevented them getting the success they deserve. A football fan seems to carry some peculiar notion that his team are one day gonna overthrow the Queen (cherish the thought) and rule the country, but with an average support of 15,000 people (for most clubs), its hardly enough to make such a serious impact on the state of the world. Once this barrier has been broken, once people's prejudice to regionalism looses all its subdued seriousness the British music scene will prosper.

In some ways, footy and music may work, look at the excellent England World Cup record with New Order but many a time it doesn't look at all the other crap football records that have come out!

Regionalism, is a dangerous thing, the football fanzine world does show a change in trends and seems to promote a "tongue in cheek" attitude towards regionalism. Thus cutting out the 'ugly' effects of hooliganism. The music scene stubbornly boasts too much about it's home grown product. By attaching it to a set of football supporters only limits the band's appeal. When asked if the music/footy crossover has any relevance at all ask yourself this question,

"Would the Beatles have swopped their placed in the musical history books for four Liverpool season tickets?"

I doubt it very much!

Mud,Sweat & Beers.

THE WATFORD F.C. FANZINE.

" WATFORD A STOP-GAP? " - by GARY PARKINS
                               Co-Editor
                          " Mud, Sweat and Beers" - WATFORD FANZINE

* *

Like a lot of clubs in the Football League, my team Watford FC can be the butt of many jokes. In our supposed "kick and rush days", we had all of the old Wimbledon gags, like the local air traffic controllers being warned when we were playing. Ha,ha! So unfunny that Jimmy Tarbuck wants to use it in his next stage scripts. I remember the bad old days of Fourth Division obscurity when we warranted ridicule even ahead of the Southports and the Workington Town's of this world. In 1975, if the Bay City Rollers weren't about then Watford took the biscuit. Vicarage Road - the greyhound stadium that had footy matches some Saturday afternoons!

However, it's bad enough that other football fans extract the urine out of one's beloved. Worse still when it's your old players who are having the laugh at your expense. " What am I getting at?", you may ask. I am sure that every player who dons a Watford jersey gives his unadulterated one hundred and ten percent effort, but my point is this. Why do so many players seem to achieve so much in their careers AFTER leaving Vicarage Road?

Of course there have been some wonderfulplayers at Watford who became integral pieces of Watford folklore such as Ian Bolton and Les Taylor. Other stalwarts such as Duncan Welbourne, Kenny Jackett, Nigel Gibbs and Lu-ther " Boomerang " Blissett have enjoyed phenominal success throughout their time at Watford. But when I look at the talented footballers that have come and gone onto better things, it's almost enough to make my bloodshot eyes cry.

It's a fact that often mediocre players can become superstars when they sign for Liverpool. If only that was true at Watford! Just look at our JOHN BARNES, an Anfield snip at £900,000, must be the bargain of the century. True he was out of contract but went on to become the best player in the British Isles. The list is endless: Pat Jennings, Tony Currie, Mo Johnston,etc. Jennings was a mere raw Irish protege in the 60's when he began his career at Watford. Before long, he was off Spurs way and onto over 100 caps for Northern Ireland.

The Sixties seemed to have started the talent exodus from the then only Hertfordshire league club. One of the most gifted players ever began with Watford, being Tony Currie. This maestro of the midfield gained England caps after kissing and playing his way past opponents in the colours of Leeds and Sheffield United. Others like Keith Eddy, Colin Franks and Stewart Scullion joined the gravy train to Bramall Lane as more talent wilted away to the benefit of other clubs.

I know it's difficult for smaller clubs like ourselves to hold onto talented players, but for the loyal fans it is still a bitter pill to swallow. In 1984 Mo Johnston, the best goalscorer I've ever seen in a Watford shirt, was sold to Celtic for a pitiful £400,000. Mo went on to score lots of goals for Nantes, Rangers and Scotland. Graham Taylor is a great manager but his main error at Watford was how he sold players too cheaply. Fees for Johnston, Barnes and Nigel Callaghan (a travesty of justice at £ 275,000 for Derby's joy) are living testimony to that policy.

Kevin Richardson arrived From Everton with more medals than General de Gaulle and used his midfield talent to good effect. So good that Bassett let him sign for Arsenal in 1987 for £200,000. Where was the missing nought? He went on to become one of the few players to win TWO Championship medals with different clubs. The instigation of the sale of 'Our Kev' and David Bardsley to Oxford helped catapult Watford to the Second Division in 1987-88. We have been here ever since! The only time we got more for a player than expected was the cash Huddersfield Town paid for Iwan Roberts in 1989.

The breaking up of Watford's solid First Division base was sad while it recouped unsatisfactory revenue in the process. In recent seasons both Oldham Athletic and Norwich City have benefitted from Hornet bargain buys. Malcolm Allen and Tim Sherwood both went to Carrow Road with youth, promise and fees of £175,000. Both doubled their values within a season. While Neil Redfearn and Rick Holden became integral parts of Oldham's promotion winning side to the top flight in 1991. To keep the trend going, Dean Holdsworth is banging home ample goalage at Brentford. Need I go on?

To be fair, Watford have a great youth policy which keeps nutruring the likes of David James, Rod Thomas and Jason Drysdale through to the first team. We also have had players signed from other clubs that have played their best football of their careers at Watford like Sims, Taylor and Joslyn to name but a few. It's just that the scales are so unevenly unbalanced. Perhaps there is not a lot we can do about it with freedom of contract, huge wage differences and busybody agents. Football is too much of a private monopoly nowadays, and that is sad. Too many rich fingers in too many pies. The wonderment of football is the unexpected, the Wimbledons of this world beating the big boys,the giant killings in the FA Cup and so on. Monopolism generates boredom when the ordinary clubs can no longer compete with the Liverpools and the Arsenals.

As a committed Watford fan, I do hope the glory days of the late70's and the early 80's return, but not at all costs. It does seem that this season, 1991-92 will be the last of the Football League in it's present format. What is sad is it's the masses that will suffer for the benefit of the priveleged few. A recipe for long-term disaster if ever there was one.

GARY PARKINS.

JOIN THE DOTS TO FIND AN ASSENAL AND ENGLAND DEFENDER?

TINY CLUE ; HEE-AW-HEE-AW-HEE ALWAYS CALLS HIMSELF TONY ADAMS.

DЯIBBLE!

THE IPSWICH FANZINE

ONLY A FOOTBALL MATCH

It was our first year in Europe, if you disregard the modest flirtation
with European football in the early sixties. The season was 1973/74 the
same season that "the Beat" was to be the P.F.A. Young player of the year,
we were to finish fourth in the league and Leeds were going to finish well
top.

In the U.E.F.A Cup we had shocked the world by knocking out Real Madrid.
We had then beaten the assassins of Lazio and the more aristocratic Twente
Enschede before fate pitted us against Lokomotive Liepzig, as dour a team
as the name suggests. But beatable, definitely beatable. I know I thought
I'll go ---- to East Germany. Never been to a Communist country, never
seen the boys in Europe ---- why not. So pre first leg, which was at home,
I bought my first ever full passport, got permission from the boss and
booked the trip.

On March 20th a small band of Town Devotees + the courier + the now late
and lamented Peter Jones of BBC Radio flew out from Stansted to the uncharted
East. I was nervous. Not out of worry that we would not hold on to the
one goal lead the aforementioned "Beat" had given us, but because this
was my first plane trip (A fogbound airport and two attempts to take off
were no help). However, a few hours and one miserable customs man later,
I was settled into my pleasant room at the hotel Stad Leipzig, and one
hour after that we were on the way to the ground, and the formality of
winning through to the next round.

There was no away end at the stadium but that mattered not because most
of the seats were in the open anyway, and as this was pre segregation Leipzig
and Ipswich fans mixed freely. These were East Germans so they hadn't
heard of pinching the best seats or pushing in at the hot dog queues.
To be honest the game itself was going through a forgettable stage when
just before half time it livened up. There was this German forward
writhing in agony as only German forwards can. The crowd booed and whistled
and bayed for blood. Those that didn't were taken out and shot. The
referee, a Spaniard, reached for his pocket. Out came a hankerchief, a
food token, his sunglasses in case of a quick getaway, his lover's phone
number and finally the red card. Off trooped Millsy. "That's a blow",
thought I. The blow turned into a gale just after half time when they
scored with waht was to be fair, a great header. All square, but how we
fought. They never again looked like scoring and 5 minutes from the end
Talbot hit the bar. Hit the bar, the goal keeper never even smelt it.
Through extra time we gave as good as we got but there came no further
goals. Another first now loomed, penalties. Even pre Pearce and Waddle
these were pretty nerve racking occasions. After the first 5 pens it was
3 each, Johnson and Morris missing but Swivell saving 2 of theirs. So
sudden death it was. They scored so it was left to Big Al to keep us in
it. Robson later described his performance as "the best he'd seen from
a centre half", and honestly Robson was right. Big Al had been brilliant
Allard would use up a whole page describing it. But ....

The Germans went mad, those that didn't were taken out and shot. The Town players stood around stunned. Millsy sat there like a Hamlet advert only without the cigar and music. Me? well the phrase "sick as a parrot" springs to mind. Not half as sick as Hunter felt though. as you can imagine celebrations after the game were somewhat muted, and it had been a long day after all. Consequently I don't think many woke the next morning the worse the wear for drink. At breakfast phrases like "it's only a Mickey Mouse trophy anyway" and "now we can concentrate on the league" were being thrown about before the whole party embarked on a coach tour of Colditz the town, visiting a school, a factory, a block of flats and the castle once a POW camp now a mental hospital. Our series of mounting misfortunes were to follow us with a puncture on the return to Leipzig. I was by now getting the impression, what with all that had happened since yesterday, that my decision to come had been a hasty one.

Neither had the misfortunes finished. Homeward bound the plane was literally 2 inches from a fogbound Stansted, when the pilot chickened out and instead landed at Heathrow leaving us to find our own way back to Ipswich. This at Midnight you understand. Some went to Stansted on a hastily arranged coach, I headed for London and the comfort and solace of a flat belonging to some nurse friends of mine. "Did you have a nice time", they enquired caringly, and so I relayed to them my adventure, regaling them with stories of heroism (Hunter), stupidity (Mills) and disappointment (Talbot), sharing with them the emotion of losing on penalties. "Never mind it's only a footbal match", they replied. Sometimes I just don't understand women at all.

Ipswich did get to win the UEFA Cup in the end: John Wark v. Alkmaar '81.

FUN PAGE!

(about as fun as running out of toilet paper)

another extract from:

JOHN WARK'S TACKLING TEXTBOOK

sponsored by TCP

---

improve your own soccer skills with......

TIPS FROM THE TEAM

#1 Frank Yallop:

"When clearing the ball from defence or passing back to the goalkeeper try not to pass the ball to a player from the opposite team."

Thanks Frank!

#32 The Wedding Tackle.

#33 The Fishing Tackle.

and remember:
always keep your eye on the ball.

It's **The Portman Posse!** D.Thomas (art) B.Mehen (story)

YOU TWO COULDN'T SCORE IN A **BROTHEL** ..... YOU'D BOTH BETTER WORK ON YOUR **FINISHING!**

OK BOSS!

HEY CHRIS, **LOOK AT THIS!**

STAR SPORT

NORWICH LOSE AGAIN! 17-0 DEFEAT!

COME TO OUR **FINISHING SCHOOL**

IPS. 9 262 9242

© 1991

LATER THAT DAY.

HOW NOW BROWN COW...... ...THE RAIN IN SPAIN FALLS MAINLY ON THE PLAIN... ...etc...... ...etc...

FISONS

end

THINGS THAT MAKE YOU GO HMMM.

A GAME OF CARDS IN BERGAMO 7-10-90

Partick Thistle's 'Johnny Flood Experience' savours the delights of Italian football ...

Thanks to B.S.B. and Clyde Cable we can view an Italian first division game live each Sunday afternoon chez nous. Today it's Atalanta versus Inter Milan. Atalanta come from Bergamo, a large town about thirty miles to the north of Milan, close enough to make it a local derby. The Scottish equivalent would be Motherwell versus Celtic at Fir Park.

On paper it looks a cracking game. It always does in Italy where even the wee teams have two or three international stars. It was dead handy, so it was, having the last World Cup there because that's where all the players are. Inter depend on the German connection with Brehme, Matthaus and Klinsmann. To help out, if things become difficult, they also have Italian internationalists Zenga, Berti, Ferri, Bergomi and Serena. By comparison the home team are a bit poverty row, although they do have the Brazilian Evair, the Swede Stromberg and the Argentinian Caniggia. Unfortunately the latter's not playing today.

It's raining and Trevor Francis, who's doing the inter-foul comments, remarks cleverly that this is unusual in Italy. We're also told that Atalanta play in 'a tight little stadium which has a great atmosphere'. This apparently means, in Italian terms, that it doesn't have an Olympic standard athletics track round it and it only holds 30,000.

The game begins. Forty five minutes later we return to a bemused-looking Andy Gray in the B.S.B. studio. We haven't exactly had the cracking first half promised us. We've had 4 yellow cards, no goals, no shots at goal and, if Lothar Matthaus <u>was</u> playing, he's better at hiding than Lord Lucan ever was.

But Trev to the rescue... He tells us what it's <u>really</u> about: "Klinsmann will be looking to get him sent off," he remarks after Contrato, an Atalantan defender, is yellow-carded. "Surely not!" exclaims the commentator, who plays naive recipient of Trev's cynical insights. "Oh, yes," says Trev, "he will." And indeed Jurgen goes into his death agonies every time an Atalanta player comes near him and sometimes when they are quite distant.

The second half is better. For a start there's a goal for Atalanta in 50 minutes. A gem of a header by Evair from a cross by Nicolini. The Inter keeper, Zenga, apparently never admits to fallibility. He's like the Pope in that respect. He and Bergomi have a 'discussion' about this as Atalanta celebrate.

The card-game continues. Ferri and Bianci of Inter receive yellows. Will they twist with another foul and burst themselves with a red? Bilardo of Atalanta does exactly that and departs the scene. Someone has hurled a huge smoke-flare onto the pitch which imparts an appropriate World War One atmosphere to the proceedings.

Meanwhile the game approaches its climax. Just on the ninety minute mark the referee awards Inter a penalty for a foul on Berti. It took me two action replays to spot the offence, but sure enough, on third viewing, it was plain that Pasciulio of Atalanta had tried to remove Berti's shorts. Strictly in the line of duty, of course.

The home crowd don't like the decision. They suggest, volubly, that the referee is on Inter's pay-roll. Pasciulio doesn't like the decision either and is red-carded. Just to even things up Berti is red-carded as well, Matthaus converts the penalty - about the only thing he's done all afternoon.

We return to the studio. "Well, Andy," says the B.S.B. anchor-man, "it certainly livened up in the second half." Andy nods, bemused-looking.

Prime Minister John Major in July of this year launched the Citizen's Charter (notice the apostrophe which denotes only one citizen) with a blaze of publicity. Although blurring the distinction between government policy and party propaganda the underlying theme was that there was a cost-effective way of improving services, which was to set targets and not provide the necessary financial investment. We at FNK appreciate the shortage of money facing many of our league clubs (see the back page financial exclusive) and are proud to offer the Football Charter which brings to football the ethos of the Citizen's Charter.

NAME TAGS

Refs and players are to wear sponsored name tags. This will bring an end to the tiresome mistakes that football commentators make, where they tell you the name of the player when you can quite clearly see it is someone else, and the banal 'number 9 passes to number 7 who in turn is tackled by number 3 for Norwich'. Referees will have to wear their name tags both on and off the pitch so they can be identified easily, and will help you to complete your Ref Spotting Guide. Great fun for the kids.

PRIVATISATION OF PLAYERS

How often have you bemoaned the performance of a player and felt frustrated because there was nothing you could do about it? Well now you can hold a stake in your favourite player. Introducing players to the free market where making a profit is essential will provide the necessary spur to improve performance in order to gain that bonus pay offered by the manager or a place on the transfer list with the prospect of a nice financial cut.

For the fans the stock market will not be a totally new experience, for in simple terms we can relate it to the buying and selling of football stickers. Now adults without the limitations of pocket money, fans can now buy and sell shares instead, and swop them with their friends. The nice thing about shares is that they also make great presents. Gift Tokens of Tommy Johnson and Phil Turner are available now.

MAXIMUM WAITING TIMES FOR GOALS

There's nothing more frustrating than coming away from a boring low scoring match, especially a goalless draw. In the Football Charter we propose a refund for every half hour without a goal being scored. This will give the fans something to cheer about before they become bored and cold, and will give the commentators on TV something to analyse at half time. A slight problem may be that the manager with one eye on the clock and the other on profits may instruct a quick own goal before the 30 minutes lapses, but we here at FNK prefer to forget about these things and pretend they never exist, just like the government. Instead we prefer to emphasise the fact that you're never 30 minutes away from a goal, and that isn't the UK a fantastic place thanks to these Charters.

OPTING OUT

A policy close to our ideological hearts. Opting out of the football league is to continue, and once opted out clubs will become grant maintained, thus receiving at least 15% more funding. This is an incentive to the other clubs to encourage them to take to the path of opting out. In the long run, if successful, we envisage a Division 1 of 93 clubs who will each play 184 games a season. Season tickets will require a mortgage to buy.

LEGAL ACTION FOR INJURIES

Legal action can be taken by players against those who injure them, because they take good players off the pitch and into the beds of an overstretched health service. The threat of being sued should take all the nasty tackling out of the game and make it flowing because there will be fewer stoppages for free kicks. Stewart Pearce will no longer be able to show off just outside the area with his kicks. This aspect of the Charter will not however apply to refs or Paul Gascoigne who deserve all the physical violence against them they get.

ALL TEAMS TO ARRIVE ON TIME

A minor proposal this because it will affect only one club. Notts County will in future have to arrive in time for the second half, or the game will start without them.

INCREASED USE OF SPONSORSHIP

Restrictions on sponsorship will be eased (in other words there will be no restrictions). Players will be able to wear sponsored baseball hats. Advertisers can buy space actually on the match ball and pitch. Goals can be co-sponsored eg. 'this cracking goal by Tommy Johnson was brought to you in association with new Radion Automatic, the powder that cleans to the very heart of your wash'. Football fans can also sell their own advertising space, with logos on their clothing. This is of most benefit when the game is televised. Critics have voiced doubts the coverage will be focused on the ball and fans rather than the match, but we dismiss this claim as being nothing new.

TABLES OF STATISTICS

We like statistics. We'd like other people to like the statistics we like. So we propose that clubs are to publish masses and masses of statistics. We'd like these statistics and we're sure the public, given time, will like the statistics too. Then they and the government will both like and appreciate the same thing, and the place will be so much nicer for it.

WINDY & DUSTY

(BUT DEFINITELY)

NOT MERRY)

THE GOOD — ROTHERHAM UNITED FANZINE

Millers' hardware is just too much

To paraphrase a Chinese soccer proverb the game played with lead balloon can be a bizarre basket of celight ("it's a funny old game" the lads of M1 Whippet's Dead might say.) Anyway thirty years ago from now (best said in a Jimmy Savile voice) Rotherham were being robbed of a place in Europe (don't check this out) and a rightful League Cup victory (perhaps). The boys from Millmoor had outplayed Aston Villa at Millmoor and assumed they'd won the Cup. Unfortunately the men at Lytham St Annes forced Rotherham to play a second game at Villa Park. The Millers were naturally gutted by this big team bias and the rest of the story is history. (Please allow for some degree of poetic licence.) (Is there any need for all these brackets— Ed.)

Since then the contest has gone down hill fast, the only exception being the Millers v Blades classic in 1989. Now the final is a bizarre no hoper contest between two pathetic teams nobody gives a knob cheese about. Even Luton have played in finals of late. This year's contest between small town Mancs and a team managed by a Sumo wrestler is the ultimate example of how the Cup has deteriorated.

To labour a point the only sex that matters is when you lose your virginity, the best marriage is the first, Neil Armstrong's walk on the moon was the only one that mattered (stuff Sting.) Inevitably the only REALLY important League Cup Final was the first leg between Rotherham and Aston Villa.

Don't believe me? Well with the wonders of modern technology I've printed the Millers team of 1961 and the probable Wednesday team into the latest hi-tech Binary International Access System (BIAS) computer. The computer then plays the game. So here's what happened.

8 mins:	A fatigued Trevor Francis limps off the pitch having played his usual contribution to Wednesday's efforts.
10 mins:	Danny Wilson signs a recording contract, re-releases "Save Me" and is never seen again.
11 mins:	Rotherham's Madden (destined to be Darlington's boss in the future) beats off a challenge, from home boy Harkes, feeds through to Kirkman, who neatly rounds Pearson finds a gap and leaves Shirtliff stranded. Turner comes off his line but cos he's crap Kirkman volleys over him. 1-0.
12 mins:	John Sheridan hammers a 45 yard free kick into the massed ranks of Wednesday fans. The East Bank Barmy Army (ha!) refuse to return the ball cos they're wooly backs and fear a hammering.
26 mins:	A Bambridge corner. Turner (cos he's crap) fumbles. 2-0

WINDY & DUSTY

	Stewart Evans replaces Webster in a tactical substitution.
31 mins:	
35 mins:	Evans gets the ball on th halfway line. Beats Harkes, Palmer, Worthington, Hirst, Eustace, Shirtliff, Pearson Hugh Dowd, Turner et al. Evans walks the ball into the net. 3-0.
36 mins:	The ball is crossed by Kirkman. Off a divot Weston collects and beats Turner. 4-0.
59 mins:	Evans, after a quiet spell, gets the ball on the half-way line. Sees a gap, shoots, scores. 5-0.
70 mins:	A Bambridge corner. Worthington fails to clear. Evans gets a hat-trick and how! 6-0.
74 mins:	Ron Atkinson tries to spend £4 million to buy some subs but it's too late now. Or is it. Atkinson in his desperation has paid £2.5 million for Stewart Evans.
76 mins:	Tension? The comeback? Evans beats Perry rounds Ironside and Wednesday have a goal. 6-1.
89 mins:	Having held out from relentless Stewart Evans pressure the Millers break. Houghton, unmarked, scores from close in. 7-1.
91 mins:	Rotherham sell the computer to Ron Atkinson for 10 million, buy loads of good players and we all live happily ever after.

And if you find all this amazing, rememeber computers don't lie. NEXT MONTH—THE ROAD TO WEMBLEY 1992— using the BIAS 2 system.

Ode
to
Clive
Mendonca

So, farewell then
Clive Mendonca.

Your surname
rhymes with
plonker.

This is
apt.

Dundee United (Falkirk Arabs) — When The Hoodoo Comes

Speke from the Harbour - Everton

I'D ROTHER BE AT MILLMOOR

Some people have ambitions to visit the Great Wall of China or Sydney Opera House. I'm a modest person and this is reflected in one of my ambitions - to attend a match at Millmoor, home of Rotherham United. In the main this was due to a friend of mine (I'll call him Peter as that's what everyone calls him) who is a lifelong Millers fan and spent many hours trying to convince me that my life would be empty without a visit to the hallowed ground.

In early 1990 a series of events conspired to enable me to fulfill my ambition. Everton were drawn away at Sheffield Wednesday in the FA Cup with a Sunday 12 noon kick off so I was able to fly to Leeds on Saturday morning, see Rotherham v Tranmere on Saturday afternoon, watch Everton beat the Owls (what's new?) on the Sunday and fly home on Sunday evening.

Peter met me at Leeds airport and we were soon heading to his house via Elland Road - a spot of sight-seeing as the ghouls were in Dublin that weekend. Having got some refreshments Peter, his son Jamie and I headed off to Rotherham, got parked and were soon approaching the ground. We had a bit of time in our hands so we nipped into the supporters social club for a look around. It was the nearest I have ever been to an Opium den. The smoke was so thick that my pocket fogometer calculated that 10 minutes in that place was the equivalent of chain-smoking 30 Park Drive. I like a beer before a game but not that badly so we made a quick exit.

I then decided to break a habit of a lifetime and buy a programme. I approached the young lady and in my best English said "Could I have a programme, please". She looked at me blankly but noticed I was holding out a £1 coin so she swiftly took it and gave me my change. I stood there waiting. And waiting. "Could I have my programme now please?" She said something in Yorkshirese and held out a programme which I made off with. I still haven't worked out what she was at. Perhaps she's used to mean coming up to her offering money. More likely some strange Yorkie custom, I concluded; probably like Morris Dancing.

Undeterred I went over to the club shop to see what was on offer. It was jam-packed and as I got closer I noticed a police car had reversed up to the shop door and was sitting there with its engine running. Either the locals demand a high intake of fumes in these parts or the Fourth Reich is alive and well in South Yorkshire. I decided to give the gas chamber a miss and we all went into the ground.

Since we were hungry I was encouraged to partake of the club snack bar. "Have a sausage roll" said Peter "they are in the club colours". I hope it's not the away colours of yellow and blue I thought to myself. Fortunately it was the red and white, thankfully, the 'meat' being red and the pastry white. Being a pie addict, I opted for a meat and potato version. These particular items are made by PUKKA PIES. Peter assured me it was not pronounced 'PUKE-AH'.

I have never been near Sellafield so my knowledge of nuclear matters is limited to the fact that the Irish Sea is full of nuclear waste. However, I am convinced that the lady in the snack bar has at her disposal a thermonuclear device for heating pies. I held the pie in the cold January air for a good 10 minutes and the ingredients were still bubbling. I made several valiant attempts to eat the pie but was losing the battle so in the end I walked up to the back of the terrace and set my pie down. I glanced back as I walked down to my friends and noted a small crowd gathering around the pie. They were not trying to eat it; rather they were using it to warm their hands. It was like a 3 bar electric fire. At that point my attention was diverted as Ian Snodin walked past followed by other members of the Everton squad. Are they here because of me or the pies I wondered?

Thankfully the teams came out and my attention was directed towards the pitch. I saw a good, top of the table, battle between the third division's two top scoring teams which probably explains why it ended 0-0. I liked Millmoor. It's a good, traditional soccer stadium and as we got ready to leave I thought to myself I must come back again. A final glance at the pie told me it had now dropped to about 95°C as the spits of rain were no longer turning instantly to steam.

The rain turned to snow that evening and I felt sure the Everton game would be off. In the morning the monsoon came and washed away the snow. It's bound to be off I thought but all that happened was a 30 minute delay because of the flooding in surrounding roads. I enjoyed the rare spectacle of an Everton away win yet as I sat in the Hillsborough stand sheltered from the rain my mind kept drifting back to the previous day. Hillsborough is a grand, impressive stadium but given the choice, I would rother be at Millmoor.

Meadowbank Thistle — Roll On 4.40

Here's an article sent in by David Windridge from Nuneaton in Warwickshire.
Well here it is, the trials of being a Meadowbank fan living in the Midlands.

PUT THE TELLY BACK ON

The next time you pass the souvenior stall at Meadowbank Stadium, laden with t-shirts and ties, scarves and mugs, spare a thought for me, the Thistle fan from the Midlands.

A trip to town usually goes like this. Enter a sports shop,
ME: "Excuse me, have you got any Scottish football shirts?"
Bloke In Shop: "Oh-yes, we've them all."
ME: "All of them? GREAT!"
BIS: "Yes, we've got Rangers AND Celtic!"
ME: "Oh, the one I was looking for was more unusual."
BIS: "You'll be wanting the Aberdeen one then"
ME: "No thanks, bye"

And on it goes. It doesn't get any better either, as every other Saturday afternoon I visit my local team Nuneaton Borough for a slice of big time football action, well, Beazer Homes League, Midlandds Division, anyway!

Just you try getting the Meadowbank half-time score from the anorak train spotter with the radio, standing next to you.
ME: "Got any half-times mate?"
GIT: "Yes, what Division do you want"
ME: "Scottish Div...."
GIT: (interupting) "Oh its Aberdeen 1 Rangers 1, Celtic 2 Dundee United 2 and Hibs 0 Hearts 7"
ME: "But what about.." but its too late, he's gone to fetch his bovril and pie.

Still, I can catch the score in the Clubhouse afterwards. Buy a quick pint, and then look at the telly, perched high on a shelf in the conor of the room.
      "Barcleys League, Division One",
   Yes, Yes, come on, get on with it
      "Barcleys League, Division Four"
The tension is too much sometimes. At last, "Scottish Premier" "blah, blah, blah " right get ready, here it comes, "Scottish League Div.." then up pops a hand from the crowd infront of the telly, horror of horror's, off it goes,
 ME: "OI!!" I scream
    "PUT THE TELLY BACK ON!!!!"
But it's too late, "Hull 12- Leeds 32" etc,etc,
Still, alls not lost, the sports paper arrives at 6.00 pm, I'll find out then; but I never do, Because it's impossible to leave the Clubhouse until at least six pints have come and gone, then its too late to get the sports paper, the shop is shut; never mind, I'll find out Sunday... Hopefully.

NOTTS COUNTY F.C.

THE FOLLOWING ARE EXTRACTS FROM ISSUES
1-5 OF THE THIN YELLOW STRIPE, A NOTTS
COUNTY FANZINE WHICH IS NOW INTO ITS
SECOND SEASON. WE HOPE YOU ENJOY THEM.

Who?!? Tommy Johnson

At last Tommy Johnson had been
noticed! The papers had
confirmed it! Selection for the
England U21 squad! But after the initial excitment the balloon burst when
Notts announced that they would take presidence over England due to the
previously arranged Charlton match. But after discussions with Mr. Taylor,
Neil Warnock had a change of heart and for once the football league
behaved sensibly and let the match be postponed, and hence Tommy was free
to join the England squad. At the following weekends game against
Middlesbrough we had a good old chin wag with Penny Morris, Tommy's
girlfriend, and decided that depending upon the team news we would
travel down to Southampton to, hopefully, witness "Skelly's" debut in the
national colours. Over the next few days we hired a minibus and kept our
fingers crossed.

When we found out he was on the subs bench everyone piled into Tony's
Taxi (a Collis minibus) and the nine nutty Notts fans, including Penny,
bravely set off for the deep South(ampton). After a relatively
uneventful journey down (a rarity for Tony's driving) we arrived at the
ground about 15 minutes before kick off. Penny took up her seat in the
main stand and we decided to stand up.

The game had only just kicked off when England conceeded a penalty,
until we saw the replay on television the next night we all thought
that the guilty culprit had been Charles from Forest, I can tell you we
were all disappointed when we found out that it hadn't been him at all.
Most of the first half was spent watching the bench for movements by
Tommy and shouting for him to be brought on. The first half ended and
we all hoped for an appearance in the second from the "Pale Genius".
But when he walked back onto the pitch after the interval with his
tracksuit top still on and his chin glued to his chest we feared the
worst, a four hour journey for nothing.

Every movement on the bench was being clearly noted. Tommy spent at
least five minutes fiddling with the cord on his tracksuit bottoms,
and then it became obvious that the bench were going to make a
substitution, our hopes rose, but to no avail, on came Robins.

By this time we were becoming desperate, shouting at the top of our
voices for Tommy to come on. Even the Southampton fans were getting
behind us, wondering who the hell this Johnson lad was. Eventually,
with the score at 1-1, Tommy was moved and received some instructions
and we began to get really wound up. Wallace, the local lad, was
substituted by our Tom! It was strange because almost as soon as he
stepped onto the pitch England scored, some Southampton fans thought
he was some sort of lucky charm, but then he went one better! With only
his third touch of the ball, and that a header too, Tommy planted the
ball firmly into the net. Scenes of what can only be described as
ecstatic jubliation followed, the journey had been worth it! The three
young Saint's fans infront of us had their first taste of "Ooh, Tommy
Johnson!", and once more they joined in!

We left the ground content with the memory of seeing a Notts player in
an England shirt...TYS 1.

DEAD WOOD!

After seeing Brian Clough's best ever England team, Robin Hood picks his best ever Forest!

1. Peter Shilton — Like the **Major Oak**, needs propping up nowadays!

2. Viv Anderson — Like a **Weeping Willow**, all gangling arms and legs!

3. Stuart Pearce — An **Apple Tree**, like the one Isaac Newton sat under. Can leave bumps and bruises!

4. Des Walker — Like a **Palm Tree**, destined for warmer climates. **Italy?**

5. David Needham — A **Tricky Tree** (dedicated to the Forest Fanzine) – there had to be some talent in this team.

6. Johnny Metgod — A **Dutch Elm!**

7. Still unable to replace **Neil Webb!**

8. John Sheridan — Like a **Christmas Tree** – one for the bright lights!

9. Nigel Clough — **Family Tree** (Enough said!)

10. Justin Fashinu — As with the **Bonsai Tree**. Needs lots of looking after but when fully grown can be worth **"Loadsamoney!"**

11. John Robertson — Like the **Broad Oak**, a player of substance.

TYS 2

MY LEAGUE DEBUT!!
(WELL ALMOST)

It was 1973 and Notts were away to Port Vale. It was in the days before we were treated like animals and penned in.

My mum and dad stood about level with the half way line and were leaning on a crush barrier. At the time mum was heavily pregnant with me.

It was just into the second half when Dad thought Mum was being quiet. He looked round to see her slumped over the crush barrier. She had fainted (something she was glad at whilst pregnant!). A young police constable saw what was happening and came over to give assistance. Seeing Mum was heavily pregnant he assumed I was on the way! Without another word he picked Mum up and set off towards the first aid room, at the end of the ground behind the stand. By the time we got to the first aid room the P.C. was dripping with sweat and gasping for breath. He sat Mum down (she was now concious) and got a glass of water, which Dad thought was for Mum, but he was in a worse state and proceeded to drink it himself!

After a rest it was decided that Mum should go home. The game still had a few minutes to go, but Mum and Dad thought it better to go before the crush. As they got to the car park a roar went up from the Notts fans – PENALTY! Dad rested Mum over a car bonnet and ran back into the ground just in time to see Don Masson put the spot kick into the net. He then, came back to Mum and picked her up from the car bonnet she was slumped over.

I managed to hang on and was born in Nottingham (where else) some days later!!!

TYS 3

A Footballing Night On TV.

4.20 pm Masters of the Universe
Starring Paul Harding as He-Man and Tommy Johnson as Skeletor.

5.00 pm Neighbours
The sound of creaking armchairs can be heard as "The Neighbours" go on a day trip to Wembley.

5.45 pm News/Weather
Read by George Foster who predicts a long gloomy period over Field Mill for the whole of next year.

6.30 pm Local News
More unbiased reports by the people who work alongside the "Evening Post" journo's

7.00 pm The Holiday Programme
Neil Warnock takes us on a visit to Scarborough *REPEAT*

7.30 pm "Trentenders"
More loveable soap opera with the cast who'll soon be moving out - Thank God!

8.00 pm Suprise! Surprise!
Arthur Cox gives us his reaction to Derby's last victory.

8.30 pm Father, Dear Father
Starring young Nigel and not so young Brian.

9.00 pm The Sweeney
The "Flying" squad try to catch Kevin B.

10.00pm Classic Comedy - The 1991 Cup Final
Relive the hilarious moment as Des "I didn't realise we turned round as half time" Walker knocks in a beauty.

12.00pm Prisoner Cell Block H
The prison football team have just set up a defensive wall on the edge of their area, when Tony A. tries to climb over it.

TYS 5

Not content with producing that marvellous series of adverts for EMEB, the Green'Un has now hit the big time with a national advertising campaign. Before we discuss the impact of Shredded Wheat, its action on the human digestive system and the connection with the team he currently manages, let us look back on days of yore, when the green sweat shirt was in its infancy and the budget was very obviously minimal.

Who can forget the Vision in Verdant jogging around the showroom and surprising everyone. Then there was the one with the Italian goalkeeper he had signed who was awful. A case of truth behind the comedy. Alfonso changed his name to Mark and now is their regular first choice keeper, though he hasn't improved noticeably. The last and probably the most controversial ad. Featured about a dozen young ladies and the Green'Un coming in from the cold. The girls go upstairs and get in the bath whilst Bri does his piece to camera. When he's done he goes up to join them. A great moral attitude from a happily married man with impressionable kids.

Now comes the crowning glory, the shredded wheat ad. No more badly delivered lines and strange jogging, this is the biz. There is still the green thing though, some habits die hard. Here he seems to be managing a Sheffield Wednesday team made up of degenerates, who surprisingly pick up after having a bowl full of a substance which to my mind has all the taste and appeal of a miniature bale of very coarse straw.

Be warned, though, of the dangers of eating three. The poor goalkeeper ages twenty years and goes on to let in seven for another team, they were all the defence's fault however.

TYS 4

Did you notice at Old Trafford the amount of groundstaff on the pitch at half-time. The TYS can exclusively reveal that they weren't replacing divets, but looking for bits of Bryan Robson which had fallen off in the first half..............TYS 5.

DERANGED FERRET!
A LINCOLN CITY FANZINE

FLICK AS A PARROT
or
IMPS LIFT THE TREBLE FOR FIFTH SEASON RUNNING

Recent fanzine articles have waxed nostalgic on the subject of table football. One DF reader, addicted to the game for years, tries to explain the attraction of a game that noone can actually play.

I starved for Subbuteo. I saved my school dinner money, in the process becoming thin and wretched, so that outside the Panini sticker season I could upgrade my ground facilities far beyond Taylor recommendations and expand my pool of teams to include, for that crucial UEFA Cup preliminary round tie, Ujpest Dozsa and Partisan Tirana. Nevertheless, despite passing the best years of my youth hunched over the tiny replicas, a celestial force attempting to manipulate balls and bodies where they simply did not want to go, it eventually became clear to me. I was, and still am, absolutely sh*te at the game.

How on earth did Subbuteo ever become popular? At least if you spend weeks practising other dork-associated pastimes, such as golf or chess, you will likely be rewarded with some level of adeptness. Progress will manifest itself in the form of a Ballesterian bunker escape or a rogered rook (or whatever the hell it is you do in chess). But, and I am prepared to argue this one long beyond closing time, mankind was not designed to express its talent on the Subbuteo table.

No doubt those participating in world championships and the like might protest at this, but these people have to remain exceptions who probably practice during their lunch-hour *and* on Friday and Satur-

day nights and I bet they never get their leg over either. However, watching 'amateurs' play Subbuteo always reminds me of the time I witnessed Coronation St.'s Mike Baldwin opening a supermarket while perched on top of an elephant. Alternating between grins, for his public, and grimaces, because he thought he was about to fall to his death, poor Mike wavered from side to side totally out of control and clearly sh**ng himself. It just didn't look *natural*. And neither does leaning over a table flicking bits of plastic that never go anywhere near where you want them to.

The reason I persevered with this ludicrous hobby wasn't because I wanted to become a colossus of the table soccer scene. In fact I rarely played against anyone apart from myself. If friends came by to play they invariably squashed players, vandalised the plastic fence surround, and mocked the paltry number of spectators spread around the vast amounts of stand and terracing I'd accumulated (my World Cup final attendance was on average ten times below that of the infamous Leyland DAF qualifier between Torquay and Shrewsbury earlier this season). Then they had the audacity to beat me, me that had all the *stuff*, the corner flags (that got in the way), the throwers (impossible to operate), the ball boys (never got the ball back), the dugout (constantly fell over and tipped the entire management and coaching team onto the pitch), the scoreboard (that only went up to nine), the floodlights (that half-lit the centre circle but left the remainder of the pitch in blackness), and for that special annual Wembley occasion, to boost the normal attendance from 42 to 47, the Royal Family Presentation set, its focal point the queen holding an amoeba-sized replica of the FA Cup. (Incidentally, there is no Prince Charles in the set, a cunning commercial ploy by Subbuteo so that when the old bat kicks it you cannot just transfer the cup from regent to regent but will have to buy a completely new set).

The only joy came from the power. Robert Maxwell must have had a dozen Subbuteo sets as a brat. You're not just in control of a complete football club, you can tamper with an entire league. This was a soccer toytown where LCFC could, yet again, lift the FA Cup. Where Percy Freeman top scored with 37 goals in 18 games, *yet again* (because the adhesive numbers always fell off you couldn't identify a player so it must have been Freeman in the striker's position every time). Then he went on to do the same for England. Bob Paisley's invincible Liverpool outfit were never going to interfere with destiny round at my place. They didn't even exist because I never bought their kit.

If I felt like it I sprayed the pitch with water to create heavy conditions. I thought that if the pitch was wet then the ball wouldn't roll into touch quite as often, but it didn't work. My dismal digits still displayed about as much control as Mark Hateley. An experiment with flour as ersatz snow was even less successful.

Snowed in for a whole weekend during the recent chilly spell I instigated a revival tournament for the benefit of three friends, all of us in our mid-twenties. Surely just a bit of a laugh.

Far from it. It was only a matter of minutes before controversy raged and tears almost gushed. Neil, who has a steady job and a steady girlfriend and is a full 26 years old, complained bitterly about one of my refereeing decisions (does anyone, by the way, have a copy of the rules?). When I dismissed one of his small plastic figures for consistent dissent, he whined, 'I'm not playing any more if you're going to be like that.' Only a handkerchief and some chocolate digestive biscuits diffused a potentially tearful scenario.

After this the ball was booted more or less constantly into touch, tackles reported late again and again, petty bickering never ceased, and the amount of genuine skill displayed was lower then the temperature outside. However much you slag off Subbuteo at least it's not too distant from the realities of English league football.
Ian Plenderleith

****
<u>PUBLIC AWARENESS SURVEY</u>

We attempted to ask 100 ordinary people *"What do you think of the Deranged Ferret ? "* The replies were reassuring

1.	Great value at only 50 pence	49%
2.	* * * * OFF (or similar)	23%
3.	No opinion/comment	10%
4.	Couldn't do worse that Mrs Thatcher	2%
5.	Best pub in Stoke on Trent	1%
6.	Roland Rat is nicer	1%
7.	Why did Kylie leave him?	1%
8.	Je ne comprende pas	1%
9.	No match for a rotweiller	1%
10.	Guaranteed to help you score	1%
11.	I can do that,Gi's a job	1%
12.	I'm going to see Mr Henderson	1%
13.	It's £15 with a condom	1%
14.	You can't beat a good cr*p	1%
15.	Pure fabrication.Should be banned	0%
16.	Allo,Allo,Allo,you're nicked	1%

Total 95

A.S   28/12/89

****

UNITED WE STAND
An independent view of Manchester United
(Number 17)

THE VOICE OF THE FANS

NORTHERN NORMAN

ARE THOU TRYIN' T' TAKE THE PISS?... O' COURSE SOUTHERNERS AREN'T LIKE US!! TESTS 'AVE PROVED THAT THEY'RE A TOTALLY DIFFERENT BRANCH O' HUMAN RACE!

NO DOUBT IN A COUPLE O' HUNDRED YEARS TIME THEY'LL 'AVE ARRANGED THEIR EVOLUTIONARY DEVELOPMENT SO THAT SOMEBODY ELSE WILL DO THEIR BREATHIN' FOR EM!

I CONCEDE THAT THEY LOOK T'SAME AS US, BUT IT'S ALL SURFACE! UNDERNEATH THEY'RE EVOLVED DIFFERENT... IT'S A FACT THAT ANY ADVANCED OF 'EM ARE BORN WITHOUT ANAL ORIFICES 'COS 'AVIN' A CRAP'S NOW BENEATH THEIR DIGNITY!)

IT'S THE WAY THEY LIVE THAT DOES IT THA' KNOWS! THEY'RE TOO BLEEDIN' SOFT! I'VE SEEN 'EM WHEN THEY COME UP 'ERE FOR A MATCH ... SOUTHERN BLOODY FANS DON'T YELL ABUSE ANYMORE ...

... THEY GET THEIR SERVANTS TO DO IT FOR EM!!

THE MASTER WOULD LIKE TO THROW 'HER LADYSHIP SUGGESTS 'DOUBT ON YOUR LEGITIMACY! THAT YOU ABUSE YOURSELVES!

SIR THINKS THAT YOUR TACKLING LACKS DIPLO-MACY!

... OH AYE!.. THEY MIGHT LOOK LIKE US, BUT SOMEHOW Y'CAN ALWAYS SPOT A SOUTHERNER!!

POOR SOD!

A WIFE 2 KIDS AND 2000 MANCHESTER UNITED SHARES TO SUPPORT

ARSNUL
v
UNITID
KIK OF:
SATERDAY 3·00PM
TIKITS: TEN POUND
(NO FIGHTING ETC.)

THIS IS A VERY POOR ADVERT FOR THE GAME!

LANGSTON⦵⦵

(BONY)

2 MILLION YEARS B.C.F.C. OR HOW FOOTBALL BEGAN..?
THE TROUBLE WITH LIVING IN SUCH A PRIMEVAL SOCIETY, WITHOUT THE BENEFITS OF ANY FORM OF ADVANCED TECHNOLOGY, IS THAT IT'S BORING... I'M FED UP!!
YES, WE ARE SIMILARLY DISPOSED!
HEY LADS! .... LOOK WHATS HAPPENED TO UG! ... ..SILLY SOD GOT INTO A DEEP AND MEANINGFUL CONVERSATION WITH A T. REX! IT BIT HIS HEAD OFF!
I'M NOT MUCH OF A DOCTOR, AND MEDICAL SCIENCE HASN'T TAKEN OFF YET... BUT I'D HAZARD A GUESS AND SUGGEST THAT HE SHOWS ALL THE SIGNS OF BEING DEAD!...
COMPLETELY BUGGERED IN FACT!
IT'S A SHAME THAT WE'VE NOT INVENTED PAPYRUS YET! .. THE ONLY USE FOR HIM NOW WOULD BE AS A PAPER WEIGHT!!
BYE BYE UG!
HEY! I DONT WANT IT!
KICK!
PITY UG'S NOT ALIVE.... HE'D HAVE ENJOYED THIS, IT'S FUN!!
AT LEAST HE'S JOINING IN!
HOLD IT LADS!... I THINK THAT THIS HAS GOT POSSIBILITIES... WITH A BIT OF ORGANISATION AND A FEW RULES WE CAN TURN THIS INTO A MAJOR SPORTING EVENT!
WE CAN MAKE UP TWO TEAMS AND KICK UGS' HEAD BETWEEN OURSELVES
THAT SOUNDS PERFECTLY RIVETTING!
HOW MANY A SIDE D'YER THINK?
SINCE WE CAN'T COUNT YET, IT'S BARELY RELEVANT!
THIS LOOKS LIKE A GOOD PLACE TO PLAY THE GAME .... THOUGH.. THE GROUNDS A BIT STICKY!
AYE.. IT'S AN OLD TAR PIT
OK.. SO WE'LL CALL IT THE PITCH!
LOOK,.. I DON'T WANT TO DAMPEN YOUR ENTHUSIASM.... BUT IF WE'RE EVER GOING TO EVOLVE INTO SOME HIGHER SOCIAL ORDER .... SHOULD'NT WE BE TRYING TO DO SOMETHING A BIT MORE INTELLECTUALLY STIMULATING THAN JUST KICKIN' SOMEONES HEAD ABOUT?
HMMM... YOU'RE RIGHT!
HEY!... HERE'S YOUR MAIL! YOU'VE GOT FOUR LOTS!
BLOODY 'ELL!.. NOT ON THOSE TABLETS OF COAL ARE THEY? ...THEY'RE DEAD HARD TO READ.. ..WASTE OF TIME.. OK! ..JUST PUT 'EM INTO SEPERATE PILES.. THEN, ... SOD OFF!!
THAT'S IT!!!
WHAT EACH TEAM HAS TO DO, IS TRY AND KICK THE HEAD BETWEEN EACH OTHERS COAL POST!!!
YOU'RE A GENIUS! THATS BRILLIANT!
SO THAT'S HOW IT ALL STARTED.... ON THAT FIRST MATCH, MUCH OF OUR MODERN TERMINOLOGY WAS COINED..
STRIKER
CENTRE FORWARD
CRACK!
FOWL
WOW! ... IT'S A FABULOUS GAME!! BUT WHAT ARE YOU GOING TO CALL IT?
I'VE THOUGHT VERY SERIOUSLY ABOUT THAT.... AND REALLY THERE CAN ONLY BE ONE NAME....
IT'S CATCHY AND EPITOMISES THE WHOLE SPIRIT OF THE GAME....
...UGS HEAD!!

MONTE CARLO OR BUST !!

ONE OF THE PECULIARITIES OF BEING A WELSH CLUB PLAYING IN THE ENGLISH
LEAGUE IS THAT YOU CAN FIND YOURSELF BOTTOM OF DIVISION THREE AND FACING
ONE OF THE PREMIER SIDES IN EUROPE.AND SO IT CAME TO PASS THAT THE WELSH
CUP WINNERS,SWANSEA CITY,WITH 2 POINTS FROM 6 LEAGUE GAMES CAME TO FACE
MONACO,FRENCH CUP WINNERS AND TOP OF THE FRENCH LEAGUE WITH 9 WINS OUT
OF 10 GAMES.IN TRUTH FROM A SUPPORTERS POINT OF VIEW IT WAS A BIT OF
LIGHT RELIEF FROM THE HORRORS OF A LEAGUE CAMPAIGN WHICH STARTED WITH A
0-5 THRASHING AT EDGELEY PARK,STOCKPORT AND HAS BARELY GOT BETTER.

MONACO VISITED THE "PALATIAL" SURROUNDINGS OF THE VETCH FIELD IN MID
SEPTEMBER,COMPLETE WITH A V.I.P. SUPPORTER,PRINCE RAINIER IN THEIR
RANKS.A POOR CROWD OF 6,208,STILL TWICE THE NORM WATCHED IN HORROR AS
THE SWANS CONCEDED A 7TH.MINUTE PENALTY,FOLLOWED BY ANOTHER GOAL
BEFORE THE HALF HOUR.VISIONS OF A STOCKPORTESQUE RESULT LOOMED.
BUT SUDDENLY A CHANGE OCCURRED.THE TEAM RALLIED AND EVEN CREATED A FEW
CHANCES BEFORE HALF TIME.AND ALL THIS FROM A BELOW STRENGTH TEAM.
THE TABLOIDS TALKED ABOUT THE PROBLEMS THAT LIVERPOOL,MANCHESTER UNITED
AND GLASGOW RANGERS HAD SELECTING A TEAM WITH ONLY 4 "FOREIGNERS".
SWANSEA'S 12 WELSHMEN INCLUDED 7 TEENAGERS,AND OUR 4 FOREIGNERS INCLUDED
CHRIS MCCLEAN,A TRIALIST RELEASED BY BRISTOL ROVERS AT THE END OF LAST
SEASON,AND TERRY CONNOR,PLAYING HIS LAST GAME FOR THE CLUB BEFORE A BIG
MONEY MOVE (WELL £192,000) TO BRISTOL CITY.HARDLY A STABLE LINE-UP.

THE SECOND HALF SAW A REMARKABLE TRANSFORMATION.EFFORT AND DESIRE
WERE THE ORDER OF THE DAY AS THE TEAM DEVELOPED A WIMBLEDON STYLE
APPROACH WHICH HAD MONACO DISTINCTLY WORRIED.KEEPER MARK KENDALL'S
KICKS AND ANDREW LEGG'S LONG THROW-INS WERE BOMBED INTO THE PENALTY AREA
WHERE MCCLEAN AND CONNOR PUT THEMSELVES ABOUT WITH GREAT RELISH.
MONACO DEFENDERS WERE SUDDENLY STARTING TO BACK OFF IN THE FACE OF
SWANSEA ASSAULTS.AND EVENTUALLY THEY CRACKED,A RUSSELL COUGHLIN
CHALLENGE LED TO A BACK PASS WHICH LEGG GRATEFULLY ACCEPTED AND CRACKED
INTO THE MONACO NET.THE GROUND ERUPTED.WE EVEN CAME CLOSE TO AN
EQUALISER,A LEGG CORNER FLICKED ON AT THE NEAR POST BY MCCLEAN WHICH
FLASHED ACROSS THE FACE OF THE GOAL.

WHEN THE FINAL WHISTLE CAME IT WAS MONACO WHO WERE GLAD TO HEAR IT.
O.K. SO WE STILL LOST BUT FOR 45 MINUTES WE LIVED WITH ONE OF THE BEST
TEAMS IN EUROPE,IF YOU BELIEVE THE PAPERS.AS I WRITE THE SECOND LEG
IS 10 DAYS AWAY,AND THOSE OF US WHO BOOKED OUR TRIP TO MONACO BEFORE
THE FIRST LEG,TO GENERAL RIDICULE,AWAIT IT WITH BAITED BREATH.
THE CHANCE OF AN UPSET MAY STILL BE TINY,BUT IT EXISTS !!

WHAT HAS ALL THIS TO DO WITH REALITY,I HEAR YOU CRY ??
WELL I HAVE A PLAN TO ENSURE THAT SWANSEA CITY RISE FROM THE FOOT OF
DIVISION THREE AND BECOME GREAT AGAIN:-

1.   ALL TEAMS PLAYING THE SWANS,FOR EXAMPLE,SHREWSBURY,TORQUAY,OR
HARTLEPOOL WILL BE REQUIRED TO WEAR CONTINENTAL STYLE STRIPS AND PLAY
WITH A SWEEPER OR LIBERO.

2.ALL DIVISION THREE PLAYERS WILL CHANGE THEIR NAMES BY DEED-POLL TO
RUI GIL BARROS,JEAN-LUC ETTORI OR YOUSSOUF FOFANA ETC.ETC.

3.BEFORE EACH GAME MANAGER FRANK BURROWS WILL INSIST THAT WE ARE
PLAYING MONACO,REAL MADRID OR A.C.MILAN.

THUS ORDINARY THIRD DIVISION PLODDERS WILL BE TRANSFORMED INTO THE
COMMITTED AND SKILFUL PROFESSIONALS THEY APPEAR TO BE ON NIGHTS OF
EUROPEAN GLORY AND THE COME-BACK WILL BEGIN.

Editor's note: Swansea lost 8-0 in the second leg.   DAI HARD II.
                                                          NOBODY WILL EVER KNOW...

Aberdeen

An exclusive TNL survey reveals average height of players in Premier League clubs.

Team	Average Height
Motherwell	6'1"
Dunfermline	6'0"
Hearts	5'11.5"
Rangers	5'11"
St. Johnstone	5'11"
Aberdeen	5'10"
St. Mirren	5'9.5"
Dundee United	5'9"
Celtic	5'9"
Hibs	5'8"

Yes, it's true! Hearts are the third biggest club in Scotland.

THE NORTHERN LIGHT

PLAYING FOR CELTIC NUMBER N².

NO WAY WIS THAT HANDBALL REF! IT JIST DEFLECTED AFF THE CHIP OAN MA SHOULDER.

Morton FC — Treble Chance

Small is beautiful

Alex "Turgid" Cameron wrote an article last season in the Daily Record in
which he suggested that League reconstruction was a bad idea for various
reasons, including the fact that "the transfer market has nearly died."
Leaving aside the coherence or relevance of such a contention, I'd like to
question an implicit arguement contained in this article. Mr Cameron
seems to feel smaller clubs (i.e. all those outwith the largest 4 or 5
teams in the country) have no right to a say on the future of the game.

Unfavourable comparisons are made between Ibrox Park and "smaller clubs
with little more than herring boxes." I'd have my doubts about whether Mr
Cameron has much recent experience of football stadia outwith the Premier
Division, but if he has then he must know that he has committed a gross
libel on a number of Scottish teams. Certainly there are some dire
grounds in Scotland (painting the outside of Albion Rovers ground does not
amount to an upgrading exercise.) but no attempt is made to differentiate
between the good and the nightmarish.

The bold Alex then goes on to make the point that "what's best for the big
boys should be good for the others." It is a sad inditement of the
standard of sports journalism in this country that this statement was
allowed to pass an editor. It is patently untrue that what suits the big
clubs will benefit the smaller ones. It never has in the past so why
should that change? What suits the big clubs is that they stay big and
everyone else stays small. In this way publicity,revenue and power are
concentrated upon a small "elite."

This fascination with the powerful takes many forms in sports journalism.
It is fostered by the cult of the individual which reached it's most
ridiculous in the deification of a fat guy called Gascoigne. It affects
the coverage of football in that both TV and the press assume that
everyone barring a few cranks will be totally fascinated by anything even
remotely concerned with the Old Firm. For me it reaches its logical
conclusion in the almost total lack of coverage given to the fanzine
revolution.

The received wisdom is that the only ideas of any worth, or originality
come from the powerful within the game. Thus we end up with a view which
suggests that Forfar or Albion Rovers or Morton are not capable of taking
informed, disinterested decisions about the future of the game,but Celtic
or Rangers are.

Surely if football is to survive then the views of everyone need to be
canvassed. It may be that the most original ideas will not come from the
biggest clubs. I would suggest that, in fact, they are less likely to
seek change since the status quo favours them so completely.

The press and TV would rather publicize the views of Wallace Mercer or David Murray, than recognise that radically different views may be held by you and me. True to form Alex wheeled on both Wallace and David to have their say. Mr Murray's contribution was particularly enlightening. "If they win their point it will certainly be democracy at work but I cannot see how a club like ours can play 44 league games." Are we to assume that democracy should be set aside when it doesn't suit those currently holding power? It's certainly an interesting concept and one I'm sure could be transferred into the wider society. Look out Neil Kinnock it might not matter how many votes you muster at the next election! This doesn't even address the idea that Glasgow Rangers are unable to cope with the number of games demanded of every team in divisions 2-4 in England.

A journalist worthy of the name would not simply spout the official line. He ought to challenge the propaganda and be aware of alternative views. Such views need the " oxygen of publicity " if they are not to wither away. Mr Cameron is not alone in his sycophancy. To one extent or another almost all sports journalism in this country is warped by the incestuous relationship between newspapers and our biggest clubs. It makes life easy for lazy journalists, but doesn't exactly encourage them to challenge the power structures at work within the game.

So come on guys how about doing us all a favour: stop being seduced by the glamour of power and actually do something to challenge its validity. Remember as I'm sure you've been told many times "Size isn't everything dear."

Morton hero Willie Pettigrew

An Analysis of the Game of Association Football

By Professor Ivor E. Tower

Professor of QuantumChromoDynamics & Tricky Sums
University of Harddnockes

Synopsis: I am pleased to present a scientific analysis of the natural phenomena which have been observed to occur in football. These observations are based on an extensive study of video tapes of English league games, visits to grounds ("field trips"), and conversations with the bloke in The Drysalters.

Introduction: On first appraisal, football might appear to be a topic not amenable to scientific analysis. This, however, is to ignore the importance and relevance of the game to British society. What I hope to show in the following is surprisingly how much of our formulation of many natural physical processes can be directly applied to help us understand the game.

The Game & Teams: Two opposing forces ("Us" & "Them") tend to act in opposing directions within a field, attempting to deposit a spherically symmetric particle, by various potentially exciting modes of exchange, into one of two quantum wells located at opposition along the rigid field boundary. The nature of these opposing forces can be considered as strongly electric (e.g. the team known as "Leeds United"), or gravitationally weak (e.g. the team known as "Halifax Town Nil")

The motion of the electron/ball particle depends not only on the relative line strengths of the opposing forces, but also on the order of the forces. Highly ordered sides produce a **L**aminar flow of the particle, which will move smoothly from point to point. These sides are referred to as the L-teams (e.g. **L**eeds and, grudgingly, **L**iverpool). For highly disordered, or **C**haotic, forces, the net motion of the particle is a random walk, which averages out to zero displacement over time T, where T tends to monotony. These are the C-teams (e.g. **C**helsea and **C**oventry). Between these extremes lie the **W**eak, or Whack and Hack, teams (e.g. **W**imbledon and **W**atford) which comprise of discrete units known as W-Bozos.

The Players: Whilst the above gives an overall picture of the game, of great importance are the individual professional players, or protons, which hope to mediate the activities of the ball.

For example, in the English national team for many years was a **Shilton**. This massive and somewhat immobile particle had a half-life of forty-five minutes. Despite this, the Shilton was generally regarded as safe, although English goalkeepers in the 70's were known to be prone to sudden transitions involving low cross-sections in the vicinity of moderate Poles. Another example from the national team is the **Robson**, a very active particle well known for its sudden and total disintegration at regular intervals, followed by long periods of recuperation, and guest TV commentary. Other interesting particles, of a less recent era, are the **Charltons**. These had great natural consistency which belied their endurance of the morale-breaking torture of parity non-conservation (their hair only grew on one side of their heads).

Just A Quick Word Lads, Please — Leeds United

Transitions: Whilst the elementary particles can change from one type to another by means of large expenditures of energy, the footballing equivalent is a transition from one field to another, involving ridiculously cosmic quantities of money. For young players, this transition is normally from a low to a high field, while for older players - who've received most of the applause coming to them[*] - the transition is usually indicative of a decay. An obvious exception to this rule is the long-lived **Strachan**, which cunningly managed to quantum tunnel across the pennines to a field of much greater potential.

Producing a team of players is a difficult task, since the natural state of many players is complete isolation - many players have a marked preference for playing with themselves, especially when red quarks are predominant in their internal structure. The same has also been true for a complete team - the once greatly despised **Lutons** - although this error has since been rectified by the ejection of their limiting and obstructive **Chairman**.

The job of keeping the Leeds particles organised at present is performed by a **Wilkinson**, a footballing pi-meson if ever there was one (it should be noted that the mean life of a meson is around one millionth of a second - just longer than that of an average football league manager). The manager often has to contend with large, seemingly neutral particles, called **Directors**, which often appear to serve little purpose, except to provide large amounts of inertia to the club's activities.

Catalytic Particles: With the game and components rigorously defined, some note should be taken of a whole range of attendant particles which seem to influence the outcome of the game. These are often seen before and after the match thriving on the absorption of highly renewable fluid energy sources which include the **Burtons**, the **Marstons**, and the **Theakstons** (a very peculiar particle). The author intends to vigorously and rigorously research these particles further once this article is over.

Conclusions: In conclusion then, I feel that a season ticket to an executive box at Elland Road is clearly the most logical route to real progress and understanding of the game of football. However, since no academic sponsor has come forward, this project will have to be funded at a lower level (about row F) on a shoe-string budget. Still, as we rather smart chaps in research say about football once dusk arrives - it's a really mildly amusing game of two 0.5 ($\pm$ 0.001)'s.

[*] i.e. Clapped out.

GRORTY DICK
AAAAARRRRRRGH!!!!!
the independent WBA Fanzine

So, it's happened. I wasn't surprised, though it hurt all the same - a bit like when someone you love dies from a disease recognised as terminal long ago, you know it's going to happen, but it still guts you when it does.

4.45, Twerton Park. What thoughts were running through YOUR head? Mine was a shed, an empty one. Like a radio that had closed down for the night, the carrier wave was there, but of the programme, nothing. I looked around, all I saw was a toga-clad sea of broken, beaten faces. It's not pleasant either, seeing good Black Country blokes weeping tears of bitter despair. Seeing Baggie people I know well reduced to that - Richie Brentnall resting against a crash barrier looking like he'd been simultaneously hit by a half-end brick, and Hamlet's ghost. Images. The scene struck a chord in my memory - where had I seen the same thing before? Then I remembered the old newsreels. All Our Yesterdays, an ITV programme a long time ago. I was a child, they were featuring 1940 - Dunkirk, and General Gort's battle weary troops looking much the same as they disembarked from the little boats. I was witnessing it again, Albion's Dunkirk.

Much to my surprise, I didn't shed tears. I simply entered into a state of shock, exacerbated by a considerable intake of alcohol that night. On the way back, we paused at a pub in Gloucester, where we bumped into a possee of Potters en-route post-match to Stoke. "Welcome to the Third Division," they said. It wasn't a hostile gesture, they genuinely felt for our plight, as we quaffed ale and commiserated well into the night.

The following day I awoke with a king size hangover and a terminal case of depression. Stockport, Hartlepool, Darlington, Wigan, Exeter.... A negative feed-back cycle that fed itself endlessly. It was not pleasant.

I spent that Sunday morning restlessly pottering about. I listened to Alan Freeman's Radio 1 oldie show - then he played Labe Siffre's "Something Inside's So Strong" - and then I nearly cracked. Listen to the words some time - if you're a genuine Albion fan, you'll reach for the hanky.

Something needed to be exorcised, so I got Simon to drive me to the Hawthorns, where I stood and screamed. Yes, dear reader, screamed. If you don't believe it, ask Simon - he was there.

It is now June. The grief is behind me, all I want to do now is get stuck into a few Third Division sides- and win. Our Chairman talks glibly of getting out in one season, but I'm not that optimistic. It's going to be a long hard struggle. Look at Stoke and Blues.

As for the future of the club, unless there is a radical rethink of policy at the Hawthorns, I fear the worst. It seems to me that the current Board are totally out of touch with the supporters - witness the away strip changes proposed for next season.

When was the last time any of the Board stood on the Brummie Road terraces, used the toilets, the tea-bar, came through the turnstiles, sampled the policing? In the name of God, gentlemen, DO IT. Listen to the supporters. They are human beings, they have a voice too! Care about them, for they will be there, come short time or dole, long after the executive box holders have departed to the richer pastures of Seal Park. For too long they have been a forgotten race. West Bromwich Albion is facing the future with it's back against the wall, the last thing we need is disunity. Come on, gentlemen, let's fight this thing truly together. In another age the love poet John Donne expressed similar sentiments- "We must love one another or die".

What about it, Members of The Board?

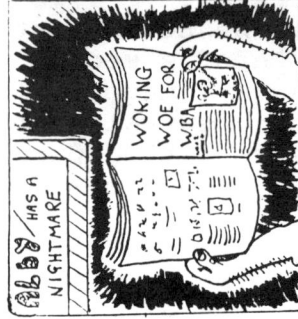

THE KING

Everybody knows that it's always sunny down Memory Lane. Even allowing for that, I can't help but believe we left a better world behind in the 1960's. There were plenty of problems around then of course, but it remains an optimistic and idealistic era compared to the late 70's and early 80's when the Black Country suffered more than most from industrial decline; proud men on their knees. Sad to think that many of Albion's younger supporters have never lived through a hopeful time. I remember debating whether the Stones were better than the Beatles when I heard that Jimmy Hagan had signed a new centre forward. He turned out to be a gangly, powerful No. 9 with axle greased hair, and neither he nor the Baggies supporters could guessed that he was to be Albion's greatest hero for the next 25 years or more.

It wasn't a particularly good first season (10 goals in 32 league games) but he immediately endeared himself to the supporters by opening his account for the club with a brace in a 5:1 mauling of Wolves. Season 65/66 saw a much better return, 18 in 27 league games and 6 in 9 league cup games. The following season saw another respectable tally, but it was 67/8 which was his pinnacle... 26 league goals and 9 FA Cup goals. In one week he scored 2 hat tricks and one of the goals in a semi-final win over Blues. "How do you spell 'goal'?" people asked... A.S.T.L.E. It seemed Alf Ramsey was illiterate for a long time however, as Jeff earned a mere 5 caps for England, despite the fact that every shot and header hit the net or came very close.

He had a very powerful shot, underestimated control and was brilliant in the air. (Even in retirement he seems reluctant to keep his feet on the ground, earning his living up ladders). His most renowned cap was against Brazil in the 1970 World Cup, when he came on as sub and missed an absolute sitter. The media had a field day crucifying him for that, conveniently forgetting the two simple chances he made for other players, and Ramsey's cock up in not playing him from the start as Brazil were notoriously weak in the air. Also forgotten too often is that the miss did not stop England qualifying, they went out 2:3 to West Germany after leading 2:0. Nevertheless it's one of football's maddening ironies that despite all the wonderful goals Jeff scored, he'll probably be best remembered for the chance he missed.

To Baggies supporters of course he'll be best remembered for his Cup Final winner in '68. But there is more to being a hero than that goal alone. He was the main scorer in a very good side. From the same team, Brown scored in every League cup game in '66, Clark in every round of the same competition in '67 and Jeff in every round of the FA Cup in '68. He averaged a goal in 48% of the games he played, comparing favourably with Brown 40%, Allen 51% and Kevan 59% (though way behind the remarkable 74% achieved by WG Richardson). He benefited too from the media. Games were broadcast more frequently then and his name was a commentator's dream for, invoking excitement whenever he had a chance. "ASTLE!!"

Stan Foggo

SEAL SALES

Although it is regularly pointed out on football fanzines that West Bromwich is not in Birmingham, there is no denying the fact that there are a lot of Albion fans that hail from the city. Having been brought up in Brum (Longbridge and Weoley Castle) I was one of the many who regularly caught the 74 or 79 down the Soho Road to see my boyhood heroes in action.

A couple of years ago my wife and I sold our house in Halesowen and invested our saving in a General Store in Great Barr (much to my Mother's disapproval "What you moving over there for?", she said, as if we were emigrating).

Now as I mentioned earlier I was brought up in South Birmingham, very much a Blues' stronghold, so one of the first things that struck me about Great Barr was the large Seal count. A Blues fan keeps himself to himself (for obvious reasons, what has he got to talk about?) but Villa fans have different beliefs, like Jehovahs Witnesses, they have to preach to every non-convert about why they are the biggest and best club in the Midlands.

Maybe my problems are all my fault, when we bought the shop Albion were climbing the Second Division and Villa were struggling in the First. I showed the door to the Villa lottery rep, replacing them with Albion ones, things were looking very rosy.

Then Villa clicked and suddenly out of the woodwork they came to tell me about their side, more and more claret and blue was spotted, youngsters corrupted at an early age. Then on that fateful day last February when I came back from the Hawthorns they were queuing outside the shop door to have a dig at me. My enjoyment of the World Cup in the Summer was tempered by 'We're only doing well thanks to Platty' remarks.

Albion fans do come into the shop (there are a few in Great Barr); we often discuss problems but in contrast to the Villa fans there is an air of quietness about our discussions which will suddenly end if someone else enters.

Suddenly things have changed, one night in Milan and the after effects have had a devastating knock on the food industry. The school playgrounds have gone back to red and white and our trade has suffered terribly,

Since we moved into this line of business there have been major crises over eggs, beef, pate, clingfilm etc. but none of these have affected trade as much as this 'mad seal disease'. I was so concerned I wrote to The Grocer (trade magazine) about my problem, they sympathised and said it was something restricted to North Birmingham, although apparently shops in the Wolverhampton area went through something similar in the mid 1980s. They went on to say that there was a Doctor from Eastern Europe who was trying to solve the problem, but in the meantime it would help if I offered discounts to Villa supporters or even supported them. It's either that or sell the shop.

I am now trying to sell the shop. Listen to your Mothers, they are always right.

DAVE THE GROCER

"We don't come from Birmingham"

Teach yourself Black Country by Baggie Bert

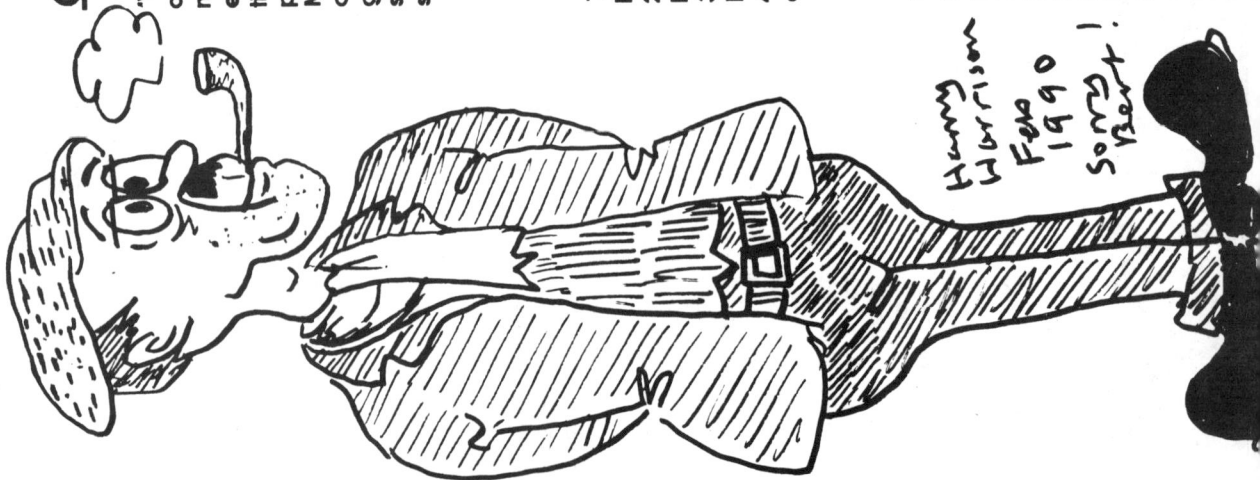

"We don't come from Birmingham!" is our own indignant response to geographical ignorance on the part of opposition supporters. Of course, WE all know WBA is based in the Black Country, NOT Birmingham and is part of the rich culture of that region. Many phrases heard around the Hawthorns could be indecipherable to visitors, so Baggie Bert has come to the rescue with this simple guide. The phrases are Baggie Bert's, so is the translation.

EXPRESSIONS OF JOY AND SORROW

1) "Bloody bostin' Splendid bit of football lads

2) "We give 'em a roite lompin' Albion have WON by a surprisingly large margin

3) "We bay 'arf bin thraped!" Albion have LOST by a surprisingly large margin

4) "Ee day 'arf gi 'im a palling!" Our winger constantly outclassed their defenders.

INSULTS

1) "Goo 'an bile yer yead, referee" That was a rather silly decision on your part old man

2) "Yer bloody great WASSOCK!" Did you REALLY have to fall over in the six yard area Mr Goodman

3) "E's loike a bloody great fart on trespass!" His contribution to the game has been minimal.

4) "E's yampy 'ee is!" The opposing side possess a neanderthal man centre half.

5) "What's 'ee blartin' on about?" Me thinks the opposition doth protest too much.

MISCELLANEOUS

6) "Ballyache referee!" q.v. "Goo an bile yer yed"
7) "Yo' grate lummock!" Reference to Ian Ormondroyd's general build.

1) "I bay arf clammed" I could eat a horse with spots on.
2) "Ee ay arf a bobbydazzler" A description of Benno Bennett smartly dressed and ready for a night on the town.
3) "Put a cogwinder on 'im, ma mon!" Robert Hopkins afficianados should be familiar with this one.
4) "Thrussle =thrush= thrustle = (guess who?)"
5) "He do' arf tek atter 'is brother" Description of Gary Robson after a good game.
6) "Gi' 'em a good tankin' our kid." Put a few past the Wolves Mr Goodman please.
7) "E's ony skraged 'imself - gerrup yer big babby" You have only grazed yourself and are therefore malingering.
8) "----, Yo'm rodny idle 'yo am (insert which ever player's name you like). He might as well be sat in the stand, such has been his contribution to the proceedings.

AND FINALLY

Grorty Dick - Albion fanzine full of poisonous and peurile prose!
Many thanks to the lads who sit in Block K seats J 93-96 whose assistance with research into this article was invaluable - the doctors tell me my hearing will return to normal in time!

DID YOU KNOW...

Tranmere Rovers tried a limited computerised ID card scheme this season. It was quickly abandoned as the cards were susceptible to the weather. Bent soggy cards could not be machine read.

Newport County of the Hellenic League are run by a committee democratically elected each year by supporters.

Harry Harrison
Feb 1990
Sorry Bert

Price 50p

No3 Sept '91

Still, MUSTN'T GRUMBLE

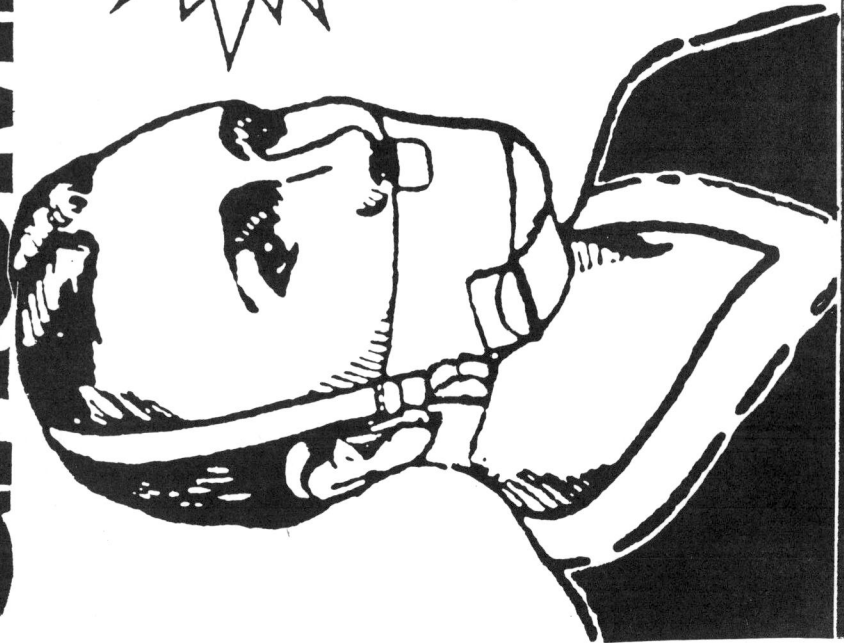

Season 91/92. We're gaggin' for it.

THE HEARTS FANZINE SEAN CONNERY COLLECTS. POSSIBLY

ABSENT WITHOUT LEAVE

If you were one of the few who bothered to go to Tynie on the 13th of May this year, I hope that you were as disappointed as I was when I looked around the ground and saw nothing but empty terracing. A turn out of 5575 for any Hearts game would be considered bad, but for a testimonial for one of the clubs most loyal and devoted players was disgraceful.

The excuses served-up by so called Hearts fans when asked why they hadn't gone ranged from the sublime to the bloody pathetic; "Oh, I was playing football down the park"; "I was doing the gardening," and worst of all "I couldnae be bothered, that Mackay's crap anyway."

Everybody is well aware that Gary's performances a season or two ago were not exactly awe inspiring, but please remember that over the piece Mackay has been, and hopefully will be again, one of Hearts most influential players ever since his debut in 1981. I find it hard to believe that the missing thousands (Hearts average attendance for '90-'91 was 10,263 for all games) have forgotten that a few seasons ago it was not an exageration to say "when Mackay plays Hearts play." The season that has just elapsed witnessed Gary return to form and link well with Degsy Ferguson which augurs well for this season. So why desert him?

Loyalty breeds loyalty, so how can we as Hearts fans expect the players to remain loyal when we cannot be bothered to turn up to honour our most loyal of players.

Unfortunately Mackay's match is not unique in this respect. Zico was 'insulted' with a crowd of only 8171 for his testimonial versus Everton in 1987, and only 9001 made the effort to honour Eamon Bannon, a player that maybe didn't spend the majority of his career at Gorgie but remember he left in order that the club would receive a much needed financial lifeline.

It may be time to rethink the whole Testimonial idea (time of year, opposition etc.) but until such time as this occurs please remember that benefit matches are not handed out willy-nilly, but are given to those who deserve them, those who have given themselves to our club, those who, most importantly, deserve your thanks.

See you all at Henry's.

Pollok — Fulton, 1-0

NEW BALLS PLEASE !

Having endured the full horror of our West of Scotland exit
to Largs Thistle, as I left Newlandsfield that evening it hit me
like an Ally Marshall volley in the private parts that it was no
more football - the end of the season.

The creeping paralysis of the close season was upon me and I
had about seven weeks to endure before another football fix
could be had. What does a Pollok supporter do in the close season
I ask? Does he/she draw their black and white scarf closely round
their body and retire to a darkened room in a cocoon like
state for seven weeks, or does he/she find alternative amusement
on a Saturday afternoon, playing or watching the many other sports
on offer.... or indeed is there anything else?

The coccon option was not open to me as my wife found the
prospect of a black and white body lying around the lounge for
seven weeks a bit inconvenient and not a little untidy, so I was
forced to seek alternative amusement during the close season.

The first couple of weeks of the close season are often the
worst having just come off a heavy diet of 3 games a week to
nothing. That's what you call cold turkey.

If possible, a summer holiday should be fitted in to the close
season and this must be taken in early June so as not to miss
the pre-season (top secret miles from anywhere) friendlys and
the start of the League Cup in August. Holidays duly taken and
three close season Saturdays out of the way, it was time to seek
out some alternative fun on a Saturday.

On with the telly..... Oh Geez! Bloody Wimbledon - Robo Tennis.
Hairy muscle bound foul mouthed oafs slogging a ball back and
forth over a net - and thats just the womens tennis. No real
action in the crowd either, no chanting, no singing, not even a
Mexican wave. No pies, just strawberries and sugar !

It is an interesting thought, that if there was a Mexican wave
round the Centre Court, would wee Betty be on her feet with the
rest of them?

No, Tennis was not the answer. So the next available sport on
offer was the Open Golf Championship. Now, I'm no glof expert.
In fact I can kick a glof ball further than I can whack it with
a glof pole (as you can see, I have a firm grasp of the technical
terms) but watching the Greg Normals and the Sandy Pyles of this
world made it look so easy, I was nearly tempted to load the
hickory golf poles into the car and show off prowess at the
Royal and Ancient Deaconsbank, or Royal Deekers as we in the
golfing world call it. But then why spoil a good walk by trying
to hit a wee white ball?

It is very strange to watch golfers being interviewed on TV.
They never say things like.... 'It was a round of two halves' or
'Over the moon, Peter' or 'The boy done good'.

'Sick as a birdie' or 'Playing for the jersey' (pringle, of
course) never cross their lips. No style or imagination these
golfing boys, let's give cricket a go.

Now, I've played cricket, and believe me, it is not a game for
softies. When you are standing at the crease waiting for some
fast bowler to rearrange your dental work, then a little fear
creeps into the game to keep you on your toes.

Watching cricket is a different story.I'd rather watch the
Test card than the Test match.Five days of rubbing your balls on
your trousers and bowling maidens over - can't touch you for it.
No,the 'Morning Jim,Morning Brian' clink,pass the gin bottle
scenario is not for this Pollok supporter.

So,what was left,apart from three blank Saturdays of the close
season.The sports channel on Sky TV is an interesting option,but
flounders on too many minority sports.After a while the delights
of floodlight Dominoes from Ramsgate or Synchronised Fish
Supper Eating live and exclusive from Harry Ramsdens begins to
lose it's appeal.

No,no more telly,it was time to reach for the boots and get out
and about and down to the Social Club.Let's hear all the usual
round of rumours of who we were signing,who was leaving and
which country the pre-season friendlies were in.Of course,every
one has their own list of departures and arrivals,all allegedly
passed on by the highest authority,but we could all cross off
Mikhailichenko from our list as he had opted to sign for another
South Side Glasgow club.However,speculation was rife that we had
just this afternoon signed the entire Ayrshire League and
re-instated our ex-players Dougie Arnott and Chic Charnley.

A few beers and much speculation successfully leaked,whiled
away the remaining close season Saturdays.

With one more Saturday to go until the return of football,
what was I going to do after sampling the joys of summer sports
and developing terminal boredom.

Ah well,there was only one thing for it.Slowly winding my
Pollok scarf round my body I entered my darkened lounge and
adopted a cocoon like state on the settee.

The wife couldn't complain about a weeks hibernation.

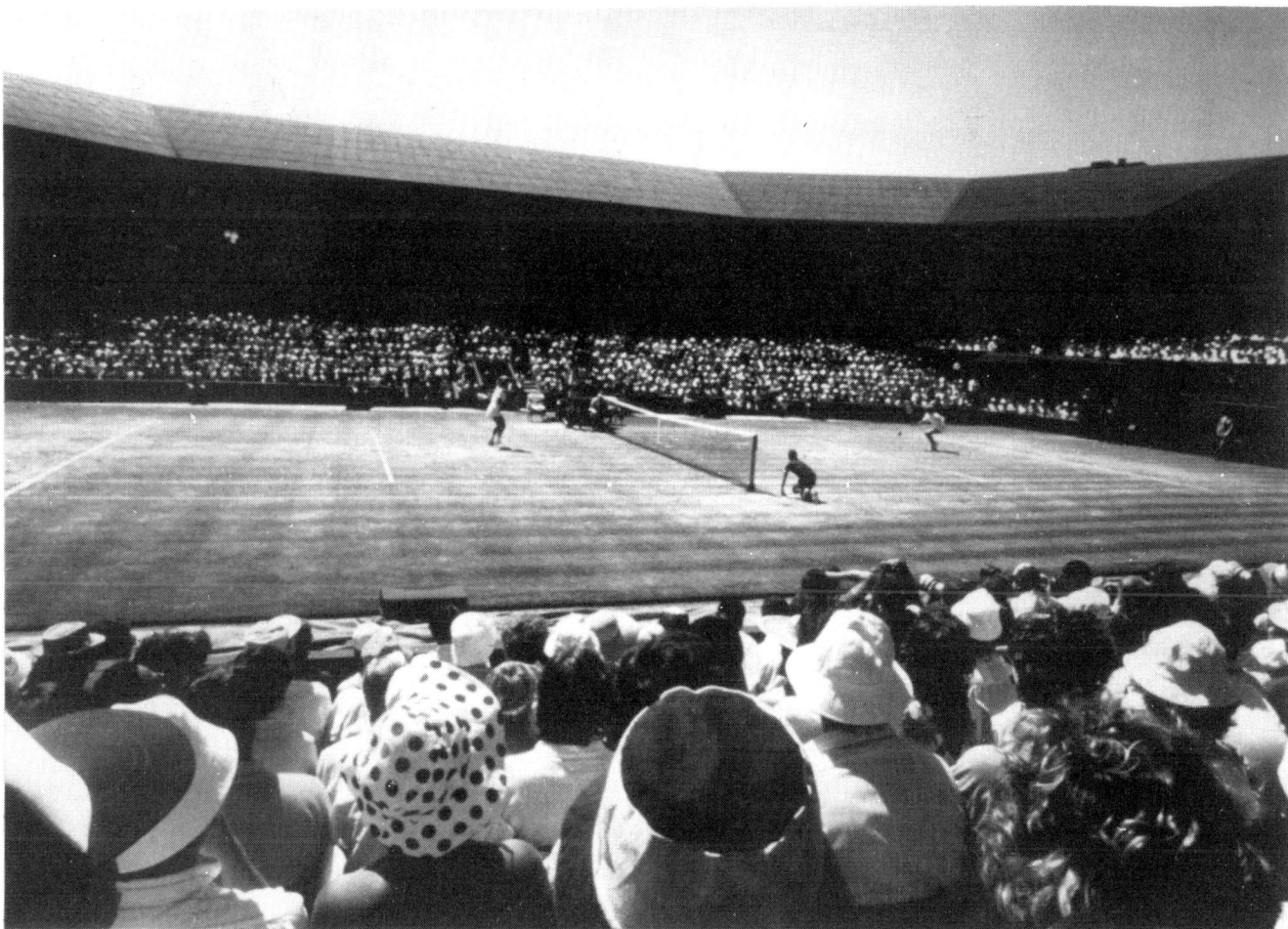

ON THE MARCH

ON THE MARCH

ON THE MARCH

an alternative view of southampton f.c.

WRITTEN BY THE FANS FOR THE FANS

WHY WASN'T JESUS BORN IN SKATESMOUTH?
CAUSE THEY COULDN'T FIND A VIRGIN,
AND CERTAINLY NOT THREE WISE MEN.

BENALI'S MOUSTACHE ESCAPES

> CALM DOWN, ITS ONLY FRANNYS TASH

> OH MY GOD WHAT IS IT?

> ARRRGH GET IT AWAY FROM ME

GIVE DONNY A NEW HAIRSTYLE • SID THE SKATE •
GRAHAM BAKER IS A DUCK • WHO FRAMED KEVIN MOORE •
ALL THIS AND MORE IN YOUR FUN PACKED O·T·M

makes the rest
look very **80**'s

EDITION TWO

COULD THEY BE RELATED →

Dear OTM,

I've been a regular at the Dell now for somewhat 25 years and I just couldn't belive my eyes at the Man utd home game this season. The two wingers our Rod Wallace and their Danny Wallace, I mean would you credit it, not only a striking resemblence but they also share the same surname, they couldn't possibly be related could they?

> OUR MIDFIELD JUST CAN'T GET INTO THE GAME TODAY!

> SORRY JIMMY, FULL UP MATE!

> MCLOUGHLIN HAS JUST MISSED THE POST

THE LAD done brilliant

Police officers, firemen and ambulance crew were punched, kicked and urinated upon by, a hooligan element in the crowd.

Some thugs rifled the pockets of injured fans as they were stretched out unconscious on the pitch.

Sheffield MP Irvine Patnick revealed

Sick Reporters Making up POISON

-- "journalistic thugs" --

THE EXECUTIVE Glassman

"IT'S RIDICULOUS TO SUGGEST THAT I AM OUT OF TOUCH WITH THE CLUB."

WHAT DO YOU GET IF YOU THROW A SET OF LEGO UP IN THE AIR?

Get the yobs into uniform

WE'LL continue to have football hooligans so long as we don't bring back National Service.

That would teach the young self-discipline and a sense of duty to the community.

The country is in favour of National Service. The Conservative and Labour parties are against it in mistaken fear of losing votes.

I don't share Mrs. Thatcher's wish to opt out of the football World Cup finals. If football louts disgraced us in Italy the case for National Service would be overwhelming.

WORLD CUP STICKERS

PART ONE : FREE WITH THE GAAARRGGHH!! WORLD CUP SPECIAL.

1. PELÉ
Real name Edson Arantes Di Nascimento. The Black Pearl, as he was known started his World Cup career when he was very young. And finished it some years later when he was older.

BRAZIL.

2. GEORGE BEST
Flairs, talent and girls were all to be associated with Georgie on his way to the top. His Kings Road boutique was visited by all the groovy cats in the sixties.

IRELAND (N)

3. JAMES GREAVES
The Lad columnist is probably better known as a goal scorer and TV presenter; but in all three jobs he is always likely to crack a joke.
He is a funny old geezer.

ENGLAND

4. Some bloke.
I don't know who this chap is, but he's sure to have been a top player in the fourties or fifties, judging by his hairstyle.

WALES

5. JOCK STEIN
I wonder how good a player he was? He was certainly a great manager, Under him Scotland qualified for every World Cup that England didn't.

SCOTLAND.

6. BOBBY CHARLTON
Unaffected by the foibles of fashion, Bobby has remained true to his roots (what few he has) by staying with Manchester United.

ENGLAND

7. SIR ALF RAMSEY
Most famous for being the only manager of B'ham City NOT to be sacked. He also invented defensive football and won the world Cup.

ENGLAND

8. COL. GADDAFFI
The only international terrorist/ folk hero to play for Uruguay in the World Cup. He surprised the world when he took on dual nationality.
HAS NEVER BEEN BOOKED.

LIBYA

PART TWO : FREE WITH THE NEXT WORLD CUP SPECIAL. (1994)

Maybe It's Because

Football Supporters Association London Branch

WE DONE THESE IN THE PUB....

Actors

Jeff Goldblumfield Road
Richard Burton Albion
Robert Tooting & Mitchum
Kiefer Sunderland
Harrison Bradford
Steve McQueens Park Rangers
David Nevin
Charlton Athletic Heston
Wimble-Don Johnson
Lee Marvinny Jones

Horror

Nightmare on Emlyn Street
Hullraiser
Exetorcist
Pet Sematerry Butcher
Drill Field Killer
Hallowstein
The Eagle Dead
The Jimmy Hills Have Eyes
Whyte of the Living Dead
The Gowling

Actresses

Meryl Filbert Streep
Shirley Anfield
Julie St Andrews
Jamie Lee Curbishley
Michelle East Pfeiffer
Deborah Wingers
Leigh Remick Mills
Vanessa Redgravesend & Northfleet
Tuesday Weldstone
Elizabeth Taylor Report

Films

How To Murder Your East Fife
North by North West Bromwich Albion
Day of the Jackal Charlton
Witches of East Stirlingshire
San Siros of Telemark
Neil Webb of the Spiderwoman
Dance With A Ranger
Love Street Story
Lennie Lawrence of Arabia
Clive Alien
Manon Le Saux

War, War, Bloody War!

DunFalkirk
David Kelly's Heroes
The Cruel Chel-sea
633 Squadron Hotspur
Cross of Come on you Irons
A Stamford Bridge Too Far
Andeers Limpar in Tumbledown
Feyenoord Rotterdambusters
Reach for the Sky Blues
In Ipswich We Serve

Art

Whistlers Motherwell
The Haywaine Clarke
Birmingham's Blues Period
Jim Bone - a - Lisa
Irving Gernonica by Picasso
The Fallen Maradona With The Big Boobies
Richard Van Gough
Monet bags Tottenham

Vietnam

David Plattoon
Hamburger Jimmy Hill
Apocalypse Howe
Full Metal Kenny Jackett
The Deer Norman Hunter
Stan Cummings Home
Bournemouth on the 4th July
Full Members Jacket

Good Morining West Ham

Books

Tess of the d'Urbervillas
The Man U Never Was
Aylott on the Landscape
Northanger Abbey Stadium
Jane Eyre United
A Tale of Stoke Cities
Southen - Dune - ited
Billy Stark
The Last of the MoJohnstones

Plays

Alls Well That Oakwell
Montrosencrantz and Guildenstirling are Dead
Agatha Christie's Offside Trap
Ablett - Prince of Denmark
Tony Henry IV Parts 1 & 2
A Woman of Substitutes
Bordeaux Calcutta
A Mansfield For All Seasons
Look Kingsley Black in Anger
Who's Afraid of Virginia Wolves?

Singers & Groups

Frank Ifield Road
Belinda Carlisle United
Deborah Harry Bassett
Madonnacaster Rovers
Guns 'n' Montroses
The Bobby Charlatans
Joy Division Four
Iron Maidstone
New Fast Automatic Cardiffodills
Bolton Thrower

Star Trek

Captain James T Falkirk
Lt Uhereford United
De Nottingham Forest Kelley
Mr Spotland
Mr Chekhoventry City
Dilithium Crystal Palace
Perry Sucklingon
Rotherhamulon United
To Bolton Go Where No Mansfield Has Foggon be Forfar
Steam Me In Mr Scott

Westerns

Hampden High
For A Few Bobby Moores
Peter The Cat Ballou
The Good The Bad and the Sedgely
Patt Garrett & Brian the Kidd
Eric Young Guns
Butch Wilkins & The Sundance Kid
Alan Smith & Jones
Carry On Cowboybeath
A Fistful of Grobbelaars

James Bond

A View To A Kilmarnock
Dr Noades
Cascarino Royale
The Mervyn Daylights
Diamonds Are For Everton
Oxfordpussy
For York Eyes Only
Never Shay Nevin Again
The Mackay Who Loved Me

Fairytales

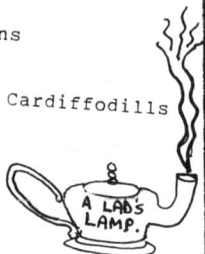

Brothers Grimmsby
Palace in Sunderland
Keith Cinderweller
Birmingham Getting Promotion
Guy Dick Whittingham
Babes in the George Wood
Puss In Bootham Crescent
Peter Pan-cev
Hans Christian Viv Anderson
Ross Jack & The Beanstalk

The Unofficial Fanzine of Carlisle Utd.

C.U.F.C. The CUMBERLAND SAUSAGE.

DOWN AND OUT IN THE FOURTH
The Fanzine : Responsibility & Dissent

'Orwellian' sticks in the English mind largely as a nightmarish vision of absolute social control. Orwell, the man, though preferred the more honest virtue of dissent, "telling people what they did not want to hear", os so he defined liberty. What relationship then to football and the attendant presence of the fanzine ?

Visions, if not, of absolute control but of greed and power monopolies currently dominate the football landscape. Perpetuated by those whose interests are entirely their own sustained by ineffectual opposition, these visions may become reality. Yet behind this veil there is dissent, murmurings. Here, the analogy with Orwell is plain. One need only look now at the FA's plans for the English Super League by way of example.

Yet the fanzine existed and thrived prior to this present furore. It did so due to the continuing adulation of the game by it's viewing public. In spite of this adulation, supporters always knew they were cheated : the arbitrary escalation of prices, crumbling facilities, infuriating absence of acknowledgement, etc, etc. It seems clear that the framework of football's bureaucracy is suffocating the voice of those so mightily placed to prevent it. Yet it fails to do so for lack of several important factors - clarity, unity, purpose for example. It is here that the football fanzine has a potentially pivotal role to play. It must not assign itself to harping sad, merely irrelevant noises it must take a self-critical look at it's ability to provide a platform for campaigning against changes and evils thrust upon us from above. Like Winston Smith of '1984' it must make the transition from unthinking object to active and dissenting citizen.

There is a natural market amongst supporters for the jovial, the humorous and the bawdy. But yet, in such afflicted and pessimistic times as these there is the need not merely to reflect, but also to lead and agitate. Throughout the 1980's football was central to government demonology. Like the miners in their traditional homes, football supporters refused to be torn from their traditional allegiances. Football was demonologized for issues such as hooliganism and racism, governments absolved themselves from blame for the existence of such ills. No-one ever really believed they cared, and thus it is a those who stand in a more direct and affectinate relationship with football to discuss and attempt to solve such ills.

To deny that football grounds harbour bigotry of all kinds is as dishonest as it isridiculous. The problem relates to how it is to be solved, and who is to solve it.

Take the issue of racism. Incitement to racial hatred contravenes legal codes, whilst racism, passive or active, should offend moral codes. I have seen individuals arrested at matches for swearing, gesticulating, some have even been charged under the Pubic Order Act. Yet I have seen no police action when frequent and vicious racial abuse is flaunted. Some PC's I have seen have even laughed. This inactivity was seen when S. Robson and I spoke to Sheffield policemen involved in policing Sheffield's football grounds. With so many in the crowd, they agreed evasively, they could not pin-point guilty individuals. Reasonable but inadequate. Because :

Most of us understand actions that contravene certain and specific legal edicts, and as a result, largely adjust our behaviour accordingly. Yet there is no law to punish ignorance. Periodically it may be consumed or transcended, but it will continually revive and grow – it is both fertile and malevolent. Law is not an active force for social education, it is a collection of prohibitions that stipulate duties and spheres of conduct The vacuum left by law where ignorance and issues, like racism, thrive is an area where the active and motivated should operate. Thus, I believe in the "dissident" role of the fanzine. Ignorance can be fought with reason, discussion. Fanzines must adopt this responsibility and be courageous enough to follow it through. In a dismal season for Carlisle, average readership of this fanzine was 350, which is an encouraging figure. Brunton Park is by no means exempt from bigotry, and our responsiblity, like charity must begin here. Only those who love the game can hope to make it attractive and hospitable to all. Thus we must fight back against both officialdom and the bigots. The limitation of the law and the blindness of the football authorities makes it our duty. The duty of all fans.

Dissent will not leave us stranded in humour and irreverence alone. Or as Orwell himself said :

'I am going to produce a work of art' I write because there is some lie I want to expose, some fact to which I want to draw attention, my concern is to get a hearing

"When I write, I do not say to myself

Mark McAlindon

"To deny that football grounds harbour bigotry of all kinds is as dishonest as it is ridiculous. The problem relates to how it is to be solved, and who is to solve it."
THE CUMBERLAND SAUSAGE

SO SAYING, THE FIGURES MELTED AWAY INTO THE JUNGLE... LEAVING A SOMEWHAT SHAKEN MELCHESTER PARTY!
THAT WAS A ODD DO AND NO MISTAKE!
MAYBE YOU SHOULDN'T HAVE INTERFERED, ROY...
I REPEAT... I WASN'T GOING TO STAND BY AND WATCH THAT KID SINK LIKE A STONE... CURSES OR NO CURSES! BESIDES, IT'S ALL A LOAD OF MUMBO-JUMBO!
ROY DID NOT HEAR THE HELICOPTER PILOT'S GRIM COMMENT...
I BEEN HERE TWENTY YEARS AND I SEE MANY STRANGE THINGS HAPPEN... NOT EASY TO EXPLAIN. THERE IS MUCH MAGIC IN JUNGLES...
WELL, DON'T SAY ANYTHING, PAL... I GET THE FEELING OUR SKIPPER MIGHT BLOW HIS TOP AGAIN.
THERE WAS ONE MORE MATCH TO BE PLAYED IN THE ROVERS' TOUR — AGAINST A CLUB SIDE. IT WAS THEN THAT IT HAPPENED...
SHOOT, ROY—!
IT MUST BE A GOAL... ROY RACE DOESN'T MISS CHANCES LIKE THIS!
BUT EVEN AS ROY DREW BACK HIS FOOT...
UUGH! I—I CAN'T MOVE MY LEG! IT'S GONE ALL... NUMB!
THE BALL WAS QUICKLY CLEARED BY A GRATEFUL DEFENDER, AND THE CHANCE WAS LOST!
BAD LUCK, ROY!
IT WASN'T BAD LUCK, THAT'S FOR SURE! SOMETHING DEFINITELY STOPPED ME MOVING MY LEG...!
9

Panel 1: IT WAS A DIFFERENT, SUPER-CONFIDENT ROY RACE WHO SWUNG INTO ACTION!

OH, GREAT BALL, ROY!

HE'S PLAYING BETTER NOW!

ENGLAND ARE ON THE ATTACK—WE COULD PULL ONE BACK HERE!

Panel 2: SURE ENOUGH, ROY BRILLIANTLY ANTICIPATING THE CROSS, LAUNCHED HIMSELF IN A SPECTACULAR FLYING DIVE!

IT'S THERE! WE'VE SCORED!

FANTASTIC! THE GOAL OF THE SEASON!

Panel 3: ROY AGAIN SHOWED HIS SKILL, SOON AFTERWARDS...

OH, GREAT BODY SWERVE! ARMENTE WENT COMPLETELY THE WRONG WAY!

THIS COULD BE THE EQUALISER...!

Panel 4: AND THEN...

GOOAAALL!

THE SCORES ARE LEVEL!

GOOD OLD ROY! HE'S MAKING UP FOR HIS POOR FIRST HALF!

Panel 5: WHEN THE FINAL WHISTLE SOUNDED, ENGLAND HAD WON 3-2. THERE WAS ONLY ONE GOALSCORER...THE REMARKABLE ROY RACE!

PHEEEEEEP!

WITH A STRIKER LIKE ROY RACE, HOW CAN WE FAIL?

THE FIRST HALF WAS TERRIBLE...THE SECOND HALF HE WAS MARVELLOUS!

Panel 6: WELL, LAD, THAT ORCHID YOU GAVE ME, CERTAINLY DID THE TRICK. IT REALLY BROKE THE CURSE!

THERE WAS NO CURSE, SENOR... IT WAS ALL IN YOUR MIND! YOU THOUGHT THERE WAS, AND THAT WAS ENOUGH TO CAUSE YOUR BODY TO PLAY TRICKS! YOU CURED YOURSELF!

Panel 7: PEOPLE OFTEN SAY THERE'S MAGIC ON THE FOOTBALL PITCH— PERHAPS, ON THIS OCCASION, I THOUGHT THERE WAS TOO MUCH MAGIC!

If ever a Swansea City player was worthy of the ultimate Welsh sporting accolade: to be immortalised in clay and become part of the Grogg collection, then that (English)man is Bob Latchford. For here is the only truly ace goalscorer to play for a Welsh club in the last twenty-five years...

big Bob came to the Vetch Field in the Summer of 1981 with an excellent footballing pedigree. Starting with his native Birmingham City as a bearded youngster he is still regarded as one of their favourite sons, second only in the St. Andrews Hall of Fame to Trevor Francis. An ex-Brum manager quoted in 1974, "Sell Latchford? I'd rather have the sack!" The manager in question, one Freddie Goodwin, was obviously not a man of his word as he did actually sell Bob four months later - I don't know whether he did get the sack - but this didn't concern bitter Brummies, they simply wanted Goodwin beheaded and some very unsavoury deeds carried out on his privates for this dreadful act of treason. The Blues fans had hoped that along with Francis, Latchford would make Birmingham City the finest Black Country exponent since 'Crossroads', but it wasn't to be,

it was on to Goodison Park for Bob in a then British record £350,000 transfer deal, and he soon started doing for Everton what a certain John Toshack was doing for their Merseyside rivals. Seven years and some truly memorable goals later after an accomplished career at Everton where he became the first divisions top scorer on more than one occasion, and gained twelve caps for England, Big Bob was comntemplating a move to Wales, and so the obvious move would be to another blue-shirted team, but unfortunately for that blue-shirted Welsh team (I forget their name), Bob knew of only one team in the Principality, and keen to try out a new colour scheme, decided to pull on the majestic white jersey of Swansea.

bob endeared himself to the North Bank with a hat-trick on his debut against Leeds United. It was the first of a few trebles for Bob, but one of my favourite memories was a magic header at Maine Road in October 1982. From the moment the ball left Bob's head, way out on the edge of the box, it was going only one way -

B in the net. Bob came up with a magnificent total of thirty-four goals in that relegation season, and his strikes were responsible for the slaying of many teams considered "better" than Swansea. But in between that term and our lousiest season on record, 1983/84, he put in for a transfer. (cue a sharp rise in the suicide rate in South West Wales, and celebratory street parties in the Cardiff area, a team often on the receiving end of Latch's golden boots). Some say it was a legacy of manager Toshack's ailing relationship with his squad, with the original stars dropping like flies from an increasingly sad side. But Latchford patched up his differences with the club, and being a true professional turned down approaches from Leicester and Chelsea, vowing he'd see out his career at Swansea.

Come early 1984 though, and our last remaining star was on his way. It became impossible for him to stay at the Vetch with the club in such a state, deteriorating as rapidly off the field as they were on. Latch was simply too good for Swansea, even at the age of 33. The class of '84, as they became known, just seven wins from forty two games, and a points total of 29, our worst ever. Not even an Ian Evans team could emulate that! It's worth noting that the three men who balls-ed up team affairs, Toshack, Phil Boersma and Doug Livermore have since managed Real Madrid, and become assistant at Liverpool and Spurs respectively?

it wasn't the last we'd be seeing of Bob mind you, for he popped up against the Swans a few years on for Newport County, Lincoln and Merthyr, after spells at Coventry and a Dutch club. I find it really upsetting to see former heroes turning out for your rivals, they always seem to look sad and overweight, and it makes you wish for their sake they'd packed it in a few years earlier.

had it not been for the financial state the club was in, I'm convinced Bob would have been happy to stay at Swansea. As it was, he stuck it out longer than Curtis, Leighton and Robbie James, and that, as well as his superb goals, is why he'll always be special to Swansea fans.

Get your pitch out for the lads!

By The DEEPDALE DISCIPLE

Lancs Evening Post: Which do you prefer Brian, astroturf or grass ?

PNE's BRIAN MOONEY: I dunno - I've never smoked astroturf.

THREE DOWN,ONE TO GO. With Luton and Oldham reverting to grass this season, only Preston North End are still spared the antics of an irate groundsman and the extortionate cost of grass seed.

September 1st was the tenth anniversary of Britain's first professional League match to be played on plastic - Loftus Road hosted QPR v.Luton (NB) on its' appalling surface with the sky-high bounce and ice-rink grip.

And oh how the footballing world grumbled and moaned when Preston and Oldham followed Luton into the world of artificial fibres and carpet burns,albeit on vastly better pitches than the one still haunting South Africa Road.

With Luton being the nearest First Division club to the family,home and Preston being the spiritual one, I have seen so much "plastic footy" that it makes a pleasant change to see a game on this real "grass" stuff. But the reasons for the installation of the plastic pitches at Deepdale and Keni Road differed greatly. Luton had suffered for many years with a very poor sloping surface which was regularly carved into a mud-bath due to the lack of air circulation and sunlight allowed to infiltrate Fort Evans. Most of the £400,000 outlay was rapidly recouped by the tremendously successful pitch-hire scheme.

On the other hand,the wide open plains of Deepdale had fostered a superb playing surface; destroying it was a crying shame but in 1986,with PNEFC on the verge of bankruptcy and 91st in the league, in stepped Preston Council with a rescue plan. They installed the artificial pitch which became a central part of the clubs new community scheme and was available to local teams for a nominal fee - payable to the owners (ie.the council).

After the initial season of success when a great new team was put together and marched victorious throughout the land - triumphant home and away, PNE have languished in Division 3 with very little to show for all the promise shown by the new regime. The amusingly dire performances on plastic of supposedly star teams such as Liverpool,usually result in the question of home advantage arising yet again. I have very little sympathy with this argument. A successful team needs to adjust to different conditions every week - lush grass,mud, ponds,ice and dust bowls plus perhaps one game a year on plastic. Preston have to learn to cope with plastic and grass, so it single week in order to alternate their style every could be argued that it is the home side who are the most disadvantaged of the two teams.

A poor team (eg Luton 1989-91) will struggle to win at home and are diabolical away - the additional factor of an artificial pitch,(as you can see in the table) has minimal impact. "It's all in the mind, innit guv."

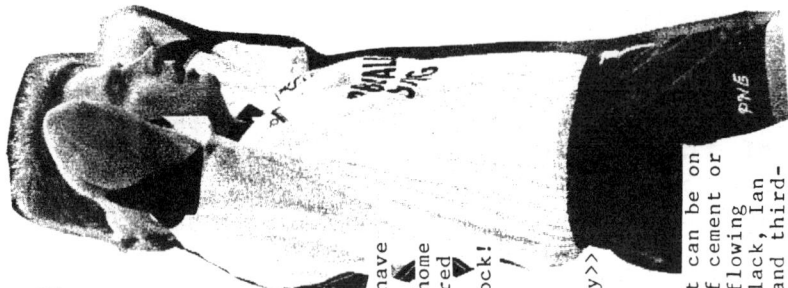

		HOME		AWAY		TOTAL	
	pos	Points max.69	Goals	Pts	Gl	Pts % at home	Gls % at home
1986/7 Great	2	75%	36	55%	36	58%	50%
1987/8 Averg	16	52%	30	32%	18	62%	62%
1988/9 vGood	6	71%	56	33%	23	78%	71%
1989/0 vPoor	19	54%	42	22%	23	71%	65%
1990/1 Averg	17	55%	33	26%	13	68%	72%

The successful teams have been formidable at home but have struggled to retain that form away. Poor seasons are characterised by gaining only half the available points at home and rarely winning on the road. The proportion of goals scored at home fluctuates wildly,but always corresponds with the relative points haul.i.e."Those who score most,win most".Shock!

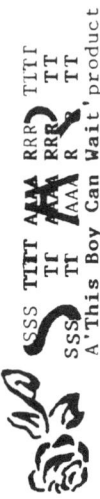

Another one that got away>>

SSS TTT AAA RRR TTT
TT RRR TT
SSS TT AAA R TT
A'This Boy Can Wait'product

Home of majestic music & fine footy

The game may also not be as pretty a sight as it can be on grass - two terrible teams who couldn't trap a bag of cement or pass the buck cause great distress for the lover of flowing football, as demonstrated by the likes of Kingsley Black, Ian Bogie and Rick Holden. A team of cloggers,half-wits and third-rate youngsters (eg.PNE'90) will struggle as much on plasky as anywhere else.

Only decent sides ever win anything. Luton 1987-8,PNE 87-89 and Oldham 89-91 have all needed to win numerous cup games off the carpet,not to mention surviving twenty-odd away games a season in order to hit the heights. How often do you hear folk remarking on QPR's astonishing change of fortune since they replaced their trampoline with a beach and finally a grass pitch three years ago?

Luton's brief respite from relegation traumas came by way of a 15-match unbeaten run in the Littlewoods Cup, which included six away wins and a draw - not exactly the stuff of the "plastic playpeople" is it ? But when the Hatters are finally relegated this coming May,the same boring comments will start up again -"It was only their pitch that kept them up" etc. Just consider the necessary sales of Wilson,Harford,Wegerle, Breacker,Dowie and now Black before joining in.

Likewise with NorthEnd - in 1987 (and again in '89) five-figure crowds regularly came to see the likes of Jemson,Ellis,Brazil,Philliskirk,Mooney and Bogie stut their stuff(or rather stagger around) in a mesmerising drunken state in the case of magical Mooney). But we sold them all for over £1 million in total - the result being three years of struggle and a recession-hit community bringing crowds down to the 3000 mark. And that is despite an early season home record of P7 W4 D3 scored 23 against 10 and an equally remarkable away run of played four,lost four.....which defeats my argument entirely. Trust North End to let me down again !!

NEVER MIND THE DANGER

The Independent Norwich City F.C. Fanzine

A Tribute to Martin Peters

I'll never forget the days of Martin Peters in a Norwich shirt and as a youngster the awe with which I held the 'great man'. Still I think of him in demigod stature because for me he is quite simply the finest footballer I have ever seen. However it wasn't just that he was a fine player but also his nature, a quiet unflappable man, modest almost to a fault and on and off the pitch a gentleman who genuinely appreciated the supporters attention.

If all this is leading you to the belief that this article is biased then you're absolutely right and I make no apology what so ever. I was at the age where most kids needed a hero and as a City fan I didn't have to look any further than Martin. As the Barclay used to sing "Martin Peters walks on water !" and as far as I was concerned he probably did!

John Bond, contrary to popular opinion, did provide our fine club with a number of shrewd signings but surely none shrewder than Martin Peters from Spurs in 1975. It brought a buzz to the City that I had never before or after associated with a signing. I was 12 years old when Martin played his first season for City during which time most clubs, including Norwich, wore 'Admiral' kit which incorporated sock tie-ups with tags displaying the players number. I would arrive 3 hours (yes three!) before kick- off and stand right behind the River End goal. At the end of one particular game Martin took off his tie-ups and walked straight toward me with his hand outstretched. I could hardly believe it, THE man himself was going to give me, a mere kid, his tie-ups. I froze ready to accept. "There you go son" whispered Martin and handed the tie-ups to a kid standing next to me!

I didn't hold it against him. Over the seasons that followed Martin more than made up for it with his footballing genius. My Dad has a very simple theory about professional footballers namely "the majority are thick!". This is unquestionably a generalisation but I have to agree. Intelligent players stand head and shoulders above the rest. Martin certainly fell into the category of 'intelligent footballer' and his quick thinking often left him one step ahead of the opposition. This was a major asset and led to Martin's nickname, "the Ghost", as he appeared from seemingly thin air to score. A fine example of his quick thinking came in the 1978/79 game at Carrow Road between City and Spurs. Spurs raced into a two nil lead with City pulling one back just before half-time from a penalty after Peter Mendham had been tripped. The score seemed destined to remain the same with only a few minutes left on the clock. City then had a free-kick awarded some 30 plus yards out from the Barclay End goal. The obvious thing to do was to float the ball to the far post for all the City 'big-boys' to try and nod in! Subsequently, all the players including the goalkeeper drifted to the far post awaiting the inevitable. Steve Perryman spotted this and ran to the near post only to think better of it and return to the far post melee. Up stepped Martin and with the inside of his right boot stroked the ball delicately inside the near post ! Who else would have thought of that, let alone have the ability of carrying it out successfully?

That was typical of the man's vision. Martin could deliver the inch perfect pass, head a ball with power and accuracy and score goals (with either feet) as clinically as any centre-forward.

If he had any weakness it was with tackling, but who the hell went to a game to see Martin tackle!

He scored many memorable goals for City, too many to mention in total but another that sticks in my mind was the superb volley from outside the box to defeat Liverpool at Carrow Road in 76/77. This won 'Match of the Week' goal of the season competition with our old friend Gerry 'Ipswich' Harrison.

Martin's example to younger players was superb; an excellent player who never failed to give entertainment but whose behaviour at all times remained impeccable.

John Bond midway through Martin's career at City, made a statement which for once made sense! He declared that Martin was still god sorry good enough for England, a sentiment echoed by all City supporters.

This resulted in Martin captaining the England 'B' team but unfortunately Ron Greenwood (just like 'Leg- over' Robson) always picked his team from the National gutter press and Martin never gained another full cap.

Martin also had his testimonial game while at Norwich and a crowd of over 18,000 turned up to see the 1966 World Cup winners play. It was a superb occasion and to go with it one of the best ever programmes was produced simply called 'Martin'. I felt honoured to have been there!

City fans showed just how much they felt for Martin when City won the Milk Cup in 1985. ITV had chosen Steve Cram to come into the studio decked out in Sunderland gear to give his opinion of the game (he just complained about his teams selection!).

To give an impression of being unbiased (they don't normally bother!) a search was started for a Norwich 'celebrity'. A phone-in was held locally and Martin won the day!

He was also strongly tipped as the new City manager during Ken Brown's era and indeed with management in mind Martin finally left for Sheffield United as player/coach and later as manager. United fans obviously have very little regard for Martin as he succeeded only in taking them into the fourth division. Unfortunately, I was not surprised. Like many City fans I felt that he would never make a football manager; he should have continued his playing career because he still had a lot to offer.

He did play several games for United and indeed scored in front of the 'Match of the Day' cameras but the added responsibility of man-management meant that he never attained the high level of play that he did with City. Martin's departure from Sheffield United also signalled the end of his involvement with football.

A sad end for one of the greatest players England has ever produced.

Finally, I think its worth including a section of a report on the Chelsea versus Norwich game of 16th December 1977 written by Rob Hughes of the Sunday Times :-

"......It was Peters' 600th First Division game; testimony to a man's ability to be ten years ahead of his time, to go well beyond that decade as a still influential player, to carry the experience of 67 caps, to evade serious wear-and-tear and finally, to prove he retains the knack of slipping defenders to save a lost game. The man is 34, tiring physically perhaps, but still a thought or two ahead of those around, and education indeed for Ray Wilkins, possibly England's future captain, who today learned that the ultimate quality of a man who seeks to control play, is above all brainpower."

If anyone knows of Martins whereabouts, what he's doing etc. please let NMTD know as I would love to get him as guest speaker at an FSA meeting, and you never know he may have an old tie-up I can have!

Gary Reeve (From issue 7 - December 1989)

And now for the less serious stuff...

Here you can see our hero – Flecky – enjoying a quick pre-match barrel with the lads down the Nags. Nice to see you Robert – you're welcome anytime!

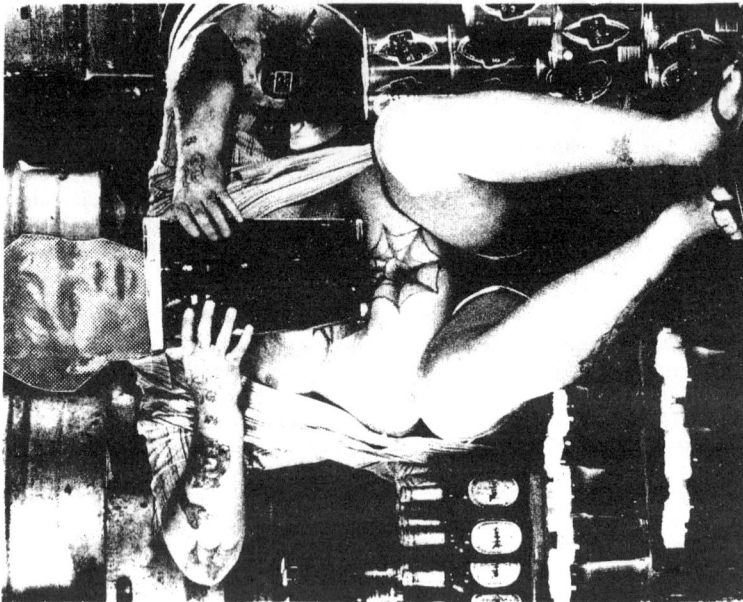

NMTD recently received a cry for help from one of our friends down there south of the border in Suffolk.

The plea comes from the head groundsman at Portman Road as he is very concerned about the state of the Ipswich pitch.

His problem is that the playing surface seems to be abnormally green and requires excessive amounts of cutting. He has no explanation for such a phenomenon.

We at NMTD are glad to be of service to our country cousins and after much investigation we have come up with the answer to the groundsman's prayers.

The answer is quite simple – the Ipswich pitch is so green because every other Saturday it has nothing but crap all over it!

ANDY THE AARDVARK

'HE'S ALWAYS GAME FOR A LARK!'

We're glad to be able to announce that following a secret inquiry undertaken by the Football League, referees have been instructed to award Norwich a larger quota of penalties this season.

In conjunction with UEFA, and the EEC, referees have been striving to reduce the Norfolk Penalty Mountain, believed to have been stored in a silo at Cantley's sugar beet factory.

Unfortunately, their remains a world-wide glut of penalties, and so Norwich will continue to suffer at the bigger clubs who can demand a larger share of the United Kingdom's allocation.

NMTD are always aiming to bring you the news that really matters. We have discovered an amazing fact brought to our attention in the pages of Chesterfield fanzine – The Crooked Spireite.

Did you know that when Fenerbache - the well known European side - walk out onto the pitch before the start of the game, they are greeted with song that contains the following lines...

"When the yellow canaries run out onto the pitch.
They make their rivals smell their shoes."

Hope they haven't stood in anything!

Under 13 Division

Ferndale Y	18	15	3	0	112	11	33
Comer P	18	15	1	2	148	24	31
Burlish O	18	13	2	3	137	18	
Bewdley H	18	11	2	5	97	23	24
Mostyn R	18	6	1	11	54	86	13
Droitwich S	18	5	1	12	62	103	11
Linden	18	5	1	12	22	77	11
Franche V	18	3	0	15	25	136	6
Cookley F	18	0	0	18	9	259	0

← Are these the worst teams in the land ?!?

Under 14 Division

Penn C	20	18	0	2	175	13	36
Comer P	17	17	0	0	127	14	34
Wordsley W	22	14	1	7	124	62	29
Worcester C	22	13	2	7	108	49	28
Kingsford K	21	14	0	7	98	49	28
Wribbenhall W	25	12	4	9	95	86	25
Forest F	21	12	1	8	118	50	25
Mostyn R	19	11	2	6	103	43	24
Franche R	25	9	3	13	81	108	21
Droitwich S	20	6	3	11	48	67	15
Alveley Y	20	5	2	13	58	85	12
Linden	22	5	1	16	84	102	11
Burlish O	23	2	2	17	36	115	9
Broadwaters S	22	0	0	22	8	413	0

→

What might have been

TODAY

CITY
v
KNIGHTON UTD.

LEAGUE DIV 1
K.O 3.00 pm
OR 3.10 pm
OR 3.20 pm
OR 3.30 pm
OR 3.40 pm

TERRACE £8.00

HAVE YOUR ID-CARD READY

IT'S THIS STUPID BLOODY MACHINE !! – IT'S ASKING IF HE WANTS A CASH WITHDRAWAL OR A BALANCE ENQUIRY !!

HURRY UP !! WHAT'S THE SODDIN' PROBLEM ??

YEAH !! WOSS THE BLEEDIN' HOLD UP ??

WOSSA TIME, CONSTABLE DIXON ??

ONE MINUTE TO KICK-OFF, SAH !! -TIME WE OPENED THE GATES TO GET THE POOR BASTARDS IN !!!

SPECIAL (SOCCER BRANCH)

THIS IS A SPECIAL B/B TO LET YOU KNOW WHO WE ARE IN CASE YOU DIDN'T RECOGNISE US

SOCCER COPS

Apron J Knick

EXCLUSIVE

CHASE IN BEDROOM SHOCKER!

In yet another thrilling hotter than hot stories NMTD can bring you all the information on the people that are at the core of activities at Carrow Road. In this issue we can reveal that Norwich city chairman Mr Robert Chase has been caught in the act in his very own home!

REFUSED

The NMTD journalists had their cameras at the ready but were politely refused entry to the Chase household. What is this scandal? What is all this about? Who is involved? Well it's only NMTD that dare to bring you the details of this sordid affair.

LONG WAIT

Having sent Mr Chase a copy of issue 6 of the super soaraway NMTD we waited with baited breath for a reply. Boy - were we surprised when we opened the long awaited letter.

ADMISSION

Typed neatly by Mr Chases PERSONAL SECRETARY and SIGNED by the man himself was a glaring admission that the most powerful man concerned with Norwich City Football club reads Never Mind The Danger nowhere else other than underneath his continental duvet in the privacy of HIS OWN BED!

ROYALTY

Never put off by a bad story we went in search of other famous readers to find out where they read NMTD. We found that even ROYALTY were involved.

The Duchess of Kent - a confirmed reader of The citizen and fan of NMTD admitted to us that she read both publications on the throne after comming back from the local curry house where she likes to have a meat phal - really hot stuff from the Duchess!

STAPLES

We even managed to track down the ex Ipswich favourite Paul Mariner. He said he also used NMTD in the toilet but always used to cut himself on the staples.

Do any other of our readers read NMTD in strange places - write in and tell us at the usual address!

ACE REPORTER : Perry Dyball

I will certainly pay particular attention to the pages you have pointed out, and I am sure that the book will prove to be very interesting bedtime reading!

Thank you once again for taking the time to write to me.

Yours sincerely

Robert Chase
Chairman

Here reproduced for you is the extract from the letter that we received that clearly shows that Mr Chase likes to fumble with his torch under the bedclothes.

The District Line

PWLLHELI & DISTRICT ARE BACK! (see page 3 for details of an inauspicious start). LET'S FILL YOU IN WITH A LITTLE BIT OF HISTORICAL BACKGROUND BEFORE ASSESSING THEIR POTENTIAL FOR THE FUTURE.

As far as I can tell, the real halcyon days were back in the 50s when ex Everton star Tommy Jones cam to Pwllheli and made them one of the most feared sides in North Wales. Not then were teams quaking in their boots at the thought of Locomotive Llanberis. Oh no, it was Holyhead Town and Pwllheli and District that were the teams to beat. Not that many did.

From a personal stance I well remember Barrow (then a league club) playing against P&D in the very early 70s. I don't know the score but shortly afterwards the Cumbrian outfit were in the Northern Premier League.

Many "name" clubs came to Pwllheli in the days of Meilir Owen, Ellis Wyn Jones and Haydn Jones (70s). These included first division Stoke City - whose fans we feared (I was only 11), Cardiff City complete with Australia's 1974 World Cup star, Adrian Alston; Shrewsbury Town in the Welsh Cup when football violence really reared its ugly head on the sleepy Lleyn Peninsula - there were more too.

I recall a 1978 Welsh Cup tie with the formidable Kidderminster Harriers which the visitors only just won, 2-0. We local lads, infuriated with the diabolical referee, planned a pitch invasion from the "Cowshed End". This act of Newcastlian stupidity was simply thwarted by a stern ticking off from the P&D trainer and the linesman. If only life was so smooth and simple in the grown-up world eh ?

Was that Brian Clough slap a leaf snatched from the handbook of Welsh League etiquette?

Local players then, as now, had a tendency to shift from side to side from season to season and in the late 70s, Meilir, Haydn et al were gone to mud-patches new. This left the dressing room doors open for a new batch of Liverpudlian heroes travelling over 100 miles for £20 a game. P&D won every cup in sight during that spell. The Cookson Cup, The Alves Cup, some other cups I can't remember and more.

Bliss!

What I do remember is organised coach trips on Saturdays to such illustrious venues as Nantlle Vale, Caernarfon, Porthmadog and beyond. I was proud to be one of a loyal band of travelling supporters (albeit spasmodic) who sampled the delights of a plastic cup of coke in the rain, in Bethesda, in the late 70s.

Things had to change of course. Players came and went, puberty set in and the prospect of similar organised coach trips to Anfield, Goodsion or Maine Road meant that P&D declined in my list of priorities. I still went to the odd game but when girls set themselves up as viable alternatives, local amateur football didn't stand a chance - do you f***ing blame me ?

Then, one day, while home for a weekend from my job as a third-rate journo on a eighth rate weekly rag, I met up with school aquaintance and college-boy extraordinaire, Dylan LL. Jones (yes, he!) who suggested a few cans of cheap lager down the Recreation Ground whilst watching P&D versus Rhos United. This was a fine way to while away the afternoon.

So it was. The cans went down smoothly and quickly while other school chum, Bedwyr Williams was playing in fine fettle for P&D - except when choice remarks from the two winos on the touchline caused him to laugh instead of dribble.

Always a loudmouth I made the mistake of questioning the parentage of the robust Rhos United number 5 after a particularly near-the-knuckle challenge on John "Poodle" Williams. The dozen or so spectators (things had gone downhill in my absence) were hushed as the abused defender pointed at me and retorted: "We see who the bastard is after the game, sunshine." I gulped as Dylan sniggered.

The home side were comfortable winners and on the sound of the first "peep" of the final whistle I was off, running out of the ground in case the vengeful centre-half was in hot pursuit. Up the road I went like Ben Johnson on crack leaving Dylan LL. Jones to fend for himself.

At the end of that, or the subsequent season, the side split up and although P&D kept up their registration with the North Wales F.A the local council decision to build a much needed leisure centre on the continually waterlogged Rec meant playing was impossible. That, I thought, was that. I assumed my days of watching a Pwllheli and District side in action were over. And they were, until September 4 1990.

The P&D team were playing an away Gwynedd League match against the side that, in theory, replaced them in the annals of local league football - Pwllheli Borough.

The District Line

It was an away match except that both sides now share the new pitch adjacent to the lesiure centre. Certainly cut down on travelling expenses!

Actually, Dylan LL. Jones and his brother-in-law, Armon, picked me up outside the Penlan Fawr at 6.25. We srove the ½ miles to the ground and were surprised to see a crowd of around 200 lining the touchlines. Almost all the old faces from 12 years ago were there. Yes, amongst those who travelled away on those draughty coaches in the 70s I saw many I recalled but one notable exception was a club official who was later jailed for certain occurances in a public toilet in Caernarfon.

The two sides were mainly made up of local players - including several nearly famous ex Nefyn United stars (see ravings about Nefyn in previous issues of Five To Three). These includes Peter Noel Jones (Boro), Adrain Williams (Boro), Wil Parry (District) and the have-boots-will-travel superstar himself, Bedwyr Williams who now sports a skinhead haircut that makes Telly Savalas look like a rather hirsute grizzly bear.

P&D, having not made a good start to the season were expected to be outclassed by the fitter and quicker and generally younger Boro team and when Wayne Jones (also ex Nefyn) headed a fine goal early on we all thought a slaughter of innocents would ensue.

But, minutes later, Ken Griffith (who was one of the 70s fans now realising his lifetime ambition by playing for P&D) was adjudged to have been fouled in the box.

Penalty!

Up stepped 31 year old Mick Pengelly to slap the equaliser.

"That makes him District's joint top-scorer," commented one wag behind us.

"Mick and Ken make the ideal twin-striking partnership," said Dylan. Quite. They have equally proportioned beer bellies.

Pwllheli Borough were doubtless the better side but then again they have had time to orgaise, pick the team and create understanding. They have not been cobbled together at the last minute due to various let-downs or other. Someone said that Mick Pengelly had turned up to watch the first match of the season with his sons and was then asked to play!.

P&D were an amorphous outfit but their commitment was never in doubt and though Borough ran out eventual 6-1 winners (lack of fitness told on P&D and Bedwyr Williams scored three!) it was almost an emotional evening for me.

The good humour continued throughout the game and one particularly choice moment was when Mick Pengelly - having been substitued midway through the second half - was asked by his son: "Have you been sent off Dad?"

The stream of spectators leaving the leisure centre at the end was reminiscent of a "proper" match and our journey back to the pub took a full ten minutes!

OK, so it was a far cry from the heady 70s when P&D stuck ten past Llandudno Swifts with (so I'm told) Neville "Once a dustman..." Southall in goal for the visitors, but any period of rebirth is frenetic and fraught with difficulties.

I'll be going to watch Pwllheli & District again, not least for to see the uncoordinated and uncalled for signalling of the home linesman Dick "The away side MUST be offside ref" Thomas.

Viva Le District!

The District Attorney

HOBBIES

Many of today's top professionals have their own special ways of relaxing after a hard morning in training - golf, D.I.Y., abseiling, embroidery, to name just a few of the more popular.

However, it has come to our attention here at Five To Three that the hobbies of players gone by were far more interesting and varied and we'd like to thank Rothman's Book of Players' Hobbies for the following information.

Did you know that ex Aston Villa star Ray Graydon was an avid mountaineer and once scaled the Matterhorn dressed as a chicken ?

Former England international Kevin Beattie liked nothing better that to mould effigy after effigy of the composer Chopin out of soap. Indeed he became so involved in this pastime that Ipswich Town's bosses became so concerned as to hire a firm of cat burglars to steal and destroy his collection.

Perhaps one of the more mundane hobbies featured in this piece was that of Coventry's Bobby McDonald. He was "into" ballroom dancing and once appeared on the TV representing the UK in an "all-comers" dance-off. Sadly for the whole country Bobby's partner - Mick Mills - was struck down by a flying bottle and the pair had to withdraw at the semi-final stage.

However, Bobby was back the following year when tragedy struck again. This time his partner was Gordon McQueen and the big blonde trod on Bobby Mac's nimble tootsies in round one.

3 MEN IN A BOAT

THE ALTERNATIVE TRANMERE VIEWPOINT

TOP REFEREE NEIL MIDGELEY (YES, THAT'S RIGHT, HE'S THE ONE WHO GAVE BRISTOL A LAST MINUTE PENALTY) ASKS YOU TO PUT YOURSELF IN HIS SHOES AND

BE THE REFEREE!!!

IN 3MIAB'S FUN QUIZ

NEIL'S QUESTION: If an opponent dives in your penalty area in a blatant attempt at play-acting to get a last-minute penalty, do you:

a) wave play on and caution the offending player during the next stoppage in the game.
b) wave play on.
c) award a free-kick against the play-actor's team.
d) give a last-minute penalty which the team scores to level the game, book 2 players and ruin a team's 52 year awaited 2nd division home debut.

Neil's answer is of course e) : cabbages.

STEPHEN McMILLAN

THE TRANMERE *PET SHOP BOYS* TOP 10

1. Being Boring — Steve Vickers
2. I Want A Dog — Dave Martindale
3. We All Feel Better In The Dark — Chris Malkin
4. How Can You Expect To Be Taken Seriously — John King
5. This Must Be The Place I've Waited Years To Leave — Mark McCarrick
6. So Hard — Dave Higgins
7. A Man Could Get Arrested — Dave Martindale
8. Opportunities (Let's Make Lots Of Money) — Peter Johnson/Frank Corfe
9. One More Chance/What Have I Done To Deserve This — Jimmy Harvey, Neil McNab, Steve Mungall
10. Your Funny Uncle — Frank Corfe

==================================

LOST

One **PLAY-OFF FINAL**. If found, please contact Phil Neal, c/o Bolton Wanderers FC.

BLARNEY STONE CAPERS GALORE

..WITH..

JIMMY HARVEY

AND HIS FIDDLE-DEE-DEE ☆☆SPOT-THE-BALL☆☆☆

Well hello there my little Frank Carsons! Uncle Jimmy here fresh from the emerald Isle to bring you my shamrock shafting spot-the-ball competition! Great prizes are on offer and it couldn't be more simple to enter. Even my little leprichaun friend Davie Higgins is having a go!

HOW TO ENTER...

1. Simply study the picture of my chrome domed self on the right.
2. Use your intelligence to identify where you think the ball is. The naughty little rascal is there somewhere!
3. Cut out the picture and put it in an envelope, but don't forget to seal it!
4. Write your own address on the front of the envelope and stick some Green Shield stamps, upside-down in the top left hand corner.
5. Then simply post your entry in your nearest toaster, go out into the garden, cover yourself in shamrocks and erect an icon of Billy Bingham . Then shout "Fiddle-dee-dee" as loud as you can...

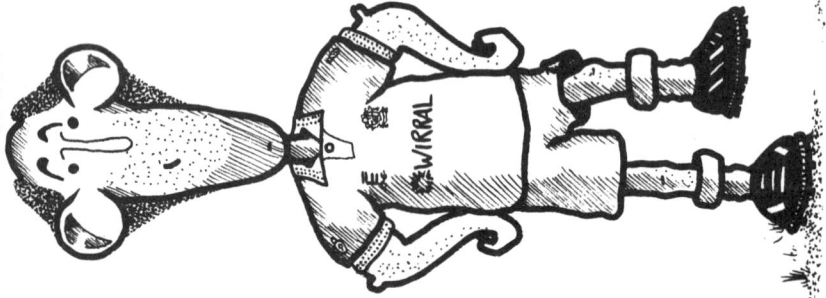

☆**FIRST PRIZE**☆ An all expenses (un)paid weekend in Belfast for two. (Or however many people you can persuade to come)

☆**SECOND PRIZE**☆ A weekend in Iraq with a free Star of David T-shirt thrown in.

☆**THIRD PRIZE**☆ Free trip to Burnden Park with your 'Forget The Cup We're Going Up' T-shirt.

ROSS McGINNES

PROMOTION REVIEW

"Say we are going up, we are going up"

- ROVERS FANS, WEMBLEY, JUNE 1st 1991

Rovers Return! We're back in the Second for the first time in over half a century. However, there were many moments during the season when I thought that we had blown it for the second season on the trot.

Following our defeat at the hands of the Notts County, and the Swindon affair, the season started in a surprisingly happy frame of mind. The bookies made us favourites for everything in the 3rd, and we believed it.

Until we lost to Stoke in the first Prenton game. Four days later, and we were out of the Rumbelows, and things were looking decidedly poor. Already! The 4-0 demolition of Preston at Deepdale helped, as did the 6-2 wasting of Mansfield in October, but the same spark of 12 months previous was missing.

Maybe this was the problem with everyone at the club. Maybe we were expecting promotion to be handed to us on a plate, because we'd done so well the last season. Of course, football doesn't take into account the past, and so we were finding out, to our cost.

Four wins in twelve games up to New Years Day saw Rovers fall out of the promotion picture in dramatic fashion, while the three upstarts from the 4th, Southend, Grimsby and Cambridge, started to pull away.

So Johnny King did what most managers do when faced with their side on a goal drought. He bought a striker. Not any striker, but Steve Cooper. Who? Exactly!

Tranmere had just paid £100,000 for a bloke who was doing nothing in Barnsley's reserves, and whose goal record was 9 in 2 years. Brilliant. His debut was on a foggy night at Prenton, and his most worthwhile contribution was to do a beautiful two-footed challenge on the Reading keeper. The match ended 0-0. Yawn!

The January 1st clash of the soccer 'pundits' Saint & Greasvie, or Rovers verses Southend, brought about the fastest, and one of the sweetest, goals of my Tranmere watching career.

Tony Thomas' 8 second strike did much to worsen the effects of the previous night's activities, but it did set us up for an important morale-boosting victory. The rest of January was also fairly decent, with us getting through a couple of rounds in the Leyland DAF.

The mixed month of February contained a 4-0 hammering at Leyton Orient, and excellent 3-0 win at Wigan in the DAF, plus a 1-0 win at then league leaders Grimsby. But this was followed by a 2-1 defeat at Huddersfield which summed up the season - annoyingly inconsistent.

The season's low was reached in March with the 'Gazza' injury which befell Ian Muir at Chester, well Macclesfield. We'd lost our best player for the run-in, and only had out-of-favour Cooperman and Chris Malkin in back-up. The season was looking bust.

Reaching the Leyland DAF final again was the highlight of April, but that was about it. Automatic promotion was dead after two defeats in a week, and our position looked vunerable for the Play-Offs.

However, going into the final week of the regular season (how American!), there was an outside chance of promotion. Coops had started to score goals and was becoming a cult figure at Prenton, and there was optimism once more.

In the end it was the Play-Offs, and once more Cooperman did the damage against Brentford with a crucial double.

So Rovers were left with the exact same last two games as in the previous season: the DAF and Play-off finals.

The DAF was a classic game, as anyone who has got BSkyB will have seen. All Brum in the first half, Tranmere in the second. Unfortunately, the fight back from two down, thanks to Coops and Steel, was in vain, as Gayle scored the winner with a stormer of an overhead kick. But we didn't give a stuff. Well, not much anyway. The big one was still to come.

And come it did. June 1st will always live long in the memory, and even now I get goose pimples just thinking about the day.

The nervousness before the game, how it increased as the match went on, and the total relief and joy at the end of 120 minutes of sheer hell.

It was unbelieveable that we hadn't beaten Bolton in a league game since we'd joined them in the Third. The only victory in six meetings had been a Leyland DAF tie in February '90. Yet we murdered them, especially in the first half.

Our old friend Keith Hackett denied us a perfectly good goal because he wasn't ready for our free kick, and Malkin and Morrissey both had great chances in the second. It seemed it wasn't going to be our day.

But then in extra-time, a break down the left, which Tranmere don't usually use, sent Ged Brannan (note the spelling Fleet Street) away. The keeper blocked the shot, and the ball spun straight to Chrissie Malkin.

15,000 people shouted as one: "Hit it! Put it in!" It seemed to take an age, but eventually Chris slammed it into the corner of the net, and we went berserk.

The next 22 minutes took the proverbial age. But there's no saying without truth, and those 22 certainly took about 22 days. Watches stopped working, hearts started missing beats, minds started wandering.

Then it happened. At 5.27, Keith Hackett blew his whistle for the last time in season 1990/91, and we'd made it. Tranmere were up. Up to the Second. Yeeeeeeess!!

Everyone was hugging everyone else. People you'd never seen before were embracing you. Tears were flowing, sirens sounding, players dancing as if they were in The Drome.

It was the greatest moment I have ever experienced, and whatever happens from now on, I shall always remember the feelings of that day.

And whilst it was Malkin that scored the goal, Tranmere had many stars during the season. Ian Muir before his injury, the emerging talents of Ged Brannan, Shaun Garnett and Kenny Irons, the excellence of goalkeeper and Wembley captain Eric Nixon, Steve Cooper going from Barnsley reject to hero, as well as the 'old' hands like Mark Hughes, Jimmy Harvey, Neil McNab and Jim Steel.

Promotion didn't sink in straight away, and I still find it hard to believe now. I was in WHSmiths the other day reading *Shoot!*, just like everyone else does, and was looking at the lists of released players.

I couldn't find Tranmere, and why? Because I was looking under Division 3. Of course we were up there with Newcastle, Derby and the rest. And that is what it means to be in the 2nd. Up there with teams who command average gates of 15,000. Teams that will bring 5,000 to Prenton Park. teams that will bring atmosphere.

And now the signing of John Aldridge has shown that Tranmere mean business, and that we're not just there to make up the numbers. We want 1st division football, or whatever it will be by then, in Birkenhead. Time will tell whether we get it, but for the moment we're going to enjoy being in the Second, take each game as it comes (!!), and hopefully be in with a shout at the end of the season. How about another Notts County? That'll do nicely!

PHIL MOSS 31/6/91

FOLLOW, FOLLOW
THE RANGERS FANZINE

MARK WALTERS

The rumours circulating amongst the Rangers' support during the close season were proved correct. Goram was destined to be a Rangers player (and for those allegedly in the know his signing at Ibrox had been assured since the close of the 1989/90 season), Woods was to depart and Mark Walters with him.

We witnessed some great players at the Stadium signed during the Souness era but arguably the most majestic on his day was Mark Walters (with Ray Wilkins a very close second). His uniqueness to the Scottish scene was not just his skin colour, although we have too few black players in Scotland (a matter I would like to return to at another time if I am permitted). His uniqueness lies in his balletic athleticism, matched with his electric pace, excellent technique and natural ball skills. It is for those attributes that I would like to contribute this short appreciation of Walters' time at Ibrox.

Along with many others I had severe reservations of Souness' managing abilities on my first sighting of Marky. An uncomfortable afternoon was spent in the woeful Parkhead terraces with an equally dismal end result. Who was this Mark Walters? Why had we signed him? He certainly couldn't head the ball (and he never will!). His tackling abilities were as good as mine - abysmal! He appeared lacking in both fitness and stamina. Yet Souness had already acclaimed him. I remained to be convinced.

Conviction came slowly but assuredly. Let me cull my own special memories.

A lovely afternoon at Tynecastle with Walters faced against an ex-Ranger, Hugh Burns. (Admittedly Burns was never a great player and certainly lacked pace). Woods launched a long kick-out which fell on the full to Walters just inside the left touch-line. In an instant the ball was killed, under foot, Marky feinted left, sent the ball up the wing while he himself headed right and infield leaving Burns stranded the whole length of Gorgie Road. Pure brilliance; sheer magic; Mark Walters! Unhappily Tynecastle was never the same hunting ground for Walters. Whether the Hearts playing staff's pride was so blunted that day that they had to restore some of it or that they discovered that physical intimidation worked I cannot tell. But shamefully thereafter any time Mark played at Tynecastle he became a target of physical and verbal intimidation. Forget the shameful racial chants from the shed at Tynecastle, they fortunately subsided over the seasons but I do recall the "workmanlike" efforts of Walter Kidd and others to do over our Marky, who too often succumbed and allowed the "hammer throwers" to get him sent off.

I remember especially his triumphs against Celtic. A caressed penalty and a kissed crest at the Broomloan end. A goal direct from a corner equal to the skill of a Garrincha or Zico, modestly put down to luck by the scorer. The decisively drilled and directed equaliser in the Skol-Cup final. The killer blow of the final goal in the 4-1 triumph running on to a defence splitting pass from Ferguson (D). The Tormenting of Anton (good title for a novel) culminating in a beautifully driven cross onto the head of "Drinks" for the powerful fourth in the 5-1 annihilation.

Despite these joyous, heart warming memories (I'm writing these notes chuckling with glee over Celtic woes) my own special favourite that I recall, because of its impact on me and all those fortunate enough to witness it, came on an evening match at Ibrox. Rangers were playing comfortably enough against uninspiring opposition then a moment of laser-light brilliance, Walters received the ball just outwith the left-hand side of the 18 yard box, a dummy to the right, a glance up followed by an exquisite chip of extreme delicacy, the ball dipped over the desperately clawing fingertips of a beleaguered keeper. It crossed the line just under the cross-bar and landed gently at the back of the goal barely disturbing the net. There followed one of those rare occasions at Ibrox, a fleeting second of total silence as those witnesses assimilated an unbelievable piece of football magic; then a deafening roar that paid rightful homage to a wonderful, wonderful goal.

These are just a few personal favourites and other fans will have their own. Was he the best winger ever seen at Ibrox? I am too young (honest!) to have seen Alan Morton; and the "Wee Blue Devil" proved himself in the international sphere. Willie Henderson in my opinion was a better "jinker" and probably more consistent entertainer and provider. Bud Johnston with his electric burst of speed and brilliant crosses on the run alsoholds special memories. Davie Wilson was a braver player on the left wing. But Mark Walters will have a special place for me. Just as Mohammed Ali as a boxer was said to have quick hands, Marky has quick feet. His double shuffle was done with dumbfounding pace. How many impersonators have you seen attempting the "double-shuffle"? They all look lethargic, clumsy and amateurish. Walters is a quick-silver sprite, balanced; athletic. A balletdancer in football boots; an entertainer. I for one will miss his special magic at Ibrox. I wish him well with his next challenge at Liverpool.

MAC

STAIRWAY 13

Supporters pay their own tributes on 2nd January 1991

twenty years ago

In issues of FF last year we raised the subject of the Ibrox Disaster in order that some of the myths surrounding that day could be dispelled. We cut the discussion off as we felt that it would be inappropriate to appear to be putting pressure on the club to do something to mark the 20th anniversary. It is not Follow, Follow's place to take it upon itself to do such a thing.

Equally we decided against suggestions that we take up a collection to provide a plaque as it would have been in very poor taste to try to claim that we somehow represent all Rangers supporters, less still the relatives of the dead.

In the aftermath of the Disaster the story of the people who died was pushed to one side as the task of re-constructing Ibrox got underway. It's said that once when asked why there was no memorial to the 66 Willie Waddell asked his questioner to look at the new stands and said "The whole ground's their memorial." That's true enough.

I doubt we would enjoy quite the same conditions we do at the Stadium if it hadn't been for the Disaster. It shouldn't have taken 66 deaths to do it though. We should never forget that the Board which neglected safety warnings back then were in large measure responsible for the deaths. That is a lesson which football fans, no matter what team they support, should ever forget.

Let's not allow enthusiasm for prestige or money to blind us to other aspects of the club.

Stairway 13 is long gone, let's ensure that the memorial to the 66 who died so horribly is not just a metal plaque. By our sportsmanship and our behaviour we should attempt to build a living memorial that will truly do them honour.

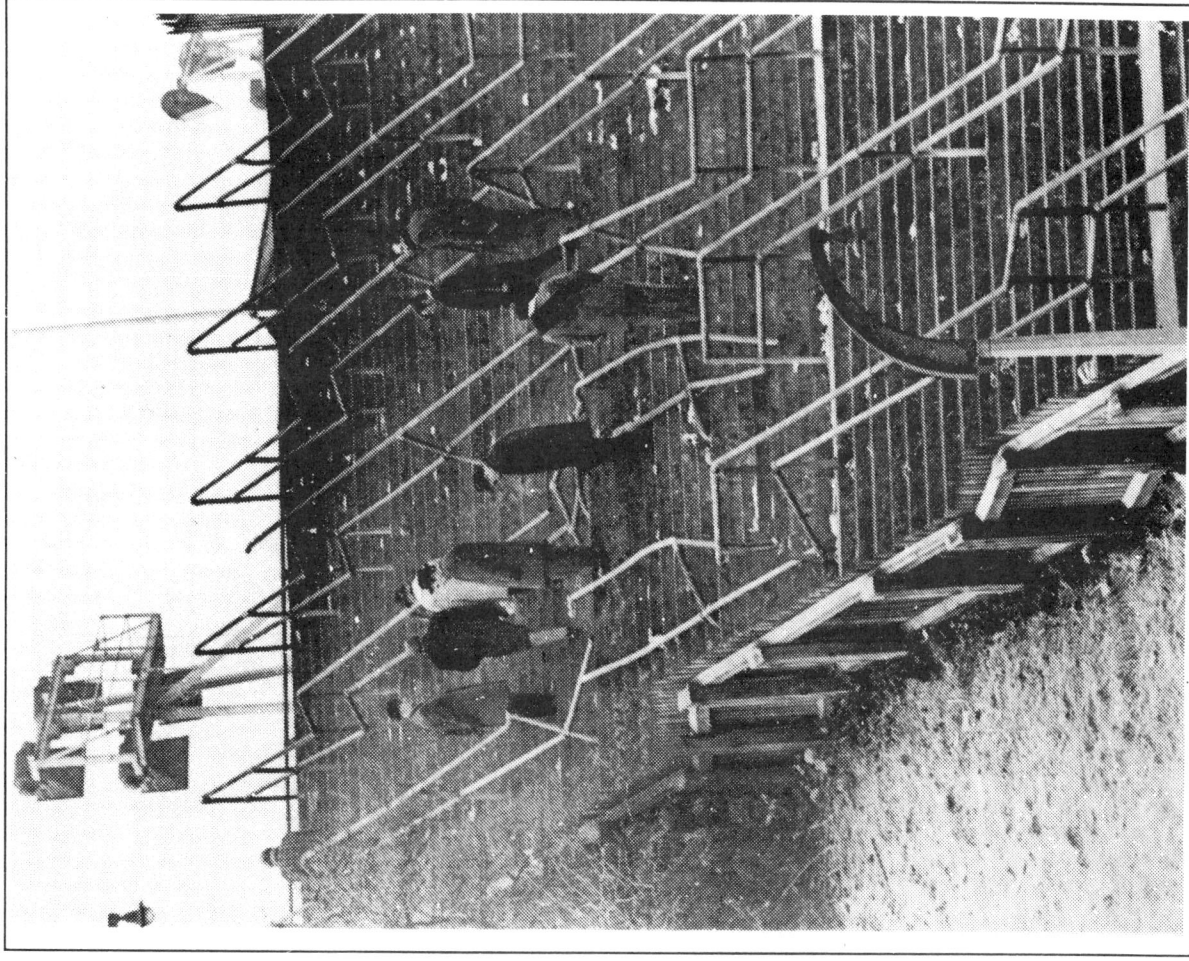

OUT ON VIDEO

STARRING

MANSFIELD TOWN FOOTBALL CLUB

IN

20,000
Leagues from the 1st.

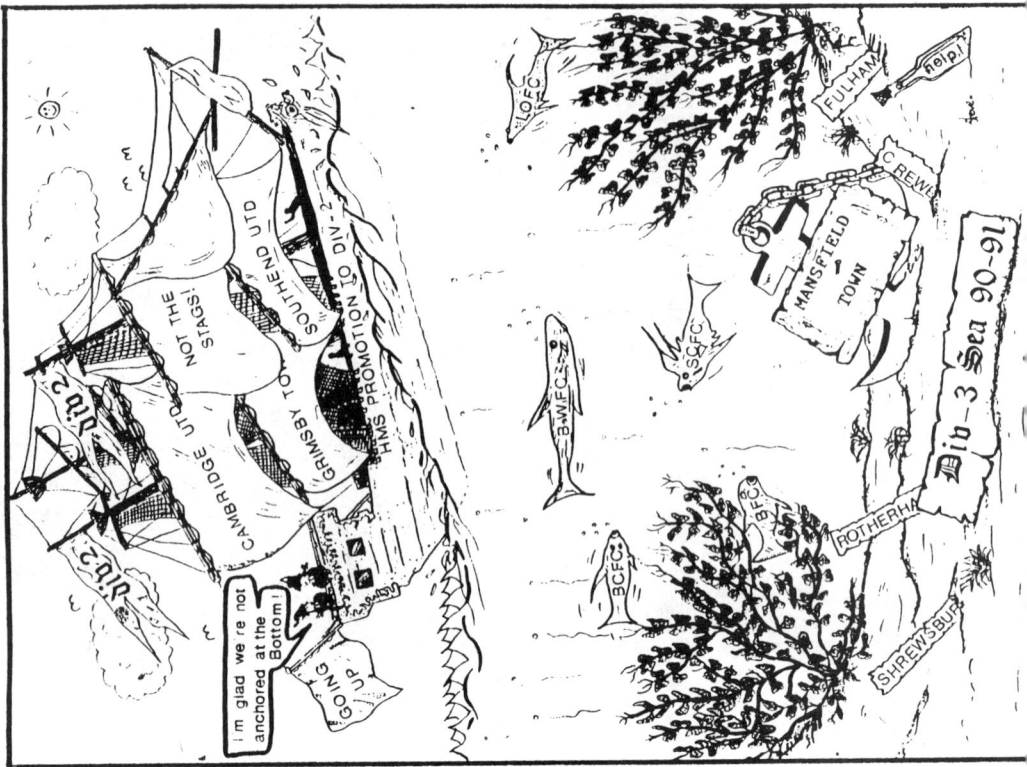

Follow The Yellow Brick Road.

An Independent Stag'zine from Ashfield.

Follow the Yellow Brick Road first arrived on the unsuspecting public at Field Mill in February 1990. It was met with fair response, for at the time there was only the established ' Size 10 ½ Boots ' available for the taste buds of the Fanzine follower. Little did we know that another Zine was on the horizon..Quickly to be followed by one more..Incredible En ? A small club such as Mansfield Town having Four Fanzines. Unfortunately, the four nave now gone down to the Two.

Admittedly the first Two issues of FTYBR were patchy affairs and there was a considerable distance between issue's 2 and 3. But now, after a hell of a lot of self commitment and help from such as, Chris Bradshaw, who has now gone on to be the official club Photographer, Mark Appleby, Brian Denton, Phil at Downing Street design and most of all a very understanding Wife, things are now looking fine.

At FTYBR, although based on Mansfield Town, we try to add our opinions on football in general and at times nave articles, containing contrasting views on the English game sent to us from other lands.

Chesterfield F.C along with our neighbours Forest and County come in for a fair amount of stick during the pages of our Zine and although certain articles may hurt their pride a little, they are all took in the way that they are meant to be portrayed...Just friendly jibes. After all doesn't everybody poke fun at a friend at work who supports another team ?

Also in our pages we try to voice the emotions, both good and bad, that are felt by supporters of a lower division club. However if you only wish to read continuous criticism, then FTYBR is not the Fanzine for you. Don't get me wrong, we do nave serious articles but we tend to centre more on the humorous side of the game.

Football to me is a case of life and death but for now, I'll just keep on enjoying the life and deal with death when it comes. After all Football is an entertainment, or so I've been told.

THE GUIDE TO THE EAST MIDLAND FOOTBALL SUPPORTER.

THE NOTTINGHAM FOREST FAN:
Can be found to be happy
and jovial and likes getting
hit on the back of the head by
their clubs manager.Only talks
about 1st division football,trips
to Wembley and about how much he
hates Derby.

THE DERBY COUNTY FAN:
Can be found to be moaning about
having no money and that nobody
wants to buy his season ticket..or
club.Thinks Maxwell coffee makes you
a fat selfish Git.

THE LEICESTER CITY FAN:
Can be found on Leicester market buying
Spudz from Linekers old man and blaming
former Manager Pleat's tactics on their
lowly position in the league.

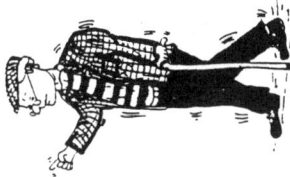

THE NOTTS COUNTY FAN:
Can be found to be extremely old,
likes talking about Tommy Lawton
and how good he was.Likes all of
Countys coloured players,even if he
gets their names mixed up.

THE CHESTERFIELD FAN:
Can be found in Nativity plays looking
for his long lost girlfriend.Has a distinct
dislike for football..hence a Chesterfield
season ticket holder.

THE MANSFIELD TOWN FAN:
We are sorry there was not enough
to do a description of.

?

FOOTBALL
A G A I N S T
MS

ARMS Action and Research **for Multiple Sclerosis**

THE WEE RED

"SOUND OF SOLITUDE"

A CLIFTONVILLE
FANZINE

P.O. BOX 429
BELFAST BT9 6PT

Turn Right At The Petrol Station, Take The Second On The Left And You Can't Miss It....

For most football fans pre-season friendlies are just a chance to watch their heroes - well, some of their heroes, a couple of reserves, a promising youth team player and as many free transfers as there are substitutes allowed - spend more time sunbathing than playing against 11 equally disinterested opponents. Hardly the stuff to set your pulse racing, especially when you realise you've just paid normal season prices to watch a 0-0 draw with your local non-league neighbours. But for Cliftonville fans our pre-season friendlies are almost the highlight of the season, and not just because we seem to spend the next nine months trying to extend our record of consecutive semi-final defeats (eight so far).

You see being a team with a largely Catholic support in a league where 13 of the 16 teams have mostly Protestant fans has its drawbacks, as you can imagine, especially when it comes to away games. Because of the reputation of a minority of Reds "fans" (à la Leeds Utd, Millwall, etc) the routine for games outside Belfast goes something like this: get on a supporters club bus, go straight to the ground, watch the match - more often than not on an uncovered terrace behind the goal with the worst view in the ground - then straight home again. Getting a pint in the social club, stopping for a drink on the way to a game or arriving early to spend all day in the opponent's town are all luxuries which we can only read about in other fanzines. OK, so I can't see many Reds fans actually wanting to spend more than two hours in a place like Ballyclare or Newtownards, but it would be nice if we could.

That's why we spend our summers counting down the days not to the start of the Irish League season, but to our pre-season friendlies instead. The club usually play two or three games 'down South' where, for obvious reasons, the natives are a lot more friendly. Since all the players are semi-professional these matches are played on Friday nights and Saturday afternoons, giving the fans a chance to go down for the weekend as well. We're able to mix freely with the home supporters, sit in the stand if we want to and even enjoy a bevvy or two before and after the match (except when we visit Bohemians where for some strange reason they wouldn't serve Reds fans in any of the four (!) bars in Dalymount Park). At least that's if everything goes to plan. But in recent seasons some of the arrangements have left a lot to be desired; indeed it's now almost an annual occurrence for the fans to get lost just trying to find a game. Never mind a few drinks before the game and all that, we're just glad to make it there, even if it is 20 minutes late.

It all started in Galway in July 1989. After losing 2-1 to Sligo Rovers on the Friday the small number of Reds fans who had made the trip went down on the Saturday to see the game with Galway United. We'd never been there before but someone said that United played at Terrylands Park, so that's where we headed for. We didn't have too much difficulty finding it and got there in plenty of time for the game, which was just as well because the ground was deserted. The dressing room windows were broken and the whole place was in a general state of disrepair, so it was back to the town to pester the locals. The first few hadn't a clue but then we bumped into a guy from Belfast who recognised our scarves and luckily enough he was able to give us directions to what was little more than a parks pitch attached to a local factory. We found it no problem as well and seen the whole of a dull 1-1 draw, but little did we know what the following year had in store.

After a 2-0 defeat by Drogheda United on a Friday night we had a game against Dublin side Shelbourne on the Saturday. Their Tolka Park ground was unavailable and the match was scheduled for Harold's Cross greyhound stadium (home of another Dublin side, St Pat's Athletic) at 7.30pm on Saturday night. Then a couple of days before the game we discovered that the kick-off had been brought forward to 3.30pm, which messed up a few people's travel arrangements. Still, Harold's Cross would be dead easy to find, I mean you can't miss it on the map of Dublin...so, of course, we discovered the night before in Drogheda that the venue had been changed as well! We'd been speaking to some of the Cliftonville directors in the United social club and they informed us that it was now some local playing field about a mile from the greyhound track. But don't worry, we were told, just be at Harold's Cross for 3pm and there'll be someone waiting there to take you to the match. Actually that was of little use to me, the minibus I was on left Belfast later than planned and it was 3.30 by the time we reached a deserted Harold's Cross; but more of that later.

About ten car loads of Cliftonville fans did make it to the meeting point on time, only to find that our guide hadn't showed. Fortunately a passer-by had a fair idea of where the match was, so the convoy headed off, much to the amusement of the locals, as one of the guys in the lead car directed the rest General Paton-style through its sunroof! They found the pitch after a while and only missed the first 15 minutes or so. Jammy gits. By the time we'd reached Harold's Cross the game was just kicking-off and there was no one about. We tried the pub outside but got little help there, so we got the map out again and decided just to drive past all the green bits and look for 11 red shirts running about. 45 minutes and no sign of the game later, we'd ended up back at Harold's Cross which was still as deserted as ever. Then, while we were debating which pub to drown our sorrows in (there was so many to choose from), a familiar face pulled up in a car. One of the fans at the game knew we were coming and we figured we must be getting lost somewhere nearby; he came to look for us at half-time and so we eventually got to the game five minutes into the second half. Just in time to see Shelbourne score once and hit the woodwork three times. You'd hardly have guessed that Cliftonville had been 3-1 up at half-time! The Reds also

lost 2-0 at Bray Wanderers the next day (as they became the first Irish League team to play on a Sunday apparently), so after travelling about 600 miles that weekend I didn't see them score a single goal. A great way to start the season!

Last summer the club broke with tradition and decided to go to Scotland for a couple of games, much to the delight of the fans - we'd never been to Scotland with the Reds before, and the pints are a lot cheaper than in the Republic! We should have known that bigger plans would call for a bigger mix-up. Games were arranged with Kilmarnock on the usual Friday night and Raith Rovers on Saturday. The Kilmarnock match had been announced three months earlier (unlike the Raith one which was finalised a lot closer to the time) so there'd be no problem there, we thought, as we booked our ferry tickets, sorted out accomodation, etc... yes, we discovered it wasn't on a week before we left for Scotland. It turned out they'd arranged a four-team tournament at Rugby Park that weekend and had a game with Sparta Rotterdam that night, which left us in the brown, smelly stuff. The club had to try to get a game at very short notice and just about every senior team in south-west Scotland was rumoured to be playing us at some stage that week. Stranraer would have been handy, or even Queen Of The South, but the day before we left we finally heard that it was definately Airdrie. Then just as we were looking for directions to Broomfield we were told that it wasn't there, it was at some junior team's pitch. Here we go again...For once, however, we didn't have too much difficulty in finding the match - the club gave us fairly good directions and everyone got there in plenty of time, unlike the Airdrie supporters, whose club presumably didn't announce the game. They were probably glad though, as the Reds upset the Diamonds 3-2 to send us home happy, despite a 1-4 reverse in Kirkcaldy the following afternoon.

God knows where we'll end up next year; the Scottish trip was a bit of a financial disaster for Cliftonville, since we had been relying on the gate from the Kilmarnock game to cover the cost, so it'll probably be back to the Republic for our annual mystery tour. Maybe we'll go somewhere new like Limerick or even Cork. No, Turner's Cross would be too easy to find come to think of it. How about Waterford ? I've never got lost in Waterford before.....

THE BUS HOME...

MOTHERWELL.
BLOODY MOTHERWELL.

*Dundee United's fanzine
The Final Hurdle attempts
to come to terms with
yet another Cup Final
defeat*

I DON'T KNOW WHY YOU'RE COMPLAINING - AT LEAST YOU'RE NOT DRESSED LIKE LAWRENCE OF *£!*!@ ARABIA!

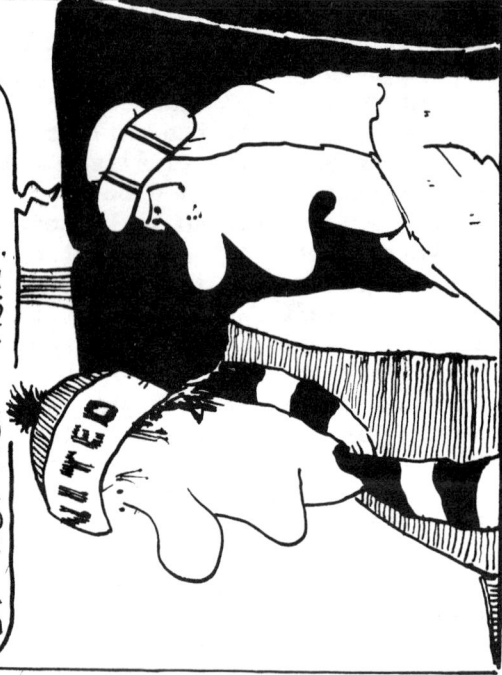

MOTHERWELL.
MOTHER-BLOODY-WELL.

WE'VE GOT TO BE RATIONAL ABOUT THIS. WE PLAYED WELL. IT MUST HAVE BEEN A GREAT GAME FOR THE NEUTRALS....

MOTHERWELL.
MO-BLOODY-THER-BLOODY-WELL.

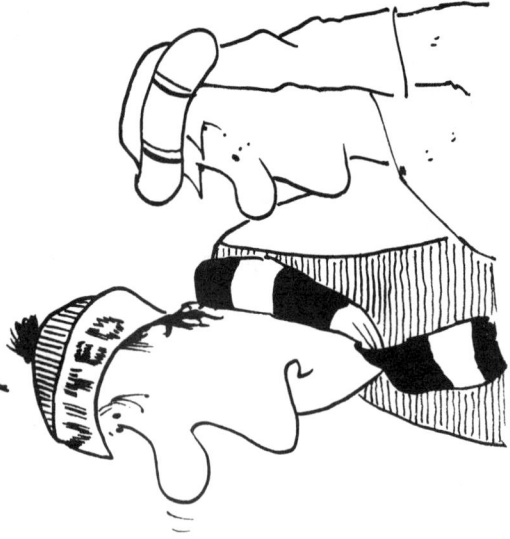

LOOK ON THE BRIGHT SIDE — WE DID WELL TO COME BACK FROM 3-1 DOWN. WE FOUGHT WELL AND NEARLY DID IT.

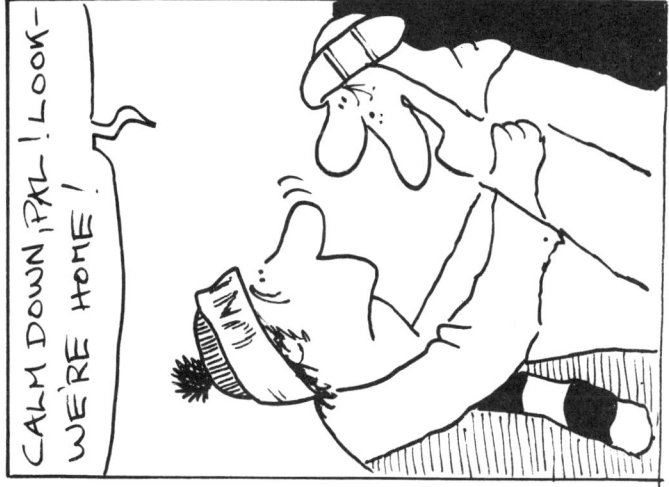

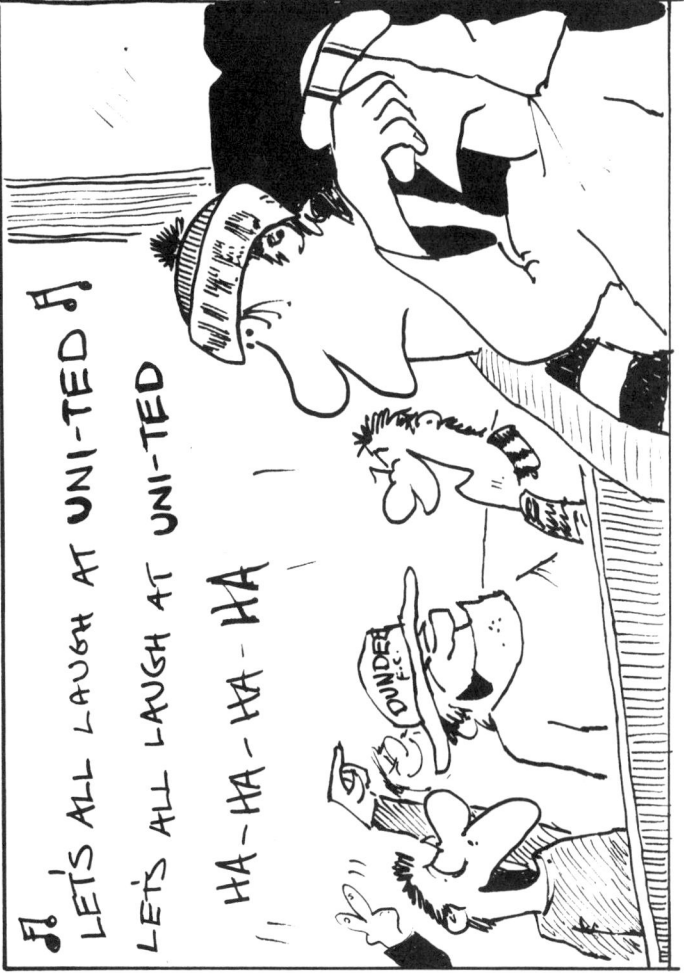

GREAT GAMES OF THE PAST
March 31 1986: QPR 6 Chelsea 0 by Martin Booth

Ah, QPR. The bumfluff on the top lip of football, the bell-bottoms on the trousers of the First Division, the fluffy dice on the rear-view mirror of sport.

Something about the Superhoops just shouts "naff" at you. Probably it's that stadium, taken straight from a Meccano fan's wet dream.

Once you've queued halfway down South Africa Road, borrowed a shoe-horn to get through turnstiles designed for anorexic stick insects and taken the scenic route direct to the terraces via the panoramic tea bar and the atmospheric gents' bog, you finally reach the away end.

Getting in is bad enough. Getting out again on the same day is virtually impossible. There are probably Chelsea fans still trapped in there from the Milk Cup game in January 1986. Which is unlucky for them, because they were thus still there for our next visit, on Easter Monday.

Chelsea came to the game fresh from a 4-0 battering two days before at the Bridge by West Ham. Don't let's talk about it. The previous Sunday the lads had won a genuinely thrilling Full Members' Cup Final against Man City, and we're still talking about the piss-up that followed that one.

By Easter the bubble had burst. We weren't to know it then but Kerry and Eddie's long-term injuries marked the start of the break-up of John Neal's side. Wembley was the last hurrah, Loftus Road the writing on the wall.

Taking Eddie's place was Steve Francis, who clung so long to his line he made John Phillips look like Dave Beasant. And after just 7 minutes 40 seconds he was at his goal-hanging best as Gary Bannister - whose middle name is not Tall - headed the first from all of three yards.

Bannister must love Chelsea, he always scores against us. He'd get off his deathbed for a game at the Bridge, he'd be sure of a goal or two even if he played on crutches.

He got another after 25 minutes, Byrne got a third and at half time Chelsea fans in the 18,584 crowd (about 17,000; remember, we were at QPR) were taking bets on which Rangers forward would get to double figures first, so crap was our defence.

Bannister had his hat-trick in the hour and Byrne soon made it 5-0. It was all too much for

Dave Speedie, who promptly got his first kick on target all afternoon. On Terry Fenwick. Quite reasonable, but Speedie was sent off the pitch by the ref.

The pitch, of course, the pitch. Notice how every visiting manager whose team has just played on the Loftus Road ploughed field this season has said *Yes it's bad but for Christ's sake don't bring the plastic back*. We could have told them years ago, long before QPR's players got thigh muscles like Schwarzenegger.

Anyway, after 81 minutes Rosenior got the sixth. 6-0. I'd never seen a side dumped 6-0 before. But now came the moment that made the whole day worthwhile. Somewhere in the deathly hush on the terrace, one bloke sang "We're gonna win the League." Everyone laughed, then joined in. We sang ourselves stupid for ten minutes solid. You name it, we sang it. By the end you almost felt we hadn't lost. What a moment, what a memory.

Chelsea went on to win just one more game, at Old Trafford, while QPR lost to Oxford in the Milk Cup final at Wembley. Now, does anybody remember that game? Anybody ...?

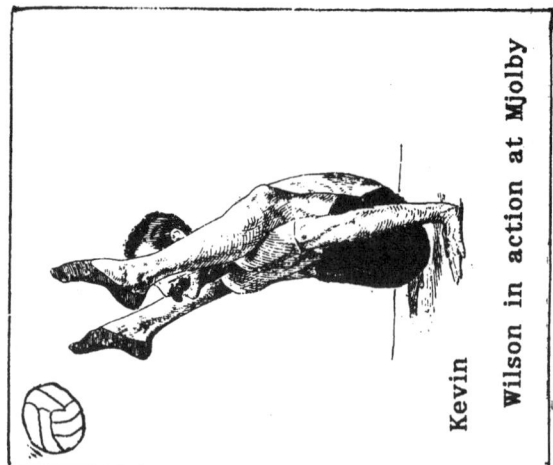

Kevin

Wilson in action at Mjolby

CHELSEA independent

THE CHELSEA independent

A TRIBUTE TO THE GREAT DOUG ROUGVIE

An era will end this coming season as Chelsea take to the field without Doug Rougvie, a man feared by Blues fans everywhere, and regarded with affection by wrestling buffs the world over. The gentle giant signed for Brighton and Hove Albion, where he will link up with old Chelsea favourites: Dale Jasper, Chris Hutchings and Robert Issac - as well as new assistant manager Martin Hinshelwood - as the Seagulls consolidate their push for Fourth Division status. According to Hinshelwood, Dougie may be in line for Brighton's captaincy, and is likely to be playing at centre-back, a position from which, as all Chelsea fans are aware, the gentle giant inspires such confidence.

Predictably, the move brought an angry response as Rougvie's fans flooded the Fulham Road to protest and an extra policeman had to be called upon to disperse them both. Throughout West London grown men were seen to cry with relief, whilst on the south coast fans queued to throw themselves off the Brighton pier.

Rougvie - or "Rubbish" as the Shed came affectionately to call him - moved to the Bridge from Aberdeen in July 1984 for a fee of £150,000. Brighton paid £50,000 for his services. Opinion is divided as to his true worth, though it is clear to most that £50,000 is the closest to zero. In a three year spell at the club Dougie played 99 first-team games for the Blues, bringing new meaning to the word finesse and making Chelsea fans long for the sure touch and delicate manner of Mickey Droy, a man who could frighten the ball out of the penalty area.

Like many others Doug Rougvie has written himself into the Stamford Bridge folk-lore. Who will forget the amiable Scot's displays at left-back? In this coveted position Rougvie became so well acquainted with the pitch, that there was talk of switching him onto the groundstaff. At centre-back he was a model of consistency, magnificently partnering Colin Pates or Joe McLaughlin and dispossessing them at every opportunity. And what of the punch that laid low John Fashanu during the 0:4 defeat at the hands of Wimbledon? Will the like ever be seen at Chelsea again? I fear not.

His pre-match warm-ups have now become legendary, yet hardly seemed necessary to achieve Dougie's standards, and who could doubt his love of a challenge. Remember how he conceded a penalty at Hillsborogh denying Chelsea an historic win, just so he could have another crack at them. For many of us however Doug Rougvie's finest moments came in the heady atmosphere of a Full Members Cup Final at Wembley, as he single-handedly attempted to wrest the trophy from Chelsea's grasp in the dying moments of the game. Surely it was only the fact that we were playing Manchester City that foiled his valiant attempts to give away three penalties.

Dougie will be sorely missed, particularly by opposing forwards - there may never again be so much space in a Chelsea defence - but also by the scores of Blues fans who thrive on the hours of frustration and despair he gave them, a commodity rarely in short supply in this part of London. But what Chelsea have lost, Brighton have gained......

Pete Collins.

Remember Our Last *Proper* Cup Final?

Inspired by Jim Ross's 'That Was The Week That Was' article in issue no. 21, I decided to look back at another eventful week in Chelsea's history; 26 February 1972 to 4 March 1972, as described in my diary at the time. I was 16, and the following is a verbatim account.

Saturday 26/2/72: ORIENT (1) 3 CHELSEA (2) 2 F. A. Cup 5th Round. So, we're out of the Cup for another year, which makes next week all the more crucial. Webb & Osgood with headers put us two up after 35 minutes, but a goal from their back, Hoadley, right on half-time, put them back in the game. Then, 4 minutes after the interval, a terrible mix-up between Webb and Bonetti let in Bullock for the equaliser. There followed a period of tremendous Chelsea pressure - Ossie hit the post, a Dempsey header headed off the line, Hollins shot saved inches from the line, Ossie header saved, etc. etc..... but then, with two minutes left, Fairbrother, after Bowyer had pushed Harris, slid in the winner. Some Chelsea ran on the pitch, but the Bill got them off. There was still time for Webb to put over an open goal, but... it was not be. Thousands of Chelsea ran riot through Leyton, and on the train smashed windows, took lights out etc.. Another riot at next station, Stratford. Tried to forget Cup defeat in evening. TWO MINS. LEFT ! It was agony watching it all over again on *Match Of The Day*.

Sunday 27/2/72: Yesterday's defeat really began to sink in more and more today. We would've played Derby or Arsenal at home in the Round 6. Not looking forward to tomorrow & all the c***s taking the piss. (*A reference to schoolfriends who supported such successful teams as Brentford, Fulham, etc...*).

Monday 28/2/72: And it was as bad as I had feared. It's obvious what the best 17th birthday present would be : The League Cup !

Tuesday 29/2/72: Garland for Kember is the only likely Team change for Saturday.

Thursday 2/3/72: CFC team announced : Bonetti, Mulligan, Harris, Hollins, Dempsey, **Webb, Cooke, Garland, Osgood, Hudson, Houseman. Substitute: Baldwin**

Friday 3/3/72: Tomorrow is so, so, vital. If we lose there's not much chance of CFC getting into the UEFA cup next season through League placing. I'm really shitting myself now with all this anxiety. Wonder what I'll feel like this time tomorrow. All the "experts" say Chelsea are going to win (*which means they won't ?*). No, don't despair - hope.hope......

Saturday 4/3/72: LEAGUE CUP FINAL at WEMBLEY
CHELSEA (1) 1 Osgood   STOKE CITY (1) 2 Conway, Eastham

So, after all, we lost - but what a way to lose it was. We had 70% of the game, but from Stoke's few chances they got two scrambled goals, and Chelsea just couldn't come back twice. The day started well enough...... birthday presents included Chelsea record 'Blue is the Colour'. Left about 10.30 with coat (*white butcher's coat with CFC all over it*), 3 scarves, 3 rosettes, 2 banners and 25 badges. I met all the others at The Red Lion, Greenford. Hijacked a bus on the way to Wembley.

The match......After only 5 'minutes a scramble in Chelsea's goalmouth ended in Conway luckily heading home. Understandably, Chelsea wilted, but soon began typically to fight back - Banks had to save from Garland, Osgood, Cooke and Hollins twice shot just wide. Then, right on half-time, Ossie, on the ground, lashed home the equaliser and it seemed as though we were on our way. With Baldwin on for Mulligan, we kept the pressure on, but Stoke held out, and, with 18 minutes left, took the lead again when Eastham shot home after Bonetti had saved from Greenhoff. From then on it was all Chelsea. Banks saved from Webb, Ossie, & in the last minute, Garland - ...so Stoke took the Cup. Lucky Bastards. Going home and everyone was in mourning; in the pub it was terrible, with the Stoke celebrating. I eventually got home about 8.30. What a day..!! I lost a scarf, a banner and a hat as well ! But being LOYAL to a team means supporting them through THICK AND THIN, so..... life will go on. Nothing now left for CFC this season. But Chelsea, WE'LL SUPPORT YOU EVERMORE.

TIM SUGDEN

"YOU'RE GONNA CRY IN A MINUTE"

'Gazza'

So nice to hear the Liverpool fans offering 'Fat Boy' a sympathetic chant to show how much they appreciate him.

ADE C ndy can do! CR N

AT FOREST IT WAS OBVIOUS THAT JOHN BARNES WAS NOT WILLING TO GIVE UP THE CHAMPIONSHIP WITHOUT A FIGHT

BEEN THERE BEFORE?

Somehow, it seemed as though I'd been here before, even though I knew I hadn't. The three mile walk from the only available car parking space gave me a good idea of things to come, and I knew it wasn't going to be my day, even though I was in quite good spirits.

Before actually reaching the town, we had experienced difficulties with roadworks and defaced signposts, so the arrival at this slum didn't surprise or affect me much. The locals were useless when we asked for assistance, and the so-called 'AA Recommended Route' wasn't exactly helpful either. The signposts we were told to follow were either facing the wrong way or had been scrawled on with graffiti, and the best roads to use were blocked or closed off.

On arrival at the town, we were directed by 'helpful' stewards and police, who only succeeded to confuse us further, and sent us right round the edge of the town, rather than through the middle where we needed to go. We were told there was street parking only, and that there would be ample space around the ground. After about an hour looking for this 'space', we settled on a spot in someone's driveway - we didn't think they'd mind. We were then miles from the ground, with no floodlights in sight. One assistant in a corner shop told us we were only a few minutes away.

did they know that I was not carrying a weapon or a glass bottle? I showed my ticket and struggled through the now familiar stiff turnstiles, only to be faced by more officials. This time I had to empty my pockets, but I still wasn't thoroughly checked.

Puddles

Once past this stage, I found myself in a line of fellow fans trying to make their way to the actual terrace. The walkway was narrow and fenced on both sides. At the top I had a choice of views - the gents' door to my left, or the far left hand corner of the pitch which was slightly to my right. I didn't choose either at this stage, so I walked over as far as I could, and guess what? - no ladies' toilet! It's probably just as well, because if there had been one, it would have puddles on the floor and no roof. I don't mind the graffiti, as it often makes good reading to take your mind off a crap game.

I decided instead to sample the 'cuisine'. The queue stretched back to the gents', and once at the counter, I got a puff of smoke in the face from the woman behind the frying pan who was smoking over the food. The pies looked harder than the concrete I was standing on, and the coffee was still floating on top of the cups, so I decided on a packet of crisps to avoid poisoning. I was charged 35p - quite reasonable for such an established club, I thought. Then I made my way along the steps until I reached a point where I could see over the person in front.

I actually had quite a good view of the pitch, the whole of the left hand side was visible, and I could just make out the near goalmouth if I moved my head down slightly and to the

A LOAD OF BULL

Wonder where Elgar went for his pre-match pint? Was "Pomp And Circumstance" intended to be performed as the Wolves came out on to the pitch? And is "Enigma Variations" a reference to endless permutations whilst trying to find the best defensive line-up?

CHARLES ROSS

An Alternative View of Wolverhampton Wanderers

Oui Bully Bully!

Dear ALOB,
I recently went to France for the weekend. I found the frogs were so impressed with Bully that they've named a town after him just South East of Calais...

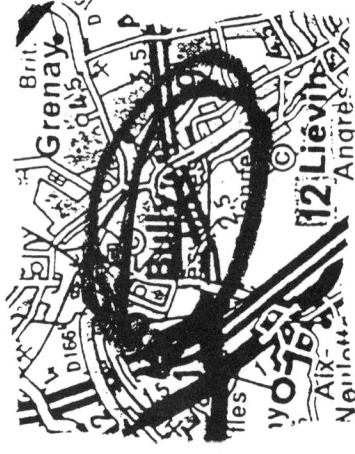

STEVE, BIRMINGHAM

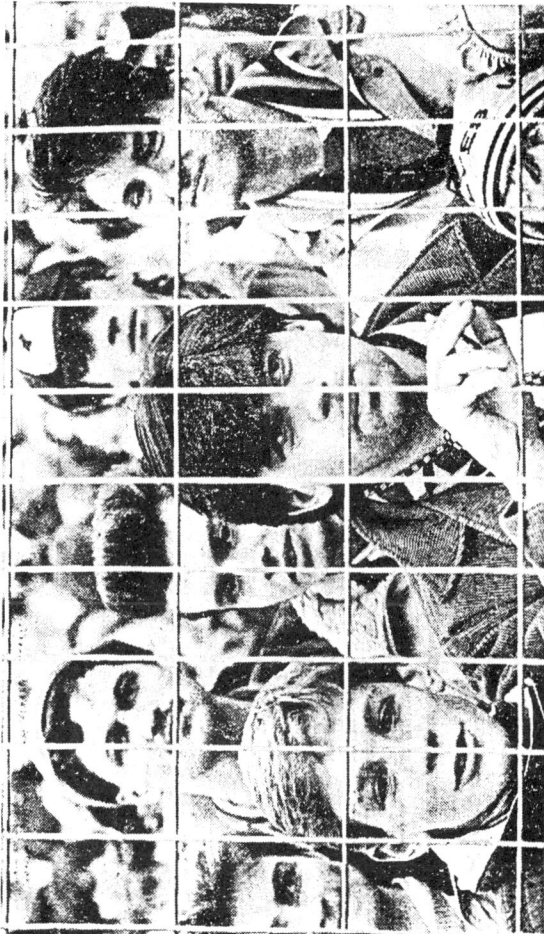

right, so as to avoid the roof which was obscuring my view (A roof? Luxury! - ed). I don't mean the roof we had (oh!!), we don't expect such luxuries in these hard times. It was for the home fans who were in the same end as us, only they had the covered middle section. We were fenced and caged into the back left hand corner.

At five to three, a six foot tall man and his short fat friend came and stood in front of me (we'll say hello next time! - obtrusive ed). Now only the far left hand corner and near goalmouth were visible, and that at a struggle.

Rain

The weather had been warm for the two or three hours that we had been travelling in the car, so none of us had bought coats or jackets. It rained at 2.58pm, only lightly to start with, but it got heavier at 3.23pm when the opposition's number 4 hit the back of our net. Just as it seemed as if things couldn't get much worse, the home faithful began a chant I hadn't heard before. It went something like

"Bullshit, Bullshit" and drowned us out as we only had 2,000 fans in the 20,000 crowd. A few more were in with the home fans, but they had to hide their loyalties. Suddenly a great roar came from behind me, and the floor shook with vibration. Bully obviously heard us, as we watched the net ripple at the far end. 18,000 people were stunned, but 2,000 were jubilant in their celebrations as the sun came out.

Great pressure followed after half time, as Steve Bull, Paul Cook and Andy Mutch all went close. Colin Taylor came on as sub and hit the post with his first touch. Dennison's free-kick went inches over the bar, and the trip on Mutch inside the box went unpunished. In the final minute, Paul Cook pulled a tremendous save out of Mike Stowell, and then put Bully clear with a great ball from his clearance at the corner. No words have been invented to express the anger at the professional foul that was committed on him. Instead, everyone politely stated that the defender should have been punished, not given the free-kick. Everyone that is, except

for the lad behind me who was furious with the decision and hit me over the head in his anger.

Roamed

After the game, we were detained for a short period of half an hour inside the cage before the officials kindly let us out. We were released from a different part of the ground into a different street, so none of us knew where we were. The mounted police were very kind and offered to help take us to the station. We explained that we needed to find our car, but were told that was our problem not theirs. We roamed the streets for an hour or two until we found our vehicle, and then set about finding the way home.

On finding the main road out of town, it was blocked anyway,

so we needn't have rushed back. Again the local constabulary directed us around the edge of town into the suburbs. Fed up after a while, we headed for the nearest pub to drown our sorrows. In one, we were refused service incase of trouble, and where we could go, we had to be sectioned off and sit up a corner for similar reasons. Eventually we settled for the local chippy before joining the motorway. Road works held us up on the way home, and traffic lights in my home town only stretched the waiting longer. When I did get home, I had the consolation that at least the S**t had lost again.

Which game was this you ask yourself? Take your pick - it's happened often enough!

- LISA FROM TELFORD

WOLVES TOP TWENTY

1. My Cook-Ca-Choo - Alvin Stardust
2. Eves of The War - Jeff Wayne
3. Gouldon Years - David Bowie
4. Dancing In The Streete - Martha Reeves and the Vandellas
5. Being Bulled - Human League
6. Hurdy Purdie Man - Donavan
7. McAlle Or Nothing - Small Faces
8. Just Be Gooding To Me - Beats International
9. Do The Bartram - The Simpsons
10. Hegan Don't Bother Me - The Tams
11. Lay Your Hansbury On Me - Thompson Twins
12. McCalliog Park - Richard Harris
13. Ain't Love A Birch - Rod Stewart
14. Concrete And Gray - Unit 4+2
15. Take Me Holmes Country Roads - Olivia Newton John
16. A Walk In The Parkes - Nick Straker Band
17. Move Over Downing - Tracy Ullman
18. Hibbitts And Pierces - Dave Clark 5
19. Making Plans For Nigel (Vaughan) - XTC
20. Yes Sir I Can Dougie - Baccara

GWILYM MACHIN

Confessions of a Mince Pie Eater

It sure is a funny old game, Sainty. Let's face it, if it wasn't for the humorous antics of the motley cast of characters who act out the drama of our national game, the football itself wouldn't be nearly so attractive. You're never certain of seeing a wonderfully exciting game with thrills and spills galore, but you're usually pretty sure of getting a good laugh when you're watching football. The sources of the mirth-making entertainment are many and varied, and you're never quite sure where the laughs are going to come from. To that extent, Tommy Docherty was surely right when he said that you needed crystal balls to predict what's going to happen on Saturday (at some grounds you need cast-iron ones) -- as perhaps the following random selection of incidents illustrates.

First of all, let's go back to the Doc. He himself has provided more entertainment in his off-the-field role as court jester than any of the preening million-pound prima donnas who've fallen under his control from time to time (Dalglish and Best excepted, OK). Older readers may fondly recall an occasion about 15 years or so ago when Tommy found himself as a panel guest in the Scotsport studio while Celtic were engaged in the away leg of a European cup-tie in Hungary. The match was allegedly to be broadcast live and the programme was presented by Alex 'Candid' Cameron. Shortly before kick-off an embarrassed and flustered Cameron had to admit to the viewing millions that "there are some problems with the Eurolink" (i.e. somebody at Cowcaddens had wired a plug up the wrong way). Consequently the usual mindless chit-chat amongst the panel was extended beyond the statutory ten minutes,

with Docherty becoming more fidgety than usual. The final straw came after about half an hour with no sign of live football. 'Candid', clutching at straws, asked Docherty, "Tommy, you've got a vast wealth of experience in these situations; if you were Jock Stein, what would you be saying to the players in the dressing room just now?" Summing up all the experience and tact for which he was renowned, the Doc replied, "Well, Alex, I'd be telling them to get out on the park, the game's been started for 20 minutes." Time for a commercial break, methinks.

Talking of Jock Stein, one anecdote concerning the big man has unaccountably been missed in the various biographies and tributes written since his death. This was an occasion featuring a pal of mine which illustrates the brilliant repartee and natural earthiness of the great man. Big Jock was a solitary spectator at the side of a pitch in a public park watching an otherwise nondescript amateur game in progress, when my pal spotted him and approached for a bit of a chat. "How's it goin', Jock" says my pal. The big man retorted wittily, "F*** off sonny." Ah, the camaraderie of football!

In the early days of jovial Jim McLean as Dundee Utd supremo, United had even more difficulties in attracting Dundonians into Tannadice than they do now. The enterprising United board came up with a number of schemes to try to get the bums on to seats. This usually took the form of some novel pre-match entertainment, ranging from women's football internationals to sky-divers over Dundee attempting to hit the centre circle from 10,000 feet. This latter proved less successful than anticipated when

one of the intrepid parachutists came to earth on the centre spot of a deserted Dens Park, while another apparently became entangled with a television aerial somewhere east of Broughty Ferry. The most hilarious entertainment I remember at Tannadice in these far-off days was one occasion when a game against Hibs was hyped up in advance by the announcement that local amateur boxing hero, Dick McTaggart, would give us an exhibition at half-time. Some of the more cynical amongst us wondered how this was going to be achieved without a boxing ring. But wait, as the players trooped off at the interval, on rushed a squad of workmen armed with planks and bits of rope. As the crowd whistled and jeered approvingly, they set to work with a will to construct a makeshift platform where the pugilists were to perform. It seems that some of the planks didn't fit together as intended. A saw was called for. A few cuts here and there, but still no joy. Some vigorous blows with hammers produced no progress. Eventually, by dint of brute force and bloody-mindedness some semblance of a boxing ring was proudly erected in the centre circle just as 22 fairly bemused players re-emerged for the second half of the main entertainment. The referee emerged to insist quite forcefully that the erection be dismantled forthwith.

Up to that point not a glove had been thrown in anger, though for a few moments it looked like a few unofficial non-Queensberry blows might be landed, as there was an earnest discussion about whether the ring was to come down. Most of the crowd would have been content for both events to continue simultaneously. The

by Burns.

prospect of seeing Tommy Traynor dribble round, or even better, through, the boxing ring was one to savour. Unfortunately the referee got his way, and those few extra fans who'd turned up primarily to watch the boxing went home for an early bath.

Of course, you don't have to go anywhere near a football ground to get your amusement from the game. One source of fun for West of Scotland residents was/is the Radio Clyde phone-in. For those of us who like a laugh after the game, the untimely passing of the late James Sanderson was a much lamented event. One of wee Jimmie's techniques was to skim through the dictionary each week to find a word with which to bamboozle the listeners on a Saturday. He'd than use the word at every possible opportunity, confident in the knowledge that no-one would dare challenge him. Thus we'd be treated to "Celtic have scored at a very piquant moment" and "Rangers' victory has added a hint of piquancy to the title race". My own personal favourite was when Jimmy confronted a caller who had a complaint to make about Graeme Souness. The conversation went something like this --

Caller: "See, eh, ma point is that, eh, Souness was never in the game against St Mirren."

Wee Jimmy: "Well you can't expect the Rangers player-manager to be refulgent all the time, can you?"

Caller: "Naw, I suppose not"!

Subtlety wasn't Jimmy's strong suit. When he got hold of an idea he just wouldn't let it go. On one memorable programme, reference was made to Lawrence Marlborough, then the owner of Rangers. Wee Jimmy graphically referred to Marlborough as "Mr Lawrence Marlborough, currently sunning himself in Reno, Nevada". So pleased was he with this off-the-cuff characterisation that from then on he was incapable of mentioning anything to do with Rangers without referring to the sun in Reno, Nevada. Thus we'd get a caller phoning in asking whether Rangers would be signing Maradona/Platini/Pele/John Paul II, being met with "well why don't you ask Mr Lawrence Marlborough, currently *etc*."

Another illustration of Wee Jimmy's obsessional hammering of a single theme was when the vexed question of players' agents arose following one of Maurice Johnston's transfers. Jimmy was particularly condemnatory of agents. Well-known agent about town, Bill McMurdo, phoned in to cross swords with the wee man. Having verbally gutted McMurdo, Jimmy than took every opportunity during the rest of the programme to regale us with "I remember the great days of Billy Steel, there's a man who didn't need an agent..." and "Denis Law was the prince of goal-scorers, all achieved without an agent" etc.

By comparison, the current crop of radio men weree a pretty dull lot until recently, though John Greig and Derek Johnstone continued to make appearances in *Colemanballs*, mixed metaphors being Greig's speciality (e.g. "fresh pair of legs up his sleeve") while big Derek began every answer "well that's right...", whatever the question. Johnstone has now been the subject of a million penny transfer from radio to TV so that we can watch as well as hear his strangulation of the English language.

One of the media men who occasionally talks some sense is Bob Crampsey. Crampsey has a seemingly inexhaustible knowledge of the minutiae and trivia of the game, and he used to (for all I know still does) provide the answers to the questions posed in the Saturday Evening Times by such as "Bluenose, Coatbridge" and "Happy Hibee, Muirhouse". Some of the queries from readers were so arcane that the suspicion was that Crampsey made them up himself to fill the page. A standard type of question would be "Please settle a pub argument -- who played left half for Bonnyrigg Rose when they beat Arthurlie in the 1929 Miners Fellowship Trophy quarter-final replay." The answer would be "It was David Forbes, and not as many people think, his brother Peter. Hope that settles the argument." The mind boggles as to how many people have been going around for the last 60 years under the mistaken apprehension that it was Peter Forbes who wore the number 6 jersey on that famous day, only to have their illusions cruelly shattered by some smart-arse writing to Bob Crampsey after a particularly fierce set-to in the bar on a Saturday night.

Back to Tannadice, though. This one's for those who are sufficiently malevolent to be amused by the suffering of others. When Andy Gray was a mere teenager (God, I'm getting old), United evolved the interesting but unsophisticated tactic of punting high balls into the penalty area for young Andy to perform his kamikaze trick of leaping like a salmon right on to the end of the opposing goalkeeper's fist. This tactic reached a spectacular high-point one Saturday against Hearts. United kicked off. As soon as he'd touched the ball to the inside forward, Gray took off as hard as he could for the opposition penalty area. In the meantime, his colleague lofted what rugby folk would describe as a "Garryowen" in the same direction. The ball and Andy arrived inside the 18 yard line simultaneously, where an obliging Hearts defender tripped the onrushing Gray. Only five seconds on the clock and the ref is pointing inexorably to the spot. Excitement indeed, but one young ruffian in front of me was reduced to a state of near apoplexy, as he was the holder of the ticket entitling him to £100 if a goal was scored in the first 30 seconds. He and his mates performed an impromptu watutsi at the thought of the beer flowing like water later that night. As Doug Smith's penalty

attempt described an arc which would have done credit to a frisbee, eventually coming to rest quite close to the corner-flag, the disappointment of the crowd was mitigated substantially by the extravagant gnashing of teeth and tearing up of the erstwhile drink-voucher.

Traditionally Firhill's a place where the entertainment has very little to do with the football on display. In 87/88 season the Jags pulled their biggest crowd of the year for the cup-tie with Celtic. One aging Thistle fan had obviously kept in touch with the comings and goings at Parkhead over the previous few years. Each time Frank McAvennie approached within spitting distance of the ball, this old boy would let loose a volley of abuse, the main import of which was "McGarvey, you're a b******". Eventually, 2 uniformed officers of the law pushed their way into the crowd and had a word with him. We presumed that this was a warning to watch his language, but as Strathclyde's finest looked on smiling benignly, the old boy shouted "McAvennie, you're a b******, an' McGarvey wiz wan tae." Satisfied that things were now in order, the polis moved off to another part of the ground.

A couple of years ago I was in a pub enjoying a post-match refreshment. The walls of the bar were liberally sprinkled with signs saying "NO FOOTBALL COLOURS". A large youth colourfully bedecked in Rangers scarf, Red Hand of Ulster badges etc. approached the bar where a steely-eyed mine host greeted him with, "Are you dyslexic?" Large youth replied with, "Naw, I've no' had a drink a' day, honest."

I started with Docherty, so I'll finish with him. While he was still the supremo at Old Trafford, there was much talk in the media of proposals to subject football hooligans to corporal punishment. When the Doc was asked for his views, he succeeded at one fell swoop in inappropriately mixing up his military ranks and performing an arithmetical improbability by pronouncing, "I'm in favour of capital punishment for football hooligans. This would halve the problem by more than 50 per cent." Now there's an idea. To hell with women's internationals or massed pipe bands, let's have a few public executions. Make it a family game again. Why has the Government not thought of this already? You've got to laugh, Greavsie.

Alastair McSporran

CLYDE-O-SCOPE

THE ALTERNATIVE MAGAZINE FOR SUPPORTERS OF
CLYDE F.C.

"Pressure is it? Pressure? Don't you talk to me about pressure. See you, you know nothing about pressure. But I will tell you this boy, I will tell you this, see me, see pressure, we go hand in hand boy, **hand in hand.**" If Rab C. Nesbitt were a Clyde supporter he'd probably put it like that - and who could blame him? For it is only when you support a small club like Clyde that you really know what pressure is.

It really makes me laugh when the experts rabbit on about the stresses the big clubs suffer - like worrying where the next million will come from to import yet another foreign star, or the terrible strain of having to decide which international to leave on the subs bench, or the agonising uncertainty of whether the crowd will drop below 20,000 because your next game is live on T.V. My heart bleeds for them.

If you really want to know about pressure then ask the supporters of the clubs in soccer's basement. Take my club, Clyde F.C. The events of the last 25 years have exerted so much pressure on Clyde fans that many (too many) have fallen by the wayside i.e. home crowds of 5,000 have dropped to 500! I've lost count of the people I've met who have said,"Clyde - yeah I used to support them."

Sharing Glasgow with Celtic & Rangers certainly hasn't made life easy. However, in the 1950's we carved a niche for ourselves in Scottish football as a team that always tried to play a cultured passing game. In this decade we won the Scottish Cup twice in 4 years and boasted 3 Scottish internationals in the side. Our fortunes dipped in the early 60's, but by the mid-60's we again had a team to be proud of, again based on the 'keep-the-ball-on-the-deck' philosophy. At the end of the 1966-67 season the big time seemed like it was just around the corner. We reached the Scottish Cup semi-finals only to go out to Celtic after a replay and in the league we equalled our best-ever placing of 3rd behind Celtic & Rangers.

At last we had qualified for Europe in the shape of the Fairs Cup...or so we thought. Sad to say we were robbed of our chance of glory by an obscure rule that no two teams from the same city could play in this competition. Rangers got the place having finished above us.

Within a few seasons we'd sold our best player (Harry Hood) to Celtic and Rangers had nicked our manager! We still had good players - most notably veteran goalkeeper Tommy McCulloch who played in the '58 Cup winning side - but lack of foresight allowed them to grow old together. In fact since Tommy retired in the early '70's, we've struggled to find a keeper of his stature and ability. Only Derek Atkins in the mid to late '80's came close.

When League reconstruction took place in the mid 1970's we failed (miserably) to make the cut for the Premier League. From then on it has almost all been downhill. Between 1975 & 1982 we yo-yo'd between the 1st & 2nd Divisions, being relegated twice and promoted twice. The 1981-82 season heralded a slight upturn in our fortunes. We won the 2nd Division thanks largely to the skills of Pat Nevin and Danny Masterton's 23 League goals. Indeed, this was the last time a Clyde player would break the 20 goal barrier and Nevin (as with Hood some years earlier) was snapped up by a big club (Chelsea) for a paltry fee (£95,000).

For the next 9 seasons we somehow managed to cling on to our 1st Division status. During this time we were turfed out of Shawfield Stadium, our home for almost 90 years (in April '86 to be precise). The upheaval was made worse by the fact that for the next 5 seasons we had to play 'home' games at the dreaded Firhill - the worst pitch in the country, the other side of Glasgow and home of our arch-rivals Partick Thistle. We fans knew that no good would come of it and we were right.

In every season at Firhill we lost more games than we won and conceded more goals than we scored as we veered between mid-table obscurity and too many relegation struggles (most notably in 1988-89 when a penalty 6 minutes into injury time in the last game of the season saved us from the drop).

1990-91 was (mercifully) our last season at Firhill and we 'celebrated' by finally going down to the 2nd Division. Not surprising really as we registered only 1 win in our first 18 games! This season also saw relations between the club and its supporters hit an all-time low. The Board were perceived as lacking ambition - a case of part-time committment to match the club's part-time status. The same old lame excuse was trotted out, i.e. "injuries and suspensions were our downfall". Basically it was a case of interpreting bad play as bad luck.

Taking all this into consideration, you'll perhaps forgive me for believing that you only experience real pressure when you support a small struggling club. However, hope springs eternal etc, etc, and there are one or two signs that Clyde might just be on the road to recovery. We are temporarily sharing Douglas Park with Hamilton Accies (a much more pleasant arrangement) and hope to be moving shortly to a new all-seater stadium-cum-sports complex in Cumbernauld a la St Johnstone & McDiarmid Park. Just look what happened to them! From the 2nd to the Premier in double quick time.

There is a much better atmosphere at the club, witness the fact that at a recent away game Clyde players who weren't selected joined Clyde fans on the terraces. Much appreciated lads. At last we have a shirt sponser and of course our own fanzine! It is just possible that the good times are all set to roll again for the Bully Wee. I hope so, they are long overdue.

ALTERNATIVE MANSFIELD MATTERS

THE LAST SCRIBBLINGS OF A TEENAGE MUTANT FANZINE EDITOR

Back in April 1990,the fanzine scene saw the birth of Alternative Mansfield Matters,now,a year and a half later,the death.When I was asked to write an article for the book you are now reading,AMM was still alive but slowly dying,now the dream is over.

I am still only 15 going on 16,and so have plenty of life left yet,but I feel,as many other ex-editors,I'm sure will have felt,as tho' part of me has died.Running a fanzine is an expensive,time-consuming,hard exercise which - altho' you must have heard it a million times on begging letters,which us fanzine editors are famed for - we recieve very little credit or praise for,never mind money.

I suppose at a tender 14 years of age,running a fanzine of my own was,to be honest,a kamikaze exercise but I rode my luck,churning out four badly-typed and pretty atrocious value for money issues,and as time went on,it proved worthwhile.Okay,so to most people a good review in another fanzine or an invite to the first national fanzine fair may be nothing,but to the strange breed,that are fanzine editors,and in particular the teenage mutant variety,it is everything and it was that sort of acceptance amongother well respected stalwarts of the zine-scene,which spurred me on to those 4 issues and many late nights spent tapping away at the typewriter.

A fanzine becomes part of your life,it takes over a huge amount of time and effort especially when,as I did,95% of everything concerning the zine has to be done by you or it won't get done.That can become one of the many problems of fanzine editorship,eventually you begin to lose contact with alot of life away from the zine-scene and the fanzine becomes your identity.

It is hard to pinpoint a certain moment or factor which signalled the death of AMM,in fact it is probably true to say that the zine became too big for me.As I have said earlier,95% of work was done by me,this was because contributions and offers of help from the outside were next to nothing.I ran the fanzine with only a bit of help from my 'sub-ed' and 49% shareholder,who wrote and typed his article (Any of you who actually read AMM will know him as the author of 'Awayday' ie.our chance to make wild and rash predictions on the outcome of forthcoming away games) plus a Stags fan, who wrote a couple of articles for issues 2 and 3.Actually I did manage to con a mate of mine,who like everybody else in my area supports Derby,into writing a few zine reviews,to lighten my load slightly.In fact,it was he,who introduced me to the zine-scene....so,blame him !

Another major factor,was our popularity !... our final issue (altho' I didn't know it at the time) was photocopied 200 times and at that I thought I'd have some left,but as I chose to sell the zine at the near sell-out Sheffield Wednesday cup game and following Stoke Daffy cup game,the copies went like hot cakes and I was left with the headache of having to photocopy approx. 100 more rapidly so my contacts and distributors elsewhere didn't think AMM had died premturely.Unfortunately all didn't go to plan as the photocopier started playing up and no more copies could be produced.Time was the killer tho',I was trying to juggle GCSE coursework with running a fanzine and it just wasn't on.I was left with too many loose ends and one just had to go.

The one and a half years,I spent in the zine-scene were mostly enjoyable altho' sometimes I wondered whether it was all worth it and it is thanks to the encouragement and enthusiasm of many other editors which kept me going as long as I did.I suppose the moral of this tale is that,you,the reader have got to get involved.The amount of work done by the editors is immense and it is for the benefit of you,the normal fan,so please put pen-to-paper,write down your views and show the editors that you appreciate their work.....don't let the scene die because of your laziness !

Signing off for the last time...Ian Martin (Ex-Ed AMM)

Scarborough Warning

As you can see, we have made every attempt to make Hartlepool fans feel at home.

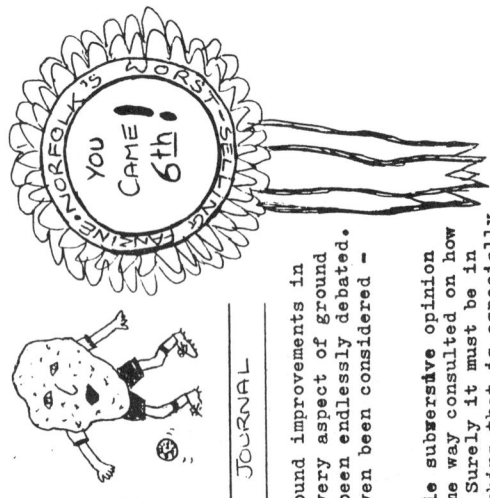

YOU CAME 6th !

NORFOLK'S WORST-SELLING FANZINE - NORWICH

SPUD INTERNATIONAL

THE NORFOLK & NORWICH SUPPORTERS' JOURNAL

During all the recent discussions on ground improvements in the Barclays League, & beyond, almost every aspect of ground design, building, usage, & funding has been endlessly debated. But one factor doesn't appear to have even been considered - yes, you've guessed it, the fans.

Is it really too much of a radical leftie subversive opinion to suggest that we are, at worst, in some way consulted on how our grounds will look in years to come? Surely it must be in the club's best interests to build something that is especially popular with its supporters, to ensure that they will continue to turn up to the stadium every other week.

Clubs also overlook the potential resource they have in their committed fans. Examples of hard-up clubs relying on local businesses & die-hard fans to actually construct their own stands are fairly common in non-league football. So why not in the Barclays League? It saves money, lets the fans feel involved, & can even give unemployed fans (the most likely fans to be able to help) useful skills training.

CUT-OUT-AND-KEEP!

Yes folks, just follow our instructions to build your very own ...... PAUL MARINER!

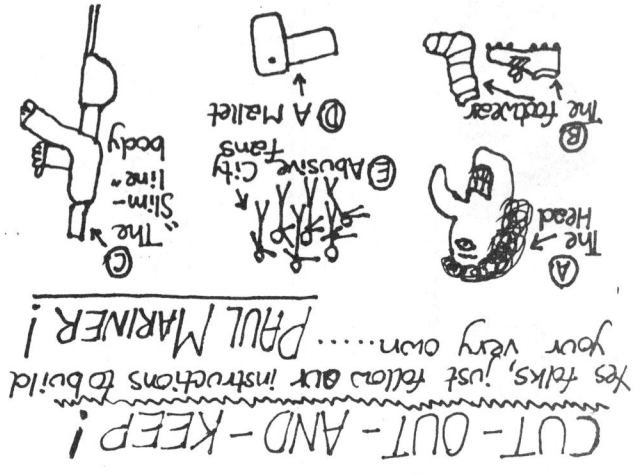

(A) The Head
(B) The Footwear
(C) The "Slim-line" body
(D) A Mallet
(E) Abusive City fans

STEP-BY-STEP INSTRUCTIONS
TO BUILD PAUL.......

1) Fold a. across b.
2) Twist across c.
3) Fasten a. & b. to c. &
   remove pullover, as its a
   bit warm in here, int it?
4) Get some glue & stick
   your hands to the table,
   cos the glue leaks.
5) Find out where 5) got to.
6) Aaah, here it is.
7) Carefully tear the paper
   in totally the wrong place,
   & realise you've ruined
   the whole thing.
8) Screw it up & chuck it out.

So there you have it. As
much use to you as Paul was
to Ipswich Town!

THE FIRST TIME - By JAMES EMERSON

What was the first fanzine in Norwich ? The Citizen? - no! Never Mind The Danger? - no! In fact, the first one in Norwich was one of the first fanzines in the country, although very few people knew about it. The story goes like this..............

When Keith Bertschin signed for Norwich City in the Autumn of 1981, he was immidiately marked out for abuse by the boo-boys. The first reason for this was that his initial performances as the proverbial donkey while on the pitch were not playing well, did not exactly inspire confidence in the supporters. Secondly, & more importantly, he was an ex - Ipshit player. This handicap had always been a nigh-on impossible one to get over, but some sympathetic & forgiving (!) fans decided that he would, given support & confidence, become a useful player in City's hoped - for promotion push.

So, they formed a Keith Bertschin Supporters Club; printed car-stickers; organised a coach to away matches; presented a trophy to the man him- self (many people believed the organisers only did it so they could legally walk out onto the hallowed Carrow Road turf to present the trophy!), and they started a fanzine, after getting the idea from the music fanzines that were springing up all over the City in the early 80's. Only 3 or 4 issues of the fanzine were ever produced, & from all accounts (the copies we had in our family have disappeared, which is a shame as certain members of my family were the prime movers of the organisation) it was a very amateurish production. But such was the novelty value that the group became quite well-known, even though very few copies of each edition were produced.

A rival 'Dixie' Deehan fan club was set up. They didn't do a magazine, but they did start running a coach to away games. It delighted the Bertschin supporters club members when their full coach sped past the half-empty Deehan fan club one. And once, at the ground, when the announcer called the team names out on the PA system, there was a great competition when the respective numbers of the two men were called out. Keith Bertschin always got a bigger cheer!

As the Bertschin supporters club gained more support, so Keith's form improved, & the need for a supporters club diminished, so it was gradually run down until all that was left was a few car stickers & a trophy somewhere in Robert Chase's melting pot (maybe it was the one that got burned during the great fire of 1984!) & a few editions (I hope!) of the first football fanzine in Norwich.

PRROOOOGRAMMES!

OO-I, IS THAT THE FANZINE, IS IT?

Spud Collective Member

SPUD INTERNATIONAL-
"Reproduced without permission."

Written, performed, &
produced by the SPUD
COLLECTIVE:-

c.J. - writer,seller.
A.R. - drawer,seller.
J.Emerson - writer,
            music editor.
F.B.Placard - ideas.

Review - Crates

We felt it was time to blow the lid on one of the most important, but least mentioned aspects of football supporting. The 'crate' is the most essential item of football equipment for any young fan. If your scarf is frayed at the ends or your 'Poll & Withey' era replica shirt is far too small for you these days, the worst thing that could happen is your mates taking the mickey – but if your crate is poorly crafted or badly designed & maintained, it can prove TRULY DISASTEROUS!

In order to put you in know regarding the whys & wherefores of the art of crate-making & crate-standing, we decided to do a 'Which?'-style exposé of the best & worst models on the market & some dos & don'ts on how to utilise this most important & sophisticated piece of technology.

THE KITCHEN STOOL is not, technically a crate, but as any under-10 fan will know, it performs largely the same function. The advantage is that it is generally higher than it's 'true crate' relative, but suffers from usually having very thin, aluminium or low-quality steel uprights. This can, with wear, lead to severe dis-figurement & ultimately instability which could be potentially nasty as the youngster lurches forward to spot Fleck putting in the winner, from the back of the River End.

Much better than this is the HOME-MADE STOOL, usually crafted from wood by the father, left over from construction of his son's Subbuteo table and/or Hornby railway layout. These vary considerably in size & style but can be easily customised by painting it green & day-glow yellow, thus adding to the scarf & bobble hat as the primary sign of dedicated (& slightly insane) support for the Canaries.

Now we come on to the 'real' crates. Starting with the down-market wooden crate. These are probably cheapest to construct (or 'borrow'),& are made entirely of thin wooden strips. These usually collapse after about ½ a season and/or a particularly exciting cup-tie, but their ease of use & availability make them ideal for the beginner.

Probably the market leader is the BEER CRATE. These are not only made of high-strength plastic but have the added advantage that parents can carry their pre-match refreshments in them, before emptying & handing it over to the Canary-mad offspring.

Similar in design, but slightly more up-market is the Rolls-Royce of the crate world, the MILK CRATE, which unfortunately usually come in a tasteless shade of Ipswich Blue, though a couple of coats of Canary Yellow model paint should rectify this oversight on the part of the Dairies.

So, to sum up, here's one of those pointless little chart thingies:-

TYPE OF CRATE	MANUFACTURER	AVAILABLE FROM	MARKS/10
Kitchen Stool	Habitat/MFI	Your Kitchen	
Home-made Stool	Father	Garage	
Wooden Crate	Unīveg/Father	Local Grocer/ Numerous Spud-fields in South Lincolnshire	
Beer Crate	Breweries	Round the back of your local, in a dingy corner	
Milk Crate	Local Dairy	Off back of Milk float,when he's not looking.	

Once you have your piece of equipment, the next crucial step is to learn how to use it most effectively. So here is a rough guide – some dos & some don'ts:-

DO paint your crate, no matter what style it is, in bright green with yellow stripes. The paint salesperson may try & fob you off with some squit about 'Canary Yellow' being most suitable. Ignore them & go for a nice flourescent shade.

DON'T make the mistake of trying to paint it 'tastefully'. Considerations of taste or colour-clash will only reduce the finished article's authenticity & shock-value.

DO take up a lot of room on the terraces with your crate. It is easy to deal with moaners by simply telling them that you represent the future generation of Norwich supporters & how, as a firm believer in football being marketed as 'family entertainment' you feel you deserve preferential treatment.

DON'T be put off if the moaner isn't convinced by the above arguments – just call him a 'traitor to the game's best interests' & wack him round the head with a rolled up copy of this fanzine.

DON'T get yourself arrested for doing the above.

DON'T pick up your crate & chuck it at Chris Kiwomya during the Hospital Cup clash with Ipswich. Not only is this illegal & not the sort of behaviour one would expect of a youngster, but also, you'd be much better off aiming it at Jason Dozzel!

We hope this wad of hints & tips has made your spectating life that little bit easier & wish you all many happy crate-standing years to come!

CONSUMER aDVICE

As we keep being told that football is a business & we are not supporters but simple consumers, could we suggest that every football fan reading this magazine who is disgusted by the fact that the business of football is made up of monopoly enterprises & restricted practices, writes to complain to; The Monopoly & Mergers Commission, Whitehall, London.
European Commission HQ, Brussels (or wherever it is)
Checkout '91, Channel 4 TV,PO Box 4000,London, W3 6XJ.

But please,please,please do NOT write to Esther Rantzen!

dREAM COME tRUE

Readers from outside East Anglia, along with the slightly less observant local devotees of this fab mag, may not have noticed the startling fact that the fine city of Norwich is gradually sliding into the remains of football all the old chalk works below the city. Insurance firms are now apparently charging exorbitant rates to home-owners in some areas of Norwich because of the risk of their insured house disappearing below, overnight!

However, it did occur to me that for professional footballers this may prove to be quite useful, as there is the increased chance of their dream coming true when, after a particularly embarrassing miss-kick,etc. they wish – to quote the old cliché – that the ground would open & swallow them up.

Campaign For Safe Terracing

The Campaign For Safe Terracing is an independent campaign, sponsored & supported by SPUD INTERNATIONAL & THE CITIZEN fanzines in Norwich. In the absence, at time of writing, of a concerted & effective PSA campaign, we are trying to work against all-seater stadia & in favour of safer terraces on a local level.

The Hillsborough disaster was not caused by the existence of terracing at Football League grounds throughout all four divisions. This may come as a shock to the Football Licensing Authority & other self-appointed/Government-appointed experts, but it was caused by too small a ticket allocation for Liverpool fans & some obscenely poor stewarding & policing. It was also partly caused by badly designed terrace entrances/exits & those horrendous spiked fences at the front. All these factors can make any terrace potentially unsafe, but terraces themselves are NOT inherently unsafe at all. In fact, regardless of wether you stand or sit, a badly designed/maintained/stewarded ground is unsafe.

The crass knee-jerk reaction of banning all terraces is a usefully easy way in which the authorities can ignore these real safety factors & push the blame onto something as simplistic as wether you stand up or not. In the process, they can help the FA & the Superleaguers with their masterplan of 'phasing out' football as we know it, & replacing it with an all-seated,all-televised,all-sponsored,middle-class alternative,in which there is no place for the die-hard fan. If you think I'm being unduly pessimistic then consider this :- It is widely accepted that £8 or £9 is a realistic figure for admission to the cheapest seats in the first year of all-seater stadia in Norwich(though this figure could be more like £12 in Southern England & London). The enormous price increase to £6 this season has seen a reduction so far in our average attendance, in line with similar reductions over previous years, as prices have risen. This has been happening during a period where League gates as a whole have been rising, & Norwich City have enjoyed their most successful spell in the entire history of the club! As attendances fall further, the prices will increase further in an upward spiral until only the rich will be able to afford to follow the 'peoples game'.

The Hillsborough disaster, rather than being the catalyst for sensible & long overdue change in football, has been reduced to the significance of an 'excuse' by the all-seater advocates. The other primary excuse seems to be hooliganism. Have we not forgotten the Luton/Millwall riots? Those pictures of loonies disguised as Millwall fans throwing seats at police? Hooliganism is/was as common in seats as on terraces. The hooligan argument (surprise,surprise!) is irrelavent.

If you are reading this & then planning to turn over the page & do nothing more about except mutter "mmmmm, he may have a point there" then you can count yourself as an all-seater supporter. They are relying on people to do nothing but moan in private. They rely on the fact that most people read whinging articles in fanzines & then do nothing more. That's why they don't ban fanzines anymore. Please don't prove them right.

YOU CAN GET INFO ON THE CFST FROM THE SAME ADDRESS AS THE FANZINE, OR JUST COME UP TO ONE OF US OUTSIDE THE GROUND & ASK FOR SOME LEAFLETS.

We support the PSA in their efforts, but are not officially connected.

READERS POLL

We've never done a reader's poll in this fanzine before, but we decided to do one now, just to fill up a bit of space. So here goes, please have your answers into us by January 1977 at the latest.

QUESTION 1 : Do you think anyone will actually bother to reply to this poll?

    a) No way.
    b) Definitely not.
    c) I doubt it.
 or d) No chance, mate!

QUESTION 2 : So there's not much point in doing one, is there?

    a) No, I s'pose not, really.
    b) Nope.
    c) I wouldn't bother if I were you.
 or d) Please find enclosed a £10 note.

Send your replies to the usual address & remember, we don't accept credit cards - cash only,please.

Yes, Folks! It couldn't be easier! There's masses of money to be won in this highly original, not to mention totally rigged......

SPUD INTERNATIONAL SPOT THE BALL competition!

In the picture below, there is not a ball. All you have to do is mark, with a small turquoise oblong, where you think the ball would be, had there been one there, which of course there isn't, as you can see.

Then all you have to do is send away the coupon & who knows, you might be in the money! (or we might just sell your name & details to a junk-mail company.)

BODNEY TOWN
versus
WANGFORD FLOWER
ARRANGERS

Name -
Address -
Shoe size -
Favourite time of year -
Number of Johnny Mathis
LP's you own -

QUAINT NORFOLK SAYINGS - NO.4
****
'We hent gotta hoop wi this loart, hev we?' - South Stand phrase, meaning "Oh, dear we haven't won the championship yet - so we must be crap." This quaint saying is usually best ignored

GREAT TOILETS OF OUR TIME

Carlisle's August away-days unearthed two unexpected treasures. The first was victory at Doncaster, which immediately equalled the number of wins United managed on their travels last season. Mind you, it has to be said that any team fielding the legendary Billy Whitehurst in its ranks, as Doncaster did, is likely to lose. And when he's employed as the play-maker, it's arguable that the team deserves to.

The other jewel came at Rochdale the following Tuesday. Forgive me, but from here on it the article becomes, by necessity, height— ist. Let me explain. With a physique which makes Ian Ormondroyd seem overweight, I was never going to take professional football by storm. It was once said of Tony Adams that he spent all match chasing his first touch. Well, if that was the case, I've been after mine all my life.

There are however, advantages. Whatever the crowd I can usually see most of the game most of the time. Having said that, even the smallest of the seven dwarfs would have a panoramic view of any ground Carlisle have played on in recent years. United are not yet the sport's biggest crowd— pullers.

But whatever our size, we spectators share a common dilemna: Dare we respond to nature's call during the game, or wait till half—time? For if there's one way to guarantee a goal, it's to leave the match to seek the boy's room. Even if you're only gone as long as it takes to list the benefits of a Super League, you know a goal will have been scored before you return. For female fans it must be even worse — by the time you've found a toilet, the groundsman will be taking down the nets.

On the Tuesday night in question, this problem inevitably arose at Rochdale. It was my first visit to Spotland, and the kindest compliment I can pay the ground is that there's covering on all four sides. The handsome new electronic scoreboard only seems to make the rest of the place sadder and shabbier.

But Spotland's saving grace is the toilets at the away end. They would not merit any architectural award, and their position at the top of the corner terracing is a little too conspicuous. And yet, providing you are a male over six feet tall, you can still see while you pee the whole of the pitch! Okay, you can be seen too, but the football's likely to be more interesting than the top of your head, even at Spotland!

So the periods of post—pint pain on the terracing are over. Rochdale heads the League in its effort to improve the comfort of standing away supporters! If for no other reason, Spotland deserves its place if football folklore.

Oh, the result of the match? Appropriately Carlisle, beaten 5-1, were watered on from a great height.

Tim Pocock (Each Game As It Comes)

Plastic

The 'Plastic Cockney' is a phenomenum which has developed in many of the satellite towns around London. They are particularly common in London overspill new towns such as Harlow, Peterborough or Haverhill but, sadly, are not unheard of in Cambridge.

The root of the problem lies in the troubled personality of the 'Plastic Cockney'. He suffers from an identity crisis which usually stems from the fact that, though he may have been born in London, he has spent 95% of his natural life in Cambridge. This is where the confusion in his mind begins and where Mr 'Plastic Cockneys' often eccentric behaviour comes from.

A dead giveaway is the accent which usually sounds something similar to that of Pete Beale or Lorraine Chase. Conversation will also be littered with rhyming-slang, the more obscure the better. Puzzlement at a certain phrase such as 'Alan Whickers' or 'Jimmy Hills' is a source of much satisfaction to the 'P C' as he triumphantly illuminates you as to what it means. He is always likely to come out with something like; 'Let's go down the Frog, around the Jack Horner, into the Rub A Dub and throw a few Pigs Ears down our Gregory Pecks and get well Elephants, and then go for a Pete Murray." A good response is "We all know you're from Cambridge really so cut out the plastic cockney rhyming ✳✳ before I deck you, me old China."

An influential source for his accent and rhyming slang knowledge is the television. Videoing and tirelessly re- running repeats of Minder, Only Fools and Horses, Grange Hill and Birds of a Feather reveals a multitude of phrases and expressions which he can store in his unstable mind for use in the pub later. Once in the pub, Mr P C comes into his element. This arena offers a great opportunity for him to assert his fake identity. He will drink 'light and lager', 'light and bitter' or a 'VAT' and takes great delight in explaining to any, preferably Northern, barmaid what the drink consists of and where it originated from. Then it's over to the juke box for a spot of Chas and Dave, Spandau Ballet, or some obscure B side which apparently is really big on the London Club scene. If you're really unlucky, he'll start singing himself after a few drinks, churning out religiously learned classics like 'Doing the Lambeth Walk', 'Roll out the Barrel' and his party piece, an all time favourite 'Maybe it's because I'm a Londoner', preferably with a tear in his eye.

Mr P C also knows all the best pubs down in London and everyone who drinks in them. All his best mates go to The Blind Beggar or the pubs down the Fulham Road and he always meets up with them when he's down for a football match to support Chelsea or West Ham. The P C of course can only support one of the London teams, usually the one which he was born 'a stones throw' from. The streets which immediately surround Stamford Bridge or Upton Park must have the highest birth rates in the country.

Taking a trip to London with Mr PC to visit a club, concert or to watch Cambridge United play is a mistake. As you venture down the M11, a Capital Radio sticker in the back window, and some inaudible pirate show from Brixton on the radio, Mr P C becomes excited. Months of meticulously studying an A to Z come to fruitiion as he nonchalantly twists and turns through back street mews and alleyways. Hours of study, planning and research for those magic words in his ears - 'You know London really well, don't you?' As he beams inwardly he bores you about some uncle who did 'The Knowledge' and drove a London taxi.

The alternative is to take the train, though Mr PC is usually prepared for this. He knows that London Underground map better than he knows his own

Cockneys

mother and as you disembark at Liverpool Street he assumes command. He emphasizes the fact that he doesn't need to follow any signs or look at any maps or directions by keeping his eyes fixed firmly on the ground. There is not a single moment's hesitation at any passage, junction, escalator or platform as he casually brings you to your destination, and he always knows the correct type of ticket to buy. "You should of got a Network South East, Awayday, Inner-Zone, Off-Peak, Subsidized, One Day Travel Card", he announces knowingly as you queue for yet another ticket.

Once at your destination, which is usually one of those brilliant local pubs he is continually going on about, Mr PC is keen to show you how well known he is. He chats at the bar to the bemused landlord like a long lost relative and shouts in a loud accent across the pub to supposed mates whilst 'letting on' to everybody who passes your table. Curiously, though he seems to recognise everyone, nobody seems to recognise him. The P C lives in a sad and confused world.

If you know someone like Mr Plastic Cockney, please write in, and send a photo as well if possible. If you are unsure as to whether they are eligible here is Norman Tebbit's 'Cambridge Test'. If the answer is yes to two or more of these questions, he is Mr Plastic Cockney!

Norman Tebbits 'Cambridge Test'

1. Does he continually bring up his London birthplace during the conversation?

2. Does he support a London team, especially Chelsea or West Ham, and wear the football strip all the time?

3. Does he have a pronounced London accent and use rhyming slang to an annoying degree?

4. If you were walking along the road with Mr PC and a car pulled up to ask for directions, would he say, "I don't know mate, I'm not from Cambridge"?

5. Does he only shop in London and buy terribly trendy and supposedly fashionable clothes, saying things like, "Everyone in London is wearing Lionel Blares now!"

6. Does he have mates in London who you've heard loads about but never actually met?

7. Have you ever seen him with a 'London Evening Standard' in a Cambridge pub or seen a 'Time Out' in his front room, especially as you know he can't read very well?

8. Does he know the words to classic London songs and does Chas and Daves's 'Down to Margate' provoke Bank Holiday yarns about when he was young?

9. Have you ever been in a London taxi with him when he has annoyed the driver by instructing him as to the best route and bored everyone with stories about his uncle who used to be a cabbie?

10. Is he overexcited about the film, 'The Krays'?

THE GLOBE

CAMBRIDGE'S FOOTBALL & MUSIC MAGAZINE

BISHOP'S STORTFORD — THE (ALMOST) GLORY GLORY YEARS

I started supporting Stortford at the beginning of the 1981/2 season ; the previous season had ended with the side lifting the F.A. Trophy at Wembley with a 1-0 win against Sutton in front of 22,000 people , the majority of whom came from Stortford. The season had seen the side complete a League and Cup double by lifting the Isthmian League Division 1 championship to regain their place in the Premier Division after a gap of three years.

1981 wasn't the first time Blues had reached Wembley ; seven years before in what was probably their best season they beat Ilford 4-1 in the last Amateur Cup Final and lifted the London Senior Cup as well as the Herts Senior and Charity Cups. The intervening years were not a success , with only one county cup win and, in 1978, relegation.

The 1980's were to prove a much more successful time with a total of ten trophies and three runners-up medals. The season following 'The Double' year saw the side win the Charity and East Anglian Cups , hardly the stuff legends are made of , but together with a reasonable league position in spite of an horrendous injury list most people were happy.

The 1982/3 season saw Stortford achieve national fame when , after beating Harlow (after a replay), Reading and Slough, we were drawn against Malcolm Allison's Middlesborough at Ayresome Park. After going 2-0 down in the first half all seemed lost , but thanks to two extremely rare goals by Richie Bradford we fought back to earn a home replay two days later. A packed Rhodes Avenue (estimates vary , but the crowd was certainly over the 6,000 limit) saw Stortford go 1-0 up just before half time through Marvin Hagler lookalike (as the Press repeatedly told us) Lyndon Lynch. Two second half 'Boro goals ended our dreams but there was some consolation when we retained the Herts Charity Cup and were runners-up in the East Anglian Cup after an appalling final at Gorleston.

During the following season the trophy cabinet remained empty and with a limited budget it was getting increasingly difficult for manager Trevor Harvey to keep quality players at the Club. Harvey finally resigned in April 1985 after a humiliating home defeat by rivals Harlow Town , who had only won four games all season and played the final 75 minutes without a recognised 'keeper due to injury. Ironically we finished the season by winning both the Herts Charity and Eastern Floodlight Cups. The latter was greeted with such enthusiasm by Blues fans that , after playing eight games to reach the final , only twelve fans travelled to Margate for the second leg on a Thursday night !

The 1985/6 season saw former Stortford and Arsenal player Tommy Coakley take over as Manager and despite limited resources, a small squad and no reserve team he took the side to 7th in the League. Towards the end of the season our injury crisis was so acute that our first choice 'keeper Martin Taylor played eight games as centre-forward (scoring three times) despite having a broken hand and on one occasion our only substitiute was on crutches due to a broken ankle – suprisingly he wasn't used !

Tommy left Stortford at the end of the season to lead Walsall into the second division and was replaced by his assistant Pat Feary (also a former Blues player). After an uninspiring run of results cullminating in a fine 4-0 defeat at home to Hitchin on New Year's Day , Feary was replaced by former Blues Coach and midfield general John Radford , who became Stortford's first full time general manager in January 1987. His first season ended with a 2-0 Senior Cup final win at Hitchin against Letchworth. The 1987/8 season saw a gradual rebuilding of the side and final placing of 13th was disappointing. The team did win the Charity Cup in our final season of entering it with a fine 3-0 away win at St. Albans City.

The following season proved to be our most successful for eight years. With an increased budget Raddy was able to sign several class players. The best player was undoubtedly ex-Colchester striker Tommy English who hit 43 goals as he formed an impressive strike force with Andy Weddell (35 goals) and Carl Zachhau (32 goals). In the Anglian Cup match against Arlesey English scored four with Weddell and 'Zac' hitting a hattrick each in a 10-1 win. After spending much of the season in the top four we faded towards the end to finally finish 7th. If the league season was a disappointment our progress in the cups certainly wasn't. We lifted the A.C. Delco (league) Cup with a 1-0 against Farnborough at Hayes , reached the Clubcall Cup semi-final before losing to Barnet in a replay, and lost to a Watford side containing several first team players in the Senior Cup final. The season also saw the emergence of Carl Hoddle (brother of Glen – yawn!) as a truly class midfielder and it came as no suprise when he joined Leyton Orient for 10,000 pounds. Zac also left at the end of the season to join Harrow Borough for 6,000 pounds.

Any hopes that the success of the previous season could be built upon we crushed at the end of July when John Radford resigned as Team Manager (he remained as General Manager) after being told to sell his best players and cut the wage bill by 70%. Obviously the announcement that the side was to be broken up caused a lot of resentment amongst Stortford fans , especially when it was revealed that even if we had won the League we couldn't have accepted promotion to the Conference. Radford's assistant Terry Moore (who kept goal in both our Wembley appearances) took over , initially on a temporary basis, and was faced with the task of dismantling a successful side while avoiding relegation. Despite selling English , Weddell , McCayna and Cowley he , together with his new coach Tony Bass (yet another ex-Blues player) , achieved this and towards the end of the season the team were actually spotted playing some good, entertaining football ! Undoubtedly Terry's finest achievement occured in the Clubcall Cup when after disposing of Grays , Hendon , Wokingham , Worcester and Marlow the team played brilliantly to beat Hyde United 4-2 at Bromsgrove in the final.

Although last season saw (yet) another cup final victory , the season couldn't really be considered a success. The Club's Board of Directors seemed to stagger from one crisis to another with frequent resignations and shareholders meetings. It transpired that the wage cuts ordered the previous year had not been fully carried out and several more players were transfered mid-season. Whilst the majority of the supporters had sympathy with Terry Moore's problems, he didn't help himself by appearing to be keen to get rid of any player with flair , and for much of the season we played dull , negative football.

With the Board spending more time squabbling amongst themselves and the likelihood of more wage cuts on the horizon , Moore resigned prior to the last league match of the season. His final match in charge (the following Wednesday) saw the team lift the Loctite Cup with a 5-4 penalty win against Chesham United following an entertaining 2-2 draw. This victory at Hendon gave the Blues fans another chance to show just how good at celebrating they had become, but was marred by troubles in the Boardroom.

After much infighting and a stormy Shareholder meeting , a new Board of Directors were appointed. The new Board have re-appointed John Radford as team manager , together with Ray Wickenden as Coach and have gaurenteed that the Club will live within it's means. Early results have shown that survival in the Premier Division is going to be difficult but seeing as the other option was inventual oblivion most people seem to understand that watching Blues in Division 1 is better than there being no Bishop's Stortford F.C. to watch at all.

CROSS RHODES

The Billy Harrigan school of
Tackling

BRIAN MOORE IS A CARMELITE

Groundhoppers nationwide can reel off yawn-inspiring visits to the grounds of Rainworth Miners Welfare, Tiptree Town and Bristol Manor Farm. But it's not often you hear the likes of St Bernard's Abbey or Coelian Hill, Rome. For these are the playing fields of teams never mentioned in Tony whatsisname's Directory. The grounds belonging to teams made entirely of monks.

Unbelievably, four teams make up the little-known and sensibly-titled "Western Homes Monks Alliance".Founded in the year 984, it is in fact the oldest league in existance. For your interest, here follows details of all four teams as they might feature in the Directory.

BENEDICTINES   Founded 5th Century

Nickname The Dics or The Penguins

Home Colours   Black
Away Colours   White or Dark Blue

Home Ground   Coelian Hill, Rome

Leading.scorer   Father Francis (12)

Facts: The Benedictines have generally monopolised the League over the past nine centuries. Playing most games at night without floodlights, their black kit tends to confuse opponents and the referee.

CARMELITE FRIARS   Founded 1210

Nickname The Slapheads

Home Colours   Brown

Away Colours   Brown

Home Ground   St Joseph's Asylum, Slough

Leading scorer   Father John (1)

Facts: Being a thoroughly miserable bunch, the Carmelites never join in with the usual post-match bevvies. As a consequence.they are disliked.by.all other teams. Their supporters are renowned for their constant moaning during games. The ground is in a poor state of disrepair and an ambitious "buy-a-brick" scheme resulted in half an outside toilet being built.

CISTERCIAN MONKS   Founded 1358

Nickname The Trappists

Home Colours   White
Away Colours   Brown

Home Ground   Mount St Bernard Abbey,
               Leicestershire

Leading Scorer Father Bob (7)

Facts: The Trappists usually show up well in the League due to their life of good health, both bodily and mental, a lifestyle diametrically opposite to the life of a Carthusian.

FRANCISCANS   Founded 1209

Nickname   The Franks

Home Colours   Brown
Away Colours   Brown

Home Ground   St Joseph's RC JMI,
               Peckham, London.

Leading Scorer St Francis of Assisi (8)

Facts: The Franks are sworn enemies of the Cistercian Monks - both sides refusing to play in any colour except brown this reults in every game between the two ending in a draw. Due to strict observances of meditation, all games are played at 4.00am and attract paltry attendances. The Franks crossed swords with the ruling body for Monk Football recently when they were approached by leading boot manufacturer Nike. The company offered to produce a revolutionary open-toed boot for the players, who were on the verge of accepting, when the ruling body decreed that only League and Cup games could be won only wearing sandals.

1988/9 League Table

	P	W	D	L	F	A	PTS
Benedictines	6	6	0	0	30	7	18
Cistercians	6	4	0	2	21	15	12
Carmelites	6	0	2	4	9	18	2
Franciscans	6	0	2	4	5	25	2

A. Phair

Lesson one - The 50/50 challenge

Lesson two- The Sliding tackle

NEXT MONTH:- WELTERWEIGHT BOXING, THE GAYLE WAY (PROBABLY!)

Will they listen to us now ??

In the aftermath of Hillsborough it was very noticable that amongst all the 'experts' that were asked to give their opnions on the tragedy the one group of people whose views were not sought were the Supporters. We were inundated with quotes from players , managers , chairman , MP's and Colin Moinahan but the very people who were affected were totally ignored. The people said that fences must come down had never even stopped to consider this until 15th April 1989 , but for years fans have known how totally unnecessary these fences are at the majority of grounds. Having travelled all over the country watching Cambridge and Wednesday I've been forced to stand in prison-like conditions just because I'm a football fan. No other sport or entertainment would treat its paying customers with such utter contempt. Some Police treat fans like they are some kind of vermin who have reliquished all rights they would enjoy ouside of a football ground. I'm not suggesting that there is not trouble at matches but if you treat all supporters like animals there will be times when they act like animals.

Last year Football League Clubs had a total income of 135 million pounds , of this 85 million pounds came directly from gate receipts , ignoring other revenue such as souvenirs and programmes that are bought exclusively by fans. If any company or group of comapnies were to contribute such a large sum they would be treated like Royalty (ITV have the power to change fixture dates yet their contribution is peanuts compared to that of the fans).

It seems quite clear (to me anyway) that if football is to continue as the mass spectator sport it currently is , the supporters MUST be given a large say in the running of OUR game. The fact that there are now over 150 independent football magazines shows that supporters are not stupid. Football's current administration can hardly claim to have made a good job of running our national game, the time is now ripe for real democracy with properly elected officials. Directors of Clubs may claim that they own the Clubs yet they the clubs could not survive without fans whereas they could with elected oficials rather than Directors. I'm not suggesting that all directors should immediately resign by a couple of supporters representatives (and not neccessarily Supporters Club representatives) would be a step in the right direction , the clubs are willing to take our money at the gate and it's time they listen to our views.

Before you turn the page and think that this has nothing to do with us as we aren't caged in at home or away games and we are run by a democratically elected committee (stop laughing, this is a seriousl article), just think one day we might be in the Football League. This may sound unlikely but the area is growing , and even if we never reach the League we will undoubtedly play League sides in the F.A. Cup. Do you want to stand behind fences with barbed wire and spikes on top (dry moats would keep any morons off the pitch in all but the most extreme cases). Do you want to sit in all-seater stadiums ? Do you think it would be reasonable to ask the people who will be directly affected , rather than those people who sit in their centrally heated little boxes and control our game, what they think of the changes proposed ?

Football will undoubtedly survive as a major spectator sport hopefully the comfort and , above all , safety of supporters will finally be considered and one day we may even have a say in the running of our game. However , it's tragic that the lessons that many people have been pointing out for a long time, were only learnt after the deaths of 95 people.

Dave Ryan (May 1989)

LIKE MOST THINGS THAT MEN SAY ABOUT SEX THIS IS ENTIRELY FICTIONAL

A leading sex therapist from the the Stevenage and Hoddesdon Association of Gynachologists (S.H.A.G.) who must unfortunately remain anonymous on the grounds of his non-existance has been specially commisioned by Cross Rhodes to investigate the links between sex and soccer. The staggering findings of his survey are likely to shake the football world to its very foundations and some of them are published below , exclusive to this magazine.

The major, and most startling conclusion of the survey is that there is an an irrefutable link between sexual activity and winning trophies. Dr X cites BSFC's 1981 F.A. Trophy winning side as an example. All 12 had sex before the match and only four admitted that it was with each other. However six wives or girlfriends of the Sutton team were late home from a Womans Institute meeting and were too tired , whilst a further 3 had headaches. Two of the Sutton players allowed the pressure of the next day to get to them and unfortunately plated host to 'Mr Floppy'. John Rain whose disasterous defensive error let in Terry 'still smiling from the 7 A.M. blow-job' Sullivan for the winning goal, had been sleeping in the spare room since his wife had caught him wearing a Laura Ashley dress with his hand up the Au Pair's skirt.

Dr X has scores more examples, shortly to be published in his book 'Soccer players must use their balls' , and it is surely the case that his conclus--ions will change to way that managers and teams prepare for matches. It is already rumoured that Blues next signing will be a maseuse to help relieve the player's pre-match 'stiffness' , and reports have reached my desk of several big name League players insisting on having concubines written into their contracts.

Dr X's book will be published in Rampant Thrust in mid-September and will be available from book sellers nowhere.

THIS PIECE WAS INTENDED TO BE HUMEROUS AND IS 100% DEVOID OF FACTUAL CONTENT
LLOYD PETTIFORD

SPORTS MINISTER IN I.D. SHOCKER!!

The Government has announced a major plan to to combat violins at football matches , by implementing a national identity card scheme for fans.

Sports Minister Mr Yehudi Moyniham said last night 'The football authorites have fiddled around for too long. It is vital for the future of the game that we Grappelli with this problem — we have widespread evidence that incidents of violins have been orchestrated by groups of hooligans. 'There are Stradivarious reasons for outbreaks of violins. Often drink is to blame , with fans arriving at the matches completley pizzic--ato'.

But not everyone has welcomed the government's overtures. Some have criticised the scheme as a viola of civil liberties. However , one progressive club , Bishop's Stortford of the Vauxhall League , have gone a step further thàn Mr Menuhin. They have decided to ban ALL of their supporters from home and away matches until the end of time.

ANDY CHARLES

CROSS RHODES

MUNCHED IN GLADBACH

No sooner had Herr Helmet Showin', aka Mathaeus Hamann, come and gone than a germane offering from Herr Traveller came to light. He takes us back more than twenty years at which time England were kings of the football world, Fulham were in Europe and the Traveller still had all his own teeth...

Utilising the basis that a change is, just occasionally, as good as a rest I thought that for this edition I'd recall a continental fixture where Fulham were well and truly turned over - tonked, stuffed, call it what you will. But please don't become alarmed, it can happen to the best of us. Many of you, like myself, have followed the Club's fortunes over a lengthy period of time and in off-setting the 'ups' against the 'downs' one soon realises that all human emotion is there. Just like life, it wouldn't be Fulham without the odd mishap.

The following account covers the initial game of a three-match pre-season tour of West Germany in 1967. To preserve the status quo I should remind you that the outstanding fixtures of the tour's itinerary, versus Arminia Bielefeld and Tennis Borussia Berlin, were won handsomely by 3-2 and 4-0 respectively.

But first an apology. The statistics are not up to the usual standard. I was only a kid (well, twenty anyway) and the full works of a pukka 'Travellers Kit' were still in the infancy stages. Talk about embarrassed - my wrist has been well and truly slapped!!

Sat 29 July '67 - Friendly match
Venue: Bokelberg Stadion
Att: 15,000 approx
BORUSSIA MOENCHENGLADBACH (1)4
FULHAM (0)1
Borussia:Danner,Wittmann,Kempers, Poggeler, Milder, Dietrich, Winmer, Winkler, Meyer, Netzer, Baumann, sub - E.Kremers.
Fulham:Seymour, Mealand, Dempsey, Drake, Callaghan, Jim Conway, Haynes, Brown, Earle, Clarke and Ryan. sub - Ryan.
Scorers: Poggeler (pen)[1-0], Baumann [2-0], Barrett [2-1], Winmer [3-1], and Netzer [4-1].

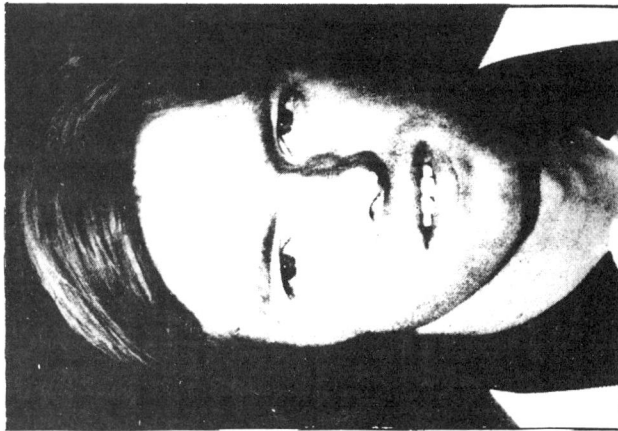

Les Barrett - on target despite being in suspended animation.

To this young Cockney sprog, one of only five fans who made the trip (including incidentally the legendary 'Mick the Beard') the pre-match forecast could only go one way. "Just oo the 'ell are this bunch of Krauts, anyway?" quoth I. A remark made with some justification I can assure you. Borussia had not yet entered the European arena where they would play with much distinction over many years, the Bokelberg was little more than a shack - sans floodlights, sans grandstand, sans just about everything - and the likes of Herbert Winmer and the immaculate Gunter Netzer (to my mind only Bobby Moore could touch him) were yet to make their international debuts.

The opposition, our good selves, were in the in the First Division of the toughest League in the world. Wembley '66 was still uppermost in the mind. And we had Johnny Haynes and 'Sniffer' Clarke in the side - it just goes to prove how insularly biased and inexperienced I was in those days and how much water, figuratively speaking, has flowed under Putney Bridge since.

Ask any professional what the first competitive outing is like after a long lay-off and he'll grimace and tell you of aching muscles, stiffness of limb, etc, etc. This fixture was our first of that season whereas the hosts had just returned from the tone-up of a South American tour. In retrospective analysis we were like lambs to the slaughter... there for the taking.

For the first half we were in the hunt - just. Only behind at halttime to a dodgy penalty (believe that if you will). Come the second half and it was a totally different ball game. The Germans stroked and caressed the ball around with almost arrogant authority, and the harder we tried the more difficult it became. Okay, so the grass may have been a bit long, in need of the joint attentions of Steve Magee and the Billy Goats Gruff, but at the end of the day that's no excuse. I can still picture Les Barrett running down the wing, slowing down as if in suspended animation with a puzzled across his creased features and the ball teasingly rolling away over the touch-line for a Borussia throw-in.

Boy was I glad when the ninety minutes were up - although One lives to fight another day so to speak. We five hurried, heads down, from the the stadium with derision from the locals ringing in our ears. When one understands that the garrison town of Moenchengladbach is inhabited by many of our servicemen and a large slice of that scorn was directed at us in the English mother tongue you can envisage why I shudder when I resurrect the events of that day more than 21 years ago.

Mind you, as completely unrehearsed Jackanory with no back-up documentation barring the match programme, it can't have been that bad...can it? To sweeten the pill somewhat, the programme did contain a very nice article entitled 'George Cohen, Fulhams Weltmeisterschafts - Held' - need I say more?
The Traveller.

WE CAN DREAM...
FULHAM UNVEIL NEW STRIKER TODAY
Borough Blurb
APPARENTLY WE'VE GOT HIM ON LOAN FOR A MONTH, WHOEVER HE IS. SOURCES CLOSE TO THE CLUB SAY HE'S OUT OF THIS WORLD!
THEY WEREN'T KIDDING!
GLEEB!
AT NUMBER EIGHT TODAY, FROM THE STAR SYSTEM OF ORION, PLEASE WELCOME ERGOL!
WELL, HE'S CERTAINLY COME A LONG WAY!
YEAH, BUT IS HE ANY GOOD?
FWEEP!
WE'LL SOON FIND OUT!
ERGOL'S BALL!
BOMP!
GLEEB!
NO! NO! NO!
HE HASN'T GOT A CLUE!
I KNOW. HE SHOULD FIT IN NICELY HERE.
LOOK AT THOSE FEET!
THEY MUST BE A DRAWBACK!
NOT IN THIS DIVISION! HA HA!
BLUP! BLUP!
ZOB! ZOB! ZOB!
HA HA!
HA HA!
THEY'RE TAKING HIM BACK! WHAT'S WRONG?
YOU LAUGH AT OUR PLAYER!
SO? WE LAUGH AT ALL OUR PLAYERS!
WE COULDN'T AFFORD THE TRANSFER FEE, ANYWAY!
GLEEB!
PING!
Paul Johnson 3/91

WE CAN DREAM...
THE CLUB CONTINUES ITS SEARCH FOR A NEW GROUND...
FFC
SITE OF NEW FULHAM SUPERSTADIUM
OKAY, IT'S NOT IN THE BOROUGH, BUT LOOK AT THE CAR PARK SPACE!
MEANWHILE, AT F.A. HEADQUARTERS...
YOU NEED MORE MONEY? OKAY.
ARSENAL AND LIVERPOOL SAY THEY'RE FINDING IT VERY DIFFICULT TO MAKE ENDS MEET ON THEIR PRESENT INCOME. ANY IDEAS?
COMPLETELY OUT OF IT
HAVE THEM FORM THEIR OWN LEAGUE AND PLAY EACH OTHER UNTIL THEY DROP!
MOTION CARRIED!
SWEET F.A.
WHAT ABOUT THE OTHER TEAMS?
WHAT ABOUT THEM?
DID WE VOTE JUST THEN?
LEGAL NOTE:- ALL CHARACTERS IN THIS STRIP ARE FICTITIOUS. ANY RESEMBLANCE TO A GROUP OF OFFICIALS WHO POSSESS THE COLLECTIVE BRAINPOWER OF AN AMOEBA IS ENTIRELY COINCIDENTAL.
HERE'S ANOTHER GREAT IDEA - FROM NOW ON, ALL CLUBS WILL PLAY HOME GAMES ONLY. THIS WILL CUT DOWN ON EXPENSIVE AWAY TRAVEL!
HOW DO WE DO IT?
PLUS - EVERYONE MUST BE SEATED FOR SAFETY!
INCLUDING THE PLAYERS!
I WANT TO SEE THE DEATH PENALTY FOR HANDBALL!
SIXTEEN A SIDE!
F.A. HQ
WAIT! I THINK I'VE CRACKED IT!
WE'RE GOING TO DIVIDE THE LEAGUE INTO NINETY-THREE DIVISIONS, SO THAT EVERY TEAM CAN WIN THE LEAGUE!
DEAD IMPRESSED
WILL YOU PLEASE LEAVE MY GAME AND MY TEAM ALONE?
DID YOU HEAR THAT?
JUST SOME PUNTER.
OH.
WHERE WERE WE?
PING!
THE VOICE OF ONE LITTLE MAN WILL NEVER BE HEARD.
BUT MAYBE, IF WE ALL SHOUT LOUD ENOUGH...
Paul Johnson 8/91

The Tricky Tree

The Tricky Tree is an independent Nottingham Forest Fanzine established in 1989 and published 6 times a season.

Thanks to all our contributors whose stuff is reproduced over the next 3 pages.

THE ADVENTURES OF MARC CROSSLEY

Leadership Challenge Special

The End of an Era : Brian Resigns

"It's a funny old world Saint"

The resignation of Brian Clough following a challenge for the management of Nottingham Forest Football Club has sent shock waves through the world of football.

In this special section:

We look back at the events of the days surrounding the shock resignation.

Gary Baldy presents a personal view of the man.

We interview former Tricky Trees and anyone else we could get a printable quote from.

We have a few drinks.

And we look at those management challengers.

And for those of you who like high tech graphics, we explain the voting system, using fancy pictures.

The Man Who Transformed Nottingham

from our on the spot correspondent - Gary Baldy

A week is a long time in football. It was only seven days ago that I was forgiving the first half showing against Sunderland and looking forward to another three points from Derby. Yet here we are, having lost the man who has been described as the Greatest Post War Manager - no matter what the war. The problems of the last year or so have been minor ones, considering that we won the League Cup Twice, and we can look back over his reign with pride: we have much to be greatful for.

Brian Clough became manager of the Trees in 1975 and by1979 our team was Number One in Europe. His years at the City Ground have seen a League Championship, Two European Cups, Four League Cups, a few minor trophies (does anyone actually own a Simod shoe?) and the odd victory over Liverpool. He is a man of enormous stature, never afraid to speak his mind, never afraid to criticise, yet capable (so he tells me) of praise where it is due. Even though he failed to put the Stags back on the Garibaldi shirt in place of that ridiculous tree, he will be remembered with great affection by those who have loved the Beautiful Game. We shall never see his like again.

Pointless Graph

8.89%
20.00%
22.22%
6.67%
13.33%
2.22%
26.67%

Countdown to Resignation

18.1.89
First signs of the trouble to come, as BC mistakes fans on the pitch after the QPR game for Arsenal players and starts a punch up.

14.6.89
Forest midfielder and holder of 18 England Caps, Neil Webb signs for Man Utd.

26.7.89
Forest sign Irish International John Sheridan but he departs to Sheffield Wednesday 3 Months and one League Game later.

4.11.89
Terry Wilson makes clear his feelings on the Sheridan affair by scoring Wednesday's first away goal of the season, giving them victory at the City Ground.

7.1.90
Man Utd fluke a cup victory at the City Ground with Neil (18.5 Caps) Webb in the stand.

4.4.90
Forest seen on television advertising Flowers by Interflora during a match with Everton. BC urges all fans to "Wear your Pansy with pride."

29.4.90
Talk of Leadership Struggle is postponed as Forest win their League Cup yet again.

25.8.90
The new season begins. Forest are still unable to win at Anfield or get a point at home to a North London club.

13.11.90
Having resigned as goal keeper and proggie columnist Steve Sutton makes a devastating press statement in which he reveals that goalkeepers generally tend to come out for crosses and occasionally catch the ball, rather than punch it straight to opposition forwards.

20.11.90
Neil Fat Wallet Webb, having advanced his collection of England Caps to 20 during the previous 17 months, announces his intention to challenge BC for the Forest job, saying "Harry says the only way back is to the England team is to come back to Forest".

24.11.90
We can't even beat Derby

25.11.90
BC resigns.

Clough Remembered

John Robertson

"I remember me and Bri used to go round the chippy for a crafty fag and a meat pie before each game."

Cap'n Bob Mismaxwell

"Sorry, I don't keep track of such petty games as football. Who is this Clough guy and what relevance does he have to Derby County anyway?"

Larry Lloyd

"I used to say to him, before we won the League, 'Here's the man who won two League Championships on the same day - his first and his last - with Derby in 72'. Well it worked: he went out and won another!"

Special Agent Dale Cooper

"Damn Fine Manager"

Kenny Dalglish

"What's important is Liverpool Football Club. We've just got to get our house in order before the next game." (Translated by B. Rice).

Frank Clark

"I thought I was going to be the next manager."

Don and Phil

"Never knew what I missed, 'til he kissed me."

The Management Candidates

Neil Webb, The Challenger

Fat former Forest midfield star, now with Manchester United trying to recover the England place he lost to an equally fat Geordie. He can be seen trying to effect the spontaneous tear when things don't go right for him. He has recorded a version of the Happy Monday's classic - "Fog on the Manchester Ship Canal".

Ron Fenton, the Establishment Candidate

Therefore boring has Bobby Charlton as role model. Keep an eye out for him outside Wembley before any final.

Archie Gemmill, BC's choice

Former Forest player who has support from both sides of the club (those who supported us before '75 and those who came across from Derby). Could play himself if Terry Butcher starts getting all the press.

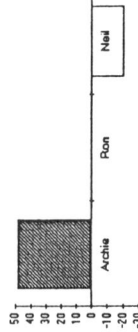
The Voting System

Many people have expressed surprise that Fat Wallet could mount a successful challenge on Brian Clough based on Manchester United's form last season, however the rules clearly state that in order to force a second ballot the challenger's club needs only to have won as many serious competitions in the preceding season as the incumbent's. In the League, Cup and League Cup last year, both clubs won 20 games.

The second ballot is based on a vote of all current players signed from non-League clubs, plus all main stand Season Ticket holders younger than 50 on the first day of the season (providing they can both make it to the ground to cast their vote).

If no-one achieves an outright victory, the three leading contenders go to a third round in which all Exec Stand and Trent End regulars also vote. Bridgford Enders are excluded on the "No Rood, No Vote" clause.

If there is still no outright winner, the result shall be decided on penalties (which should not have to happen at this level of competition so how about a one on one from the half way line, Jim?).

The Clough Years...

1975	We beat Spurs
1976	We win a Cup
1977	We win promotion
1978	We win the Championship and a Cup
1979	We win two Cups
1980	We win two more Cups
1981	We sign Justin Fashanu
1982	
1983	
1984	
1985	
1986	
1987	
1988	
1989	We win two Cups
1990	We win a Cup

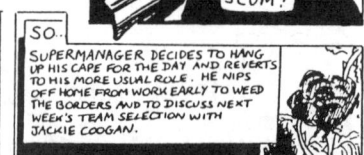

SUPERMANAGER

AN ACTION ADVENTURE

Katherine Shortland

ORDINARILY THE BOSS IS THE NORMAL, DOWN TO EARTH MAN IN THE STREET WE'VE ALL GROWN TO KNOW AND LOVE...

"WORLD'S NUMBER ONE GRANDAD... BUNCH OF PANSIES... PRUNE THE ROSES... FIX THE BACK KITCHEN... UMM... MMM..."

"DROP DESSIE. PLAY OUR 'LIZBETH - MORE TALENT IN HER LITTLE FINGER..."

BOSS

BUT, IN TIMES OF GREAT CRISIS AND DANGER FOR THE CLUB, UNBEKNOWN TO ALL BUT HIS CLOSEST ALLIES, THE BOSS CAN CAST OFF HIS FAMILIAR GREEN SWEATSHIRT, AND BECOME — SUPERMANAGER.

THE TEAM IS IN NEED OF A NEW STRIKER TO MAKE UP THE FINAL COMPONENT IN A SIDE OF CHAMPIONSHIP POTENTIAL. THE SCOUTS HAVE BEEN WORKING OVERTIME, AND THE BOSS HAS SPOTTED HIS MAN...

"GOOOAL!" "YESSS!"

"NOW THEN YOUNG MAN, DO YOU WANT TO JOIN MY CLUB?"

"I'M THE LAD'S AGENT, ANY NEGOTIATIONS WILL BE DONE THROUGH ME."

ONE QUICK CHANGE LATER... "KAPING"

AND... "NO! THAT'S NOT THE WAY WE DO BUSINESS AT THIS CLUB."

THEN... "OOF!"

"TAKE THAT, SCUM!"

"WELL, IF YOU THINK YOU'RE GETTING MY CLIENT NOW YOU'VE GOT ANOTHER THING COMING, AND YOU'LL BE HEARING FROM MY LAWYERS ABOUT THIS..." "WHOOSH"

"DAMN, ANOTHER ONE SLIPS THROUGH MY FINGERS."

SO... SUPERMANAGER DECIDES TO HANG UP HIS CAPE FOR THE DAY AND REVERTS TO HIS MORE USUAL ROLE. HE NIPS OFF HOME FROM WORK EARLY TO WEED THE BORDERS AND TO DISCUSS NEXT WEEK'S TEAM SELECTION WITH JACKIE COOGAN.

WORLD'S No.1 GRANDSON

THE END

Cloughie's Scrawling

Now then young men - hic! The new season is here and despite what the press say Old Big 'Ead is raring to go. And I'll tell you summat else for nowt - hic - these reporters know about as much about me as Robert Maxwell knows about slimming and I'm not joking either. It's just too daft to mention - hic - hic!

Take the other day for instance. I had to go to the Palace for some award or other. It's strange you know, I looked all over but I couldn't find Steve Coppell anywhere - hiccup!

Anyway, you know what our Barbara's like - she insists on dressing me up. I'm telling you, I looked more like one of those nancy boy Chippendale's than the world's greatest - hic - football manager- hic. And I'll tell you summat else, she still takes the Nº 9 to Mothercare for his fittings. I keep telling her there's no way he'll ever be fit enough to score as many goals as I did.

Well, there I was all dressed up ready to get my award. Incidentally, I'd sent someone to ask Stuart Pearce if he minded me collecting it and he said yes of course or piss off or whatever - hic.

Suddenly, a mad woman with a funny hat jumped out of the dugout with a big stick and tried to hit me on the shoulders with it. Blow me, if I'd done that I'd be fined five grand and banned from the touchline all season - hic.

I'll tell you what though, those dugout benches are impressive - hiccup - velvet lined and covered in gold. I'll have to talk to the chairman about them.

I'm telling you though - I wasn't hanging around after that - hic! I ran outside where I was swarmed by a bunch of jumped up press photographs. I couldn't let them photograph me like that, I dived into the limo, - hic - which Des kindly lent me, and sped off.

Down the Mall, young Crosby was waiting with his lovely smile - hic - and the new wardrobe he's made me - hic! I pulled on my green sweater and my trackie bottoms and got back in the limo.

I told the driver to go back to Selhurst Park - hiccup - but when I got there, everyone had gone. They should know by now I can't work without the right clothes - hic - still it's their loss - hic.

Anyway, onto the new season and we've made two big signings this summer -hic - or at least that's what it said in the Evening Post.

The first one is some defender from Barnsley called Tayler or summat -hic. Still, if he's as good at keeping the ball out of the net as his mate Currie, he should have no problems.

I'll tell you what - hic - we may have some communication between the goalie and the defence at last - hic. The rest of the back four can't understand a damned thing they say but Tiler and Norman seem to comprehend every grunt and groan - hic. I'll tell you they sound like a pair of gorillas. Alan Hill says they roam free up in Barnsley - hic - I think he said they call them miners - hic!

And I'll tell you summat else for nowt - I haven't decided who's signed him yet - hic - me or that clown Fenton - hic. I'll tell you next year but as you know - hic - I sign the bad ones - hiccup - and he signs the good ones - hic - or do I sign the good ones - hic - Oh I don't know - hic - I can never remember - hiccup!

As for this Sheringham bloke - hic - I'm sure I've already told Ron we don't want him - hiccup. In fact I had to sell him to Wednesday at a loss - hic - after Ron had gone and bought him from Leeds two years ago -hic.

Oh well, I'll buy him a new red nose for his birthday - hic - it'll keep him occupied all season.

Anyway, that's all for now - hic - I'm for a shower - hic!

They're on the -hic - march in - my - army - hic ....

Brain.

Twenty Things You Never Knew About Notts County

Free cut out and keep guide

> The current chairman of Notts County, who was once on the board at Forest, was the founder of the 4th Rainworth Brownie pack. He left Forest to join an outfit that would remind him of his earlier happy days at Rainworth.

> Justin Fashanu signed for County after he had heard that the club were going to be sponsored by KY Jelly

> The thin yellow stripe on the shirts on the Notts County strip is actually to prevent people from parking on the players heads between 8am and 6pm.

> Don O'Riordan appeared in several episodes of Crossroads during the late Seventies.

> Notts County manager, Neil Warnock, began collecting stuffed seagulls during his time at Scarborough and has continued ever since. He now has a collection of over 300 which he keeps in a garage in Worksop.

> Meadow Lane was once the site of a Pagan festival held for several hundred years where grown men dressed up as witches and performed hideous dances whilst chanting the blind syphilis ridden donkey keepers ancient cry of Yuuu Peyes. This ritual continues, almost unaltered, on Saturday afternoons when County are at home and sometimes during the week.

> The Notts County fanzine, "The Pie", is run by a group of ex-Mr Kipling cake factory workers who were unable to think of an original name for their oracle.

> Insomnia has never been experienced by any Notts County fan - ever.

> Notts County's nickname, "The Magpies", was inspired by the ITV children's television programme featuring Jenny Hanley and Tony Bastable, hence why the main stand is made out of old corn flake packets and egg boxes.

> The film "Apocalypse Now" was filmed entirely on location at Meadow Lane.

> Notts County turned down a five year sponsorship with Skoda as they thought it would present the club with an image they could not keep up. Besides which, the chairman already had one.

> Noddy and Big Ears both hold executive season ticket passes with Notts County.

> Blindfolds are regularly handed out to home supporters by the St. John's Ambulance Brigade at all Notts County matches.

> County goalkeeper, Steve Cherry, is well known for being superstitious and always keeps a tin of John West sardines in the glove compartment of his Reliant Robin.

> The official Notts County Club motto is "In Boredom We Trust".

> Jimmy Sirrell was eighteen times world guming champion.

> At Meadow Lane, police always hold away fans in for ten minutes after kick off to avoid anyone being trampled to death in the rush to leave the ground.

> The half time announcements at Meadow Lane are always read by Katie Boyle and John Noakes.

> Notts County inform striker, Tommy Johnson, once appeared on the Radio One Roadshow as a replacement stylus.

> Notts County's longest serving season ticket holder, Mr Geoff Psychotic-Gambler, has recently been awarded the George Cross for outstanding bravery.

Next Issue: 20 things you did not know about Rude Gullets Hamster!

EXCLUSIVE: NIGEL CLOUGH'S VIEW

JELLY!

Why Stevie Hodge will be sorely missed...

Alot of youngsters these days are saying to me "Oi Nige, ya comin' dahn Madison tonight? - The birds there are well fit! "

But, leaving aside such examples of youthful exuberance, every now and again someone pipes up with "Excuse me Mr Clough- Sir, exactly what does it take to become a top professional footballer and a terrace idol for many thousands of spectators?", and may I say that's more the sort of attitude I would have expected from the Junior Reds Summer Soccer School.

★ four-pack

But seriously, don't get me wrong. I'm in no sense an old stuck-in-the-mud, fuddy-duddy whose idea of an all night rave is a Wham compilation and a four-pack of Irn-Bru, no way bruv, I'm well groovin' and chillin' with all the other young people of the street, and so on whenever the opportunity arises.

Still, enough about that. Make no mistake, I'm always keen to pass on any handy hints and tips that I've acquired during my years in 'The Biz'. First and most important is the adoption of as many bizarre and time-consuming pre-match superstitions as possible, in order to provide something to talk humourously about during TV interviews and features in 'Match'.

Another vital attribute every aspiring young player needs to cultivate is a good name for terrace chanting.

Top tips here include having an easily abbreviated surname, a namesake who sang popular songs in the 1940's, or a tendency for extreme violence.

★ Tipp-Ex

Here at Forest the departure over the summer of Steve Hodge will be keenly felt on several counts. Firstly by the woman in the club shop who has to work overtime to Tipp-Ex his autograph off all the souvenir mugs, and also by the fact that the "Ohhh, Harry Harry..." chant becoming obsolete has now severely depleted the Trent End choir's repertoire.

Tipp-Ex: much in demand

★ Kidney Bean

Whilst Harry's loss may be lessened on the field by the presence of Roy "he's a lovely young man" Keane, on the terraces his arrival has done nothing to improve the variety and vocal range exhibited there on matchdays. And, believe you me I'm the first to admit that the fact that he's nicked my Big Ben chimes does not greatly endear him to me. However, never let it be said that I'm one to bear grudges, so if someone out there were to come up with an alternative we'll say no more about it. (Bear in mind his name rhymes with *Mean, Unclean and Kidney Bean.*)

Thirdly any soccer hopeful must go on enough exotic holidays in order to be able to compete in the traditional start of season 'Who's got the most impressive tan ?'competition.

Only the other day, Jemmo (or "Hey everybody, remember me?", as he likes to be known these days) was down Trentside displaying his tan to a gaggle of admiring girlies, or 'training' as it used to be called.Sadly (for him, anyway),I had to tell him that he had been disqualified from the competition on the grounds that he was at an unfair advantage, having had the second half of last season free to go on holiday as well.

★ Marmite

On top of all the qualities mentioned previously a sensible diet and a sound knowledge of the sport are of paramount importance.

Personally I never start a match without Margaret making me a plate of Marmite soldiers, preferably followed by jelly & ice-cream and a going -home present.

As far as a sound knowledge of the sport is concerned, that is of most use if you want Saint & Greavsie to describe you as a'great student of the game'. I always find a quick flip through my 1978 Shoot Annual just prior to a big match is sufficient to give me the edge over most of my opponents. However, for real devotees a study of suitable'Well Fancy That's from vintage Walkers Crisp packets or a perusal of the 'Interesting and little known facts' section on the back of those cards you used to get with bubble-gum should do the trick.

Speaking of which, swap you two Ray Kennedy's for Alan Sunderland?

Nigel Clough: lost his chant

SHOP TILL YOU DROP...

Never ones to sit back and rest on their laurels, NFFC staff have been beavering away over the summer to bring you the very latest in designer-wear and gift-ideas suitable for every member of the family.

As ever replica shirts are very popular with style-demons everywhere and both Home and Away kits are available in sizes Large, Medium and Gary Crosby. In addition to these, our comprehensive range has been extended to feature specialist shirts, including:

The Stuart Pearce -with enlarged arm holes to allow for bulging biceps.

The Nigel Jemson - featuring foam padding to prevent serious injury when diving for penalties.

The Nigel Clough - thick and woolly with a fleecy lining and mittens sewn into the sleeves.

Also on sale :Psycho stick-on tattoos, Des Walker stick-on moustaches, Learn-to-speak 'Roy Keane' tapes and many, many more.

©KP.

Alex Ferguson is Jive Bunny Shocker

Following minutes of extensive research, we can reveal that the brains behind chart phenomenon Jive Bunny is none other than Manchester United's Alex Ferguson.

Commentators have noticed the similarity between United's style of play and Jive bunny's music, namely that unique ability to take the best bits from everybody else, such as Garry Birtles or the riff from Eddy Cochran's "C'mon Everybody", and turn them into pure garbage.

Just as thousands of music fans are getting used to turning on the radio, hearing their favourite music, getting up to dance round the kitchen and then having to hide their embarrassment as the truth dawns "Oh no! It's Jive Bunny" so too are Norwich, West Ham, Middlesborough and Southampton fans are having to justify their allegiance to Phelan, Ince, Pallister and Wallace; claiming 'Honest! They were good once.'

We here at Forest have suffered more than most. Losing such greats as Ian Moore and Peter Davenport as well as the aforementioned Birtles, at least Jive Bunny have missed out reworking Paper Lace.

Confirmation that the similarity was no coincidence has come in an interview with a small Scottish ball player who escaped the clutches of the United production line. Obviously he wishes to remain anonymous so we will call him Gordon, although that is not necessarily his real name.

"It's a real business empire you know! They have got everything under control. They know it's easier to sell rubbish than quality - I mean Jive Bunny consistently outsell Birdland. That's why I left - I couldn't keep up the wayward pass. I really admire McClair - he's perfected the Slice Shot and the Blastover-from-six-yards and it's only his form that has stopped him buying Lee Chapman. Of course, it's tough on the body, it's unnatural playing all that naff football, look at Webb and Robson, never out of hospital."

Sadly all you get on TV nowadays is the same monotonous junk week in, week out. A repeat of the late Seventies is long overdue, when a group of brash upstarts shook the establishment to become number one throughout Europe.

Next Week: Paul Gascoigne is Bart Simpson..

Franz for the Memories

The Oxford English Dictionary describes an enigma as a puzzling person or thing. The words Franz Carr, unsurprisingly, are not given the honour of an entry in the OED but were they to be then I'm sure their definition would be a direct synonym for enigmatic.

To me, Franz was an enigma. One minute he would be leaving his full back for dead, beating him for both skill and pace down the touchline, the next the ball would be floating harmlessly towards Row C, the result of yet another overhit cross. I first set eyes upon a very young Franz Carr in a pre-season friendly at The Baseball Ground in 1985. News had broken of this raw, exciting teenager with exceptional pace whom Forest had snapped up from Blackburn Rovers, apparently landing his signature ahead of the likes of Manchester United and Everton. The fee was minimal but would increase as Franz reached a certain number of appearances in the first team and yet more would leave the Club coffers when (not if but when) young Carr donned the white of England. That night at Derby, Franz played on the left wing and we lost 2-0. After the humiliation of losing to the then (and again now!) Second Division Rams had subsided, we were left to ponder as to why such an obviously predominant right footed player should be handed his first team debut out on the left! Looking back, that night set a precedent for what was to follow in his ensuing years at the City Ground.

Franz made his League debut at Villa Park in September 1985 but it was his home debut the following week which had the media heralding yet another Clough discovery. Just turned twenty, Franz was up against Kenny Sansom of Arsenal, then left back for England. To put it bluntly, Franz destroyed Sansom that day. I don't think anyone present will forget the sight of Franz sprinting clear down the right, looking up and actually having to wait for Peter Davenport (who was no slouch) to arrive in the middle, before the necessary cross could be provided to enable Davo to complete his hat-trick. During that first season of regular first team action, Franz was a revelation. It takes a very rare breed of footballer to get people out of their seats but Franz had that ability. Standing in the Trent End, it was a great sight indeed to see the bottom tier of the Executive stand rise like a wave as Franz set off on yet another run towards us. That was the joy of Franz. In those early days he was direct in his approach play and the crowd responded to him. The following season he destroyed Chelsea almost single handedly at Stamford Bridge as Birtles and Fat Wallet helped themselves to hat-tricks in our 6-2 win..

It was about this time, however, that Franz started to show signs of change in his play. He wasn't as direct any more, he'd still beat his full back but then he'd stop and try and beat him again. He'd wait too long before crossing the ball and when he eventually got round to doing so he invariably failed to find a red shirt (unless we were playing at Anfield, Highbury or Old Trafford). Franz was starting to think too much and, in doing so, was forgoing his greatest asset - speed. Give Franz 30 yards in front of him and any defender in the League (save for our Des of course!) a 10 yard head start and it would always be the Garibaldi which was first to the ball but give him the ball to his feet and Franz was in trouble. Gone was the prodigious youngster with no other thought than to get to the byline and send over a cross. In his place was a mature player looking to contribute more to the team. In most players this would be a good thing. In Franz it most definitely was not. His ability to get the crowd on their feet as soon as he received the ball was all but gone and returned too rarely but his ability to throw the opposition into fits of panic remained.

I remember him being sent on as sub at Leicester in a League Cup tie in 1988. Psycho had been sent off and we were under the cosh. Nigel was brought back to bolster the midfield and Franz was left on his own up front. The ball was continually booted up front to relieve the pressure and for Franz to chase. He could, and should, have won the game for us that night but he caused so much havoc that Leicester were forced to leave two men back to mark him, thus virtually nullifying their one man advantage. We held onto a 0-0 draw, won the replay 2-1 and went on to beat Luton 3-1 in the final at Wembley where Franz was a mere spectator, the hamstring injury jinx which plagued his final three years at the City Ground having again struck. Franz did make an appearance at Wembley that season, coming on as a sub against Everton in the Simod Cup Final and whipping over the last minute cross which Chappo converted to give us a 4-3 victory but by this time it wasn't only injuries which threatened Franz's regular first team spot. In December 1987, Gary Crosby had been signed from Grantham Town and it soon became obvious that the N°1 requisite to fill the Garibaldi N°7 was not pace or skill but a "nice smile" and the ability to put up shelves. If Bing was fit then Bing would play, it was as simple as that. Brian once said that "you can't get away with playing two wingers in the First Division nowadays" but that did not stop him trying on numerous occasions. When he did, it was always Franz who drew the City Ground's equivalent of the short straw, the N°11 shirt. If Bing was out of sorts he'd have five or six games to regain his form. Franz was lucky if he got 90 minutes.

A three month loan period at Sheffield Wednesday during the 1989-90 season brought praise from Ron Atkinson but not a permanent move, Franz returning to claim his place in the side which defeated Oldham at Wembley. During the summer of 1990 Franz stated his desire to move abroad but a trial at French Club Cannes came to nothing. Last season there was a loan spell at West Ham and talk of possible moves to both Coventry and Wimbledon but Franz turned them down, saying he didn't want to play for another side against Forest. Dare I suggest that statement had something to do with the left back he would be up against?! Yet despite all the speculation about his future, Franz turned in some fine performances during the last season, the undoubted highlight being a vintage one at Carrow Road on January 2nd as the Welsh international left back, Mark Bowen, was time and again left for dead. Not long after, the hamstring jinx was to strike again and his career at the City Ground was all but over.

Franz played his last game in the Garibaldi on May 14th 1991 against Leeds United Reserves at the City Ground. Midway through the second half a precise pass down the middle of the park sent Franz scurrying off in pursuit. The United N°5 headed the chase but not for long. Franz was there first, entering the penalty area and despatching the ball past the advancing 'keeper and into the corner of the net. The sparse crowd of just over 1,000 were out of their seats applauding and somewhere in South-West London Kenny Sansom felt the proverbial someone walk over his grave.

BILLY the FISH
CD 3/86
THIS SPACE FOR SALE
CRUNCHY BISCUITS
BORN HALF MAN, HALF FISH, FULCHESTER'S BRILLIANT YOUNG KEEPER BILLY THOMSON'S UNCANNY ABILITY HAD EARNED HIS SIDE A DRAW IN THEIR VITAL CUP CLASH WITH MUCH FANCIED ROSSDALE ROVERS. WITH £500,000 SIGNING SHAKIN' STEVENS SET TO MAKE HIS DEBUT UNITED WERE CONFIDENT OF VICTORY AS THEY SET OFF FOR THE REPLAY AT ROSSDALE ROAD. BUT VITAL ROAD SIGNS ALONG THE WAY HAD BEEN SWITCHED, AND WITH ONLY SECONDS REMAINING TILL KICK-OFF UNITED FOUND THEMSELVES IN THEIR OWN FULCHESTER STADIUM, 200 MILES FROM ROSSDALE!
FU FC
WE'LL NEVER GET TO ROSSDALE IN LESS THAN A MINUTE!
WAIT A MOMENT. THE CLOCK ON THE GRANDSTAND SAYS 6:30. OF COURSE! THE CLOCKS WENT BACK AN HOUR LAST NIGHT! I MUST HAVE FORGOTTEN TO CHANGE MY WATCH.
IN THAT CASE WE STILL HAVE AN HOUR TO GET TO ROSSDALE
FULCHES
YES, AND WE MIGHT JUST MAKE IT, IN OUR MILLIONAIRE POP STAR CHAIRMAN RICK SPANGLE'S HELICOPTER!
HOP IN LADS, AND HOLD TIGHT!
UY A TATTY HOUSE
GET SOME PETROL
RS001
MEANWHILE, AT ROSSDALE ROAD...
WELL, FULCHESTER HAVE ONLY GOT TEN SECONDS LEFT TO GET HERE 10... 9... 8... 7... 6... 5... 4...
HEY! WHAT'S THIS?
THEY'VE MADE IT- AND IN THE NICK OF TIME TOO!
WE'RE READY WHEN YOU ARE, REF!
OKAY. LET'S GET STARTED
FULCHESTER MADE AN IDEAL START
GOAL! AFTER ONLY FIFTEEN SECONDS.
IT'S AN IDEAL START FOR THE VISITORS
SOON ALL EYES ARE FOCUSED ON NEW BOY SHAKIN' STEVENS
LOOK AT THAT BODY SWERVE!
NEAT FOOTWORK! HE CERTAINLY CAN MOVE.
OH NO! HE'S LOST IT!
COME ON STEVENS! YOU'RE RUBBISH!
BOO!
UNITED BOSS TOMMY BROWN LOOKED ON EAGERLY
STEVENS' MOVEMENT OFF THE BALL IS IMPRESSIVE, BUT HIS CONTROL IS LETTING HIM DOWN.
YES BOSS. HE HASN'T MANAGED TO TOUCH THE BALL YET!
SUDDENLY...
WHAT A PIN POINT PASS!
THAT PENETRATING THROUGH BALL LEAVES STEVENS WITH ONLY THE KEEPER TO BEAT
IT'S A ONE AGAINST ONE SITUATION
HE'S ROUNDED THE KEEPER!
WHAT A TERRIFIC GOAL SCORING OPPORTUNITY
OH NO! HE'S TRIPPED ON THE BALL!!
BAM!!

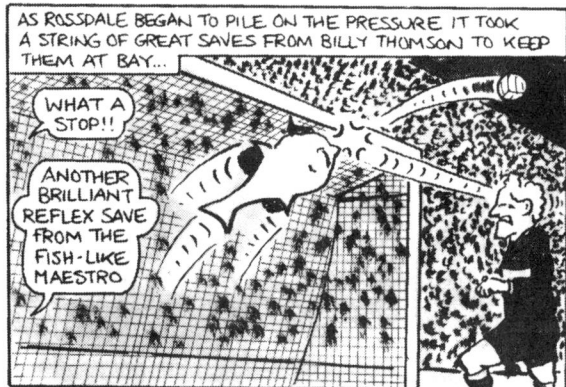

Billy The Fish reproduced with kind permission of House of Viz

The Jolly Green Giant Armchair Football Fanzine - RUNCORN

DANNY'S DILEMNA

Can you help Danny Wallace back to the halfway line after the corner
kick has been cleared ?.........

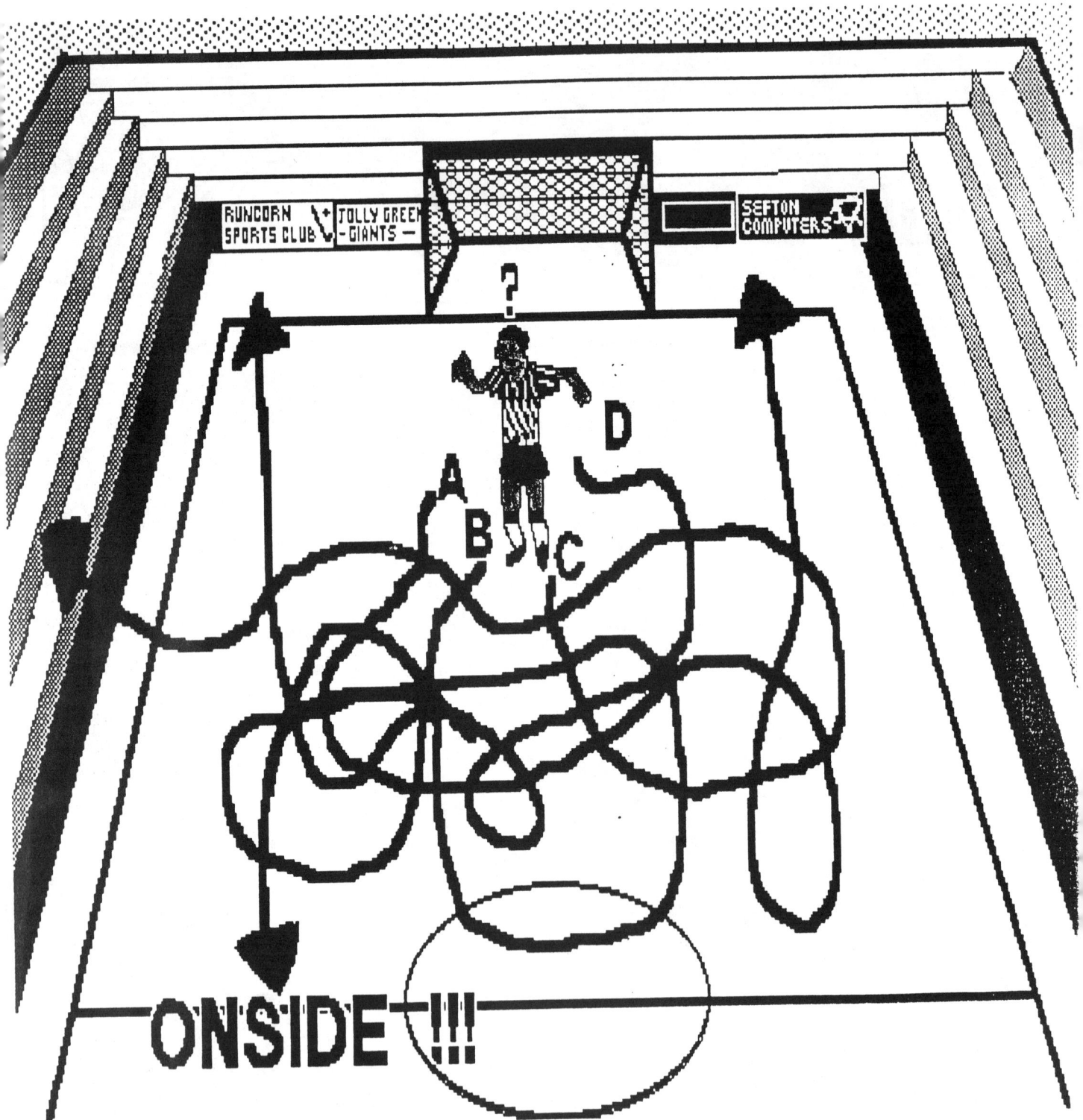

NO MORE INJURY PROBLEMS

As a result of the current injury crisis which has hit Canal Street, **the club** is desperately seeking new ways by which the problem of injuries can be kept to a minimum. Probably the most interesting proposal which has been put forward is the idea of an injury application form, which must be completed by the player prior to the injury taking place. Unfortunately these forms will not be available for public viewing as they will contain insider information, but we have managed to produce the likely layout of the form - FOR YOUR EYES ONLY.

APPLICATION TO BE INJURED

This form must be completed at least 7 days before the date you wish to be injured.

Name .... Position played ....

Nature of injury ....

Date on which you want the injury to commence ....

Have you ever applied for the injury before ? ....

Do you wish the injury to be :-
   Slight/Severe/Crippling/Fatal*

* Applicants wishing to suffer a fatal injury should indicate at the foot of the page whether they would like any opponents to be involved and if so which team they would ideally represent.

Have you ever been refused permission to suffer from an injury ? ....

If so, please give details

....
....

Do you wish your wife to be informed of your injury if she contacts the club regarding your whereabouts ? ....

- -

I, the undersigned, declare that to the best of my knowledge the answers given above are both true and accurate.

Signed .... Date ....

Applicants are reminded that all applications will be considered on merit and that more than 3 applications in one season will be considered excessive and not in the best interest of the club.

PAYING THE PENALTY ?

They're controversial. They can make heroes and villains. They should be easy to score with. Female strippers, no, sorry, penalty kicks. Or to be more exact, penalty kick shoot-outs. For this is one area of the modern game that continually causes many heated discussions on its merits.

Who would have thought that after all these years, they still wouldn't be accepted as the best way to settle drawn Cup games, at every level. We have them everywhere after all, from the World Cup down to schoolboy level. So why are they still considered to be unacceptable in some quarters?

Every season, without fail, at least one big mouthed, bad loser of a manager will be up in arms about the shoot-out system. "It's not fair" he'll moan. "After 120 minutes of football, it's not fair to get an outcome with a system that will be determined by the failure of one player" he'll whinge. "There surely must be a fairer way of settling matches" he'll grumble. What of course he'll not happen to mention in such post-match cries is "we lost". With many managers it's a case of a 'we won - good system', 'we lost - change it immediately' standpoint.

The hysteria in the English based media following the England - West Germany 1990 World Cup Semi-Final was comical. Television pundits derided the shoot-out system. Columns upon columns of newspaper space was given over to debating the issue, with old players trundled out of the woodwork to examine how the English lads had been robbed of glory by a cruel and unfair system. To those of us looking on in Scotland, the whole thing was brilliantly hysterical, for we knew what the reaction would have been in the media had England not had two donkeys taking their penalties - no-one would have given a toss about the Germans or felt that they had been put out unfairly.

One thing that penalty shoot-outs certainly do is to bring out the bad losers - and there certainly seems to be a lot of them!

All the bad losers out there should look no further than to East Fife fans for the way to react to a penalty shoot-out defeat. For we on the Bayview terraces have had to watch our beloved team lose out in the Skol Cup on penalties for the last six seasons on the trot. 1986-1991, penalty shoot-outs have been our downfall against Rangers, Albion Rovers, Dunfermline, Queens Park (twice - once very controversially, but that's another story!) and most recently East Stirling. Not only this, but the Mighty Men from Methil have also lost numerous Fife Cup ties on penalties in recent seasons. Do we cry for a rule change though? No we do not, because the penalty shoot-outs add much excitement to often dull games and keeps the fans right till the end of the ties. That's why the Skol Cup has been such a big success in Scotland. Mind you, East Fife fans have become very used to failure in penalty shoot-outs, as we haven't seen the Fife win one since the early eighties! This has given the old wags in the crowd excellent fodder for comment upon, with cries like "can we have the penalties first this time ref" booming out at Skol Cup time.

For those that do want to change the rules away from shoot-outs, what are the alternatives?

East Fife — Away From The Numbers

One idea that has been put forward, and has gained much support it seems, is to play until someone scores. No missus, titter ye not! Whilst this would see the game played to a finish, if the game was between teams like Dunfermline and St Mirren, this may not actually be on the same night that the match started and you could still be there when Saturday's opponents turn up.

This would save the fans a fortune in admission prices though and boost the local economies no end by the roaring trade that camping shops would do in sleeping bags. It would also bugger up the TV schedules, so any idea that could keep Prisoner Cell Block H off our screens can't be all bad! Seriously though, the idea shouldn't even be considered because of all the hassle it presents to travelling fans, particularly for midweek games and for fans relying on public transport.

A variation on this idea is to take a player from each side off the pitch every five minutes or so until someone scores the deciding goal. This is an idea already practiced during normal time by Celtic and Rangers in Scottish Cup ties, leaving fans wondering if they are watching an 'Old Firm' game or the action screens from the computer game 'Football Manager'. A similar effect size-wise can also be achieved by watching any game at Meadowbank Stadium.

FIFA's favoured shoot-out replacement idea is that of a corner count, and if reports are to be believed, this will be in force during the 1994 World Cup in America. Well that's going to make for more exciting games isn't it?! Players will develop new skills. At free kicks over thirty yards out, instead of trying to score an unlikely goal, players will now aim to smash the ball off the wall and out for a corner. Count number one. Someone should really tell East Fife though that the rule hasn't actually started yet and even if it does become law, it won't be in force for league games. As another new tactic, players running along the wing with three men around them will now just hit it out for a corner off one of them, maybe not even on purpose. Count number two. Brilliant idea FIFA. Keep it up.

FIFA are rumoured to be looking into further possibilities for replacing penalty shoot-outs though.

They have still to rule out the playing of a post-match blow football game. This though must surely be even unfairer than penalty shoot-outs. Teams with players like Paul Gascoigne in them have a distinct advantage over the others. With the amount of hot air he has, the game would be over in a matter of seconds, unless of course he tries to draw breath before the game starts, then swallowing the ball would be a major problem. You could overcome this by using a ball of around two feet in diameter, but even this may not be enough. Meanwhile, at wind-swept Arbroath, keeping the ball on a surface at all would be an even bigger problem.

Scots comic genius Craig Ferguson's comments on blow football should be enough to put FIFA off this idea for a shoot-out replacement though. "It shouldn't be called blow football" argues Craig, "it should be called 'inciting a riot' because it always ends in a fight". Thinking back to my own childhood, he's right! Take note FIFA. Penalty shoot-outs aren't all that bad after all. I certainly wouldn't be without them.

MICHAEL McCOLL

("Away From The Numbers")

A LOOK BACK AT THAT NIGHT OF WELSH MAGIC

WERE YOU WATCHING ENG-ER-LAND??

Well, well, well! They are the most powerful economic nation in western Europe - we are a nation racked by economic depression too dependent on declining heavy industry. They picked their team from a population of 80 million - ours from a few million. They are the current World Champions, and have qualified and indeed won the two major internationaltournaments on seemingly countless occasions, whereas we have . . . . . oh well, never mind. They beat the mighty Eng-er-land,(and if our British press is anything to go by, is the ultimate achievement of only a super-team) in the semi-finals of the 1990 World Cup on the way to winning the aforementioned tournament - and . . .WE BEAT 'EM!!

My day started off well, little did I know then it was going to end in sheer ecstasy. I want down to my local bright and early, so as not to miss the bus - which was due to pick us up 3hrs later! Our plan was to set off early and hit the Cardiff hostilries for a few bevvies before kick-off but this plan was kicked into touch when one of the lads turned up tell us that the City centre pubs were to be closed hours before the match; an alternative plan was quickly devised, and Leominster was selected as the place bestowed with the dubious honour of quenching our thirst. After eventually finding a pub which was open, we sank a few extortionally priced beers, before once again boarding our executive coach, where we settled down with the results of a shopping trip to the off-licence - and watched the brill' videos thoughtfullyprovided by the Llansantffraid boys - this is the life - this is the way to travel to a footie match.

After chips in Hereford, a couple of piss stops and another couple of hours of Simple Minds and Phil Collins (yes, it did take us bloody ages to get there) we finally got to Cardiff.

Bloody hell! what a transformation, how different the streets looked today compared to that Sunday a couple of weeks ago - West Gate, a seething mass of Taffs, Gogs, Exiles, flags and more Umbro shirts than I care to mention (one of the F.A.W.s better decisions). Even though the weather was shitty, the atmosphere certainly wasn't and as we neared the stadium, the occasion began to take us all over - win or lose, this was one night the first sell-out crowd for donkey's years, was not going to forget in a hurry.

Jeeesus Christ!. . .what a sight - not even Wembley was this good; on my previous three visits to the National Stadium (Simple Minds concert and the two Cup Finals) I had sat in the lower tiers but this time, I was upstairs, the view was awsome - what a ground - what a noise.

When the teams took to the pitch, everyone around lost their inhibitions to get behind the lads; who said we'd forgotten the war! And but for a few Cardiff dotted around our area, who (once again) mistook their magnificent surroundings for the Shay or Spotland and chose to urge on their blue shirted heroes! (come on Buds - get wise, change the bloody record).

Anyway, back to the story. The Jerrys probably realised they were in for a rough ride - from the crowd that is Bertie! I had no idea the Germans were so unpopular - well I've never been on a Club 18:30!

I'm not going to have a go at the people boo-ing the supposed World Champions' national anthem because, I must confess, in a moment of madness (honest!) I added a few whistles and hoots of my own to the now deafening noise. I know there's no excuse but I was simply carried away by the occasion; and besides, I'm sure the Krautes will return the favour at the Nuremburg "trial" in October. Then it was our turn, and after the ritual singing of "Mae hen wlad fy'n nhadau" - three bars behind the band, the build up was complete.

For me, the match itself was too tense to enjoy, although there were a number of high-points, such as Horney's (??) shot against the bar, the Mexican waves, the excellent refereeing (there's a first by a Wrexham fan) and of course Rushie's goal. And then there was Dave Phillips' back-pass;which worked better than any laxative I've ever tried; Big Nev's "Gordon Banks" save from Klinsmann's header was quit effective too; and finally of course, the relief that spread around the Park - a few minutes before time - when we realised that the aforementioned Mr Karlsson hadn't given the sausageeaters a free-kick (inside the area) for Nev's (now legendary) time wasting, but had given us one (free-kick - not a sausage!).

The final whistle ended the longest 20 minutes of my footballing life and to a crescendo of "Are you watching Eng-er-land?" repeated time after time, the V.E. (victory in European Championships) celebrations started in earnest, Rushie in his German shirt on his mini lap of honour, Peter Nicholas' one man disco, big Eric kissing everyone in sight, and I think Barry Horne smiled!

After applauding our heroes off the pitch, we made our way on a sea of exhaltation and exhuberance (poetic eh!) before eventually bursting onto the streets to join celebating throngs making their way back to the valleys - only for a group of us to find - that we couldn't find (eh) our bus. After spending an hour roaming the streets in the pissing rain, we eventually met up with our search party, who after a few choice words, escorted us back to it, which we eventually boarded, soaked through, thoroughly sober and well and truly knackered but all with smug cheshire cat smiles (we must have looked like a coach of Japanese tourists) on our faces, made all the more lunatic-like due to our red and white face paints having run in the rain. unfortunately, because of our impromptu "walk about" we were too late to stop and really celebtate in style, but I needed nothing, I was on a "high" which was to last for the next three days. So girding our loins, we prepared for the long journey back to the Tanat Valley, entertained by Charlie Sheen in some Baseball film or other (major league I think) and the one and only and very apt LIFE OF BRIAN which ended just before the journeys conclusion with the immortal song ALWAYS LOOK ON THE BRIGHT SIDE OF LIFE. This had been the greatest night of my footballing life.

Like most major occasions, an award or two is usually in order, so I'm going to dish out a few of my own, and I'll start off with Big Nev as the Obvious choice for "man of the match". But a mention should also be given to Bodin, who appart from the obvious "pass" to Rushie had a cracking game. Young Andy Melville, although a little green at times came through his first major test with flying colours. Horney and Aizlewood also deserving of a little praise.

Celbration of the evening has to go to the bloke behind me, who even
after I'd smacked him on the side of the head when Rushie scored simply
laughed it off and went crazy - like the rest of us.

The atmosphere was made all the better for me by the non-stop singing,
which sadly didn't come across too well when I watched it on the T.V. the
next day. "Where's Matteus gone - Where's Mattheus gone?", "Stick your
World Cup up your arse!" and that never to be forgotten, and best of all,
"Are you watching Eng-er-land?" boy(o) was it one in the eye for the so
called "British" press, Jimmy-goat Hill and not forgetting Saint and bloody
Greavsie for their shitty coverage of the game and their non-stop Gazza,
Italia 90 crap we've had to endure for the last 12 mind numbing months.

SWEDEN HERE WE COME ??

D.M.

*   *   *

*   *

*

THE
SHEEPING
GIANT

● only 50p.
and cheap at
double the price ●

THE WREXHAM F.C. FANZINE

EDITORS: Darren Morris & Gavin Evans.

THE MAN WHO WOULD

So often in the past, especially in the self-destruct days of Allison's second coming in the late 70's/early 80's, City have bought players and the first reaction has been, "Who the hell's he?" Daley, Lee, Shinton, Silkman and Stepanovic – who the bloody hell were they? Very often, unremarkable players at remarkable prices. Billy McNeil too, made one or two dodgy signings; Cunningham and Dalziel, McIlroy and Tolmie, as did Mel Machin when his turn came with Biggins and Bradshaw. Who were they? However, despite Machin's strange days and stranger ways - which are documented elsewhere such as the sale of Paul Moulden - the man has never really been accorded the credit that he surely deserved for some other inspired signings: Andy Dibble, Paul Cooper, Colin Hendry and.... and Ian Bishop.

Everybody was aware of Dibble, Cooper and Hendry but Ian Bishop? While hardly being a household name, every City fan who was at that notorious 3-3 draw with Bournemouth last season was well aware of Ian Bishop. He stood out a mile, as apparently he had done in the Cup game at Old Trafford earlier on in the season. With the acquisition of Bishop for £750,000 and Clive Allen as well in the summer, there could not have been a City fan anywhere who wasn't looking forward to the new season with fresh optimism. For an indication of what was to come, we all traipsed off to Burnden Park to catch our first glimpse of the new signings and while Allen was unlucky not to score, we were rewarded with Bishop and Trevor Morley scoring in the 2-0 win. Then at Old Trafford on the Sunday, Bishop returned to his happy hunting ground and with his undoubted ability to put his foot on the ball, gallop through midfield splaying the ball all over the show and above all, getting stuck into Captain Marvel, Bish was an instant hit as City beat the reds 2-0. Superstardom was guaranteed.... or was it?

Despite so many early season setbacks, the general concensus was that things could only get better and that it was only a matter of time before City would take off. Shades of "the good times are just around the corner" perhaps but it was apparent that here were the makings of a good team and this was bourn out as never before on Derby day in September. With only one previous win behind us, team confidence was nevertheless growing and so was Bishop's - even if his hair wasn't! Green with envy, Mel Machin had ordered our new hero to get his hair cut. What difference a player's hairdo makes is beyond me, after all, Gary Pallister's got a lovely haircut and he's rubbish. Still, Bishop - long hair or not - managed to get his name on the scoresheet on this day to end all days, when he got on the end of David Oldfield Oldfield's right wing cross to head an absolute beauty past Slippery Jim Leighton in the 36th minute, giving City a 3-0 half time lead. Bishop's role in the game still wasn't over, in the 61st minute he picked the ball up in the middle of the pitch, made a 30 or 40 yard pass to David White who, in turn, crossed to Andy Hinchcliffe to head in the fifth. Not only was this one of the most memorable goals of all time, it must have worn a million video recorders out since! For £750,000, Bish' looked a bargain. The following week against Luton, he scored again and scored one more against Norwich in the Littlewood's Cup a month later.

Not long after that, Machin, who had already been given football's equivalent to the kiss of death - the infamous 'vote of confidence' - was sacked. Following the comedy of errors that ensued and the eventual appointment of Howard Kendall as manager, it was soon spotted that it was Kendall at Everton who had sold Bishop to Carlisle for £15,000. Bish' appeared on 'Kick Off' on the Friday before Kendall's first game in charge, ironically at Goodison Park. Reading between the lines, it was obvious that Kendall wasn't a Bishop fan at all even if we all

From "Electric Blue" No. 5 - A Manchester City fanzine.

BE KING

were. Despite having been an ever present in the team up until then, he said that he didn't know if he would be playing on the Sunday. Even his mum had phoned up, he told us, so she was obviously worried too. Meanwhile, we consoled ourselves with the knowledge that all that business was years ago, water under the bridge. Bish' had obviously come good and was well on his way to becoming the next undisputed 'King of the Kippax' in the true sense of the phrase and that Kendall could never sell him again anyway.... could he?

It was a lunchtime start for the trip down the M62 for the televised game on the Sunday. Arriving at Goodison, disbelief hung heavily in the air due to the fact that Bish' had been dropped to make way for Gary Megson or was it Kendall's mate, Peter Reid? It was almost as if Kendall was trying to make a point, show us who was the boss. In what could only be described as a non-event, the only exciting moment came when a plank of wood fell out of the back of the scoreboard, with one or two City fans narrowly missing decapitation! Everton fans obviously lack the fabled wit and passion of their counterparts across Stanley Park as once again, Goodison remained largely silent and you could almost be forgiven for thinking that it was the graveyard of the neighbouring church. Of course, it was a different story where we were as the Park End reverberated to chants of "We want Bishop" and "There's only one Ian Bishop" interspersed with songs regaling in the exploits of Neville Southall's wife. We got what we wanted, albeit briefly, when Bishop appeared as sub towards the end of the game. The songs aimed at Southall however, didn't have the desired effect as he retained sufficient concentration to keep a clean sheet as did Andy Dibble and the game ended at 0-0 to be referred to as a 'Bore draw'.

Anyway, after a week of rumour and conjecture as to the futures of both Bishop and Morley - who were both linked to West Ham in a swop

deal for Mark Ward - they were still included in the team that played Norwich on Boxing Day. With the Ward deal put on ice over the Christmas period, we were given fresh hope that they wouldn't leave especially when Kendall said of them after that game, "Bishop ran the show for twenty minutes in the second half and I could not fault Morley". Three days later and our hopes were shattered when both left for West Ham. Certainly Didsbury, and probably half of Manchester as well, was plunged into the kind of despair not seen since Dennis Tueart went to New York. Ian Bishop - where did it all go wrong? After all he DID play for Everton! Hopefully, one day he'll come back to play for City and then he can lay claim to his crown as the undisputed 'King of the Kippax'. Until then, we can only reflect on what might have been....

SO THIS IS ANFIELD

"In British mythology, Liverpool has three things for which it is famous - football, fighting and comedians". So said Hunter Davies in his introduction to 'The Beatles - The Authorised Biography' way back in 1969. In the intervening years, nothing much has changed it seems. Liverpool Football Club dominate the domestic football front more so than ever, especially since their flights of fancy into Europe and beyond were curtailed following Heysel while the likes of Stan Boardman and Jimmy Tarbuck are dragged from the comfort of the Cup Final bar every year to tell us the same old gag for the millionth time and what of the fighting? Well, we shall see later on....

I know dozens of people who won't go to Liverpool for a match whether it's Anfield or Goodison. "Too much bother" they say, or "I've not been for ten years". Of course, ten years ago things were different.... or were they? We've all heard the horror stories about the Stanley knives and the razor blades hidden in lumps of putty and I can think of at least one person who was ambushed by Everton 'fans' at Corley Services who carved their mark through the back of his leather jacket. But surely, things have changed now in these post Hillsborough times.... or have they???

I've been to Liverpool dozens, hundreds of times for all kinds of reasons; passports, parties and pubs as well as football. Usually, Scousers will talk readily and knowledgeably about football and even your team as long as it's not United, although you will never be left in any doubt at any time as to who is the greatest team in the world. You will be frequently and gently reminded of the honours Liverpool have racked up over the last twenty-odd years and even with the wickedest intent in the world, you will humbly have to agree with them. But then again, this isn't match day anyway, so it doesn't really matter!

However, on our last visit to Liverpool for last season's Everton match, we left Goodison with everybody remarking on how Hillsborough had had a remarkable calming effect on their fans only to see them attempting to attack City fans by the time we reached the car park. At least it's different at Anfield.... or so I thought. We arrived at Anfield this season at dinnertime by way of the M62 and a myriad of architectural nightmares that pass themselves off as spires and steeples on virtually every street corner. After parking outside what looked like a mortar bombed house that had been plucked straight off the the streets of Beirut, we dived into the nearest pub. There, we met the 'Electric Blue' Think Tank comprising of Bibby and the near legendary Steve Worthington amongst several other Blues. Naturally, most people in there were Liverpool fans but even so, there wasn't the slightest hint of bother.

Everybody in the world knows how the game went but it was interesting to see how the celebrated humour and knowledge of The Kop stood up to City going a goal up (not to mention the ref giving us a penalty in the first place!) Like any other terrace anywhere, you could have heard a pin drop on The Kop - it's just that you notice it more at places like Anfield and Old Trafford. We all know that the Koppites love opposition goalies particularly when they're either Gary Sprake when he's just thrown the ball into the back of his own net or Perry Suckling after Liverpool have just slammed nine past him. A winning goalie, on the other hand, might just find an empty bottle landing on his cranium. Once Rush had fluked his goal past Dibble while trying to get out of the way of a Barnes' shot and Rosenthal had come on and scored, Grobbelaar could barely contain himself and Ronnie Evans jumped so high out of the dugout that it's a wonder he didn't find himself on the TV gantry. Meanwhile The Kop were "gonna win the League" and "never walking alone" once more thus providing the assembled paparazzi with the kind of stirring display of pageantry you find in every football book until.... Niall Quinn's last gasp wonder goal succinctly, if metaphorically, summed up by Peter as this, "Quinn headed the equaliser with the last kick of the game!"

After being kept in long enough for time to have been called in the local pubs, we walked back to the car. Anfield Road, I have to say, is not the most welcoming place on earth. Hieronymous Bosch could have had a field day down there. It was here, in the doom and gloom, that we met them: the idiots. It's not just Liverpool or Everton that's got them but EVERY club and no matter how long the police keep you behind, they hang about in packs of a dozen or more, for as long as it takes in all weathers to pick off one or two kids strolling down the street. Not for them the skills of Barnes or the agility of Grobbelaar and certainly not the merits of the opposition's play or even the comfort of home or the nearest pub. Martyrs to themselves alone, their only opposition are shadowy figures in the neon gloom, minding their own business as they make their way home. "Come on then, Mancs" they shout as they outnumber their prey four or five to one. They ignore me, running past and the bravest of them cracks a young lad on the back of the head before running back to the pack. A cowardly action if ever there was one - taking anybody from behind yet this is a tactic the police use to arrest people in a Home Office approved headlock. The only irony here unfortunately, is that they never arrest the idiots. No doubt in some Liverpool alehouse that night, the conversation wouldn't have been about a great match but about how "we took the Mancs". If this is Anfield, I'll probably give it a miss next season along with dozens of others.... it's too much bother!

*Adapted from "Electric Blue" No. 8. Both articles by Noel Bayley.

...what other First Division ground offered a free view to upper deck bus passengers stuck in the traffic outside, would you find "Yeovil" graffitied in chalk on a concrete terrace support at any of the superleaguers homes,and what other stadium could hold memories of your team playing the Jimmy Hill All Stars,or performing dogs as part of the club's centenary celebrations?

I hope I'm proved wrong,but if things start to go awry on the playing front it would seem a formality for the already pathetically low attendances to diminish even further as the poor youth of Wimbledon are tempted by the fruits of football grounds more suitably located just a few stops up the District Line.Then,if the famed Wimbledon "spirit" should ever be allowed to drift away an aimless downward drift would seem inevitable. I hope you're reading this Hammam!

FOR THOSE WHO ABSOLUTELY REFUSE TO COMPROMISE.

YIDAHO!

'Enchanting...for Womble addicts of all ages.' *Children's Book Review*

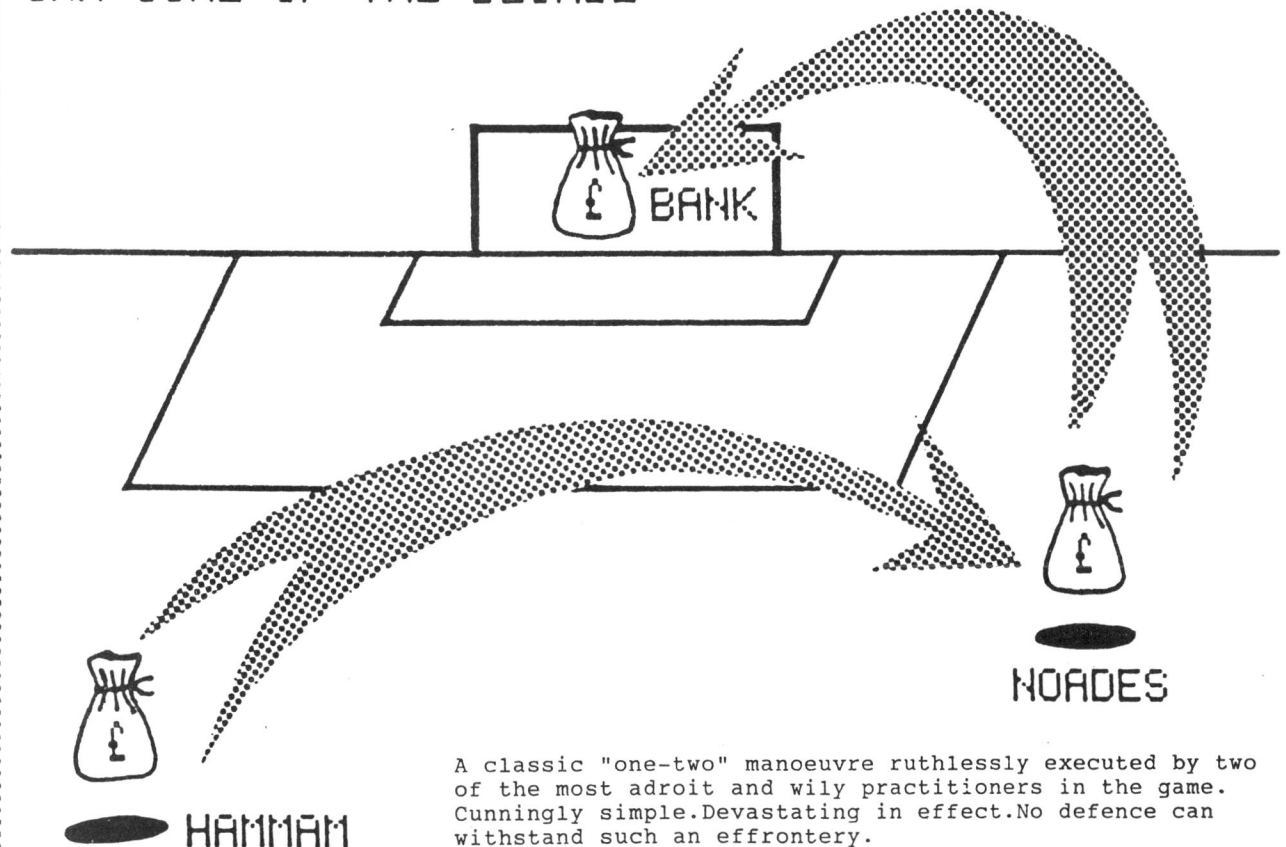

OWN GOAL OF THE DECADE

BANK

NOADES

HAMMAM

A classic "one-two" manoeuvre ruthlessly executed by two of the most adroit and wily practitioners in the game. Cunningly simple.Devastating in effect.No defence can withstand such an effrontery.

SEEHURTS PARK 91.

FRASER BEAM

In 1989 - 90 it was Jim Duffy. Last season another Prodigal son returned to Dens. Admittedly not in as great shape as when he departed, but what he lacked in leanness Cammy Fraser more than made up with meanness. The Editor squints into the sun and reflects on how a very uninspiring trip to Clydebank became the day when Cammy Fraser once again donned the Dundee blue, and turned the air blue to boot.

Cammy Fraser's return to Dundee in late March was the result, many assumed, of a bout of March madness on the part of Gordon Wallace. Further proof that the man had gone completely, irrevocably troppo. Or so we thought.

The sight which greeted yours truly as I entered the footballing mecca that is Kilbowie Park was one I won't forget in a hurry. What was that bulky, dishevelled and, frankly, unathletic figure doing in the dark blue of Dundee? The number 4 shirt clung tightly to his upper torso. It wasn't figure hugging though. What would want to hug a figure like that, I ask you?

Were Dundee so short of talent and depth in squad that a hardened Bluenose had been plucked from the spacious Kilbowie surroundings, handed a dark blue shirt and told to get on with it? By the looks of things, a Bluenose with an unhealthy penchant for pasta and alcohol. Had Gordon Wallace taken literally the anguished cry from a cynical Dees fan during the pre-match kick about - "*I kid dae better thin that s*x*t oot there!*". Or had the S.F.A. decided that, due to the possibility that a team from the East Coast might gain promotion at the expense of Airdrie, we would have to play the remainder of the season saddled with a handicap. A large (and heavy) one at that. The handicap being forced to include in the team for each game a stout, rapidly aging man with a waistline befitting of a darts player and the mobility of, well, something not very mobile. (No Stuart Beedie jokes please). Little did I know at the time, but I had just described Cammy Fraser.

Slowly I shuffled down towards the Kilbowie Park pitch and took my place in eager anticipation of another 90 minutes of ghastly football. I was not to be disappointed.

A song tentatively began behind my left ear. The first dulcet tones of which floated high into the smog-filled sky above Clydebank, before dying a rather undignified death. They try again. It gets better. The words begin to assemble themselves in some sort of coherent order and I managed to make out the curiously doom laden chorus of "*Cammy, Cammy......Give us a wave!*" Cammy? Cammy? Cammy who?

Cammy Duncan was the first name that sprung to mind. Must be Clydebank's new goalie thought I, as I turned blinkingly towards the sunlight and squinted in the direction of the Clydebank goal. A bright flash emanated from the figure positioned between the goal posts. The glint of sunlight hitting shiny pate confirmed the Clydebank's custodian of the sticks was not; indeed, Cammy Duncan but Jim Gallacher. The bald one was still there. Play then duly started.

My eyes did another spot-check of the pitch and then fell once more upon the figure bearing the number 4. That face, that walk, that....groin high challenge as a Clydebank player was given the invitation to take a closer look at the pollution filled atmosphere. I knew then that it could only be one man. Cammy Fraser.

"*He's back, Cammy's back!*", shouted one exciteable Dees fan beside me in response to Cammy's 'tackle'. The linesman, however, was not as glowing in his interpretation of said challenge and duly gave a free-kick. Fair enough in my eyes. Fair enough in the eyes of most of the crowd. But, not so Cammy. He dusted himself down, turned towards the offending linesman and just, sort of, *glared*. The kind of glare that the phrase '*If looks could kill*' was coined for. Cammy then walked towards the linesman and stopped at an intimidating distance, it has to be said, away from him. Like 2 cm's away from his face. You could tell the man was already regretting his decision. Faced with the wrath of Cammy, who could blame him? Cammy paused for a moment. Perhaps he had gone soft in his old age and was willing to let the poor man be? Wrong. A vehement stream of abuse came forth from the mouth of Cammy, spat out with venom at the unfortunate linesman. All the expletives you would expect to hear, and many more besides. Once Cammy had satisfied his malignant urge he turned, visibly pleased at his skilful elocution, wiped a globule of sweat from the tip of his nose and waddled back to his position in the middle of the park.

And yeah, I thought. I guess Cammy *had* returned.

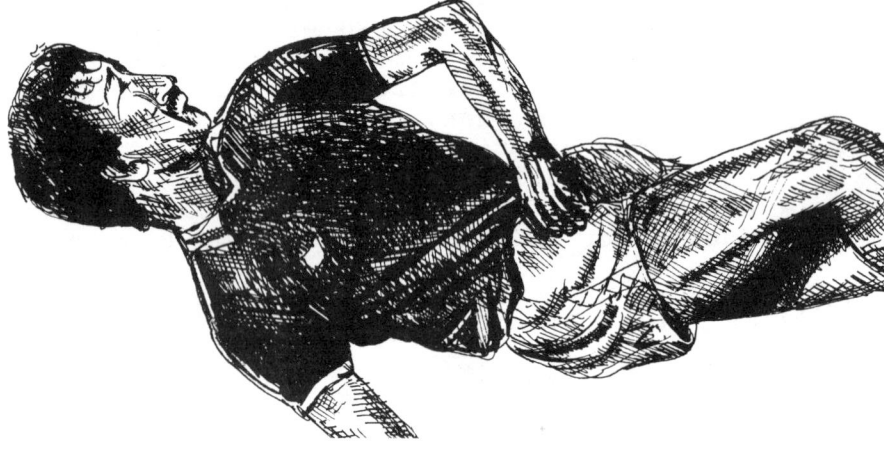

**It's half past four.......
and we're 2-0 down.
The alternative Dundee F.C. fanzine.**

THE WORLD'S A STAGE - II - AND ALL IT'S MEN & WOMEN MERELY PLAYERS

Then where did Vince Mennie fit into the great scheme of things?

The first in a series (fat chance - Ed) of articles which examine the various conditions of the human psyche and unearth those searching questions you always wanted, but ultimately could not be bothered, to ask.

EUROPE....?
What's the big deal?

O.K., so it sounds nice. It's what we lie awake at night and fantasise of. Visiting some lovely Italian city, soaking up the culture, the sunrays and the alcohol. And just to top it all, the chance to see our team in action against some crack Italian outfit. But is it *really* such a big deal? Is it *really* important enough to worthy dedicating a life to? When a manager is asked to outline his aims for the coming season one word is more likely than any other to spill forth from his mouth. *"Europe!...,"* he'll foam, saliva dribbling down his chin in gleeful anticipation. And that's it - a whole season's expected accomplishments precied down to one word. What makes this scenario even more ridiculous is that this manager's team will invariably spend the entire season battling against relegation whilst having been unceremoniously dumped out of both major cup competitions in the third round. Milan, Madrid and other exotic locations could not be further from the player's minds as they contemplate yet another 'relegation crunch match' in the driving rain on a mud-bath excuse for a pitch deep in the wintry clutches of December. The only whiff of things European they are likely to experience is the aroma emitted from the local Italian Restaurant which hangs almost mockingly above their noses.

Yet, on the other hand, perhaps the situation occurs where your team does achieve its sole aim in life and, yes, a European place *is* finally achieved. The street parties, celebratory dinners and civic receptions continue at a pace, rich pageants of success and glory. Yet, just around the corner, the terrible truth lurks ominously.

The players, manager and fans congregate around radios waiting for the draw, expectant looks imprinted upon their faces. Vienna perhaps?...Paris?...Rome?...Or maybe the south of France? Their and your hopes are, however, shattered when the man with the peculiar voice drops the ultimate bombshell. It's final. It's irreversible. Your team had been paired with some unknown outfit which hails from the North Eastern tip of Siberia. A location so remote that not one inhabitant has even heard of Angus J. Cook, never mind seen his photo. A place still in the throes of the *Teddy Boy* era. A place where to visit requires taking a month off work. It is not so much a trip, but a *trek*. And you thought travelling to an away fixture at Ayr was tricky.

On your return (if, in fact, you ever do...) there is no suntan to brandish boastfully in front of your frier's. Your skin tone may, indeed, have changed but only to a rather unfetching bluey-black colour; a more lasting impression of the inevitable frostbite being the fact you now resemble a stage extra from *Treasure Island*. Half your leg having been left in a Siberian hospital.

And what's worse, your team loses.

That's the European experience over for another season, but come August that craving for the continent returns, your roving instincts once more renewed and refreshed. Once again the manager in a frenzy of uncontrollable excitement cites Europe as "...Our aim, our ultimate aim..." This he proceeds to repeat over and over in an almost trance-like state.

For Dundee my aims are perhaps rather more modest. Winning the Scottish Cup would be nice, and *then* we can look forward to the added bonus of a trip to Europe, where we can enjoy its accompanying delights - *the food poisoning, the alcohol poisoning, the language barrier (..."Can eh hae a pinto lagerplease?..), your accommodation in a hotel yet to be built, the fact that every mode of transport you decide to take in order to get to your team's appointed destination is invariably late, cancelled or non-existent. And then the ultimate ignominy - your team loses to Jeunesse D'Esch of Luxemberg in the Preliminary round.*

Knowing Dundee's luck as I do, we'd be pitched against some dark, satanic insignificant mining village in the south of Wales if ever we got back into Europe. Makes a trip to Airdrie in November sound vaguely appealing.

A friend of mine once commented on the strange phenomenon of European football competitions (he wasn't a Dundee supporter obviously). *"Europe is like a continental breakfast",* he stated philosophically. *"It always sounds nice but when it arrives it never aspires to your expectations yet constantly leaves you wanting more".* I pondered upon this unexpected and unprompted outburst, and then smiled. A more fitting analogy for the whole European experience there could not be.

FROM **FOOTBALL UTOPIA** ISSUES 6 & 7:

Those Now Gone (1)

Bexley's League Dream Sinks Without Trace

It is particularly galling to chart the downfall of a once ambitious club which definitely had potential. **Bexley United**, who were formed and indeed reformed as 'Bexleyheath and Welling', were confident enough to twice apply for league status in 1961 and 1962. By 1976 hope had been transformed into despair and amid financial turmoil the club was emphatically out of business.

Originally formed well before World War Two, 'Bexleyheath and Welling' were forced to stop operating in 1939. After a gap of some eleven years, a number of town luminaries decided it was time to reform the club. A meeting was coverned on 7th February 1951 and the highly influential Harold Tanner appointed chairman. A certain Edward Heath (yes, that one!) also gave some enthusiastic backing to the scheme. The club hastily gained a council lease for the Park View Ground (now Welling United's home ground) and, despite being rejected by the London League, gained acceptance to the Kent League for the following campaign. The team's strip was rather quaintly described in the local press as "red shirts and white knickers". At this stage everyone stiffly insisted that it would remain a strictly amateur outfit.

A steady development in fortunes saw the club join the Southern League in 1958, and within 3 years they had clinched promotion to the Premier Division. The third promotion slot being secured by two resounding victories (6-1 v Trowbridge and 4-0 v Rugby). This season must rank as the most glorious in the club's history, for it also saw the side capture the Kent Senior Cup in fine fashion. That Easter Monday triumph over Sittingbourne quickly went into club folklore, as reports spoke of immense support and the players being swamped at the end. Guided by former Charlton star, Charlie Vaughan, and with talented men like Terry Gill and MCC cricketer, Brian Taylor, the side seemed set for more honours. However, it was still no surprise when their application to join the League got no votes. The audacious attempt was prompted by the evidence that Peterborough were forced to apply 21 times before being accepted, and they wanted to 'get in early'.

Still it was a sign of ambition. So was the decision to change the club's name in 1964 to Bexley United. Although wanting to keep the name of Bexley, the directors were looking for a more modern image, and at the same time revamped ground facilities. The mood was one of progression and optimism.

1965 was a turning point as one director lamented "everything we tried to do seemed to go wrong". Bad weather interfered with a ground levelling scheme and managers started to come and go with infrequent haste. The culmination was inevitable relegation. The rot had set in, and income was now not matching expenditure. The team never regained its place in the Southern League Premier Division and although Brian Kelly brought stability to the management, support dwindled. When the colts team was axed in 1967, the stalwart Chairman, Harold Tanner, resigned.

Bexley United began to stumble from crisis to crisis, including the shock resignation of the Chairman, Jimmy Mulvaney, in 1974. In a period when a whole series of Southern League clubs (including Dunstable and Stevenage) were wound up, the summer of 1976 saw the club finally cave in. A mass of resignations by directors, secretaries and even the Chairman (again) left chaotic scenes. The Inland Revenue and a local brewery were owed vast sums. Poignantly the official winding up order was found "fluttering in the breeze on the pitch". It was hoped local businessmen might, in the time-honoured phrase "put together a rescue package", but these hopes were soon scuppered. Firstly some vandals burnt down the clubhouse and main stand, and finally all rescue hopes were stifled when only a handful of loyal followers attended a meeting designed to get the club moving again. Apathy had taken over and even Harold Tanner conceded that "with the present economic position this was bound to happen".

Bexley United had disappeared, but perhaps the success of Welling United, who took over the ground lease, is some consolation. Whatever, I feel sure that the day Bexley United won the Kent Senior Cup at Maidstone is still remembered by some supporters with glowing affection. These days are surely what supporting non-league clubs is all about.

My thanks to Hall Place, Bexley for their help in compiling this feature.

Those Now Gone (2)

In Search Of ... Nunhead F.C.

Investigating the story of how the little known club of **Nunhead** rose and eventually fell proved to be as elusive as finding a cut price Cup Final ticket. Football Utopia's very own version of 'Mission Impossible' began with a trip to Nunhead in the borough of Southwark. It immediately became apparent however, that there was no conceivable source of information in the area. Next stop was to be Peckham Library, only to discover that the district's main centre of archive information lay in à building opposite London Bridge station!

Once there I was aided by an extremely courteous curator, who got out a series of maps and cuttings, but to little benefit. From these scraps of information we did ascertain that Nunhead played in the Isthmian League until the 1938-39 season having made their first appearance some thirty years earlier. Historical maps of the town showed that a ground had been established by the 1890's. An old team photograph suggested that Nunhead players often made a habit of moving on to Arsenal. Most famous of all was that cricketing legend, Denis Compton. Other standard reference books show that Nunhead reached the proper stages of the FA Cup on 4 occasions from 1926 to 1936, including a 9-0 home win over Kingstonian.

And sadly that was where the trail ran cold. My heart sank when I was assured that no-one else had ever researched the subject! All other leads proved unavailing and so that was that. My guess would be that the club simply drafted apart during the war. However, it seems that the exact details may remain hidden for some time yet, if not for ever.

ARTICLES BY MARK LE-FAYE. COPYRIGHT UTOPIAN PUBLICATIONS 1991.

SIZE 10 1/2 BOOTS

No.9 50p

THE

MANSFIELD

TOWN

FANZINE

Speech bubble: "Look, its Bruce Rioch and George Graham... Notts must be worth Millions these days"

Speech bubble: "Yeah.... its strange that they have spent £3/4 M on Stags"

RANK BEER

Size 10 1/2 Boots Pen-Pictures, 91/2

When Stags are away I often get very disgruntled when, having travelled 220 miles to see my team in action, I turn to the page in the match day programme entitled 'Welcome to Our Visitors'. This page invariably includes a load of nonsense known as pen-pictures. Well, my friends, imagine that West Stand Stan the Stags Cynic was to write this feature. This is how it might go.......................

Andy "Suicide" Beasley

Many goalkeepers will assess their performance over the course of the season by counting how many clean sheets they had managed to keep. However, Andy judges his personal success by counting the Saturday nights spent out of hospital. An account of the injuries sustained since his arrival at Field Mill in the Summer of 1983 would shock our younger readers. Andy's most memorable suicide attempt was when he lunged at the feet of Spireite striker 'Bruno' Morris. Andy was carried off on a stretcher and Keith Cassells completed his final appearance at Field Mill between the posts.

Paul "Unknown Quantity" Fleming

No first team squad is complete without a player who can be refered to as an 'unknown quantity'. What exactly does it mean to be an unknown quantity? Perhaps it is that the player concerned has never done anything worthy of merit. A more generous interpretation may be that the player has not yet had ample enough opportunity to show his full potential. Supporters hope that Stags latest defensive acquisition (signed from Halifax) does not follow a succession of disappointing defensive signings : Smalley, Murray, Prindiville, Hunt, etc and instead fits into the latter category of 'unknown quantities'.

Chris "Swap Shop" Withe

I always pitied young kids who came out worse off on Noel Edmond's Swap Shop. You know, the sort that swoped their £200 Hornby train set for a poster of John Travolta. Well the same applies in the case of the swop deal involving Mark Kearney and Chris Withe. Admitedly Kearney was an important cog in the Mansfield Machine in his early days at Field Mill, but like John Travolta he aged and became unfashionable very quickly. Chris Withe, however, is more like the Hornby train set in that he has stood the test of time. Unlike Kearney, Withe has the ability to pass the ball more than 10 yards without giving the ball away to the opposition; can refrain from offering words of friendly advice to referees; and, doesn't attempt to convert rugby kicks when he has an opportunity to shoot at goal.

Greg "Demo" Fee

Greg graduated to the Stags team via Polytechnic. He would have liked to have gone to university but couldn't match Steve Charles A-level grades. Never mind the international caps, Stags players have more O-levels than most. As a student Greg was never one to miss a demonstration and enjoyed throwing up in traffic cones. Greg's move from Sheffield to Mansfield meant that he avoided paying his poll tax last time around. Expect Greg's stay at Stags to be a short one, as he will have to move on again soon in the event of the local authorities catching up with him at his new abode.

George "Columbus" Foster

George is not just (even?) a football Player Manager but is also a keen explorer and discoverer. He recently discovered America and this season is looking forward to visiting new pastures in Scarborough and Maidstone. Future plans include ventures to Blyth and Ashby-de-la-Zouch (hopefully not with Stags, unless they are friendly matches). Amongst many fine discoveries George has brought Steve Prindiville to Field Mill. This Spireite species was captured from a Peak District Nature Park, discovered after a drinking session in Derbyshire. However, perhaps George

Mansfield Town — Size 10 1/2 Boots

Foster's biggest virtue of all is that he gets right up Notts County fans noses whenever Stags play their Meadow Lane neighbours.

Kevin " 63 Minutes" Gray
63 minutes is the average amount of time Kevin spends on the pitch before he upsets the match officials and retires for the afternoon to the dressing room. I know George Foster likes to 'blood' his players in slowly but he is surely going a little too far if he is suggesting that Gray should get himself sent-off each time so that he doesn't have to play a full 90 minutes. Indeed Gray is very much Foster's protegy in central defence - strong, hard working, honest and reliable, but also slow, heavy footed, and temperamental.

Steve "Xmas Lights" Chambers
If West Ham come down with the Chistmas lights then surely the same can be said of Steve Chambers. A player that shone bright in last season's matches early few matches but faded until he finally went out completely in the final run-in. Chambers has never really settled at Field Mill since joining Stags from Sheff Wed, and unless he performances and consistency improves he will surely follow others that have failed at Mansfield and moved on to Chesterfield; like Messrs Gunn, Williams, Ryan, and Caldwell. A player who demonstrates that quantity is not as important as quality.

Martin "Costa Rica" Clark
Martin Clark missed the final few months of last season when he went off injured mysteriously during the match at Exeter. Reports indicate the Stags sweeper was reminded of Scotland's World Cup horror defeat against Costa Rica when during George's half time chat Martin was told to "express yourself, when your one on one". There was a cruel irony in those words of advice and Martin found himself on a stretcher concussed reliving bitter memories of Scotland's sad few weeks in Italy.

Steve "Spireite" Spooner
Steve has taken a lot of unfair criticism since his transfer from Rotherham, when popular winger Ian Hathaway moved in the opposite direction. Okay, so Hathaway was a skilful match winner and Spooner is slow, negative, and a little on the geriatric side, but come on he is not a Spireite anymore so he deserves to be given a chance. Anyway, strategically the signing of Steve Spooner could be a wise move since next time Stags try to off load an old lag to our Spireite neighbours they can point out that they also come to Mansfield via Chesterfield, as opposed to just moving in the opposite direction.

Wayne "Player of the Year" Fairclough
Probably the highest accolade any player can receive is a Stags Player of the Year award, and so Wayne can feel very proud of his achievements last season. In a close contest Wayne pipped the award narrowly ahead of the Crewe supporter who raced into the penalty box to kiss Ian Stringfellow's knee at Gresty Road. Wayne is one of a batch of Stags players who have been attracted to the bright lights of Mansfield after playing for more unfashionable clubs like Notts County, Nottingham Forest and Sheff Wed. A major reason, in fact, for Fairclough deciding to join Stags was that he had been very impressed with the facilities at The Village and Digby's when shown around.

Steve "Casio" Charles
It was a tremendous relief to Stags fans everywhere that George persuaded mathematician, and occasional midfielder, Steve Charles to sign a new contract in the summer. George knows that he can rely on his man to tell him how many points Stags are away from the top of the table. It is certainly a clever man who can handle numbers as big as that. Stags miraculous escapes away from relegation in recent seasons are due largely to to "Casio's" points calculations. Unfortunately his batteries seemed to run out last season - this might also explain his disappointing performances on the pitch. After his playing career ends "Casio" is hoping to join The Chad sports team so he can improve on the woeful inaccuracies in Stags On Tour reported at away matches.

Gary "Laidlaw" Ford
Any comparisons with former Mansfield wizard on the wing Joe Laidlaw stem rather than in the resemblance in physique rather than in terms of footballing ability, thankfully. Whether or not Stags rise to the challenge of Fourth Division football largely rests on the shoulders of this man. Gary Ford proved to be a good replacement for Kevin Kent in the latter part of last season, and if he can watch his weight he will prove to be every bit the match winner the likeable Kenty was. Like many of George's signings Ford does not have the benefit of youth on his side, but unlike many of the others he does have genuine ability.

Steve "Davis" Wilkinson
Why does this man always look so bloody miserable? He barely even managed a smile when he scored five goals against Birmingham City in one match a couple of seasons ago. Perhaps the lack of a striking partner has upset Wilkinson since he joined Stags from Leicester City. Well, possibly the signing of Phil Stant will bring a smile to the face of this unhappy man. Steve Davis can be the only sportsman who appears more melancholy in his play. It is just a pity that our man doesn't pot as many balls away as Davis.

Phil "Forgive and Forget" Stant
Phil Stant will be remembered by those Stags fans who, like me, were daft enough to travel to Craven Cottage, Fulham, last April for his exuberant celebrations after scoring the only goal of a drab match. Stant, playing for Fulham, seemed quite pleased with getting one over a team he had played against a number of times before while with Notts County. Stant's gestures to the travelling Stags fans were not really appreciated as he had hammered another nail in the Mansfield relegation coffin. Similarly, I don't think Stant was too impressed with the plaudits he received in return. Life is too short to bear grudges so I think Phil Stant can expect some hearty encouragement from the Stags faithful, just so long as he provides the 20+ goals needed to get us out of the football basement.

Ian "Kiss my Knee" Stringfellow
Stringfellow was responsible for the best moment of light relief last season when he fell down in the penalty box at Crewe. A caring Crewe supporter came to our striker's rescue and raced on to the pitch to kiss Stringfellow's injured knee better. At the time not everyone saw the funnyside of this incident, not least the spectating Stags supporters who thought there may have been something more sinister in this strange show of compassion. If only Stringfellow's exploits with the football were recollected with such fond memories.

Paul "International" Holland
The Stags are not reknown for producing international players, so it is perhaps surprising that Paul's success has been played down. The young midfielder who made his league debut at Crewe on the final Saturday of last season has two Under 18 England caps to his name. I suppose that makes him "a player for the future" and I'm sure "the Club expects big things of this player".

Wayne "Who?" Davidson
How many supporters remember this man? He was signed from non-league obscurity over a year ago and has been out injured ever since. Wayne was tipped by many to break into the first team at the start of this new campaign, but a pre season injury picked up in a friendly may keep him out even longer. Is this man just scared of playing in front of the partisan Field Mill crowd?

Jason "Forgotten Man" Pearcey
Jason completes Stags first team picture. He is largely a forgotten man since he came on the scene with an outstanding debut at Aldershot a couple of years ago. A one hit wonder? I think not. Jason will become a permanent fixture in the Stags goal, if and when he is given the chance.

Bernard Savage (an occasional Stags Cynic, and editor of 'Size 10 1/2 Boots' - a Mansfield Town fanzine)

The A-Z of American Soccer

A is for **American Soccer League**. Not the current pseudo-professional entity, but the old American Soccer League, which began in 1933. In the booming seventies, it shed its ethnic image in search of a more mainstream audience, despite operating in the shadow of the mighty NASL. Mounting debts and dwindling financial support, however, forced the ASL out of business in 1983. A funny way to celebrate your 50th anniversary.

B is for **Bahr**. Specifically, Chris Bahr, the talented American midfielder who in 1975 was voted NASL Rookie of the Year. So impressed was Chris with this honour that he gave up soccer to pursue a career kicking field goals in the National Football League.

C is for Paul **Caliguiri**, who scored the goal which put the U.S. in the World Cup Finals for the first time in 40 years. His speculative effort against Trinidad & Tobago in the decisive qualifier produced the only goal of the match, and sent the 40,000 or so rabid T & T fans home in fits of depression.

D is for **Dorrance.** Anson Dorrance is head coach of the University of North Carolina women's team, which has won the national championship nine out of the ten years it has been contested. En route to their first title in 1981, they won all 23 of their matches, and finished with a goal difference of 172-8.

E is for **Ertegun.** Ahmet (chairman of Atlantic Records) and his brother Nesuhi were the driving force behind persuading corporate conglomerates Warner Communications to buy the New York Cosmos NASL franchise. The ensuing razzmatazz surrounding the Cosmos made the Mardi Gras look like positively dull by comparison.

F is for **Foreman.** Back in the late seventies, Earl Foreman decided it might be possible to make a lot of money by bastardising soccer to suit American tastes. Thus, the Major Indoor Soccer League, a six-a-side, rock-'em, sock-'em affair, was born, with teams like the Baltimore Blast and the Phoenix Inferno, blue cards to compliment red and yellow ones, players entering the, er, rink, through clouds of dry ice, and obligatory organ music to get the crowd going. Twelve years later, the league (now inexcusably called the Major Soccer League) still survives. But only just.

G is for **Giorgio.** Chinaglia, that is. He was a run-of-the-mill Italian League striker who was lured to America in 1976 and went on to become the most prolific goalscorer in NASL history. His prowess: 243 goals in 256 games, including seven in one match. Chinaglia, thrilled beyond repair with his superstar status, became a naturalised U.S. citizen. Despite having earned 14 caps for Italy, he then pressed FIFA for clearance to play for the U.S. national team. (They never gave it to him.) When the Cosmos folded, Chinaglia returned to Italy and Lazio, where he went on to lambast FIFA for awarding the 1994 World Cup to the U.S.

H is for John **Harkes**, the first

native American to play proper football at Wembley. He is not, however, the first Yank to play for a Football League Club: that honour falls to Brent Goulet, who got in a few games with Crewe Alexandra during the 1987/88 season. Perhaps G should have been for Goulet. Sorry.

Soccer League after seventeen seasons as a professional. Tony Meola, who was supposed to wind up playing in Italy after the 1990 World Cup, also makes the ASL his home these days after failing to land a job in Europe. He's not 37, though.

I is for **interruptions**. Interruptions are the life blood of American television, and one of the reasons it is claimed soccer does not go down well with the TV networks is there's no opportunity to sell beer or automobiles every ten minutes. The fact that nobody watches soccer on television has nothing to do with the networks' lack of interest. Nothing. Absolutely nothing.

N is for **New Jersey**, which is where the "New York" Cosmos played from 1977 to 1983. So there.

O is for **Olympics**. In the 1984 Olympic Finals, 101,799 saw France beat Brazil to take the gold medal. This is the largest crowd ever to watch a soccer match in America, and is only 743 less than the number of Americans who have heard of Gary Lineker.

J is for **jerseys**. America prefers player surnames on the backs of them, and numbers on the front and back. So, when the World Cup comes to America, guess what's going to happen?

P is for **Pelé**. And you certainly don't need to be told about him.

K is for **kids**. There are lots of kids playing soccer in America - millions in fact - and when they grow up they will all become rabid soccer fans and transform the game into a major spectator sport. This argument has been used for twenty years now, and frankly it's wearing a bit thin. Don't these kids ever grow up?

Q is for, er...**Quincy**. A small college soccer powerhouse which won national championships nine times from 1971 to 1981. Phew. Got that one out of the way.

L is for **lady linesmen**. There was one in the NASL, I think. But I can't remember her name. Or perhaps I'm only dreaming.

R is for Kyle **Rote**. Jr., the son of a famous gridiron halfback, who became a professional soccer player with the Dallas Tornado. In his first season (1973), he was the league's top scorer, and was named Rookie of the Year. But Americans remember him because he was so bloody good in those "Superstars" competitions.

M is for **Mausser** and **Meola**, perhaps the two best goalkeepers America has ever produced. Arnie Mausser, at 37, is still active in the American

S is for **Shootout**. The phrase was used here first, folks. The original "shootout" was the NASL's ultimate

The A-Z of American Soccer

« continued »

way of deciding drawn matches. You started with the ball 35 yards from goal and were given five seconds to beat the keeper and put it in the net. Shhh! Let's not put any more ideas into FIFA's heads.

T is for **Tatu.** You know...Tatu, the famous Brazilian footballer. Oh come on now - surely you've heard of him? Readers of "Soccer America" voted him as one of their Top Twenty Heroes, for crying out loud. Beat out Stanley Matthews. Tatu plays for the Dallas Sidekicks of the Major (Indoor) Soccer League, and when he scores a goal, he takes off his shirt and throws it into the crowd. Yes, he does go through a lot of shirts. But what idol doesn't?

U is for **UCLA** - the University of California at Los Angeles, who in 1985 won the longest single championship match ever played. They defeated American University in the National Collegiate Athletic Association Division I final after eight periods of extra time - 179 minutes of play. Lest you begin to envision players melting with exhaustion from such prolonged activity, it should be pointed out that in American college soccer unlimited substitution is permitted. Thus, **U** is also for **unlimited substitution.**

V is for **Veee.** Julie Veee played both indoors and out with the San Diego Sockers. Nothing too unusual there. But how about that surname?

W is for **Woosnam.** Phil Woosnam ran the NASL as Commissioner for 13 years. In 1970, with the league down to just five teams, he ran its operations from the basement of Atlanta Fulton County Stadium. Eight years later there were 24 teams in six divisions and his league's offices were in midtown Manhattan. When the NASL folded in 1984, Woosnam worked for the U.S. Soccer Federation for a time, but with less success. Where is this man now? Caddying for distant cousin Ian, perhaps?

X is for bugger all as far as American soccer is concerned. But if you insist, it is for, um, **X-Ray Facilities**, which are sometimes required during particularly nasty matches. Perhaps.

Y is for **Youth Soccer.** This is not poor kids from run-down neighbourhoods playing pick-up games in their street clothes on some derelict piece of land. No, no - we're talking proper Youth Soccer here. All those kids referred to in **K** wear full kit and nice boots (which they outgrow every other year). Someone's buys them that. They play in organised leagues, on neatly-manicured pitches, with trained coaches and referees. There's money there, too. And many teams travel up and down the country or even overseas to play in tournaments. Travel agents love youth soccer. Hmm...are you sure all this isn't how Maradona got started?

Z is for **Zungul.** Steve Zungul, the Giorgio Chinaglia of indoor football. We won't go any further about him, because quite frankly we're sick of talking about indoor football. But he's a good Z.

DAVE WANGERIN is an American living in Britain who produces a fanzine about German football called ELFMETER.

SEASONS OF MISSED OPPORTUNITIES AND MELLOW UNFRUITFULNESS - BRIGHTON AND HOVE ALBION

They say that football passion is more red blooded and intense the further North you
go. The feeling of jubilation or dejection is felt deeper within and expresses itself
more visibly. Metaphorically, the Northern heart is an erupting volcano while the
Southern one is a garden sprinkler. Whatever that makes the football heart of the supporter in the heel area of England one can only speculate - equivalent to a bucket of
stagnant water perhaps.
And Brighton - does one get passionate about Brighton?
I will tell then. I will tell of tears, chins drowning in disillusionment on train
rides home, ecstatic laughter that echoes in manic delirium down foggy backstreets and
speech that is garbled so fast it sounds like a thousand cats mewing over a tape re-
cording of splashing water.
Yes, the South rests sedately, its spectators temperamental and tepid or so it seems;
deserting in droves when those twin brothers, Failure and Bad weather arrive like bull-
ies in a playground of happy kids.
The stomach of the Goldstone rumbles hungrily, unsatisfied by five and a half thousand
and the atmosphere so often as electric as a spent match.
Then, as two thousand visiting Geordies roar lustily in their corner, adding yet more
fuel to the Northern fires, i look around.
Grown men with age lines like battle trenches on their faces, weep. Their tears follow
these skin rivers and like canoes going over a waterfall drop onto shoes and concrete
terracing. Young girls, and men with stubble, blubber gently into their programmes and
pretend to be reading the pen pictures of these invincible visitors.
Hearts are bleeding salt water that escapes through tear ducts and dampens the air even
more.
I muse and consider and crushing the lump in my throat croak, "you do care!"
In that unit of time i knew that The Albion faithful felt defeat and victory in a different way. The numbers may be few but the sensibilities portrayed exposed an internal
constitution more akin to Shelley, Woolf or Eliot; at times Kafka or Orwell even.
Football at the Goldstone you see had left the realms of mere physical recreation and
succeeded to the level of appreciation reserved for theatre, painting or literature.
Many consecutive seasons of adroit passing movements and fertile, constructive defending had attuned the audience away from boisterous vocal howls and thunderous bellow-
ings.
Of course chanting and song still played a part, but in a context of mellow approval
or stern rebuke for a fluffed rendition of the ninety minute script.
Once I'd penned my thoughts on the back of my railway ticket one cold October evening
while whizzing home from a performance akin to 'Frankenstein and the revenge of the
rice pudding spawn' i decided to see just how defeat rested on the shoulders of the
spectators on the train.
Wandering the aisles of the train opened my eyes. I didn't see faces, i saw rows of
heads, seemingly resting on upturned palms like fruit on a plate; i smelt disenchant-
ment hanging in the air like cordite from a gun; i felt pens burning lines on paper as
homespun poetry soothed the fraughtness. I watched passengers bound for Eastbourne get
off at Lewes to walk dark lanes flaying their bare backs with rolled up programmes.
When perfection was attained and emphatic victory was taken from terrace to home i watched the same people converse with rampant conviviality in quarter of an hour stints
each. Each stint involved barely a pause for breath and employed a rich tapestry of
adjectives. I taped whole hours worth and had to deliberately slow the tape down on
replay to unravel the words, such was the frantic speed of delivery.
In the course of my prognostication i wandered various haunts in Sussex and Kent,
mainly when misty evenings rested on the land. I well remember the walls of Horsham
being bombarded by an acoustic barrage of demented laughter after one win. It seemingly went on and on; hoovering all other noise into its balloon of joy. A touch of
Shelleyan wildness.

Across the border in Kent some keen avant-garde painted blue seagulls on the leaves of all the trees at Winston Churchill's old residence of Chartwell.
Perhaps the boldest stunt and one that never quite came off was the attempted transformation of The Long Man of Wilmington, that chalk carving in the South Down hills near Eastbourne, into a large engraving of Clive Walker. When the hairstyle looked just a little like Clive's wispy barnet a police guard was placed around the hill to prevent further improvements.
So you Northerners when you're being loud and fervent and us Brightonians seem meek and typical of supporters from a 'non-football area', don't worry about us we're immersing ourselves in Josef K comparisons!

LIFE OF RYAN

My dad is not noted for his intensity of feeling towards football. He casts fleeting gazes across the back pages, mainly checking headlines, and has been known to ask the Albion score. Apart from that, he lets football drift past; it may shout and scream, but it'll only be a whisper to my dad.

However, Say Gerry Ryan and his face will show as much recognition as if Garry Nelson, John Keeley or Robert Codner had been mentioned to present day afficionados. Gerry Ryan is on the pedestal where stand Brian Horton and Peter Ward from that much remembered Class of 1978/9.

In those blossoming days when I was accompanied to football to prevent me ending up in outlandish places like Portslade or Wivelsfield, Gerry Ryan was the type of player first division dreams were built upon.

He arrived sometime in September 1978. His first home appearance was in the 5-1 spanking of Preston North End.
This was a winger who could blaze a path along the touchline as devastating as a new road through Brazilian rain forest.
Baxter was the name of the Preston full back that day and he was subjected to trickery   that should have cast Gerry into such a nationwide figure that Paul Daniels would never have been necessary.
Baxter scored one short of a hat trick of own goals that day, Gerry got one and those raging, untamed Irish locks of hair and nose that if subjected to the laws of symmetry would have created a fine arrowhead, had indelibly left their mark on my pre-teenage mind.
Gerry played a key role in Brighton's ride up nthe escalator to the footballing top floor and despite initial problems of vertigo suffered by the team as a result of these dizzy heights, they and Gerry survived.

One of my most endearing memories of Mr Ryan was in the game versus Manchester City on December 29th 1979. That game was the one in which the Albion finally unpacked their suitcases and hung up their attire in the grand wardrobe that is division 1.
Following superb wins at Wolves and at home to Crystal Palace The Albion proceeded to dismantle Manchester City 4-1. The final screw was extracted by our Gerry. He had the ball just inside the City half and made a run that took him past defender after defender until he was faced with only the goalkeeper. He flicked the ball as nonchalantly past the goalie as Desperate Dan flicking away Dennis the Menace's mate Walter in the boxing ring. Then he turned, spat and walked away as if he did that sort of thing daily to unwind after a gruelling day at the office.
29000 people bawled spontaneous personal poetry in celebration of this goal. I clearly remember my teenage physique being powerfully pressed by surging fans into the metal terrace barrier as I yelled "Wonder goal!" at this colossus of a footballer.

Mullery only gave the bohemian ex-Bophemians star two full appearances in season 1980-81 and in both these he was substituted. Yet in the close season as Mike '40 yard back passes' Bailey assumed the baton dropped by Mullery as he left Chairman Bamber's office after tendering his resignation, dear Gerry signed a new contract and made me a proud and happy man.
His appearances increased and so did the goals; from none in 80/81 to one in 81/82.
The following season — the one we completed our infamous double, Gerry combined a midfield/striker's role with that of supersub and finished second highest scorer.
The happiness at seeing him be one of the first to congratulate Gary Stevens after his late Wembley Cup Final equaliser, was a source of joy to those who felt the final wouldn't have been complete without an appearance of Ryan.
It was on then into division 2 and a run of centre forward appearances, of which the exquisite finish versus Liverpool in the live on T.V. F.A. Cup game that we won showed an unaware nation that the moustacheoid sharp shooter was a silent and deadly assassin.
In the season of the 'semi-promotion' push the following year (1984-85) disaster fell over the land; the shadow of the Dark Lord Sauron fell upon some Crystal Palace chugger in the Mordor of Selhurst Park and he committed the atrocious injury on Ryan that ended his career at the tender age of 29.

Needless to say his skill, his Albion loyalty and his goalscoring prowess were lamented by myself and others.
Gerry was never a big blaster of the ball; his goals were often a result of being in the right place at the right time, or of a delicate, fleeting stroll into the penalty area. He was a danger with his excellent footwork and will be remembered also for being a thorn in Liverpool's early 80's F.A. Cup sides.

Remember to, the winner at Forest that ended a marathon unbeaten home run from Clough and Taylor's team?
The one at Newcastle when we went up to division one?
The man, the memory, the conclusion: I leave you with a February Saturday in 1984, the week after beating Liverpool in the F.A. Cup for the second season running. The Albion are at Charlton. The team come out to warm up, to buoyant acclaim. All save Gerry. He does eventually come out. The away section in the all-seated stand rise to their feet and loud rapture pounds out from many hand clappings. Von Ryan's especial!

THE 'SUPER-LEAGUE';
THE DEATH OF QPR?

I write this article following yet another dismal display, this time at home to Southampton. Of course, by the time it goes to print, events...(hopefully!)...will have overtaken what I have to say. QPR will have already signed Paul Walsh and Clive Allen!

However, I feel that I must point out to the heirachy at QPR that it is *they* that have decided to put their name on paper in favour of the proposed plans for a 'Super-league'. With this in mind, it is *they* who must ensure that our club still enjoy 1st division status come next May! Recent reports in the National press quote QPR as saying they're ready to listen to offers for Andy Sinton and Roy Wegerle. This, to me, is a clear indication of QPR's apparent lack of ambition, these continuous quotes by the press concerning the availability of QPR's main assets only increase the supporters mounting disillusionment with the club. If the quotes are untrue then it is the club's responsibility to let the supporters know!

Let's remember, as QPR have resigned from the Football League, if we were to be relegated just what sort of football can we expect next season? The Diadora League, playing the likes of Maidenhead and Chertsey Town?

The QPR LSA have recently circulated a questionnaire to ascertain the supporters point of view on the proposals. The results have yet to be formulated, although I can say with 100% confidence that of the 100's of completed questionnaires already received, the supporters of QPR are overwhelmingly firmly against the proposals.

QPR don't seem to have grasped the fundamental principle that to become part of the so called 'Super-League', you have to buy your way in. Many clubs are already in the process of spending vast sums of money to insure their inclusion, but not all are 1st division clubs. Take Blackburn Rovers for example. They have made a positive decision that they wish to be a 'Super-League' club and have made it known they're willing to pay for the 'privilege'.

With the current season just 9 games old, one thing is abundantly clear; the present 'strike-force' is just not good enough! The euphoria of Gerry Francis returning to Loftus Road has already evaporated. Supporters are asking questions. For many, the season is over. Only one thing brings the crowds flocking back to Loftus Road – <u>SUCCESS</u>. Only one thing will assure us of success – a positive effort by the Board of Directors of QPR to build a squad capable of achieving it. The present board have done much to put matters right off the pitch and deserve our praise. Sadly, on the pitch the same cannot be said. They share the same aspirations as the supporters. We all want our club to be the best. The supporters wish for success because it's **our club** – we differ from the Directors of QPR in so much, as with success comes **profit** on their investment.

If we are to believe that the Directors of QPR are good business men then they have got to realise, as we do, that you must 'speculate to accumulate'. Unless they start to grasp the basic principle, QPR will end up out in the cold next season.

The supporters of QPR deserve better than they're getting at the moment. The Board might well be able to take their money and run when things go wrong, unlike the supporter who remains loyal. We'll still be here when they're gone!

Although I've always strongly opposed hyper-inflated transfer fees, I am a realist. This season is the big one. If QPR are to realise their dream of becoming a 'big-club', then this could be their last chance...I hope they take it!

Trevor Kingham, Chairman, QPR LSA

RAISE THE ROOF

ISSUE 12 MARCH 91 50p

HELLO BILLY!

HELLO JOHNNY!

Billy Whitehurst and John Muir

GW/391

ROVERS NEW STRIKEFORCE GET AQUAINTED

A DONCASTER ROVERS FANZINE

Albert Rossington.

A DONCASTER ROVERS SUPPORTER OF OVER SIXTY YEARS STANDING
(and a good few sitting down!)

"Raise T'Roof? Don't make me laugh! When I were t'lad we din't even 'ave a roof on t'outside privy. It rained, we got wet. End o't' story. In them days you din' t go to t'footy for things like shelter or entertainment. You went to escape from t'missus. It allus poured down in them days, and you 'ad snow, real snow then, three foot deep. One game, New Brighton it wa', they 'adn't brought a keeper wi'em, so they built a ruddy snowman an' stuck it in t'net. It wa' so life like that no-one noticed while 'alf time when they 'ad to rebuild 'im at t'other end! Even then t' Rovers din't get a shot on 'im in t'second 'alf. 'Appen they 'ad five snowmen playin' in t'ruddy forward line! Some things never change. These days though, a drop of rain an' its pitch waterlogged, game off! Jessies, thats what they are! Mind, its were baking 'ot all summer an' Yorkshire allus won t' Championship. These days they could'na win a raffle. They're all soft they are!

"Modern Footballers? Don't make me laugh! In my day t'players put in a good shift down t'pit then walked t'ground. None of these 'Executive coaches' - not even if they were playin' in t'South. I recall walking all t'way down to Exeter for a cup tie to see t'Rovers. We lost, mind but t'were worth it. There were none of this long ball nonsense either. Tha could'na kick t'owd casey more than five foot wi'out bustin tha leg. If tha 'eaded it, tha'd be off wi' t'concussion. They're all soft they are!

"'Ard Men? Don't make me laugh! In my day we 'ad real 'ard men. Big lads at full-back who'd kick t'winger over t'Main Stand an' onto t'Racecourse. An' that were before t'game ad' started! Aye, an' they played in proper gear - shirts wi' proper collars, shorts a decent length an' real boots, not yer carpet slippers. Aye, an' t'centre-forward could knock t'keeper over. Nowadays if they do it, ther's 'ell to pay.

"Leeds United? Don't make me laugh! Ten blokes who can kick t'ball an 'undred yards and one footballer (young Strachan) 'an they think t'Glory Years are back! I'll tell thee summat abaht Leeds - they've alers been t'same. My mate Rodney Smurthwaite - 'e wa'a smart lad, 'e failed t'eleven plus by ten marks. 'E wa'a Leeds season ticket 'older for twenty years. 'E said te me "Albert, I don't know why tha bothers wi' that shower o' thine - 'e meant Rovers I think - "t'best times I've ever 'ad 'ave been at Elland Road". Turns out that 'e wa'a bad insomniac an' t'only way e' could get any sleep wa' to watch a Leeds game! Perhaps that's why they go on abaht t'crowd bein' so noisy - they're all snorin'!

"Wider Goals? Don't make me laugh! Most o't'blokes playin' football these days would'nt be able to score if they made t'goals ten yards wider an' ten foot 'igher! It reminds me o' when I worked at Blunt an' Forthright Ltd. We 'ad this gaffer in t'platin' shop called Willie Ekerslyke, who reckoned that we should make all t'spades an' shovels an foot wider. "If we make 'em bigger, folk'll be able to shift more earth wi' 'em," 'e said. So we tried it, an' it wa' a flop! T'spades wa' bigger, but they wa' so 'eavy that folk couldn't lift 'em! Well, owd Willie got discouraged after that, an' 'e went off to South America. I 'eard later that 'e changed 'is name to summat even more daft - Joe Havelange, I think! Daft bloke 'e wa'!

"Foreign 'Olidays? Don't make me laugh! I've been comin' to Brid' t'same two weeks ot'year since I wa knee 'igh to Brian Flynn. Tha don't need t'sun or ruddy golden beaches for a good 'oliday. I spent most o' last 'oliday sittin' in t'pourin' rain in a busted deckchair. Ruddy great, an' no-one about to spoil it! I saw a bloke there who wa' a dead ringer for Gerry Daly, so much so I shouted "Wek up Daly, your idle!" at 'im. Any 'ow, 'e turned round an' stuck two fingers up at me. Proves it must 'a bin 'im, as that wa' what 'e used to do when I shouted at 'im at Belle Vue!

"Football Fanzines? Don't make me laugh!

ALBERT ROSSINGTON WAS TALKING TO JOHN COYLE

RAISE THE ROOF -*- Doncaster Rovers   Issues 3, 9, 10, 11

HERR WE GO !

GIVEN THE ROVERS' RISE UP THE LEAGUE AND IMMINENT ENTRY INTO EUROPE, OUR LASS ON T' POP SIDE BLAZES A TRAIL TO BAYERN MUNICH .v. BOCHUM TO TEST DAS WASSER.

What's this I see? Beer and football fans in close proximity ten minutes before the kick-off? And inside the ground, too! Beefy Germans urinate in the bushes, flanked by amused onlookers, the armed Polizei. The fans wear a uniform of denim, spattered with red and white slogan-bearing patches. They beat drums and spray flugal horns. Its a carnival atmosphere, reminiscent of all those televised European Cup ties on sunny Wednesday nights in the Seventies.

The Olympiastadion, Munich (or Munchen to the natives), is more like Wembley than a League ground, even allowing for the fact that Bayern Munich are the Liverpool F.C. of the Bundesliga. But even with a gate of 30,000 (low for the German Champions), the fans still rattle round the huge empty stadium like twenty odd Carlisle supporters on a rainy Tuesday night in Exeter. This is a vast place with sumptuous facilities. You can get a cracking seat with panoramic views for around a tenner. Its hard to believe that just a fortnight before my high heels were sinking into the sands of The Shay.

Bayern kick-off at 3.30 p.m., but not before the massed choirs of "V2" have serenaded us with

> *"Que Sera, Sera,*
> *Whatever will be will be .....*
> *We're Champions of Germany!"*   (in English too)

There are also some chants in their own language, but they're all quite sophisticated and mostly sung to tunes we've all heard on British terraces. The German fans haven't yet degenerated to *"Wer is die Schweinhund in der Schwartz?"*   (I need not translate!)

As for the football, this match was a veritable speil of zwei halben (Eh?). Its fair, from this showing, to say that the German game is played largely in midfield. The likes of Augenthaler in this all-star team showed the skills we'd grown to marvel at during Italia '90. Predictably, Bayern were clinical in going 2-0 up before half time (which was accompanied by more beer for die junge mann at 60p a nearly pint, and fat wurst sausages for all). However, just after half-time, someone failed to inform Kohler that the teams had changed ends. His goal was a perfectly executed Gary Lineker style shot, except that the boy Line-acre generally puts them in the right net! Kohler's was the most amazing and deliberate own goal I ever did see. He then lay prone in the goalmouth, han(d)s on head, for at least funf minuten, thus giving opponents Bochum the chance to level the score to 2-2.

For Bayern to draw at home to lowly Bochum is tantermount to the Scousers going three down at Anfield to Sunderland. They're a fickle lot, the Bayern fans, sarcastically cheering Bochum whilst some bright spark plays "The Last Post" on his flugel horn. A word about the programme, the lavish and glossy "Bayern Magazin"; if the Germans can manage 44 sides of colourful A4 with a statistics section worthy of the Financial Times and extensive interviews with players, match predictions from Boris Becker, Steffi Graf, Sepp Maier et al and a "win a car" competition, all for 70p, then why can't we?

In all, with beer and delicious cheap food readily available, and even the best seats costing only about £12, it seems the English game can learn a lot from its German counterpart. Perhaps the likes of Jimmy Hill, who think they know what's best for us, should take notice.

POLLY GOERRES

Ipswich Better
Than Eindhoven
Says Robson

Former Town Boss Full of Praise

Ex-Ipswich and England manager Bobby Robson was at Portman Road recently to see Town take on Notts County. Appointed boss of crack Dutch side PSV Eindhoven, currently flying high in the First Division in Holland, Robson took the opportunity to assess that changes in his old stamping ground.

Asked for his impressions, Robson came up with some typically forthright views. 'Ipswich is definately better than Eindhoven', he said. 'Tower Ramparts Shopping Centre is one of the best I've seen and that fancy paving at Cornhill is really nice. I'd forgotten just how much I miss the Pick 'n' Mix counter in Woolworths. You can't get humbugs in Eindhoven.'

When questioned about the performance of the Ipswich team, Robson had no comment to make.

Steve Fill

Those Were The Days – Ipswich Fanzine

Do You Remember?

No. 2 - Silk Scarves

Long, long ago when 'Match of The Day' was still in its rightful slot on Saturday nights and being too skint to go out at the weekend wasn't such a disaster, people used to go to football matches in scarves in the colours of the team they supported. Scarves in those days were, however, not like the expensive and intricate woollen designs that you get nowadays (and very few actually wear). Plain blue and white bar scarves were the order of the day at Portman Road. If you had a 'college' type scarf with the blue and white going the other way you were very cool indeed. Manchester United fans became the envy of everyone with their three-coloured red/white/black scarves and were shortly followed by Leeds United with a white/yellow/blue version. A few years later Town fans were wearing blue/white/black scarves, the black coming from the away strip.

During those early years however there was an alternative to the plain old bar scarf. Yes, the silk scarf. These pathetic, thin little efforts from which the tassels always fell off within a week of purchase, were as tasteless as the era from which they came. It was the early seventies - tank tops, flares, butterfly collars and silk scarves. Some people wore them around their wrists, ironed out flat to make sure you could read the teams name on them, others wore them tied in a little knot around their necks. The real rebel however wore them like the Pat Cash headband to keep the long hair in place.

Silk scarves did however have their advantage, they were cheap for a start. But on the more practical level they could be easily concealed when leaving away grounds as opposed to the thick woolly type that when shoved inside a jacket made you look 8 months pregnant and extremely conspicuous.

The silk scarf seemed to disappear around the end of the seventies. Knitting technology obviously progressed and crests became possible and what more they had the added advantage that the letters didn't come off when your mum ironed them.

Clint West

Do you Remember?
No. 4 Rosettes

As you make your way through the streets approaching almost any football ground in the country you will see at least one, and often many stalls, selling scarves, hats, badges etc. Had this been in the seventies or earlier though, they would almost certainly have had on display a selection of rosettes. The rosette at this time was quite a common way of displaying support for a team. Nowadays if you saw someone wearing a blue rosette at Portman Road it would probably be MP Michael Irvine desperately trying to hold on to his seat at the next election.

The rosette was usually a cheap and nasty little nylon ribbon wound round a piece of cardboard, to which it was then stitched. On top of this was stapled a piece of card bearing the clubs name. Better quality ones might also carry the club crest, but more often they had no more than a tinfoil replica of the FA Cup on them.

For some strange and unexplained reason rosettes seemed to be synonymous with the FA Cup. It was noticeable that as the later the stages of the Cup crew closer so rosettes grew in size. This strange process climaxed with the final itself and the appearance of huge Cup Final rosettes a foot or so in diameter. Those, of course, were in the days when Cup Final supporters deemed it necessary to dress up as Screaming Lord Such for the day.

Times, and thankfully fashions change and the football rosette is no more. I never seriously thought that the day would come when flared trousers would come back into fashion. It was always believed that they were just too naff for that to ever happen, but youth has conspired to shatter such illusions. So, perhaps there is hope yet for the rosette. After all it was only a few years ago that football fans were to be seen wandering around in ski-hats like Norwegians such was the football fad at the time. More recently we have witnessed the unlikely craze for inflatables, so what price a rosette revival. Remember where you read it first.

Clint West

The Deserving Testimonial

In the modern marketing age when everything has a fancy package and name it should come as no surprise that 1990 should be named the year of the Deserving Testimonial. In football speak terms "the boys done good" certainly stands up.

Look at the list of deserving testimonials that football fans were served up with. Ray Clemence, Peter Shilton, Bryan Robson, Graham Rix and Liam Brady. Great players undoubtedly, but did they need or ultimately deserve a testimonial?

If 20,000 fans want to turn up to watch a nothing friendly (in Brady's case it was 40,000) then let them. What I object to is the notion that these players needed a tax free windfall.

Are they crippled? Are the bailiffs knocking their doors down? Are they struggling to pay their Poll Tax? Will they never be able to work again? No on all counts. In fact, these players were some of the highest paid in the modern pro-game. In the case of Shilton and Clemence they are now both coaches and still earning big money.

Shilton's testimonial was supposedly to say goodbye and thank you to the great British public. It's a pity his goodbye had to inflate his bank balance at the same time. Perhaps Shilts felt it would be insincere to say goodbye without turning it into a nice little earner. Shilts and his ilk were top earners for the past 15 years so why they need another payday takes a little explaining to me.

No fan takes exception to players earning big money, after all, we all want to be there. What I object to and I think most other people do,is the whole army of suited hangers-on who seem to get the clichéd quote into the papers every time a player has to have a testimonial.

It always brings a smile to my cynical outlook when I read that players care about the fans, especially when I read it in ghostwritten programme notes. Normally, fans are about as cared about (by players) as the unemployed were under Thatcher. The testimonial is a hangover from the days when footballers were poorly paid and retirement with the testimonial funds meant a newsagent or a pub tenancy. The game itself was fun, full of skill and of my contemporaries would no doubt have fans were treated to an honest spectacle.

Today's footballers, especially those in the supertax bracket, have no need for the testimonial. The argument that they have short working lives is facile and shallow - one which doesn't stand close scrutiny. It is a dated legacy which makes any modern high earning pro look like a mercenary.

Some players whose career is ended by horrific injury do deserve a testimonial. I can think of a lot better causes which football could have organised a testimonial for. How about the families and dependents of the survivors of Bradford and Hillsborough. What about Shilts and the rest donating their money earned to the football trust so that football fans could benefit. Now that would be saying "Thank you" to the great British public.

A testimonial is often cited as a reward for loyalty. Loyalty to most players is a clause inserted in their contracts which awards them more money. Players agents often ask for loyalty bonuses before a player even signs for a club nowadays. Fans are told that the testimonial is vital if our players are not to be lured abroad into better paid jobs.

How much longer will the testimonial debacle go on for? If football fans can't see that last season they were taken for complete mugs then my name is Bilbo Baggins. The sooner fans vote with their feet then the sooner this hoax will cease. Any footballer who accepts testimonial money while England's football disaster victim's families struggle along on state benefits is beneath contempt.

The next time I hear of a highly paid player getting a deserved testimonial then I will reach for the sick bucket.

Colin Ward

SUPER ANDERS AND HIS DOUBLE ENTENDRES

BY MIKE SLAUGHTER AND MIKE MURPHY

Cage aux Folles

All young Gooners reading this article would not know about the famous Highbury Cage, that most of my contemporaries would no doubt have experienced. The cage, as it was known, was situated behind the Clockend and existed throughout the seventies and part of the eighties. Now you are probably wondering what the cage is and what was its function at Highbury. Well one thing is for certain it wasn't there to keep your pet budgie or hampster in!! It was actually there to deter violence. Once a 'victim' was nicked on the Clockend, for whatever reason the ol' bill found it justifiable, then that was it matey you spent the rest of the match in the cage. It was in the open, set next to a wall with barbed wire so there was no talk of the great escape. So if you were unlucky enough to be detained in the winter months, then hard luck, you just froze your b***ocks off!! You just had to endure whatever the weather decided to be on that day. So really the best time to experience the cage would be at the start of the season in August or September, even then if it rained you didn't have to bother about washing your newly acquired 1978 Cup Final scarf, but you did go home wearing a pair of 'ankle swingers'. Yes, you did get released eventually with no charge, the idea was to put you through a humiliation process, for when the crowd were leaving the ground you were victims of exposure to all in sundry. You felt like some kind of exhibit.

You were released a little while after the game finished, the punishment being that you had you missed the game, and that could be very frustrating, especially when the Gunners scored and the ol' bill would wind you up by continually giving you the score to remind you what you were missing. The more bizarre thing I found was the fact that all supporters arrested, home or away were locked in the cage together! So you can imagine the mayhem at times because it was always 'off' between rival fans, with the ol' bill turning a blind eye. Away supporters were always inevitably out numbered so they suffered the consequences. I can recall the time when it was my time to be put on exhibit. It was around about season 1978/79 and I was standing on the Clockend vs Everton with Beverley holding on to my arm. Usually Bev would spend the entire game in the bar at the back of the clock, with all the other lads girlfriends. However, this day she decided to stand on the terraces. As the game progressed, I was getting more and more irrate at the abuse the Evertonians were giving the Arsenal. Nonchantly I eased over towards the scousers, there was no bars then to segregate the supporters only a line of cops. Almost standing on the side of the 'mickey mousers' I began to voice my opinion which attracted several of them to retaliate verbally. This form of Tete-a-Tete turned into a private argument with one scouser, who took particular concern at my presence. I was told to "shut it" by the police, which I did, but the scouser continued his bombardment of abuse in my direction. Gesticulating to one another that is what 'Guns at Dawn' after the game. I finally retaliated with "F**k off you scouse B*****d!!". I was promptly apprehended by 'Uncle Bill' and with Bev still on tow was dragged away from the terrace and taken into a small wooden hut, had my name taken and then thrown into the cage. Bev thinking we were going to be escorted out of the ground, was still holding onto me and subsequently she too was also thrown into the cage, even though we tried to explain she was an innocent party the ol' bill didn't want to listen, so it was a lock in for the rest of the game and the only lock in Bev was used to was in a pub with a white wine and soda!! Every two minutes the cage door would open and another unfortunate victim of the terrace policing would join us. Eventually, about 10 of us shared the cage and unfortunately one was an Evertonian who proceeded to take abuse followed by the occasional whack and kick and was spat on for his duration. To his relief he was eventually taken out. As the game finished the terraces began to empty and we were looked upon by the passing thousands as a form of degredation. One at a time as the ground emptied we were released without being charged. We made our way to the Plimsoll Arms - the 'in' pub at the time - to recall our experience. Bev - being the only girl I know of to have been locked in the cage - still frequents the watering holes around Highbury, notably the Barn. At least on that day the weather was at it's best which in a way acted as a consolation. The cage is no longer; however, it can be seen as a part of history along with other types of tortures in the London Dungeon, Tooley Street, underneath London Bridge. Go and see it if you dare!!

Trevor Smith

:Gooner   :Gooner   :Gooner   :Gooner

Policing the Game

We really should have seen the writing on the wall. To think, ten years back in 1991, the Metropolitan Police were languishing in the relegation zone of the Vauxhall League's First Division, more accustomed to meeting Dulwich Hamlet and Chalfont St Peter than Arsenal and Manchester United. No-one suspected the travesties that were to follow. Initially, the idea of the police dictating kick-off times and moving fixture dates around did not seem unreasonable after the Bournemouth/Leeds riot. But then this idea of changing over one hundred years of tradition in the FA Cup. It was the thin end of the wedge that would end with the Met Police as our European Cup entrants for the 2000/2001 campaign.

So only one replay would be allowed in the FA Cup, beginning in the 91/92 season. No more of those epic Cup marathons. A sad day for football. We would have to get used to the idea of the penalty shoot-out - but not for long, as the game of association football as we know it, began to change inextricably. The Met Police's own football side were in a bad way. In danger of going out of existence. But the new power they had over the football authorities offered a potential solution. The first move was to "appoint "Kaiser" Franz Beckenbauer as the new "technical director" at New Scotland Yard. An undoubted masterstroke.

The Kaiser's duties were twofold. Firstly to sort out the footballing side of what had become a bunch of obscure non-league cloggers. And secondly to exploit the opportunities that were available with the police's new influence over the running of the game. Memories of the 1986 Mexico World Cup game were to the fore in his first FA Cup run. A side lacking any real talent played a 9-0-1 formation It was a big leap from 5-3-2, but it got them to the quarter finals, with a succession of 0-0 draws being turned into victories after replay penalty shoot-outs. Training consisted of penalty practice and players throwing themselves at the ball to stop shots raining in on goal during open play.

Clawing their way out of their non-league depths was to be a different matter. One point per game was never going to suffice in the three points for a win system. A new approach was needed -but not on the field. On safety grounds, the police began to insist that Vauxhall League crowds of 200 would require three times that amount of police inside the ground. The attendant police bill to the clubs concerned saw most of them go into extinction, and the Met Police rise in the table as names like Dorking and Molesley returned to Sunday morning league public park status. Promotion to the Vauxhall Premier, and then the GM Conference followed.

The Fourth Division was the next step. Stringent safety criteria in the stadiums of those wishing to gain full League status became a must. The Met responded by building a spanking new 25,000 all-seater in Hendon - government funded. Though finishing tenth in the GM Conference in May 1994, the nine clubs above were rejected because of their grounds, and the Metropolitan Police became the Football League's latest member.

The FA Cup still offered their easiest route to glory. By now, replays had been done away with, as well as the antiquated notion of extra time. After ninety minutes, it was straight down to penalties. But the force was dismayed that their pride and joy could still not get their hands on the silverware. The reason? Everyone had got wise, and penalty practice was a staple part of any training session. Time to change the rules again. For the good of the game, the police's football committee argued, it would be best if the individuals of most upstanding character in society were seen to be the most successful in the sport. So, away with penalty shoot-outs. In future, drawn matches would be decided by the side with the cleanest criminal record.

Initially, it was a no-contest. The Met romped home in the Cup between 1996 and 1998. This three on the trot triumph saw the Zenith Data become the credible knockout trophy to win for sides more interested in playing football than checking out their youth trainees for juvenile shoplifting offences. Bert Millichip, attempting to stop these enforced rule changes to the FA's premier tournament, was jailed for ten years on the grounds of preventing the police from carrying out their public duty.

On the playing side, the police were actually improving. Beckenbauer's footballing influence had its effect over time. Added to which, the income from policing other teams' matches meant it was not long before the Met became 'the world's richest club. Eyebrows were raised when Paul Gascoigne was bought from Juventus for £25 million in the autumn of 1996, but he was neither the first nor last major Met purchase. Some of the bought players had trouble coping with the hassle they faced when they had to do their nominal weekly two hours on the beat - part of their large paying contract agreement - but the success gained on the field compensated.

Conveniently, the minimal police duties that had to be carried out coincided with international games, meaning the Met's best players were never available for international selection. No danger of playing too many games in a season for these lads. Promotion to the First Division did not take long. Beckenbauer's suggested changes to the established rules of the game were key. Amongst the new police "recommendations" were that team sheets should be handed to the referee twenty four hours before kick-off, as opposed to the previous sixty minutes, on the grounds that the police needed to know who was playing to co-ordinate their crowd control procedures. In fact, this was merely a ruse to allow the Kaiser to devise a gameplan depending on the opposition's selection.

Another tactical masterstroke was responsible for promotion from the second division. That season (1996/97) the Met players all did night shift duty. All their games kicked off ("for safety reasons") at three in the morning, every Sunday, and the half-asleep opposition they faced in that triumphant campaign could not adapt, especially as they had kicked off another match only twelve hours previously.

Incredibly, the League Championship was not to follow immediately, as the more established First Division sides were so incensed at the flagrant misjustice going on that they all played their best football against the Met. They would have to wait until the 1999/2000 season before a League Championship came to Hendon. What a chaotic season, as the police took drastic measures to ensure the trophy. In most games, the first three fouls by the opposition resulted in immediate arrest for the guilty party. Incitement to riot, the charge. Things got seriously ridiculous when the veteran Tony Adams, of co-leaders Arsenal was given a five year sentence for an offside appeal in the notorious November 0-0 draw at Highbury (with 2,592 other offences taken into consideration). Arsenal finished that game with only six players on the field - but their will held out.

It was not like an average Arsenal game. The crowd, for starters, was limited to 1500 - a level deemed acceptable by the police safety officer at Highbury. This scenario was to be repeated in most of the Met's away matches - some were even played behind closed doors. It was all concluded on May 26th, year 2000. Arsenal visited the Met's Hendon ground needing a 2-0 victory to bring about another title triumph. Beckenbauer, predictably, packed the defence to gain the 0-0 draw that would give the Met their first championship. Despite this Arsenal managed to score in the second half, and were searching for a second when the talismanic Michael Thomas was brought off the bench with five minutes remaining.

To prevent their players being arrested for decisions going against them, George Graham had pulled off a tactical masterstroke of his own. packing the midfield with solicitors. Incredibly, it worked as Arsenal finished the game with eleven men on the field. But no title. Thomas broke through in injury time, slipping the ball past the Met's keeper, only to be foiled by a pitch invasion across the Met's goal - of uniformed officers. The referee had no choice. The laws of the game meant that it had to be a drop ball where the ball had been impeded. The Met eleven crowded into their own six yard box for the drop, and a goal-line clearance resulted. Arsenal's chance had gone, the Met were the newly crowned champions.

It will be interesting to see how they fare in Europe this coming season. Especially if they come up against the giants of Italy, Spain or France, where it looks like the Carabinieri, the Guardia Civil, and the Gendarmerie are home and dry in their respective domestic campaigns...

(Police) Doctor Robert

ARSENAL FANS UNITED

Date: .... Address: ....

Dear Sir

I would like to put on record my disgust at the actions of your disciplinary committee in penalising Arsenal Football Club two league points as a result of 'the brawl' at Old Trafford on Saturday October 20th 1990.

Although I agree that discipline is an important aspect of the game, I believe that Arsenal F.C. should have all their points deducted and be relegated to Division Three. However to keep a balanced League I suggest Fulham F.C. be given the points and promoted to Division One, thus giving Liverpool some worthy opposition and ensuring a London Club represents this country in Europe next year.

I think exactly the same treatment should be given to Chelsea F.C. as a warning to other clubs.

I would welcome your comments.

Yours faithfully

Bloody Cheek!

The postcard (right) was distributed outside Craven Cottage at a recent Fulham game. One of the cards fell into the hands of our spies in South-West London and we reproduce it for you all to have a good laugh at! I thought they had a bloody cheek using The Gooner's logo!!!!

The Worst Ever Arsenal Team?

PAT JENNINGS

What ever possessed Terry Neill to waste £40,000 on this over the hill, overrated keeper we will never know. The fact that he was part of the THPLC for over 75 years speaks volumes for the man. His ball handling was very weak and always very suspect on crosses. Shot stopping wasn't too bad, but often used his legs and feet, when surely the use of the hands would have stopped many an unnecessary corner.
CLAIM TO FAME: Only keeper to have T. Brooking score a header past him.

DAVID O'LEARY

Slow moving, poor aerial ability and truly unloyal servant to AFC. He may be our record appearance holder, but this is due to the fact nobody else wanted him. Has recently worn the number 7 shirt, but has also proved a complete flop as a winger.
CLAIM TO FAME: Has applied for the record amount of transfer requests at Arsenal (believed to be somewhere in the region of 120 now).

PAT RICE

Another player who's loyalty has to be seriously questioned. Made only 397 appearances. Very suspect going forward and always weak in the tackle.
CLAIM TO FAME: Once tackled Kevin Keegan at Anfield. The ref however, for some strange reason awarded Liverpool a penalty, which rather took the gloss of Pat's big moment.

KENNY SANSOM

Overweight, slow and needed a map and compass to pass the half way line. Only 5 goals in over 300 matches (a marvellous feat considering that certain players achieved this landmark in a game ie. Woodcock and Drake). And all for a measly million and a bit quid.
CLAIM TO FAME: Won £7.50 on the 1984 Gold Cup

TONY ADAMS

Faint-hearted skipper of the current side. Has a tendency to flick the V's at opposing supporters (after they've been so friendly to him). He often attempts to head balls that normal humans would kick, usually while they are still there trying to get a boot to it).
CLAIM TO FAME: Scored a hat-trick for Chelmsford prison reserves.

FRANK McLINTOCK

'Wimp' best describes this man, who's pathetic ball distribution cost us many a match. A brilliant wing half in his early days, but due to lack of fitness and enthusiasm found himself leading the side from the edge of the 18 yard box.
CLAIM TO FAME: Appearing on 'The Big Match' with a silly jacket and tie.

ROCKY ROCASTLE

A clumsy midfield player with very little ball skill.

He has been accused of being ball greedy, maybe, but it is far more likely that he has no ability to pass the ball over 5 yards. One of the very few players to graduate from Arsenals poor youth system. However, if he is a typical example, surely we'd be better off scrapping the system and spending the millions saved on truly class players like Stewart, Fenwick and Sedgley.
CLAIM TO FAME: Played in the same England side as the Lord God Gazza himself.

LIAM BRADY

Scheming alcoholic hatchet man of the seventies. He was hated by the fans. Could have been a reasonable player had he learned to shoot straight. He possessed one of the best right feet the world would have ever seen. But chose to stay with the also rans by sticking with the weaker left foot.
CLAIM TO FAME: Teaching Rixy how to take penalties.

CHARLIE GEORGE

Had this giant amongst landlords been as good at playing the game as he now is running a boozer, then we might have seen one of the true greats. However, his whole upbringing was wrong, public school, rugger every Saturday afternoon cheering on the Harlequins. Hardly the sort of stuff to make a Northbank hero.
CLAIM TO FAME: First player to sport a permed hair style.

JOHN RADFORD

Played 23 league games between 1982-83 amassed a colossal 4 goals, and more to the point scored in every (both) European match he played in vs Spartag Mogow. Signed for a mere pittance from Stoke City and sold for a massive profit in his prime. His potential never fully seen. Never has a more classy forward graced Highbury. Ball control second to none. Shooting 10 out of 10. Passing 11 out of 10, and words cannot describe his heading. A certain sweeper mentioned earlier could learn a thing or two from Mr faithful here.
CLAIM TO FAME: Bedding Leslie Ash.

ALAN SMITH

Aggressive, dirty, bad sport, animal and foul mouthed. Just about sums up this selfish forward. He jointly holds the world record for bookings and sendings off (with that nice Mr Lineker). Still looking to score his first goal after 3 years. Not a good return for £800,000 (must have been a tax write off). Or are we being unfair judging him against the truly great legends he had to follow, like Hankin, Hawley and Chapman.
CLAIM TO FAME: Hitting the crossbar 724 times in a season.

by Ian (Dodgy) Davey

THE GREAT AMERICAN PICTURE SHOW

Picture the scene: Superbowl XXV - NY Giants v Buffalo Bills. A flighted pass finds its way over the Buffalo defence into the arms of a grateful Giants receiver in the end zone. He trips and falls over the touchline. The officials are reluctant to award the touchdown. The officials are reluctant to award the score, but by referring to an action replay they are able to see that the play is good. Touchdown. The Giants go on to win by just one point.

Picture the scene: FA Cup Round 4 - Arsenal v Leeds United. A flighted pass finds its way over the Leeds defence and onto the head of a grateful Paul Davis who nods the ball past an advancing John Lukic and into the net. The officials are reluctant to award the score because they think he is offside, but by referring to an action replay, the commentators are able to see that the goal is good. The referee has no such facility. The goal does not stand and the game is drawn 0-0.

action replays can, and do work.

Soccer, on the other hand is a completely different kettle of fish. One of it's main attractions is the fact that it is non-stop for two halves of 45 minutes. No breaks. A stoppage for several minutes in an end-to-end game would not only be unwanted but intolerable. And who is going to decide whether a decision is going to be marginal enough to require the use of an action replay? Someone will have to draw the line somewhere, and the confusion would be tremendous. Just think of the problems they're having over this professional foul law. Of course, if the system was ever introduced to decide whether a goal would stand or not, it would not be long before television cameras were used to spy on players on the pitch. Would the beady eyes of several TV cameras watching them for the slightest indiscretion have an effect on the players? It would be like the Paul Davis punching incident, only without the two week interval. Would this be acceptable? It's a bit of a grey area but I'm pretty sure that the players would object in the strongest terms.

Amazingly, both these incidents occured on the same day, and it shows how the application of modern technology can turn a game when the officials (who after all are mere humans) are lacking. But can video action replays be of any use in football? That's soccer if you're confused.

American football is a game dominated by television. The frequent stoppages between plays are an advertising executive's dream, and in the NFL there are plenty of breaks. Video evidence is viable here because there are so many stoppages that nobody will notice another, especially if it is on a play which will turn a game, perhaps even a team's entire season. Mega-bucks mean that the officials have to get it right, or there will be hell to pay. American football is of such a format that

However, the system does have its supporters. Terry Venables for one. And after the Leeds game, most Arsenal supporters. It does have its merits in the fact that controversial decisions could be resolved within a reasonable time span. But, in my opinion, it would be unfeasable to install, and the fact that it would probably start more arguments than it settled would make it impossible to run. Nice try America - now don't you dare consider putting into your World Cup.

Alistair Coleman

PG TIPS *LEARN FOOTBALL THE PERRY GROVES WAY*

LESSON 2 : THE GOALKEEPER

SHOULD HE GO RIGHT?   SHOULD HE GO LEFT?

BY MARC NORDEN AND MIKE MURPHY

JOHN WICKENS ON THE WAGON

THE Margate F.C. Fanzine

Issue Five   September'91 Edition   Still Only 50p

Taylor's Masterplan Revealed:Promotion to the Kent League!!

League!!

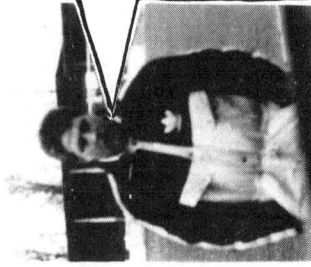

A place in the Kent League has long been an ambit-ion of mine.If only Canterbury could win a few games we'd go up as Champions!

Kent League	Pl	Pts
3.Deal Town	9	20
2.Herne Bay	9	22
1.Alma Swanley	10	22

Beazer Southern	Pl	Pts
22.Canterbury C	6	1
21.Margate	7	5
20.Gosport Bor	6	5
19.Salisbury	6	6
18.Andover	6	6
17.Baldock	5	6
16.Sittingbourne	7	7

SEE BACK PAGE FOR FULL AMAZING STORY !!!!

INSIDE: Jim Cullen sees the light,Ten things you never knew about Clive Yeo,Tommy Taylor own goal shockers,Extracts from Ian Young's diary,The truth about Gordon Wallis's programme collection,Painter George's Column and much,much more......

New League
Pyramid (from
1992-3 season)

Super Winstonlead
Kent Super League
▲

Beazer Homes Lge
(Southern)
▲

Beazer Homes Lge
(Premier)
▲

GM Conference
▲

Barclays Lge
(Division 4)
▲

Barclays Lge
(Division 3)
▲

Barclays League
(Division 2)
▲

Barclays League
(Division 1)
▲

Many Margate supporters have been a bit disappointed with the start to the season.One win in eight and out of the FA Cup hardly seemed the perfect start.However,they reckonned without the skills of their master-tactician manager Tommy Taylor.It turns out that Tommy is good mates with Graham Kelly at the FA and gets to hear all the 'whispers' at Lancaster Gate.Tommy now knows the truth behind the so called'Super League'plans!

Next summer the FA are going to turn the entire league stucture in England upside down. The Kent League will be the top league in the country instead of the lowest,and will be renamed 'The Super Winstonlead Super Kent League'.Division One will become the lowest league from next season onwards.But the FA aren't going to tell anyone until the summer so all teams who will think they've been promoted will infact have been relegated and vice versa.Luckily for us the only person outside the FA who knows anything about this scheme is Tommy.

In an exclusive interview with JW-otw Tommy said,"I first found out about the FA's plan in July.So I then had to get a squad together which I thought could do a job for us.It's gone quite well so far;own goals,needless penalties conceeded,dodgy backpasses,awful finishing;we're throwing away game after game! But you've got to get a squad together which I thought could do a job for us.It's gone quite well so far;own goals,needless penalties conceeded,dodgy backpasses,awful finishing;we're throwing away game after game! But you've got to get a squad together! But you've got to give credit to Canterbury City - they really are naturals at this game. I can't see us catching them but the runners-up spot will do us fine.I still haven't got the perfect line-up and am looking to sign some even more hopeless players - Steve Lane and Carl Laraman are top of my shopping list...."

At that moment several men in white coats arrived,took Mr Taylor's temperature,gave him his medicine and took him back to "Hospital".

MY EYES HAVE SEEN THE

GLORY

(TOTTENHAM HOTSPUR.)

AS THICK AS F.I.F.A.

Our undercover reporter, Walter Gates, reveals the proceedings from Geneva and takes a sly look at hush-hush developments to improve our game.

Well, it was the thought that counts, I suppose, although I thought it was goals that counted. And goals are a major topic here at FIFA HQ these days. Due to the lack of them in last summers World Cup (That's funny, I saw one at each end every game - Ed), the idea has sprung into the collective mind of FIFA officials to make the game more suitable for American consumption, what with the approach of 1994 and all that. Yes, so that American Joe Public will flood to the attend the matches at the greatest football tournament of them all, Joao Havelange (That's Portuguese for 'Joe-I-think-there's-a-lot-of-money-in-this-for-us') has been looking at methods to make scores higher and thus align football with gridiron.

The basis of their idea is that because goalkeepers are now taller than when football began, that goals should be made bigger to prevent them using this entirely natural phenomenon. I know some forwards who wouldn't benefit if they doubled the size of the goals, but that's a different story. Having watched most of the 1990 World Cup matches, it seemed to me that it wasn't the size of the goal that was the problem, but the amount of shots, or lack of them, that was the over-riding concern.

It was put forward by the Canadian FA that the growth of goalies could be controlled. Not by steroids or anything like that of course, but by custodians having to pass through a standard template designed by FIFA committee (so it would probably look like a camel). This would regulate the height and width of a keeper and if he did not pass through the regular cut-out shape, his team would have to find a smaller or thinner man for the job.

As an alternative to making the goal bigger, FIFA considered the proposal put forward in a recent issue of When Saturday Comes (It seems they really do look at the fans views !!!!) to make the ball smaller. They were not going to go as far as that particular contributor in reducing it to a tennis ball (Although this gained strong support from the English Schools FA), but would set up an investigating sub-group to review the possible use of a volleyball or handball(Favoured by the Argentinian FA) size ball to make a more exciting goal-wise match and to increase the skill factor.

The discussion on the ease of scoring then continued. One suggestion involved the goal keeper having to play one half of the match with one arm inside his shirt, leaving him with only one arm to protect his net or whatever else he chooses. Another more radical view to be raised was that the goalie should have his hands tied together, but in Scotland's case this was seen as an advantage.(Only joking). A proposal from the Luxembourg camp that the goalkeeper should be tied to the goalpost with a strong piece of elastic (OoohErrr), so that he could not roam too far from his line (I thought this had already been introduced at WHL on occasion), à lá It's a Knockout. This would give the attacking player more opportunity to collect the wobbly bucket full of water. Er, no, I mean,get nearer goal before having to shoot. The Chilean FA raised the idea of blindfolding all keepers, but FIFA upheld an appeal by Amnesty International. The English Schools FA (ESFA) put up a marvellous idea that was close to capturing the imagination (What all of it? - Ed) of the footballing top brass. Having had loads of experience in this field, they put forward the idea of 'one-and-in', thus, once the regular goalie had conceded a goal,he swopped positions with an outfield player and so on. The only drawback on FIFA's part was that although it gave an ideal break in play to screen more adverts, the Americans would be having enough trouble with the rest of the oh-so difficult laws, that they would lose interest. (If only we could be that lucky-Ed). This decision puzzled me, as they don't have a problem with the constant interchange of players in ice-hockey.

After exhausting the possibilities put up for discussion, they moved onto the next item on the agenda, which was the final one, the resolution of drawn matches.

With protests still ringing in their collective ears about the penalty shoot-out method, they investigated various options to define the winner of the contest using a fairer and more skillful process. These were the proposals for the FIFA committee to consider:-

1. The number of free-kicks conceded - One of our own Jimmy Hill's pet theories. The idea was a loser from the start, as FIFA,like everyone else, realise that referees couldn't spot a foul if Vinny Jones upended them himself. Too much room for argument.

2. The number of shots on goal - The problem here was who decides what is a shot on goal? Would one of Mitchell's wayward crosses that floats two feet over the bar be counted as a shot? Who knows? (I do - Ed)

3. The number of corners a team gains - It was forseen that this could result in teams running up the wing, stopping on the dead-ball line and waiting for an opponent to challenge to win a corner, rather than go for goal. You remember the Leeds team of the 70's in the last 10 minutes of a game they were winning 1-0. Again, refereeing was pointed out as a weak point in this suggestion, as how many times have you seen goalkicks given instead of corners(in the recent home game v Filth)?

4. Reduce the number of players - This seems to be a good idea, but in reality, players who have given their all for 90 minutes plus 30 mins. extra time (Not including Diego here I hope? - Ed),will not relish playing on in a dwindling team. It could bring a more defensive attitude as both teams could pull off attackers and choose to defend their goal. And how would it work? Would opposing managers choose a player from the other side to be removed every 5 minutes or would they choose one of their own players? Would the reserve official shuffle the numbers used for substitut-ions and both players of that number leave the field? Where would the removals end? Would we get to the stage where the two keepers were left to battle it out? The way refs flashed the red card around, there wouldn't be 22 players left on the pitch at the end anyway. Look at Cameroon- they beat Argentina with only 9 men! An excellent idea then.

5. Remove booked players from the game - Like i) too reliant on good sensible refereeing. No chance of working.

6. Team with least back passes wins - One of the better ideas. This would reduce the amount of time-wasting and boring football, but then again, is a throw-in to the goalkeeper a back-pass? Needs further investigation.

7. Play until next goal - A good professional way of deciding the game. Only one problem, will US TV schedules be willing to screen a 7 hour match between Egypt and Argentina?

8. Tie players legs together - After every 5 minutes of added time, two players from each side shall have legs tied together in a 3-legged race style (OoohErrr).This would reduce their pace, increase the amount of space available and provide great entertainment for the fans.

9. One touch - Another idea from the ESFA. A game of one touch (OoohErr) could sort out the more skillful teams from the dross. This was considered but with only 2 or 3 Wimbledon players touching the ball once to propel it from one end of the pitch to the other, the idea foundered.

10. Players may only use one foot - Free-kicks would be awarded if a player used the wrong foot. Problems occured in the selection of foot - with claims of 'footism' from those of the other foot persuasion.

11. Remove the players boots - This would give the players a chance to shine if their balance and skill are up to the job. However, in rainy climates this move would provide marvellous fun for the fans.

12. Do away with offside - The ESFA strike again. The installation of 2 or 3 goalhangers would lead to a glut of goals, as witnessed in the early 70's in the Watney Cup, where this tactic was experimented with. However, there would be an equal and opposite reaction with the opposition pulling back an equal number of defenders in order to counter the rule change.

13. Shoot for points - A Dutch suggestion this one. A board is placed across the goal with holes cut out to a size just bigger than a football. Each hole corresponds to a certain number of points depending on it's location in respect to the goal. So, a hole near the top left hand corner may score 20 points while one in the middle at ground level might only be worth 5. Each of 5 players has two shots each to score the maximum that they can. If still undecided after this, then the other players would have one shot each in a sudden death round. This idea is well worth thinking about.

14. Replay matches - Oh, no, no, no. Couldn't possibly do that.

****

PHRASES YOU NEVER HEAR

"No problem Andy, i'll be able to play
on Wednesday"   -   Gary Gillespie

"I'm a bit worried about your fitness,
Ally, maybe you should be on the
bench on Wednesday."   -   Andy Roxburgh

"Hello Mum, yes, I'm playing on Wednesday for
Scotland"   -   John Robertson

"Lad's, you're leaving yourselves exposed
at the back going forward like that -   Alex Miller
                                          (Mgr of Hibs)

"Great goal Brian! (McClair)"   -   Anybody

"Isn't it about time one of the Highland
League clubs were admitted to the Scottish
league?"   -   SFA Representative

"That youngster in the reserves may get
a place in the team on Saturday"   -   Any Rangers Fan

"I've got no comment"   -   Wallace Mercer

"Hey, Grandad, lets have another look
at that photo of you when Hibs last
won the Scottish Cup"   -   Any Hibs fan

"Rangers were lucky to win today"   -   Any Rangers Fan

"England were lucky to win the
world cup in 1966"   -   Any English person

"Welcome back, Ron, good to see you
again"   -   Sheff Wed Chairman

"I want Luton to stay up"   -   Any English fan

"I want St.Mirren to stay up   -   Any Hearts fan

"if you do that again I'm going to
book you Roy.   -   Any Referee

"And that was a definite penalty there, Ally
McCoist was pulled down in the box" - Commentator

"You're not physical enough, Mark. You
have to put yourself about a bit in this
league you know"   -   Walter Smith

"Fancy coming round for a coffee
sometime next week Mark?"   -   Crawford Baptie

HEARTS

GO JO, GO !!

AKA : We belong in SW19, not SE23 !!

A DAY IN THE LIFE OF A REFEREE.

08.30   Wake up and fall out of bed. Got a stinking hangover.

08.45   Finally manage to get my eyes open.

09.00   Get up, have a wash and the all important "morning after" tablet.

09.15   Breakfast ? You must be joking !

09.30   Pack my bag and check I've got everything...whistle, yellow card, red card, pencil, notebook and, oh b****y hell nearly forgot....my glasses .

10.00   Leave the house and go to the car only to realise I've left all my keys in the house !!

10.05   Oh my god, what next ??

10.20   Really cheesed off now !

10.30   Going to be late, so I decide to throw a brick through the front door to get my keys.

10.32   Discover keys....in jacket pocket all the time.

10.45   Still thinking what a complete idiot I am.

10.55   Been trying to start the car for the last ten minutes.

10.57   Decide to start car with ignition key rather than front door key.

11.00   On my way at long last.

11.01   Stalled !

11.05   And we're off again.

11.30   Pull over to the side of the road to look at map, only to
        realise that I don't even know who's playing today !

11.33   Get severe ticking off from F.A. over the phone.

11.40   Some passer-by says go to South London and it's around
        there somewhere. Talk about precise, eh !?

12.30   Would be flippin' Wimbledon - aerial bombardment and a
        .hangover never was a good mix.

12.45   Nice people around here - manage to give me a red ticket
        for stopping at a red light.

13.00   Driven everywhere in Wimbledon. Can't find the ground.

13.01   I suppose I should really have known that Wimbledon don't
        actually play in Wimbledon.

13.28   Never would have connected a stadium this big with
        Wimbledon.

13.30   Parked car. Some balding bloke asks for my I.D. I show him
        my glasses. He says "Make sure Wimbledon win, " and shoves
        some notes into my hands.

13.45   Finish reading the notes that the bald bloke gave me.

14.00   Getting changed.

14.01   Forgotten my boots !

14.02   B*****ks !

14.55   Go to check pitch, nets and balls - Bolleaux !! I'd
        forgotten to do it, alright !?

14.58   Notice bald bloke from car park warming up in a No.13
        Wimbledon shirt.

14.59   I'm feeling a right prat in my open-toe sandals, I can
        tell you !

15.00   Back into changing room   to look for a coin.

15.05   Back again to get the ball.

15.10   Blow whistle to start game.

15.20   Astounded by the quality football on display, especially
        from Wimbledon. I'm getting a stiff neck from looking down
        at the ball being passed around on the grass all the time.

15.21   Oooh !! A mistimed tackle from a Wimbledon player. Time to get the book out. Right son, what's your name ?

15.22 Z...b...i...

15.23 Zbigni...sorry ?? What was that ?

15.24 Zbigniew Kr...I missed that last letter.

15.25 Zbigniew Krusz...

15.26 Never mind, just don't do it again !!

15.30 Ball in face...hurts like hell. Broken nose...oh shove off, and stop writing down everything I do and say !!

22.35 Out of hospital.

22.37 Car been stolen.

23.45 I hate Wimbledon. (*Ed. Don't all refs ?!*)

23.55 Newspapers print Sunday headlines :

"REF COMMITS SUICIDE IN WIMBLEDON"

Jertzee Balowski
Gordon Gattling
Cinimod Giraffe

Photo : Keith Gamble

Ooo Ref!

You are awful...

...but I do love you!

The Midge Scruffy Story

Script - The Poisoned Pen
Artwork - Mike Pringle

THE STORY SO FAR...

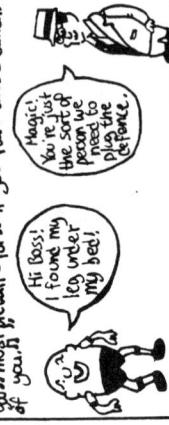

DENS-SCENE — A Dundee Fanzine —

A Question Of Loyalty

One of the most important aspects of football management is to secure the best players at a club. This forms a secure basis for the club to build on. At some clubs, they simply have to sell their best players in order to survive, but this cannot be said of Dundee. Having been relegated, all efforts should be directed towards going straight back up. We simply have to get promoted in our first season, otherwise our decline could be irreversible. But, despite this, Jim Duffy left.

In the past, when players refused to re-sign because there wasn't a good enough offer on the table, the Chairman or manager has always been the culprit in the eyes of the fans. These views have been representative of the Jim Duffy affair as well. I can fully appreciate why most fans feel this way, even though my own view doesn't point the finger at the Chairman entirely.

Dundee made £420,000 profit last year, of which £350,000 was said to be needed to use for a full time First Division. £160,000 has been taken in from transfer fees (as of 7/8/90) and £150,000 has been spent (as of 7/8/90). In total, this leaves £80,000 clear profit. The question that most fans will be asking is: if there is money available, then why wasn't Duffy paid what he wanted?

Of course, the immediate reaction to this would be to blame Cook because he wasn't paying out enough money. But even Cook isn't gullible enough not to realize how valuable Duffy is, so I believe he did make him a very good offer. This suggests to me that Jim was either asking too much, or that he had no intention of staying unless a ridiculous offer was made.

However, a lot of people could argue that buying a replacement of an equally high standard would cost far more than simply paying him what he wanted, and I would agree with this point. But if he had no intention of staying then this would be irrelevant.

We must also consider that Duffy has an inbuilt risk factor. He may have managed to see out last season, but there is no guarantee that he would last a whole season. He may say he's perfectly fit, and he may look fit, but I don't believe for one minute that there is a real guarantee that he is completely back to normal. An injury which puts a player out for 2 years (and said to be life) is extremely serious and I can't imagine that even the fittest players would be able to resume playing without any risk. Bearing this in mind, it would be incredibly stupid to gamble a lot of money to keep him here.

I also feel that he is being extremely disloyal. Wasn't it Dundee who looked after him so well when he had that crippling injury? As one of 5,905 who subscribed to his testimonial fund by going to his testimonial game, I feel betrayed. The least you could have expected him to do was to play another year for Dundee as a thank you for looking after him so well. I think that Duffy has been a bit greedy and asked for too much. He should have played 1 more year. If he had helped us to get promoted then the chances are he'd stay on anyway. If we didn't get promoted then he would be free to move; he would have repaid his debt.

But another thing that annoyed me was that he expected Dundee to let him go for nothing. Apparently, an agreement was signed stating that if he left, there would be no transfer fee involved. But can he really expect Dundee to let him go for free? He knows how valuable he is. In the end, it looks as though we'll get around £20,000, which, to put it mildly, is a disgrace. I'd be looking for at least £50,000.

But we'll just have to accept the situation as it is. Duffy is no longer a Dundee player, and will in fact be playing against us in the first game of the season. It will be interesting to hear the reaction he gets. I, for one, won't be booing him, but I certainly won't be cheering him.

Jim Duffy - the loyal, totally innocent football player who was a victim of Argus Cook's stinginess? Don't you believe it!

LEAGUE SNAKES & LADDERS

YET ANOTHER* AMAZING BOARD GAME FROM YOUR FAVOURITE FANZINE!

YOU HAVE 20 MOVES IN WHICH TO DECIDE WHETHER DUNDEE WILL BE PLAYING PREMIER, FIRST OR SECOND DIVISION FOOTBALL NEXT SEASON. ALL YOU NEED TO PLAY THIS GREAT GAME IS: A DODGY DICE & AS MANY COUNTERS AS YOU WANT. TO DECIDE WHO STARTS, THROW THE DICE. THE WINNER HAS THE RIGHT TO JUMP UP AND DOWN VERY QUICKLY. IF YOU LAND ON A SNAKE, YOU FOLLOW IT DOWN. IF **YOU LAND** ON A LADDER, YOU GO UP.

PREMIER

| 81 | 80 | ROBERT MAXWELL TAKES OVER | 78 | 77 | 76 | 75 | 74 | 73 | 72 |

| 60 GRAEME HARVEY BREAKS HIS LEGS | 62 | | 65 | 66 | BILLY DODDS SIGNS FOR CELTIC? | | 69 | 70 | 71 |

| 59 | 58 | 57 | 56 | | 53 | 52 | | | 48 |

| 36 | 37 | 39 | COOK LEAVES THE COUNTRY | DUNDEE SIGN DAVIE DODDS | 43 | 44 | 45 | GORDON WALLACE GETS SACKED | 47 |

| 35 | 34 | 33 | 32 | 31 | 29 | | 26 | | 24 |

| 12 | | 15 | IAN ST JOHN TIPS DUNDEE TO WIN THE LEAGUE | 18 | | | 22 | 23 |

| 11 DUNDEE FAIL TO SIGN GRAEME HARVEY | 9 | 8 | 7 | 6 | 4 | OWEN COYLE BREAKS HIS LEG | 2 | 1 | START |

* NOT TRUE

DIV. 2

Dundonian for beginners (with thanks and apologies to Nick McCloskey)

If you are thinking about going to a football match at Dens, here are some phrases which should come in handy. (D is for Dundonian M is for Meaning)

Before the game
A confrontation with a fanzine seller...

D: 'sthit thi programme? Much?
M: It looks like a fanzine.

D: Fuftay petrice?!!
Fowir fuftay?!!
M: I have no intention of buying it, but I'll ask you how much it is anyway.
That's quite reasonable.
I think I'll insult the seller.

At the turnstile...

D: Much tae git in?
Fowir fuftay?!!
M: I can't be bothered reading the sign.
It's so long since I've been that £4.50 seems quite dear.

Inside the ground...

D: Oot mi road.
M: You're taller than me – I'd advise you to let me sit in front of you.
You may be taller than me, but I'm harder.

D: See yi efter.
Whit taims Dundeh?
M: I haven't been to a Dundee match in years.

First Half

D: Cripullum!
Wull yiz stop yir muckin aboot an day sunhin'.
Whazzat geein eejsel a showin up?
Snoh bahd.
Nuthinzup.
M: Good tackle.
Come on lads, string some passes together.
Is that Stuart Beedie?
It's a good game.
It's completely crap.

Half Time
Acquiring refreshments...

D: Jooz hay eny pehz stull?
Um affy dreh.
Wacha skunner, yir slaberrin.
M: I'm so hungry I'll eat anything.
I'm very thirsty.
Watch it, you clumbsy prick. Can't you carry your bovril without spilling it?

Finding the toilets....

D: Heer paal, wharza lahvee?
M: I'm bursting for the bog. Where's the toilet?
If you stand there, I'll piss on your feet.

D: Oot mi road.
M: United could piss on you lot.

Second Half

D: Yizir kikin it aboot liyk a 'skwahd o' ald wiyfeys.
Eez a bit o' a skitzo.
Awa t go!
M: Oh look, there's Terry Hurlock.
The decision was correct, but I'm complaining for the hell of it.
Oh look, Stewart Forsyth's coming on.

D: Oh mah goad!
'At manky towrags mingin.
Oot mi road.
M: Who's that nearside linesman?
We're losing, there's only 10 minutes to go and if I leave now I'll get another pint in.

Dundee B&Q it

As I was walking through Motherwell in the early afternoon, a couple approached me and asked why there were so many people walking about. I explained that there was a Cup final that afternoon, and they gave me a surprised look and said, "Oh."

It was this particular confrontation that made me realize what pitiful coverage the B & Q Centenary Cup had been given. Right from the start it had everything going against it. First, and foremost, was the fact that it was a trophy for the 1st and 2nd Division teams; any competition which didn't include the top 10 must have been a complete waste of time. Even the trophy (well, the glass decanter) was ridiculed!

Basically, the competition was only as bad as the media wanted it to be. It certainly had the potential to be a successful tournament, and in my view, it was. Certainly, the crowds backed up this opinion. Although the (official) attendance of around 11,500 (it looked [and felt!]a lot more) might not appear to be a particularly large crowd for a final, in comparison with the average crowd for a League game in the First Division, it was roughly the same as a Scottish Cup Final crowd compared to the average Premier crowd. It seemed afterwards that it was generally regarded as a fairly successful competition, with much talk of how it should be continued under a different name. Of course, it still had its critics, like most Premier teams' fans, but it was also mocked by other First & Second Division teams. But let's face it - if it was their team who had won it, would they be so against it? Is it true mockery, or is it just jealousy? I was standing there after the game with a feeling of true elation, but some other Dundee supporters found it difficult to get excited over winning a competition for 1st & 2nd Division clubs, and I can understand their point. After all, they had seen Dundee winning the League and the League Cup, so this competition wouldn't have seemed very prestigious. But let's not kid ourselves - we are only a First Division team, so winning the B & Q Centenary Cup should be regarded as fine an achievement as Rangers winning the Skol Cup.

To me, the Centenary Cup was a worthwhile competition, and I regard winning it as one of my high points in supporting Dundee.Think differently if you like, but I hope it continues, and if we are ever in the position to play in it again, I will treat it as being a major tournament.

"CHAMPIONS" - At last   by Kenny Ross

For years the Dees ain't won a cup,
Recent efforts have been in vain.
But last October saw a brand new Cup,
The Centenary was its name.

Right from the start we thought we'd win,
'Cause we got a message from the sky.
'Cause in the first round,we were told
The Dees had got a bye.

In the second round, we played away,
At Recreation Park.
We beat Alloa, five goals to three,
With Dodds the vital spark.

The third round saw us go to Fife,
To play Frank Connor's men.
In extra time we got the winner,
Scored by our number 10.

The semi was away again,
This time at Kilmarnock.
We won with 2 goals from Keith Wright,
So the final was now the talk.

The final was on Remembrance Day,
The venue Motherwell.
The papers said that we'd beat Ayr,
But with the Dees you couldn't tell.

And our apprehension was correct,
When United took the lead,
It stayed like that until half time,
When the fans could moan indeed.

But in the 2nd half, the Dees came out,
With a renewed will to win.
And soon wee Billy equalized ,
When his penalty went in.

We now looked the more likely to win,
Just as the papers said.
Cause pretty soon, Dodds scored again,
But this time with his head.

But Ayr came back and equalized,
With a deflection off West.
The shot caught Carson off his line,
To make him fail his test.

But we won the match in extra time,
With the final score 3-2.
So Dodds' hat trick won the cup,
And made a dream come true.

So Chis went up to lift the cup,
And through the team it passed.
And the fans they sang out very loud,
"CHAMPIONS" - at last!

A Guide To Becoming A Football Chairman

WHAT YOU NEED & DON'T NEED

MONEY - Lots of it. Buying a club doesn't come cheap you know, and all the expensive cars etc, will cost a lot.

KNOWLEDGE OF FOOTBALL - Not Needed. You're in this for money, not because you're interested in the game. But a few of the basics may be necessary, and some research into the club you're wanting to become Chairman of is recommended so that you can pretend you have supported the club all your life and that you are an enthusiast. Be careful not to use all your knowledge in the one sentence, as this may mean more research.

QUALIFICATIONS - Unnecessary, but don't admit to not having any. Avoid any reference to this.

THESAURUS - Very important.When it comes to writing your column in the match programme, you'll need this to try and make out that you have a large vocabulary and are clever. Using the Thesaurus is excellent if you have an occasion for malingering that you're sagacious.-See?

WHAT TO LOOK LIKE AND WHAT TO WEAR

APPEARANCE - Must be fat, preferably quite small and balding. Face should be small and round, with a double chin forming.

CLOTHING - Expensive-looking suit with a hanky appearing out of the chest pocket. Black shoes, white shirt, and a smart tie.

EXTRA'S - Cigar in mouth at all times. Glasses (optional).

WHAT TO DO

CHOOSING THE CLUB - Probably the hardest thing to do. Don't go for a really big or a really small club, as with the former it's too expensive and with the latter it's a waste of time. Go for a club which has potential and a fairly large ground.

BUYING THE CLUB - What you set out to do. How to go about it will be your biggest problem. Buying it won't be, as every Chairman will accept a big enough offer. Just offer them a lot of money and that's you in the hot seat.

WHAT TO DO NEXT

SUSS THE PLACE OUT - At last you're Chairman.Now you should have a good look around the place. Get to know your way about, get to know the players, and see what the secretary looks like.

LIE TO FANS - Very important. Make sure you make it clear of your false intentions. Phrases like "I've always supported this club", "The fans deserve success" & "Money is available to the manager to buy players" should be learned and used at every opportunity in the first couple of weeks. During this time you should suss out the best players by asking the manager, but do not tell him your plans as he may resign and then you won't have anyone to sack, and it will involve all the hassle of getting a new manager.

SELL BEST PLAYERS - No problem here. There'll be plenty of takers, but don't be too greedy by asking too much, otherwise you might scare them off. There may be an outcry, but tell the press and fans some crap about being heavily in debt, and that if you don't sell them the club will go bankrupt.

SELL THE GROUND AND GET RID OF ALL THE STAFF - This is where you make the money. Be careful not to tell the Press before you've done it all. Once it's all completed, live a life of luxury. Emigrate to Australia and don't worry - Wallace Mercer's managed to live with it.

The Abbey Rabbit

Confused/amused by the official attendances given for matches at the Abbey for the last few seasons? I think I've found the answer...

Figure It Out

In Douglas Adams' series of books, "The Hitchhikers' Guide to the Galaxy", an advanced form of mathematics is explained. This theory, Bistromathics, states that just as Einstein had observed that space was not an absolute but depended on the observer's movement in space, and that time was not an absolute, but depended on the observer's movement in time, numbers are also not absolute but depend on the observer's movement in restaurants.

These nonabsolutes relate to the number of people for whom a table is reserved, the number of people who actually turn up, the number of people who subsequently join them and the number of people who leave when they see who else has turned up. When combined with the relationship between the number of items on the bill, the cost of each item, the number of people at the table, what they are prepared to pay for and the number of people who have actually brought money with them, you can see that numbers written on restaurant bills within the confines of restaurants do not follow the same mathematical laws as numbers written on any other pieces of paper in any other parts of the universe. If you don't believe me, invite a group of 17 people to the Pizza Hut after the next home match!

In line with this thinking, I can add another branch to this science; Abbeystadiumattendancemathics. This theory is based on the fact that the number of people in the ground, the number of empty spaces, and the ground capacity bear absolutely no relevance to each other.

If we look at an example; the attendance for the Derby match was 7,923 and the ground capacity is 9,998. Now you tell me where the additional 2,075 could have been accommodated. Let's now throw an additional factor into the equation - The Taylor Report. This has reduced standing capacity so that you should be able to stand in sumptuous comfort. And, as if all this isn't confusing enough, bear in mind that around 400 fans were locked out that night!

This startling discovery opens up new frontiers of business opportunities for John Holmes and Katie Loring in the Commercial Department. With figures leaping around in such an alarming way in calculations in the Abbey, perhaps the terraces could be rented out during the week to accountants. The ground would provide the ideal abstract environment for filling out tax forms (not that I would even hint at suggesting that tax has anything to do with attendance figures!). Could you imagine it - come 3 O'Clock on a Saturday afternoon the

terraces would be packed with plumbers writing up bills,
builders and motor mechanics filling out estimates, quantity
surveyors completing their time sheets and government officials
seasonally adjusting the unemployment figures. Just think,
you could even calculate a lower mortgage repayment as the
figures bounce around the concrete steps and onto your piece of
paper in erratic and alarming ways.

There is a drawback, however. This theory does mean that
should we ever develop the Abbey to increase its capacity, it
would have to be increased to something in the region of 42,042
to accommodate all the supporters who were at the Derby match.

Zaphod

Before each home match at Cambridge United, a Moose runs round
the pitch. Let me try to explain why...

Moose Story

The history of The Moose is shrouded in myth and legend with
many people claiming responsibility. I have, however, found
that the most reliable story goes as follows:

On 19th August 1989 we kicked off our (successful) Fourth
Division campaign at Grimsby Town. Amongst the travelling U's
fans that day was a gentleman by the name of Dale Collett who
had literally just stepped off a return flight from holidaying
in Spain (although the venue of this holiday is, again, an
element of uncertainty) and into a car to take him to sunny
Cleethorpes.

Because of the length of his trip and the particularly silly
number of hours it had taken he, as he said at the time, smelt
like a moose. He then promptly put a hand to either side of
his head and imitated the creature.

Alright I admit it, a little alcohol had been consumed that
sunny afternoon by the travelling fans so naturally, they all
decided that Dale's actions were quite rational so we all
decided to copy him.

It naturally followed that, maybe in an effort to improve the
image of football (or maybe because we were all feeling the
effects of a hot day and a liquid lunch) that, when the Grimsby
goalkeeper took a goal kick from in front of us, instead of
shouting "You're sh*t ahhhhhhhh" as most teams fans do, we
would simply raise our hands and shout "Moose".

As the season wore on more and more U's fans took up this habit
and it was brought via The Abbey Stadium to Wembley. From then
on the club adopted it which is why you will see a man in a
Moose Suit before every home match.

Tyke And Humberside Fatigued Sides Slide To Untimely Demise
(or 'An Alternative Look At The End Of The Yorkshire And Humberside Cup')

When Marco Polo first set foot on the beach at Botany Bay and cried "Eureka!", the world soon realised that it was the dawning of a new era in catch phrases. Little did the young Turk suspect, when he stood there in the snow, that, two thousand years later, his Dutch international namesake Van Gullit would slot in the winning goal for Halifax in the Yorkshire And Humberside Cup. In its short–lived, but meteoric, history the cup provided a lifeline for many a starved Tyke *(and Yellowbelly – eds.)*. In years to come, a vanguard of Tigers can hold their heads proudly aloft and say "We won the Cup".

Forget the FA, Apex Lieutenant–Commander Data Systems (?!) and Rumbelows (which reminds me, I need a new washing machine), the Y & H was the extra–length filter tip of Cup football!

For the likes of Leeds and Sheffield with their high and mighty aspirations, it was just a coal truck shunted onto a disused piece of time but, to the REAL teams, it was more than a mere provincial line of pac–a–mac trainspotters!

Gristle, sweat, backbone and genius. Yes, that and much more might all have been missing from this shunned and unglamorous second–rate trophy affair.

It was, however, loved, cherished and fondled slightly by all those who really care about dire, rainsoaked soccer.

As my tears fall, stinging like a swig of TCP, I wonder if this great event will ever be reinstated. Did Mr. Polo die in vain after all, that we should tarnish his memory so?

All he asked for was a decent win bonus and a new land to discover. I'm sure he'd be saddened by this greenfly-infested decision to fell the White Rose of its noble birthright.

For the unitiated there lies below, a rare, decaying document of that most glorious of days when the unique fervour and magic of the cup came to this humble parish:

Radicliffe The Healer

Hull City 2 Bradford City 0
*(Yorkshire & Humberside Cup Final,
05/09/89, Boothferry Park)*

The wind howled around the sparsely populated coliseum. Man, woman and child turned as one to welcome their gladiators.

From the West come a guttural howl, a banshee wail, as the forces of darkness from the lowlands of Bantamdom swept onto the field of battle armed with size fives and dubbin cocktails.

The shrill sound of Overlord Reffio's whistle of justice signified the commencement of hostilities. The dark Prince Yorathiccus had marshalled his riders of doom into a hardened fighting unit. The kingdom of the fish people was under siege and Handsome King Appleton knew it. He needed a champion or his people would be banished to the land of pots to writhe in perpetual torment for all eternity under the evil tyranny of the mad hunchback, Mills de Mick (MBE).

Around him grown men broke down and cried as, from the very bowels of hell, the evil Yorathiccus summoned up the hideous Adams–demon "Offsidior The Game Destroyer".

Handsome King Appleton knew he had to act fast to counter this hellish deed. He turned to wise old soothsayer Radicliffe The Healer for advice.

The wind swirled into a terrible fury as Radicliffe consulted the mystical sponge of truth.

"I see...the number....ten", croaked the healer.

Suddenly the raging storm subsided and, from a golden oasis, appeared the blonde, big bottomed, Adonis–like figure of Sir Edwards Of Keith. The people rejoiced like never before and Handsome King Appleton danced Bez–like in happiness. His kingdom was saved!

The forces of darkness and their evil leader Yorathiccus were banished to wander the lonely labyrinths of the strange "second place" for all infinity.

The kingdom of the fish people once again echoed to the sounds of laughter and singing.

Mr. Polo slept very soundly that night.

© *Karl Vint/Paul Heathcote Communique '91*

THE HANGING SHEEP

the independent leeds fanzine

Over the years football supporters have had some dreadful media coverage, some of it justified, some not. Hooliganism, racism, sexism, infact most 'isms' of one sort or another have been paired with followers of our national game - so is there a positive side to us rabble?

The setting up of the Football Supporters Association in 1985 was a group of fans direct response to yet more football tragedy - the F.S.A. was the driving force behind the anti I.D. Card campaign. A successful attempt by ordinary fans everywhere to kick the Government's idea into touch (football cliché No. 1!!) But what about the media coverage? Almost non existent, apart from a few journalists who had their heads screwed on to what was going on in football.

Though the F.S.A. is only small in numbers it's views are now being listened to by those in authority - rather then being dismissed as a "silly idea by football fans who don't really know what they want." Something which would have been the norm up until not so long ago. Similarly fanzines have expanded beyond everybody's wildest dreams - proving without a doubt that the paying masses need an independent network, and more importantly want one.

We started our fanzine 'The Hanging Sheep' 3½ years ago with the aim that all fans but in our case particularly Leeds fans could have their very own voice when it came to issues that affected them. In that 3½ years we think we've provided a reasonable service for those who've sought us out. The only real pity is that fanzines have and probably always will be regarded as "subversive" or how about the immortal, "not in the best interests of the club." It is a real pity because if those in the boardrooms and press offices around the country showed as much enthusiasm as the fanzine folk our national game would be a hell of a lot better off.

More and more supporters are realising that just because they support different teams it doesn't necessarily mean that they should have different viewpoints - but do we hear about this in 'our' national press? No, of course we don't as it would get a bit boring wouldn't it? Reading headlines such as "rival fans in pre-match kick about." Here at Leeds the fans themselves have all but smothered the life out of the racist thug that rampaged around the country a few years ago. People will point to the incidents at Bournemouth in May 1990 as an example of Leeds fans at their very "best". But if you study all the factors closely, real Leeds fans behaving badly comes well down the list of excuses, still you probably don't believe me anyway.

Finally - "Football Against MS" is yet another chance to show the vindictive press of this country that we football fans can do constructive things - and in doing so not only enhance football's better points, but blow our own trumpet as well. Lets hear you load and clear!

CHRIS STRINGER
(Co Editor The Hanging Sheep)

10

OVERSTATED 'FACTS' ABOUT LEEDS UNITED AFC...........

1) ELLAND ROAD IS INTIMDATING

2) DAVID BATTY RESEMBLES NOBBY STILES (?)

3) LEEDS ARE 'BIG SPENDING'

4) ELLAND ROAD IS A FAMILY GROUND

5) LEEDS UNITED'S AWAY GAMES ARE ALL TICKET

6) LEEDS ARE AN AUTOMATIC CHOICE FOR A SUPER LEAGUE PLACE

7) STRACHAN IS ALWAYS 'INSPIRATIONAL'

8) MAN UTD ARE UTTER RUBBISH

9) THIS LEEDS TEAM COULD BE AS GOOD AS REVIE'S

10) "IN POINT OF FACT, BATTY'S ONLY EVER SCORED ONE GOAL FOR LEEDS" (A Motson special)

Major General Ivor Screwloose VC.

In the circumstances, City three goals down and heading for another season of Third Division football, I thought their rendition of this excerpt from Monty Python's Life of Brian not only witty but good humoured. I wonder how Leeds United's rottweilers (not all Leeds fans are that) would have responded to defeat and disappointment?

"Going up, going up, going up!" bellowed Wigan's supporters.

The City fans had an answer to that too. "Staying down, staying down, staying down!"

ELLAND ROAD ... characters

Ten replacements for a pit bull terrier

A poodle with a grudge

A bonsai sumo wrestler

John Prescott with a muzzle

Hannibal Lecter

An East End pub landlady

Someone who's just been wheel-clamped *

A Leeds United supporter *

Roseanne Barr

A VAT inspector

A South African policeman

THE DOUBLE BREASTED YUPPIE

The ever impartial Mail on Sunday (above) spreading goodwill to Leeds fans everywhere!

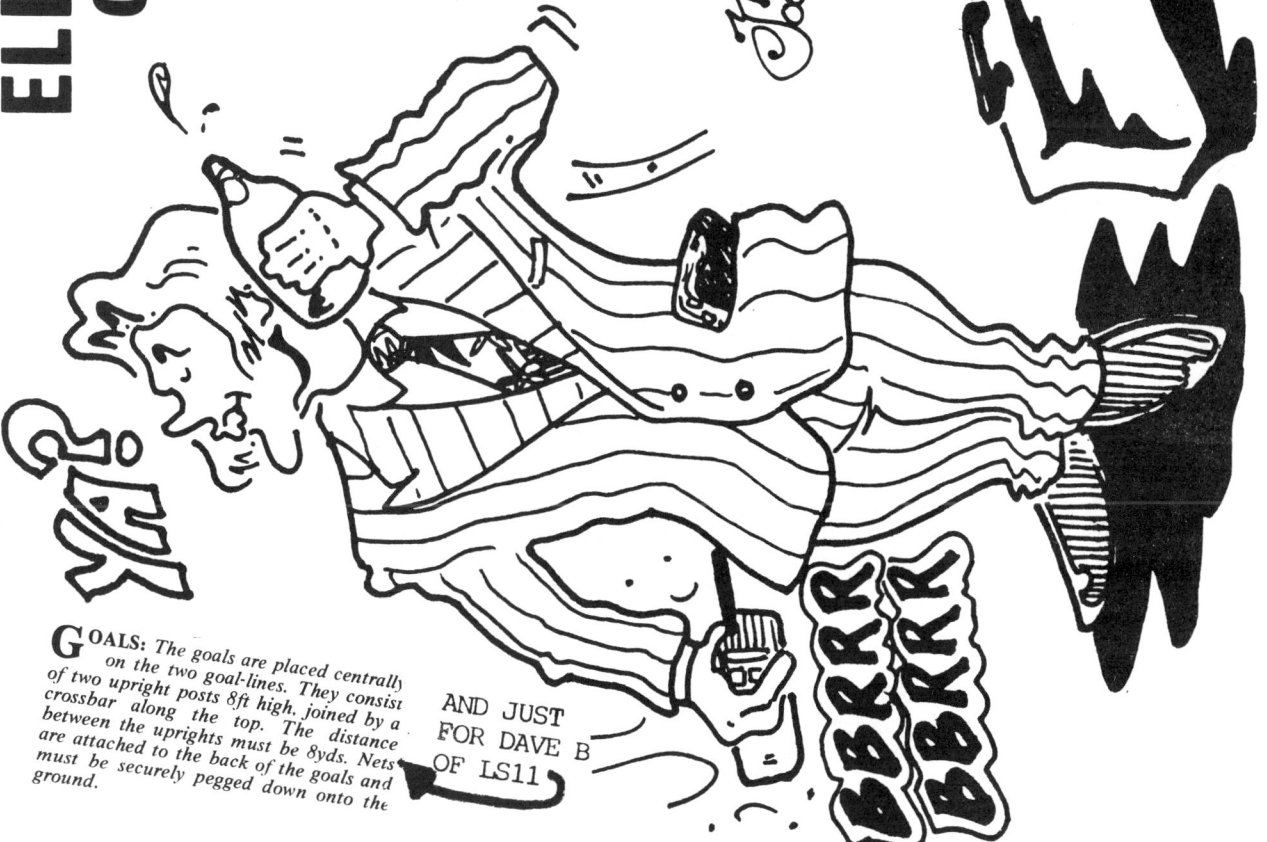

"SGT WILKO'S BAAARMY ARMY!"

PAM.

GOALS: *The goals are placed centrally on the two goal-lines. They consist of two upright posts 8ft high, joined by a crossbar along the top. The distance between the uprights must be 8yds. Nets are attached to the back of the goals and must be securely pegged down onto the ground.*

AND JUST FOR DAVE B OF LS11

BBRRR BBRRR

One Minute To Go
A Liverpool Fanzine

BLUE PETER

Hello everyone,and welcome to this special edition of Blue Peter,coming direct from Goodison Park.

first today,our lovable,bald friend Howard Kendall who is going to show us how to make a crap football team.unfortunately,we haven't got time to go out and waste £10 million now so we're going to get Colin to show us one he made earlier.

Model making time now,and we're going to show you how to make a model of Everton's fantastic away end,first you take a cornflakes box and cut off some of the front so you only have the back and side left. Then take a few matchsticks and fold them into the shape of crush barriers.Please note that this model is the actual size,for extra special effects draw on your score-board.

Next,we're going to make Everton's back 4,for this you need 4 card board players,all with their hands above their heads,stick all four players onto a metal rod and then stck them on the halfway line and you've got it,very realistic.

Sorry,we have to go now,a bomb has just gone off at Goodison Park it has caused millions of pounds worth of ground improvements. GOODBYE.

EVERTON FOR THE LEAGUE!

WE ALL AGREE, MOLBY DRIVES FASTER THAN ADAMS

LIVERPOOL F.C.

ONE MINUTE TO GO ONLY 50p (10 BOB)

MIKE '91

ARSENAL'S TITLE: THE TRUTH

THERE YOU GO GEORGE, OUR CLEANING LADY'S QUIT KEEP THE SHINE TILL NEXT MAY

MIKE

SATURDAY AFTERNOON WITH THE BLUE'BOYS'

1:00-1:30-ARRIVE IN VACINITY OF GOODISON,BUY SOME CHIPS.
1:40-SCOREBOARD BUZZES(LITERATLY)INTO LIFE.
1:45-RADIO CITY/GOODISON BLASTS OVER THE TANNOY.
1:46-FINISH CHIPS,BEST BUY AT LEAST 1 MORE PORTION BEFORE
1:50-ENTER GROUND.
1:53-BUY THE'BEST CLUB PRGRAMME'AND DEVOUR THE TECHNICAL INGENUITY
     IN THE GRAPHS.
1:55-CHECK OUT THE TEA BAR.EVEN THESE UNCIVIL NEADATHALS USE THEIR
     BETTER JUDGEMENT!
2:00-ENTER'EUROPE'S GREATEST STADIUM'.
2:15-'EVERTON,EVERTON'RINGS ROUND THE'ST.END.UNFORTUNATLEY UNLESS
     THE BOYS ARE PLAYING A TOP TEAM eg.US.OR THE OPPOSITION HAVE
     A PLAYER SUCH AS VINNY JONES,THIS COULD BE THE LAST WE HEAR
     FROM THEM UNLESS(GOD FORBID)THEY SCORE!
2:30-AWAY SUPPORT(EVEN WIMBLEDON'S)OUT NUMBER THE BOYS IN BLUE.
2:48-FIRST BRAVE(SUICIDAL?)PERSON VENTURES ONTO THE TOP BALCONY.
2:49-PARK END TERRACE PACKED.CAPACITY OF AROUND 46 REACHED.
2:49½-UPPER BULLENS FLOOR CREAKS(WOOD IN'EUROPE'S FINEST?NEVER)
2:50-GROUND NOW LOOKS ½(IF THAT)FULL.
2:53-TEAMS ANNOUNCED.MOST BLUES GET BOOED WITH ONE OR TWO NOTIC-
     ABLE EXCEPTIONS.
3:01-THERE OFF!BALL PASSED STRAIGHT BACK TO NEV'WHO HOOFS IT AS FAR
     UP FIELD AS POSSIBLE(A CONTINOUS TACTIC)
3:06-EVERTON SCORE(FICTIONAL REMEMBER)SCORERS NAME ANNOUNCED ABOUT
     SIX TIMES OVER TANNOY.
3:07-OPPONENTS SCORE(OK SO NOT SO FICTIONAL)TANNOY SILENT.
3:46-HALF TIME.RELIEF.NECK GETTING A BIT STIFF.
3:58-BACK TO THE TORTURE.RICKED NECK NOW A FORMALITY!
4:20-ATTENDANCE ANNOUNCED.THE'BOYS'AREN'T PLEASED"CONNING BUGGERS"
IS ONE TERM LOSELY USED.I'M ALWAYS SURPRISED AT HOW MANY PEOPLE
OUR CONNED INTO ATTENDING!
4:46-TRUNDEL OF HOME AFTER ANOTHER DISAPOINTING(?)DEFEAT.TRY TO
     THINK UP A FEW EXCUSES AS TO WHY LIVERPOOL WON(7 LUCKY BREAKS
     v DERBY)

TOSH
     IF THE GAME WAS AT NIGHT,THE FLOODLIGHTS,ALL 93(I'VE COUNTED)
     ARE TURNED ON LONG AFTER YOU'VE TRIED TO READ YOUR PROGRAMME.
     AND WHEN THEY DO COME ON THEY ARE A BIT TO BRIGHT.AND YOU
     WONDERED WHY EVERTONIANS ARE SO SHORT-SIGHTED.

SOUNESS:- A BATTLER

10 past 6 on Tuesday 17th April; "Paul,it's Souness!", "Ugh", I readily replied,"It's Souness." Quick as a flash it was out of bed and down to the papershop to have a look at the papers.And sure enough,large as life it said that Greame Souness was to be the new manager of Liverpool F.C. It was a decision which I was sceptical about.After all, wasn't Souness the man who bought Hurlock, Hateley and Gary Stevens?, wasn't Souness the man who turned Rangers into a team more reliant on strength than skill?, wasn't Souness the man whom I called a "bloody traitor" the day he left us?, yes,he was but he was and is also a winner,someone who will demand 100% out of every Tom, Dick, Harry and Barnes who play for Liverpool,he is a man who won't stand for being second best and these are the qualities that I think a Liverpool manager needs.If he can put the sense of pride back into Liverpool's players then he will have done his job.Too many of the current side are far too complacent; it seemed,especially in the tail end of last season that some of the players were only here for the money,not to play their heart out for Liverpool Football Club.I don't mind how crap he is as long as he gives 100% every second he's out on the pitch,no matter how crap he is,if he goes in for the ball all the time then he'll do for me.That is why I like Ablett,OK,he may not be a Hansen or a Lawrenson,but at least he gives his all, that clenched fist salute at the end of an away game shows he's proud to have that red shirt on his back,and that's what I like to see. Souness installed a sense of pride into Rangers,every player that pulled on that blu shirt knew that they had to give their all or they would be in for some secere criticism.

There has been many stories about why Kenny quit,we all know it was'nt down to the pressure,the reason I believe is that after the 4-4 he criticized one of the players and they bit back. (I AM NOT IMPLYING THAT THIS IS TRUE,IT IS JUST MY OPINION,AND FOOTBALL IS ALL ABOUT OPINIONS-in other words don't sue us please) Kenny could'nt handle that, he had let his players get on top of him and that was why he decided to quit.Kenny didn't install a sense of fear into his players,he always was one of the lads and.I believe that that was his eventual downfall.

Souness won't be like that,he will anstall a barrier between him and the players.He'll have a laugh and a joke but they will always know who's the boss.They'll have to learn to take criticism and if they don't like it,they'll have to lump it.The remaining games of the 90-91 season showed that he can install confidence into a side and with a bit of luck he'll buy wisely and we'll have a strong side that can play football next year.

My last memory of Souness as a Liverpool player was him holding aloft the european cup,and hopefully,within 3 years he'll be doing the same thing,but as a manager!

.PAUL.

Home To Home - General Irish

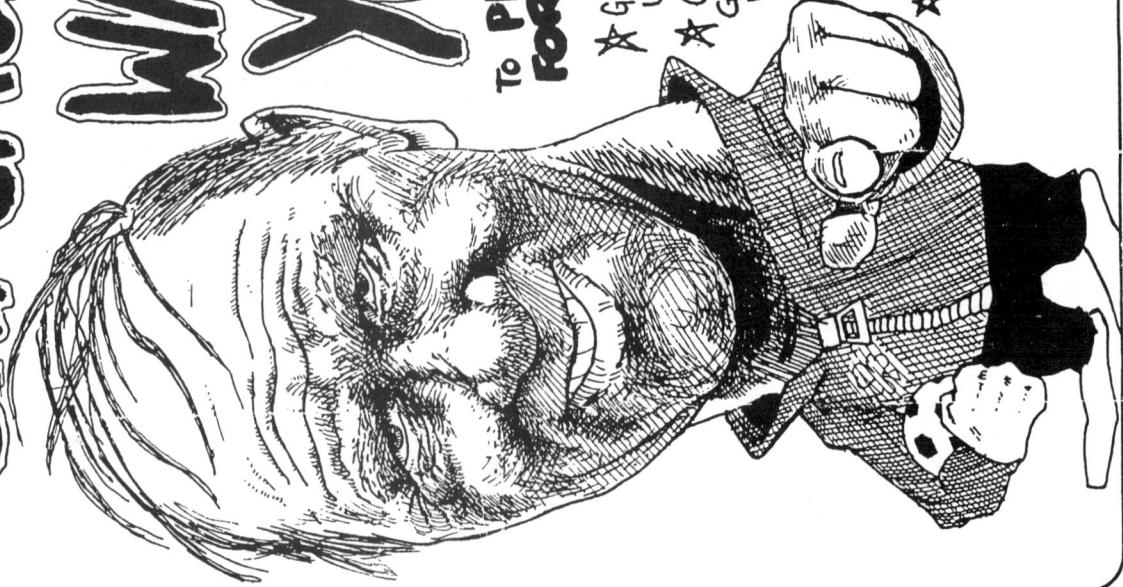

BIG JACK WANTS YOU!

To PLAY SOCCER FOR IRELAND

☆ GOOD WAGES AND UNIFORM

☆ GOD-LIKE STATUS GUARANTEED BY PRESS AND PUBLIC

☆ ABILITY TO KICK A BALL AN ADVANTAGE

☆ ALL NATIONALITIES ACCEPTED — EXEPT IRISH

Paul Bowe

THURLES TOWN REVISITED.

The faithfully gathered on a murky morning. We looked forward to visiting a foreign and seeing flyaway shirt collars and Bay City Rollers trousers. As we talked somebody out of the corner of their eye saw a certain Bob Flynn waltzing around the corner. We looked disbelievingly as a pair of bright grey trouseres with silvery bits bounded up the street towards us. We were even more shocked to see two huge pink socks that had been pulled up outside his trousers to his knees and had fallen down again. Panic immediately set in and we begged the driver to go. Despite offers of huge sums of money (10 shillin's a man) he refused and the Bob got on the bus. Hysterical laughter from the Shels party greeted him and everybody sat on the outside seat. But eventually he got a seat it later transpired that the huge pink socks were actually leg warmers and were "the height iv fasin".

We stopped at an Hotel for lunch the players went off to the restaurant and we went to the bar, a big plate of sandwiches arrived and were devoured before the barman had actually put the plate on to the table, many moons later P.J. (on one of his all too rare appearances at a shels match) remarked, " Who was the stupid bastard that bought the sambos that we all milled", "That was me!" said Jockey Duff smiling inanely and wondering why we had all burst into tears of laughter. We finished of our martini's and pints and continued on our way. Connie earlier had us squiming when we asked some of the Shels enterage for their autographs but we regained our composure by the time we arrived in Thurles. We got off in a small square and there was a girl holding a sports bag which protruded a hockey stick Peadar, decided to use his charm and chatted her up . " Are you going to play a game of hockey or wot?" the girl rolled her eyes to the sky and mumbled something sarcastic . The boys laughed all the way to the pub which was just close so we had several pints and made our way to the ground. It was still a fair while to the kickoff so we found ourselves a ball and had ourselves a little kick around on the pitch to enhance our meagre existence. A certain official of Shels who shall remain nameless ran on the pitch and ordered us off the playing surface. The Thurles fans mumbled something, after a count of 1-2-4 sang "Shell fish (clap x3) and fell about laughing. Some people are easily amused. Shels won the match amid much jubilant celebrations and throwing hats into the air, with Peadar still vainly trying to chat up the hockey stick. She turned up in a Ballybough hostelry years later and someone shouted that they "regcognised that boat race from somewhere", and Peadar cowered in the corner. The return trip had cost us three pounds (about four thousand pound in todays money). Ah me, dem was der days.

C.C.

<u>SPORTSNIGHT</u>

DES LYNAM - .... and your commentator in the San Siro tonight is of course, John Motson.

JOHN MOTSON - This magnificent stadium, venue for the opening match of the World Cup Finals, is a sea of colour for this clash between two of the real giants of European football. This is just the kind of atmosphere we used to savour back home, before our clubs were prevented from competing. In charge tonight is England's World Cup referee, George Courtney. And Mr Courtney's whistle gets this match underway.

(Various Italian, Spaniard, Dutch and South American internationalists produce stunning, one-touch, passing movements, covering the whole length and breadth of the pitch.)

MOTSON - ....and a good decision there by George Courtney, perfectly positioned to see that dreadful foul by the Spanish captain........ and Van Basten is clean through, no, the English linesman on the far side has his flag up. Excellent decision that from Mr Wilson from Guildford.

(Replay clearly shows that Marco was a good five yards on-side.)

err, these foreign TV pictures can be deceptive........ and Mr Courtney was well up with play there...... another superb decision from George Courtney....... it's easy to see why our referees are the envy of the World....... George Courtney won't be swayed by this hostile Italian crowd......

(Italian centre forward produces a dive in the box which Greg Louganis would have been extremely proud.)

PENALTY! No doubt about it. Mr Courtney was perfectly positioned yet again...... and George Courtney checks with his fellow English linesmen and blows his whistle to bring this European Cup Semi-Final to a close. And I return you to Des in the studio with the knowledge that George Courtney has done England proud.

DES - Thanks John, great stuff that from George, I'm sure you'll agree. Elsewhere on the continent tonight, Chrissy Waddle's Marseille triumphed three-nil in Belgium. The England winger's side went one up when Papin scored from 30 yards. Chrissy's mate popped up to head home number two and Waddle inspired the French club onto a third, just before the end. Waddle missed the game through injury of course, get well soon, Chrissy.

Before we go a few other results. Rangers 4 Bayern Munich 0; Dynamo Kiev 0 Celtic 3; Aberdeen 5 Anderlecht 0; Benfica 0 Dundee United 2.

We leave you tonight with the result from Milan which means that without doubt English referees are the best in the World. Goodnight.

THE DAVE MORGAN FAN CLUB

YOU'RE RUBBISH DAGGERS. BLOODY RUBBISH!

I AGREE!

Fig 4.

COME ON WARNERS YOU'RE NOT TRYING! Fig 3.

SCHOOLBOY STUFF MORGAN! Fig 1.

YOU TELL 'EM DEAR. HERE'S YOUR TEA! Fig 2.

Daggers fans are not the worst in the country but they are not the best either. The Aylesbury game apart, Daggers fans get very disillusioned very quickly. This is understandable but there is a certain section near the Seal Pound whose verbal abuse of our team is both unhelpful and crass. I stand quite near them each week and I have given them the name 'The Dave Morgan Fan Club', because it was poor old Davy they first started on. I know it's not clever to take the whoops out of our own supporters, especially with current results, but these people deserve it!

They are led by THE DES LYNAM HEAD (fig. 1) who looks remarkably like the BBC Sports figure but uses his mouth to run off a tirade of ridiculous abuse e.g. calling John Bailey lazy (and meaning it!), always blaming Dave Morgan for any goals that go in but at the same time never crediting him for good saves. MRS HEAD (fig. 2) rushes off to the tea bar several times in a game to fetch him tea for his overworked throat glands. Fig. 3 is MR MIMIC an OAP with a cap who joins in with this infantile ridiculing of our lads and his MISSUS (fig. 4) who agrees totally with everything the DMFC shout out. Maybe now I've spotlighted them they'll calm down a bit (don't think so actually, but I think more people will notice them now – Ed). My brother is fed up with dragging me away from them spitting blood!

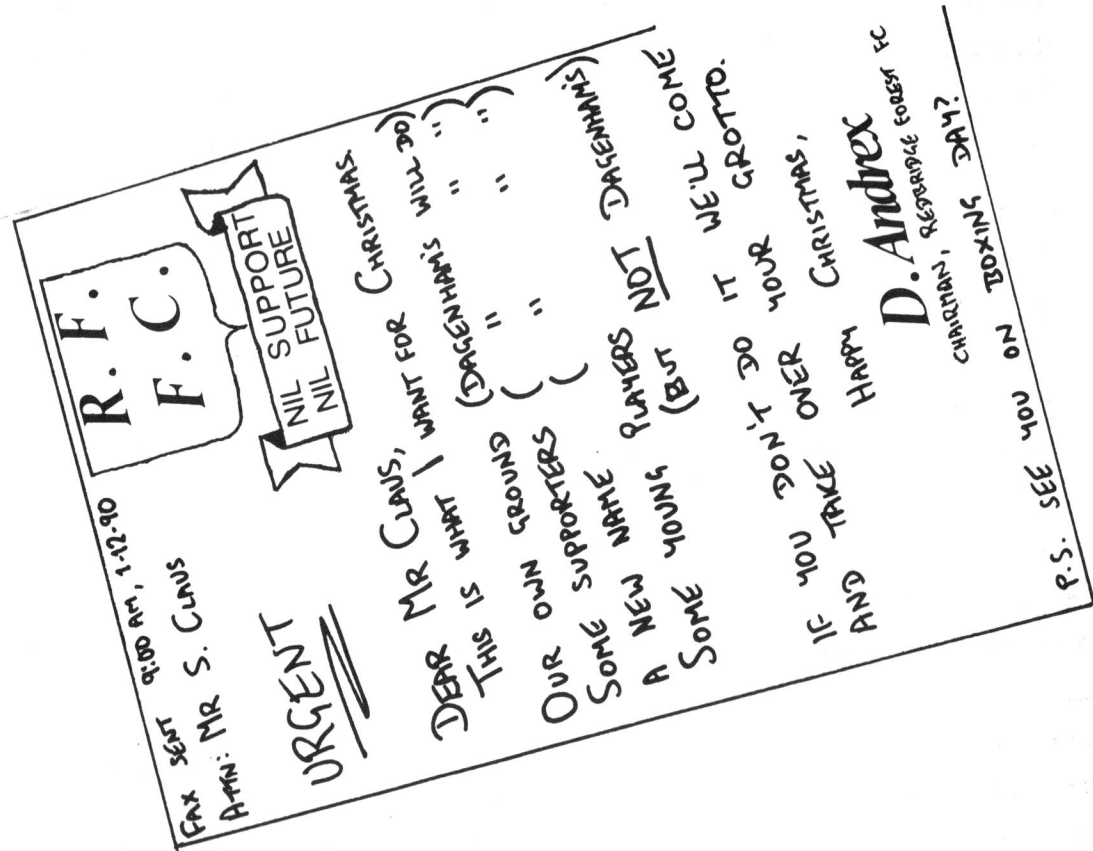

FAX SENT 9:00 AM, 1-12-90
ATTN: MR S. CLAUS

R.F.
F.C.

SUPPORT NIL
FUTURE NIL

URGENT

DEAR MR CLAUS,
THIS IS WHAT I WANT FOR CHRISTMAS.
(DAGENHAM'S WILL DO)

OUR OWN GROUND ( )
SOME SUPPORTERS ( )
A NEW NAME ( )
SOME YOUNG PLAYERS NOT DAGENHAM'S
(BUT WE'LL COME

IF YOU DON'T DO IT YOUR GROTTO.
AND TAKE OVER CHRISTMAS,
HAPPY CHRISTMAS,

D. Andrex
CHAIRMAN, REDBRIDGE FOREST FC

P.S. SEE YOU ON BOXING DAY?

COME ON DAGENHAM. USE YER FORWARDS

More fun than a
trip to Marlow

A GROUNDHOPPER'S LAMENT

(to the tune of Spitting Image's "I've Never Met A Nice South African")

I've eaten corned beef sandwiches at Weston-Super-Mare
And spent the night on British Rail stations everywhere
A friend of mine says he once saw five nil-nils in one day
And it's over fifteen years since he saw Hornchurch play away
      Last week I went to Gloucester
         in my mate's dad's helicopter
      But I've never seen a goal at Wokingham

No he's never seen a goal at Wokingham
And that's not bloody surprising man
Because he's only been there once, and the score was nil-nil

I haven't seen a goalie sent off since May '89
And it's twenty-seven matches since I last saw extra-time
I saw QPR reserves beat Chelsea 7-3 last year
And a 5-5 draw at Hythe versus Erith & Belvedere
      I've seen Woking fans with glasses
         with their brains stuck up their bottoms
      But I've never seen a goal at Wokingham

Nah, he's never seen a goal at Wokingham
And that's not bloody surprising man
'Cause they won't let him in anymore because he's so boring

I've seen West Allotment Celtic score a forty-yard o.g.
And it's ages since my goal average went down to less than three
I've done all the grounds in Essex but I haven't finished Kent
And the floodlights failed at Bognor Regis Town last time I went
      I've seen Eric Ryan sober
         (it was sometime in October)
      But I've never seen a goal at Wokingham

No he's never seen a goal at Wokingham,
And that's not bloody surprising man
Because we've never seen one either
Except for that 2-2 draw last year when he was at Cobham v Bedfont

Yes, we've seen a goal at Wokingham, but he's seen more goals than anyone
Because he's been to 1200 games in the last four seasons

Wembley. What does the name mean to you? I would wager that, despite many believing that it has passed its sell-by date, and the not unjustified allegations of tattiness, you still find magic in the word and consider the stadium to be the Mecca of sportsmen. I would hate to see it replaced by something resembling a flying saucer.

Wembley holds many memories for me. Around 1937 I lived in Wealdstone. I considered Wembley to be my local sports stadium, though I still travelled to Dagenham Speedway every Sunday. I watched ice hockey at the Pool and saw speedway racing at the Stadium regularly.

The only football I ever watched from the Wembley terraces was the 1968 F.A. Cup Final. All Dagenham's Wembley appearances were covered by me from the Press Gallery, or the Royal Box! I also covered several World Speedway Championship finals from the Press Gallery. I remember a commentator from Poland trying to hold a telephone conversation while politely standing to the British national anthem, to the amusement of seated scribes.

I shall never forget my introduction to the Press Gallery. The climb seemed endless, and I expected to see base camps on the upper landing and to be supplied with oxygen for the final assault. When the last flight was conquered, although obviously prepared for an aerial view, I was still staggered to see the bowl of the arena laid out far, far below me. I then descended a short flight into the Press Gallery, which resembled the gondola of an airship. The view was magnificent - after that first shock which, of course, was not repeated on future visits!

I also have very clear memories of my one appearance in the Royal Box. As secretary of Dagenham in 1980, I participated in the pre-match lunch, which was somewhat protracted. There was only time to meet Tom Finney before entering the Box, by which time the teams were ready to be presented - thus I missed all the exciting build-up on the terraces. Seated in a wicker armchair, I managed to observe protocol until Chris Maycock corkscrewed his way through to score the winner. I was out of my chair, arms aloft, and then realised I was the only one standing in the Box! But if I missed out by being in the Box, I was repaid when Denis Moore lifted the Trophy in front of me, as Dagenham officials brushed away a tear. I may be the only person to have covered a match from there!

One of Dagenham's appearances was soon after Wembley made the mistake of holding show jumping. The pitch was in a terrible state, patched with pieces of turf which hadn't had time to blend in. The players said it was extremely difficult to perform on. Yet Wembley now stage American Football there regularly! It is ironic that the stadium authorities decided to stop staging World Speedway Championship finals there, which only entailed lifting turf from the corners, because it interfered with soccer. Yet Wembley used to have its own speedway team without any problems.

I would be very interested to know how Wembley justifies the expulsion of speedway while providing the stadium for American Football!

THE MAD AXEMAN

A HISTORY OF FOOTBALL IN LANCASTER

(Note: Early dates are approximate due to a lack of surviving evidence e.g no programmes, fanzines etc)

BC3000: (or whenever): Life begins. Football begins in Lancaster. Burt Lancaster and Dickie Danson involved from the start; and still involved now.

AD45: Romans arrive to bolster Lancaster's defence - choosing the castle site not so much for its defensive advantages, but for the Giant Axe site just below.

350: After a 300 year unbeaten run at home, Romans leave, and sequence of managers and tribes can't halt the rot.

1066: French(Normans) beat England in international at Hastings. 1st list of British Football clubs compiled - known as Domesday Book - Lancaster feature.

1400s: Dirty game with York - known as "Battle of the Roses". Lancaster win after several replays and transfers.

1642: "Civil War" - a series of cup replays like Arsenal v Sheffield Wednesday in 1970s, except even Arsenal couldn't make a game last 7 years(Sure?).

1650: First City Cup run - knocked out by Scots under Charles 11 - who then lose at Preston.

1700s: Lancaster becomes a prosperous port town - mainly because sailors want to bring their ships to Lancaster to see the football team.

1905: After 100 years of football decline, new club formed. Dick Danson continues as Manager.

1930s: The golden years. The time to be a City fan.

1948, 1972: Cup runs, ended by Gateshead, then Notts County, only a step away from Wembley(2nd Round) We wuz robbed!

1975: Lancaster wins the FA Cup! Unfortunately, Alan Taylor, from Lancaster, was playing for West Ham at the time.

1976: City start to dictate National fortunes; Main stand burns down - causes crisis and Harold Wilson is forced to resign as Prime Minister.

1981: City Directors resign due to bankruptcy; Thatcher at lowest popularity rating.

1983: City revival, under lethal strikeforce of Dave Barnes and Andy 'good beard' Graham. Sadly, Thatcher also revives.

1985: Relegation, for the first time ever. Thatcher again unpopular.

1987: NPL 1st Division formed; things look up for City even though Keith 'God' Brindle plays his last game for City. Thatcher wins again(damn!)

1990: City, expected to challenge for promotion, don't live up to it. The social club burns down. Danson goes after 5000 years in charge(It seemed like it!). Thatcher cannot survive. (To find out what happens in the future, follow City's fortunes)

A LANCASTER CITY FANZINE

4 REASONS AGAINST ALL SEATER STADIA

1/OTHER FACILITIES WILL BE NEGLECTED: One of the things mentioned in the Taylor Report is making grounds more comfortable. This will not happen. Forcing clubs to install seats will mean that they will not have the money to upgrade other facilities. Toilets and tea-bars will be just as bad as ever. Clubs will not change their attitudes to fans due to the Taylor Report. Expect lots of uncomfortable seats at bad viewing angles, with poor access, grotty toilets, and rip-off catering.

2/TERRACES COULD BE MADE SAFE: Overcrowding at grounds has not always led to tragedy - because there are often other spaces for the fans to move onto - including the pitch. TMA safe terracing - no separation into pens without numbers being controlled at each(e.g turnstiles to all pens), clear gangways leading onto pitch or moats, no fencing, meaner calculation of capacity, more crush barriers, no restricted views through obstacle or shallow terrace, better designed approach to turnstiles for big grounds.

3/CAPACITIES WILL BE CUT: Obviously, this is an effect, restricting the numbers who can see games, possibly reducing interest in the game. Higher entrance to make up for this will have the same effect. This could only be rectified by new stadia - but no big clubs are planning these. At lower levels, effect could send some clubs to bankruptcy, for the game in general, less interest means less commercial interest, less players etc.

4/FOOTBALL'S NATURAL HABITAT WILL BE TAKEN AWAY: The game of football generates excitement on the terracing, and vice versa. Take away the terracing, and the game could become less exciting. It is difficult to generate excitement from seats, and this could harm the quality of the game.

OPPOSE THE TAYLOR REPORT. WE NEED A CAMPAIGN BEFORE IT IS TOO LATE. OTHERWISE, THE EFFECTS COULD OVERTAKE US ALL TOO SOON.

===
CITY FC ANNUAL DINNER - MAY 18 1990
===

Among the highlights of the annual senior presentation dinner was medical man, Brian Maudsley's epic monologue on receipt of his Clubman of the Year award. Receiving the Doug Gayton Trophy jointly with fellow "spongeman", Dave Hughes, Brian launched into a lengthy tirade in which he expressed his own dissappointment at the 1989/90 season.

Not for him gripes about missing key players at crucial times and seeing opponents escape with points in the face of intense City pressure. No, his chagrin concerned the lack of serious injury among players, and the all too infrequent calls on his expertise. Spattering his speech with words like pusillanimous (which provoked gape mouthed reaction fromthe bulk of his audience) Brian bemoaned the lack of success of Peter McCrae's attempts to get himself kickedby opponents, and berated his players' efforts to inflict damage on opponents. Of course, the high spot of the year was Martin Horsfield's superb pubic strain, quite the most outrageous injury he had come across in recent years. Unfortunately, the "Horse" was away checking it at the time.

===
PIE EATING CONTEST!
===

At the recent away game at Radcliffe(December 90) there was a contest of a different kind. A Pie and Peas eating contest, in fact, between Osher Williams(City skipper) who was out of the team but watching us there, and loyal supporter Jim (reknowned for his eating).

It was Jim who drew first blood, downing the first nearly half an hour before kick off, closely followed by Osher. Halfway through the first half Jim could wait no longer, and down went number 2, swilled down with a can of coke. As the half-time whistle came, Osher made a move to the tea bar in search of an equaliser. After queueing for 3 minutes he got it. 2-2. The second half started, and Jim was getting hungry again. He made his move to the tea bar. There was no stopping him now. The girl gave him a funny look as he bought his third. It was the winner for Jim, as Osher could find no reply. FINAL SCORE: O.Williams 2 Jim 3

Two clubs which we're directly involved in my becoming interested in the glorious world of non-league football we're Weymouth and my then local outfit, Weston-super-Mare A.F.C. Many people of the Avon seaside town probably don't even realise that the club exists, and those that do have probably only noticed when visiting the out-of-town shopping area which surrounds the clubs newish Woodspring Park ground. If you're a

The oval ball game is also another significant factor in the clubs low profile, with most of your physical-educational experience at the towns secondary schools comprising of 'slopping' an oversized 'egg' into a pool of mud, giving evidence of the apparant bias. Visit the Rugby ground, complete with impressive Grandstand, and further evidence will be gained, if it we're needed (it would make a nice Beazer Premier ground.....shame to waste

centre-half if ever there was one, perhaps best remembered in the football world as the man that Plymouth Argyle fans would sing, 'give us a hyphen' whilst reciting his name letter by letter.........terrific stuff although I never heard any of the old boys down at Wes' giving it a try! There was also ex-City and Rovers goalie, Ray Cashley who had a short spell as caretaker manager a few years ago and who has recently, unfortunately disappeared

unsuprisingly, he couldn't! And what about Jeff Pople? A young local lad (who even now is only 25) who had trials with Southampton (yes, the first division side!) yet I couldn't see for the life of me what the attraction was. At times, after another apparently mediocre performance I thought there might be something wrong with me, but as now he turns out for the delightfully named, Weston St. Johns in The Somerset Senior League I can sleep peacefully at

Harry Thomas's royal

schoolkid in the town, then you either support Bristol City or Bristol Rovers, so consequently if you tell them that you occasionally visit the town's local club then they automatically think that you've fallen from Mars. Many a wet lunch hour would be spent arguing with a City fan who would claim that Weston had no football team whatsoever, whilst he proudly waved a copy of The Today League's (as it was then) 4 divisional tables shouting, 'come on, find 'em on there then...'. It was almost enough to make you cry! The Rovers fans, being slightly more down to earth we're often more sympathetic to my cause - 100 miles from Brum and no cash to get me to St.Andrews every week. Just what am I supposed to do,....?

it on Rugger!).

What most people didn't seem to realise, was that Weston had a ground, a manager, a squad of players, and a league..........in fact all the things that the likes of City and Rovers had albiet on an aledgedly grander scale.

And in the mid-eighties (ah, my era!) they even had some big-names gracing the poorly drained pitch - more than enough to keep a nostalgic City or Rovers fan happy for 90 minutes. Players like Forbes Phillipson-Masters - a reliable brute of a

from the 'Weston scene'. For those that didn't know him, 'Cash' was a sort of Peter Shilton, John Burridge clone that could shout himself horse through the course of 90 minutes....if ever there was a fanzine dedicated to a man then this surely is it - boy, could that man TALK! It wasn't all one-way transfers though, because in 1983 Terry Cooper decided that Weston centre-forward, John Palmer, a huge tank of a man could transfer his Western League form to that of the fourth division. Rather,

night, knowing that my supreme talent spotting skills we're pretty hot even in them days!

Then there was the ones that should have made it; David 'Jockey' Craig, a local centre-half 2 years older than Pople and who spent 2 different spells at 'The Seagulls' sailing through each 90 minutes of Western League football as if they didn't exist. In the hum-drum existance of The Premier Division, Craig stood out as a quality act (like Pavarotti appearing at The Red Lion!). The sort of defender that when an opposition goal seemed a mere formality, he suddenly emerged (alá Des Walker) from the mud and sea mist to make a last-ditch tackle to save the points not to mention the blushes of his teammates. The highest he reached however, was

let's get
talking
an alternative view of non-league football

spells in Cyprus, Bath, Cheltenham and Gloucester until injury unfortunately brought his career to an abrupt end. At this time the manager (previously the player-manager) was Harry Thomas, the stereotyped non-league club servant who played about a million games for their clubs, except in Thomas's case it was a mere 800! For a while his able assistant was a certain Richard Harris (no, not **that** one) who had developed the unusual

some beating. Thankfully (looking back on it) I stopped short of asking him for an autograph - I don't know who would have been the more embarrassed! One player who I certainly never saw in any newsagent stroke bookshop in the town was Kim Metcalf, a centre-forward whose presence ironically helped keep Somers in the reserves, with a useful run in the 1986/87 season as the target man beside Nigel Jones. Metcalf was about nine and a half feet

being tackled. This seemed to be a deliberate attempt to avoid doing himself damage, and so instead of falling into a sprawled heap, he 'sort of' folded over in a robot-like effect then got up and trotted away.....(you'd have to have seen it to appreciate it!)

Of course, there were others - all interesting in their own individual ways. Some were merely interesting because they were so uninteresting! The supporters on the other hand were never quite as memorable, most of them being rather placid although there was one man who was in his mid-twenties and who stood out as the nearest thing 'Wes' had to a football hooligan (ya know, one of those people that the papers are always going on about!) On the occasions when I saw him (which seemed quite often, 'cos he seemed to be a regular), he appeared to be a somewhat quite sort of chap, who wouldn't have given a couple of coachloads of Leeds fans any trouble at all, if **that** F.A. Cup run had ever materialised. I did though, learn of one story about him from a school friend (a City fan, even), which told of how he, in an F.A. Cup game (probably 1982) versus the then mighty Weymouth at the clubs old Langford Road Ground, objected to a refereeing decision which went the way of the Dorset side. Our hero then preceeded to run half the length of the pitch from the corner flag, along the touchline until level

with the referee. Once he was sure that he he had the man in black's undivided attention (and **only** then) he dramatically raised his erect middle finger skywards to the horror of the conservative Weston crowd.

Yet this was Weston-super-Mare A.F.C., a whole world away from an Alan Walsh thunderbolt at Ashton Gate and a Vaughan Jones contract dispute at Twerton Park - this was **real** football played in front of usually the same 250 loyal servants every other week. So whilst the Rovers and City fans would argue on a Monday morning in a treble lesson of Social and Economic History, whether Glyn Riley was a better forward than Steve White, I could lie back in my chair safe in the knowledge that if you added them both together, they still wouldn't be a match for Richard 'Golly' Harris! But, if I tried explaining it, they just wouldn't believe me.....

blue army...

nickname of 'Golly' which was no racist comment towards the colour of his skin because he was as pale as freshly driven snow, yet there was no doubting that the nickname seemed to suit his awkward appearance in some strange and wonderful way. Perhaps those that gave him the name thought that 'lumbering carthorse' was too much of a mouthful with it no doubt doing him an injustice because somehow (God knows how) he **did** score goals, and lots of 'em too!

For a football supporter though, the first brush with stardom is never an easy thing to forget and in my case , seeing reserve team centre-forward, Wayne Somers (it really was **him**, honest!) in Weston's WHSMITH is an experience which is always going to take

tall (okay, so I exagerate a wee bit), weighing about six stone and who often resembled a horse (for some strange reason) when in action - you'd have had to have seen it to understand what I'm on about. One player who did promise more was Steve Tapp, a small winger based at R.A.F. Locking (as we're several players) and who obviously had that 'certain something', yet (yep, you've guessed it!) didn't often show it-frustrating bugger (typical winger!!!). An equally memorable player, but for different reasons was full back, Peter McCall complete with a very strong Bristolian accent and looking about 103 due to his balding appearance but who gave many steady performances on the left, often including his memorable 'fall' when

AYLOTT OF MEMORIES

You are standing on the terraces watching your team bear down on goal, but your man completely fluffs the chance. The opposing fans do not bray like donkeys nor do they release an ear-splitting AAARGH! No, with one voice they pick up the unique cry of "HELLO, HELLO- SON OF AYLOTT! SON OF AYLOTT!". You can only be watching your team play Crystal Palace!

Its over five years since big Trev skied a close-range effort in anger for Palace, but the legend lives on in the memories of long-suffering Palace fans of the early/mid eighties. Palace fans seem to enjoy making a cult (sic!) out of less-talented players- witness the Semi-Final deification of Alan "Supa-Al" Pardew, however, quite how Trevor Aylott came to be given honorary membership of the "carrot-crunching" Club when his predecessors included the likes of Tommy Langley, Ian Edwards and Andy McCulloch is open for debate. Perhaps its just that "son of McCulloch" doesn't quite have the same ring to it. Okay, so alongside Ian Wright, Mark Bright and, latterly John Salako, the Order of the Hoof seems appropriate, but compared to "the stable" of his predecessors some of those long-term supporters aren't quite so quick to pin that title on the Donkey!

Trevor was nothing if not memorable, not only for his actions, but also by the significance of goals he scored. Those hardcore fans still speak reasonably fondly of him, he is seen almost as a chink of light at the end of what was a very long and dark tunnel! They recall the time when his brace sunk Hull at Boothferry Park, one of those goals (their voices fall to a reverential whisper) was a Back-heel from three yards out! They still puzzle over the F.A. Cup replay with Millwall when he headed a perfectly good goal only to be pole-axed by the Lions' keeper and then suffer the final indignity of having the foul awarded to the Goalkeeper! They'll tell you of his last goal in his penultimate appearance in a Palace shirt away at Barnsley after coming on as Sub. helping us to a 4-2 victory. Significant because it was three long years since we had scored four in one game and a whopping nine years since doing it away from home! The game is still regarded by many as the start of the "good times".

So much for the goals he scored, just how did he get this "four-legged" reputation. Perhaps it was the application of his boot to the odd goalmouth scramble which invariably steered the ball away from its intended target, or perhaps the one-on-one's with the 'keeper that had the Holmesdale end taking bets on which post he would roll the resulting effort past, or the power-drive headers that so terrified fans on the Sainsburys' terrace, or even the moments when Trev just couldn't get out of the way of one of his team-mates screamers. He was generally good for all of those tricks in any one game!

After 55 full appearances and 13 goals for Palace, Trevor finally sought out a quieter pasture in the Third Division with Bournemouth and, yes, the predictable joke of giving kiddies rides on his back along the beach surfaced in all its glory(?). He had the last laugh there though, his goals helped the Cherries to the Third Division Championship that season! However it should be noted that his performances against Palace were of the standard that had come to be expected of him. The Palace fans always took vocal delight in his shortcomings, but he recalled after a 3-0 defeat that it was no worse than he used to get when he was here!

Seldom does a week go by without his name being chanted at some wayward opponent. We wonder if this is a some kind of record or are there other Clubs' fans who sing in commemoration of the misdemeanours of a player who left them over six seasons ago! Ironic also, to think that those fans who make most of the noise at Palace probably never saw him play for us! Other Palace players of that era are now long forgotten, but not Big Trev - a "memorable" player, indeed!

SO GLAD YOU'RE MINE!

MAD AS A HATTER!

A LUTON TOWN FANZINE

Fanzine Sharing

– The Shock Revelations

Correspondents in When Saturday Comes included letters which sought to denigrate the current state of the Fanzine market, essentially on the grounds that there are too many and therefore the available talent is spread too thinly. Well, there is a section of the Taylor Report which addresses this problem but was suppressed and never published. By a manner which I cannot reveal the suppressed section has come into my possession and it can now be revealed to the public.

Its findings show that there are not just too many fanzines but that the spread is non-uniform across the country. For example many clubs have only one whereas others have up to five, with one club, Leeds, having six. Studies of this show that, contrary to expectations, the number is not proportional to the average attendances at the clubs. This can not be better illustrated than by comparing Wimbledon with Manchester City. Both clubs have three fanzines which leads to a ratio of 2585 fans per fanzine for Wimbledon compared with 9325:1 for Manchester City. Of course this compares favourably with the Enfield ratio of 420:1 but non-league clubs are outside the scope of this Report. Incidentally the league record for the lowest is held, surprisingly, by Cardiff who manage four fanzines leading to a ratio of 910:1.

The reason then? Well it is suggested that where strong local rivalries exist the number is disproportionately large. For example look at the following clubs: Newcastle 4, Sunderland 5; Man. City 3, Man. Utd. 5; Ipswich 3, Norwich 5; Luton 3, Watford 3. The Report concludes that such proliferation is bad for fanzine standards and sets a minimum fan/fanzine ratio of 9000:1. It also goes on to recommend that fanzines should only be read sitting down and that they should only be sold to bearers of club membership cards. The lack of balance is also mentioned and it is recommended that fanzines are compelled to allow the real supporters in the executive boxes to have their say too. A national fanzine for the true supporter in his or her armchair is also recommended. These measures, says the Report, *'will lead to a reduction in the congestion in the roads leading to the ground before the match'*.

But what about those clubs which have less than the 9000:1 ratio? The proposals will mean that hundreds of perfectly good fanzines can no longer be legally sold? Well, the radical proposal of fanzine sharing is proposed, with the proviso that such fanzines should not publish material which criticises one of the sharing clubs. Indeed the Report states that *'it would not be conducive to good relations between sets of football supporters to allow criticism of football club performances to be published'*. This is perhaps the silliest notion of all and shows how out of touch the Report is with what fans really want. It is impossible to see how this would be palatable to the fans of clubs with close rivalries. How do the authorities expect Luton fans to say nice things about Watford? It is this sort of arrogance that brings disrepute on this Report.

The most controversial proposal of all is that fanzines contributors must be registered with a new trust which will be set up to regulate the industry. I can reveal that the chairmanship of this trust will be offered to none other than Robert Maxwell. To be registered the fanzine will have to pay a fee of £1 per fan, leading of course to a minimum fee of £9,000. Grants will be available from the trust but all would-be editors must possess an MA in literature or sociology. This, says the Report, *'will lead to a rise in standards that can only be good for the game as a whole'*. All contributions will be vetted by a specially selected panel of league club chairmen to, as the Report puts it, *'ensure consistency'*.

As I said above the Report has been suppressed till now but

COLD BALLS COCK-UP

News has reached us that Luton Town were responsible for a dreadful error that marred the draw for the Third Round of the Rumbelows Cup. This is how our source who was present at the draw described the shambles:

"The list for the draw was done in alphabetical order to try and make things easier for David Dent to understand. Because time was dragging on - it was already past Bill Fox's bedtime - and the Bradford-Luton tie was still undecided, we had to make a choice as to who to include in the list so that we could refrigerate Liverpool's ball to ensure that they got their usual favourable draw.

"We decided Luton would go through so David put ball number 18 into the fridge. All was proceeding according to plan until that *!?@?X Dowie missed his penalty, for Luton's defeat meant that we had to re-jig the draw in a hurry. This made Liverpool number 19 in the draw and, as Bill had nodded off, we had to make the draw straight away - Liverpool's ball was not "cold" and of course the consequences were disastrous - Manchester United v Liverpool. Ian St John was in the studio and he was fuming I can tell you - 'heads must roll' he muttered darkly as he left to catch the last bus home - But it was all on tape and even we couldn't destroy the evidence. Mind you, Nick Owen thought the whole episode highly amusing ..."

Expatriate

---

is due to be published at the end of this season by the direct order of John Major who points to the already successful fanzine share of Chelsea, Rangers and Linfield. I am afraid that those fans who thought our troubles were over with the demise of Thatcher will be sadly disappointed.

So the conclusions are controversial but do they make sense? Do they address the real problems affecting fanzines today? After all do we want to restrict fanzine contributions to the elite or should they be open to all? Surely fanzines are too important to only be read and written by fans with MAs in literature? If you feel as strongly about this as I do then write to your MP now, get your branch of the FSA to take this up and give the authorities and the doubters this message: 'We may not be perfect, we may not always be up to the standards of Shakespeare but we demand the right to say what we want, how we want, when we want. Hands off our Fanzines!!!'

TUSSAUDS BID FAILS

An audacious bid by Leisure giants Tussauds to buy the entire Watford defence for its Madame Tussauds Waxworks has been turned down by Manager Colin Lee, who would prefer an exchange deal to the straight cash offer made by Tussauds.

Tussauds spokesman Jack Theripper said of their swoop: "We have watched Watford several times recently and it is clear that their defence would be ideal for us, being a complete load of dummy's, expert at adopting a statuesque pose when caught on the break. They could go straight in to our Chamber of Horrors!"

Hornets Manager Colin Lee insisted however that the offer of £9.72 for the four players was derisory, although he confirmed he would consider an exchange deal. Negotiations are said to be continuing.

I Believe......

I'm prepared to believe John Fashanu's an international
And I'm prepared to believe Mark Dennis is perfectly rational
I'm prepared to believe that Liverpool do not bleat
And I'm prepared to believe Diego isn't a cheat
I believe Peter Reid's not old enough for a bathchair
And I'm prepared to believe that Greg Downs once had hair

I'm prepared to believe P*** G******** looks much leaner
And I believe Peter Shilton never knew Tina
I'm prepared to believe Jimmy Hill's not a prat
And I even believe Philip Carter isn't fat
I'm prepared to believe Watford aren't really shit
BUT I CAN'T BELIEVE GRAHAM RODGER IS NEARLY FIT!!

South Liverpool FC

I GUESS THAT'S WHY THEY CALL IT THE BLUES.

I GUESS THAT'S WHY THEY CALL IT THE BLUES IS A TITLE OF AN ELTON JOHN CLASSIC SONG, BUT AT SOUTH LIVERPOOL F.C. IT AS A HOLE NEW MEANING FROM 1983 SOUTH LIVERPOOL HAVE NEVER DONE TO WELL IN CUP FINALS WHEN THE OPPOSITION HAVE BEEN PLAYING IN BLUE, THE LIVERPOOL SENIOR CUP FINAL OF 1983 SOUTH PLAYED EVERTON AT GOODISON PARK, WARWICK RIMMER GOT THE ONLY GOAL OF THE GAME FROM THE PENALTY SPOT, IN 1985 IN SUNNY PRESTON AT THE HOME OF PRESTON NORTH END, SOUTH WHERE PLAYING IN THE DAIRY CREST FINAL TO THE EX DERBY COUNTY & NOTTS FOREST PLAYER JOHN MCGOVIN'S TEAM HORWICH RMI WITH NO LUCK ON ARE SIDE WE RAN OUT LOSES BY TWO GOALS TO NIL (2-0). THEN IN 1988-89 SEASON WE PLAYED TWO MORE FINALS, THEY WERE TWO FINALS YOU WOULD LIKE TO FORGET, FIRST WE LOST TO BANGOR CITY AT HOME 1-3 IN THE FIRST LEG OF THE PRESIDENT CUP FINAL THEN LOST 2-0 IN THE SECOND LEG, THE OTHER FINAL WAS EVEN WORST IT WAS THE FLOODLIGHT FINAL (EX DAIRY CREST) WE PLAYED AT CHORLEY F.C. GROUND AND LOST BY AN EVEN GOAL IN FIVE, NOW THATS GOT YOU PUZZELD, WE LOST 4-1 TO STALYBRIDGE CELTIC. I HAVE COME TO THE CONCLUSION NEXT TIME WE ARE DUE TO PLAY A TEAM IN BLUE IN A FINAL LETS JUST GIVE THEM THE TROPHY AT THE START OF THE GAME THEN WE CAN SPEND ARE TIME DOING SOMETHING LESS BORING.

South Liverpool against MS

South Liverpool FC resigned from the HFS League in May 1991.

They are now suffering from what we call "the JS decline".

Just like the people who want to help with MS, there are some South Liverpool fans trying to get the club back on the football map. If they succeed, the new club chairman, Mike "General Custer" Broken, is hoping to have the new South Liverpool FC (1991) back in a league for the 1992/3 season (note the new name).

Let's hope this is no idle talk. We have had our fair share of this over the years.

I do think South will get over their crisis, but there are people with MS who will suffer for years and years, so every little bit helps.

I am only too glad to have helped in what Football Fans Against MS are doing.

Let's hope one day we find a cure for MS.

Paul Webster, editor, *Southender* fanzine

ONE DAY THE SOUTH WILL RISE AGAIN UNTIL THEN READ SOUTHENDER SOUTH LIVERPOOL F.C. FANZINE (1991)

The Southender

Screen Sport

by Barry Normal

April has brought a remarkable crop of football-related movies out on video. Here are just a few of the better ones:-

Home Alone
The story of how a young boy survives three months on his own after being left at the ground following a Halesowen Harriers' home game.

The Comfort Of Strangers
A period piece recalling the halcyon days of Lye Town when they could look forward to money-spinning holiday games with the Yeltz.

Last Tango In Paris
Michel Platini and his search for a can of orange.

Awakenings
Maverick doctor brings Stourbridge fans out of thirty year comas by prescibing drugs with ultimately tragic consequences. A touching film, especially when the fans awaken from their trances and decide to go down The Grove to watch a decent standard of football.

Major League
Unlikely tale of an ineffectual Prime Minister who tries desparately to boost his popularity by personally sponsoring the Football League.

Killing Fields
Shocking exposé of the misery brought about by the brutal and cynical regimé of the People's Republic of Wealdstone.

My Left Foot
Tear-jerking true story of the Beazer League right back who overcomes all the odds to learn to kick the ball with both feet.

And why not?!

Halesowen Town —
Follow Your Instinct

In Strictest Confidence

Due to a Post Office mix-up, a copy the FA's previously unpublished "Blueprint for Football : The Real Version" was delivered by mistake to FYI Mansions. After much heart-searching we decided it was in the public's interest to risk prosecution and reveal the contents of this secret report.

The central theme of the paper was the creation of a new Super League comprising 18 teams with a revolutionary new points scheme. Teams with only one word in their name (ie Liverpool, Arsenal, Everton, Spurs and ManU - the latter being the new name of the current Cup-Winners Cup holders) will receive 4 pts for a win, 3 for a draw and 2 for a defeat. Teams with more than one word in their name (ie Aston Villa, Nottm Forest, Chelsea United, Southampton City etc.) will receive 2 pts for a win, 1 for a draw and nothing if they lose.

Although this scheme appears a trifle harsh on some of the teams, there will be no relegation unless a club's ground falls below the required standard of "20,000 seats and really nice toilets for the visiting Chairman's wife".

For teams outside the Super League, it was envisaged they set up regional leagues of 3-4 teams (eg Wolves, Albion, Blues and Walsall) and play endless games against each other so fans would soon lose interest and spend all their money watching Super League football.

It was predicted that non-league football would benefit greatly from the new proposals as all teams outside the Super League would henceforth be designated 'non-league', resulting in a much strenghtened FA Trophy. Semi-professional teams would be allowed to carry on much as before as long as they didn't make any money.

An FA spokesperson we phoned denied that the document actually existed, and even if it did the proposals were for the good of the game and absolutely nothing to do with the big clubs wanting to keep all the money for themselves, honest.

Let's Raise a Glass to...

Number 1 in a series of,um...er...well, one at the moment (but there might be some more in future if you're really lucky !!) recounting some of the greatest moments in Yeltz matches gone by. To kick-off with, here's one memory we at FYI will treasure for the rest of our days.

'Twas the spring of 1983 and everything in the garden was lovely. VS Rugby were lined up for demolition in the FA Vase final at Wembley in a weeks time, the West Midlands League title was all but wrapped up and we'd booked a place in the League Cup final. With a week to go to the Vase final a day out in deepest Derbyshire seemed rather a good idea, so off we all went to that centre of football excellence that is Gresley. They were around mid-table at the time but included David Nish, Roger Davies and Kevin Hector in the team. Little did these internationally famous stars realise that they would be eclipsed by the mighty talent that made up that colossus of the game - Les Frosser.

STOMACH

Now, for those who don't remember him, Les bore a striking resemblance to Clive James and was so laid back on the pitch he was almost horizontal. The only way

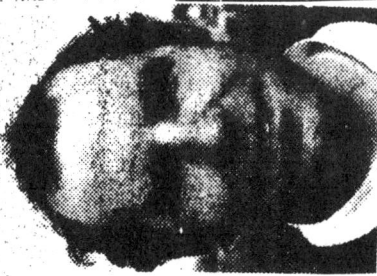

Les Prosser

he remained upright was to use his stomach as a counterweight.

INTESTINES

We're sorry to say, most of the match has been forgotten in these parts, so overshadowed was it by the piece of skill which was to follow.

It was late in the second half, Les had come on as substitute and taken up his customary position at full-back. He picked up the ball just inside his own half and, in an amazing burst of speed, broke into a brisk walk towards the half-way line. After playing a neat one-two that would have put the Brazilians of 1970 to shame, he continued on towards the Gresley goal.

LUNGS

By now, Les had reached full speed and was hurtling along at a rate of knots only fractionally slower than that of a giant tortoise as he approached the oppositions penalty area. Bets were being taken around the ground as to whether he would actually make it to the other end and, if so, whether he could reach it before the referee blew the final whistle.

We needn't have worried. With the Gresley defence bearing down on this solitary figure, Les summoned up those extra reserves of effort that only superheroes can manage at times like this, and let fly with an unstoppable, cannonball of a shot that flew into the top corner from 25 yards. The clouds parted, the sun came out and the birds started singing.

HEART

Les left us at the end of the following season and missed out on the Wembley appearance he so richly deserved. Okay, so maybe he was fat, bald and slow but he definetely knew how to compensate using his experience and his brain (a rare enough trait in most footballers). We would like to take this opportunity to wish Les all the best wherever he is now, and thank him for the memories. Cheers Les !!

Coming soon, possibly (i.e. send us enough money and we won't print it !!) a tale of three people, an umbrella, a monsoon, a field in Ledbury and 5 goals from Geoff Moss.

Every Saturday is such an exciting day for me. I wake up at half past four to let my cat, Tiddles, out. I then wake my wife up so that she can cook me a lovely big breakfast. I do so like bacon, sausages, egg and cornflakes before setting off on a long journey to a new ground. I then wake up my one year old daughter. She comes to every game with me. She never complains, so she must enjoy it. Today we're going to see Puddlethwaite Rangers Reserves. They play in the little village of Puddlethwaite - about 450 miles away. At half past five, I put my daughter, Loakes (I named her after Wycombe Wanderers old ground) in the boot and I kissed my wife goodbye. As I pulled away in my Morris Minor, I ran over Tiddles. Never mind, I can always get another cat on Monday.

Soon we're on the motorway. I especially like travelling in the autumn, as you can see the pretty leaves changing colour and falling from the trees. Whilst on the motorway, I see five naked young women, holding a sign saying "Puddlethwaite". I mustn't stop however, as I must get to the ground at least two hours before kick-off.

I pulled into the club's car-park at precisely eight minutes to one. I opened the boot. Loakes is crying. I bought an ice-cream for her, making sure that there is strawberry sauce on it, and give it to her. I then shut the boot once more. How she loves her soccer.

At exactly one o'clock, I went to the secretary's office to buy a programme. I spent an hour chatting to him, about how my Great Aunt Elsie once knew a man who had stayed for two days in a town no more than about 100 miles from Puddlethwaite. It's a small world, isn't it?

After an hour of chatting with the secretary, I noticed that he had tied his belt around his neck and was hanging from the ceiling, so I decided to walk around the pitch. I took photographs of each corner flag, the penalty spot, and the goalposts. The penalty spot was particularly well looked after, and the picture will take pride of place in my collection. Although it was raining quite heavily, I decided to stand behind a hedge next to the half-way line. Although I had to stand in a pile of cow dung, I think I had the best possible view of the pitch from here. I took two pictures of the dung, as it had a colour and texture quite unlike any other I had ever seen before.

The match started at twenty seven seconds past three o'clock, and I counted another seven people in the ground. Unfortunately, there was no public address system in the ground so I had no idea whether the teams on the pitch were as those printed in the programme. I therefore walked around the pitch until I reached the managers' benches. I went up to the home manager just as his team had conceded a very dodgy penalty, and I asked him if he could give me his team line up.

I remember waking up in a hospital just outside Puddlethwaite. The clock opposite me told me that it was five o'clock. The match had finished. I took the tubes out of my arms, and removed the bandages from my head, and jumped out of bed. I not only had to find out the result of the game, but I had to write a report of my day out for all you lovely readers of "Non-League Football Magazine".

Non-League soccer is such good family entertainment, and I promise to write more stories of my future adventures.

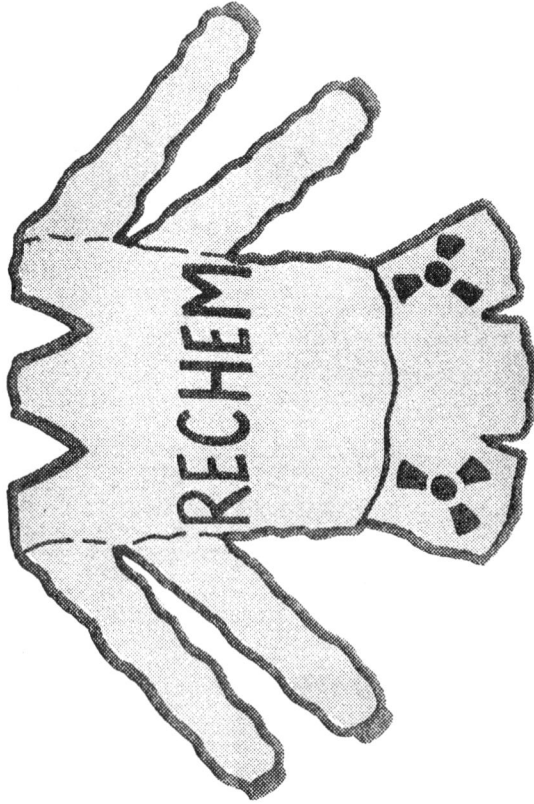

A JOURNEY THROUGH THE F.A. CUP 1988/89

<u>THE DAY GOD PLAYED FOR SUTTON</u>

In season 1988/89, fulfilling a desire I had held ever since reading Brian James' "Tividale to Wembley" a decade earlier, I followed the course of the FA Cup competition from its humblest beginnings to the Final. I did so in the traditional manner, choosing a tie (almost) at random in the Preliminary Round, following the winners until they were knocked out, then following their conquerors and so on to Wembley. I chose a good year to do it, and found myself accompanying two clubs in succession through some of the greatest moments in their history.

My trail began three miles from Wembley Stadium as the crow flies, in front of 55 spectators at Hanwell Town. Hanwell, in their first ever FA Cup tie, disposed of the renowned Corinthian Casuals 4-0, and won through to the 2nd Round Qualifying by winning at Erith and Belvedere. The early rounds, though intriguing in themselves - Hanwell lost to Wembley FC, Wembley to Walton and Hersham - gave no structure to the unfolding story until, one bitterly cold late October afternoon, Walton drew 1-1 away to a club about whom, and about whose manager, very little was known by the public at large. The manager was Barrie Williams, and the club Sutton United.

Sutton had the worst away record in the Conference, but were galvanised by the return of striker Lenny Dennis, who had recently played for Jamaica in a World Cup qualifier against the USA, into scoring eight without reply in three away ties. 3-0 in the replay, 4-0 at Dagenham and 1-0 at Aylesbury, and Sutton were in the third round draw, where they were paired with Coventry City. And everyone knows what happened next...

In the fourth round Sutton went down to perhaps the most prestigious 8-0 defeat in football history, against an outstanding Norwich City side who, to their own supporters' disbelief, were reaching out towards the Double. Following Norwich to the semi-final via thrilling ties against Sheffield United and West Ham was a privilege: there can never have been a better time to be a Norwich supporter, as their team vied with Arsenal and Liverpool for the League leadership and appeared destined for Wembley as well. Yet their season collapsed in the space of two April weeks: decisive league defeats and a 1-0 loss to Everton at Villa Park. As for the "Casuals to Cup-Winners" story, that too changed in tone, in a far more serious fashion. As Pat Nevin scrambled the ball over the line for the Everton winner, I was preoccupied listening to radio reports of what was happening at Hillsborough. The game I was watching was fated to be a footnote in football history, and football itself was never to be quite the same again.

But back to a winter's day when football really was about joy, tension, excitement and the unexpected. Back to Gander Green Lane on 7 January 1989.

Every once in a while there takes place a match of which you will boast to friends for years to come, "I was there". In my case the Arsenal v Manchester United Cup Final of 1979 comes into this category, along with a few others - Manchester City 10 Huddersfield 1 comes to mind. This third-round Cup-tie has taken its place alongside them.

Coventry City have perhaps the unique distinction among football clubs of being the subject of a famous Monty Python joke: the "Communist Quiz" sketch in which Lenin is told, "No, that was a trick question, Coventry City have never won the FA Cup". On that momentous day in 1987 Coventry ruined the sketch and ceased to be a joke. With eight of the men who won the Cup taking the field at Sutton, Coventry at last had a team whose names rolled off the tongue - if this could ever truly be said of Steve Ogrizovic. Moreover, their preparation for this match was highly impressive - a 5-0 drubbing of Sheffield Wednesday, one of the highspots of a season which thus far saw the club fifth in Division One. Sutton, by contrast, had contrived to lose in the Conference to their second round Cup victims Aylesbury United, and remained without an away win from twelve matches.

Gander Green Lane, whose average attendance is comfortably under four figures, was heaving with an all-ticket 8,000 sellout crowd, which spelt a Happy New Year to the treasurer. In the queues people were vying with each other to establish their Loyal Sutton Supporter credibility. On the terraces, a couple of inflatable bananas fought it out with a crocodile. In the programme notes, Barrie Williams suggested that "the everlasting team-work of every bloomin' soul" just might pull it off. These words were soon to become the best-known Kipling quote outside "If".

My section of terracing - or rather, grassy bank - was a veritable conclave of the "When Saturday Comes" superhero, The Bloke Behind Me. One of the best exchanges went something like: "It's all kick and rush and punt the ball upfield at this level, isn't it?" - "Yeah, that's how Coventry have always played." Another couple of chaps, eminently respectable, were calling out tactical advice throughout the game, from the pragmatic - "Kick Speedie" - to the David Pleat School reasoned coaching - "Come on, lad, kick Speedie, that's it" - to the plain psychopathic - "Kick Speedie, NOOOWW!"

As for the on-field activities, these are now the stuff of legend. Coventry started as if they meant to blow the opposition away, and Sutton, to their credit, withstood the barrage. The first real indication that the giants were not to have it all their own way came when Kilcline missed an easy header, and minutes later Hanlan beat his full-back and crossed for Dennis to shoot. Kilcline's face took the full force of the shot, and he was felled. From the subsequent corner any one of half a dozen Sutton men could have got the vital toepoke.

Nevertheless Speedie, Bennett and Regis all missed reasonable chances as half-time drew near. Then came that fateful 42nd minute: the near-post corner flicked on by Golley, and the emphatic header by Tony Rains that Kilcline could only help into the net. The crowd erupted as a hope they had hardly dared to admit began to come true. Half-time, 1-0.

Rains, in his 613th game for the club, was easily man of the match,

and only once did his defence slip. In the 52nd minute, a finely-worked move from goal via Bennett and Sedgley found Phillips exploiting a large gap in the back four for a simple Coventry equaliser. We all thought, the game's up, it was fun while it lasted. Barrie Williams' boys had other ideas. The goal was just the prelude to Sutton's moment of glory, the corner that, as the nation soon knew, had not worked in training that morning, but now turned Sutton's cup run overnight from one-inch stories to two-inch headlines. Six minutes later, Stephens, to Dawson, deep into the goal area for Hanlan, and 2-1. Another eruption.

Hanlan himself blew a golden chance created by Dennis two minutes later, and as Sutton threatened an even more astonishing scoreline, Dawson shot feebly wide after a move whose flowing arrogance had First Division written all over it. Attack was proving the best form of defence, but it couldn't play that role for ever.

Those last twenty minutes were beyond belief. Laudable as their presence was, the Match of the Day cameras, partly due to editing and partly to the limitations of the format, could not convey all the excitement of that period. They failed to show a brilliant Bennett overhead kick which was barely a foot over the bar. They could not convey the effects on a palpitating crowd of Coventry's near misses: a header won by Speedie from which Regis's shot miraculously came off the legs of Roffey; a Sedgley attempt which hit both post and bar, while the net billowed as if struck by the ball; a Kilcline header which was cleared by Robyn Jones in a manner, I kid you not, reminiscent of that Banks save from Pele. And the cameras had not a hope of communicating the tension of every Coventry attack, the ratchet-like effect of a situation where every minute passed was a mountain climbed, where hearts hesitated every time Bennett found space on the left. The suspended relief when Roffey lined up a goal-kick and we noticed the referee taking a long serious look at his watch. And the supreme moment... the final whistle.

I had followed Sutton through five matches dating back to October, and I was jumping up and down and singing the Yellows' praises. Around me, people who had supported Sutton for decades, and had the battered scarves to prove it, were utterly beside themselves. A young man whose girlfriend was sharing his moment of euphoria over the team he had supported since the age of six, was simply muttering "Unbelievable" over and over again.

As the ranks of the committed thinned a little on the pitch, and the players took their salutes in the stands, we ambled across the field of play, visualising Tony Rains' view of a hell-for-leather Coventry attack, and made our way to the bar. Backstage, Rains and Hanlan were being interviewed on the radio, Trevor Brooking beamed, Cyrille Regis passed the well-wishers on his way to a subdued coach, and Barrie Williams prepared to enter Cup legend as "the man who quoted Kipling in his programme notes the day his team beat Coventry". Perhaps the whole afternoon was summed up by a supporter who said, "Well, we had God in goal for us today". Surely nothing could top this. It was the finest day in Sutton United's history.

Or was it? Two days later Tony Rains and Matthew Hanlan appeared on "Wogan".

BRIAN SPURRELL

SUTTON UNITED
COVENTRY CITY
at the Borough Sportsground, Gander Green Lane, Sutton
on Saturday 7th January 1989. K.O. 2.00 p.m.
Admission to Ground £5
Sold subject to ground rules as displayed

THREE -ONLY- ONE

MARK -D'ARBY 91-92

FIVE OF THE BEST:A SEASON'S HIGHLIGHTS

1.6th October 1990
Sheffield United(away)2-1
Scorers:Fairweather,Fashanu.

Undoubtedly in my mind one of the season's highlights.This match had been built up as the purist's nightmare,Wimbledon against Wimbledon clones.An extra edge was added to this by the ex-player connection:Jones and Morris,with Bassett of course now United manager.
Your humble editor(Andrew)turned up at Bramall Lane at about 2.30 to meet Russell,Donna,Stuart and friends on the terrace.I was all prepared for the big match,and before the kick-off,I proceeded to hand out 60 Vinnie Jones masks on the terrace,to commemorate the occasion.So,to the match itself.

With 11minutes gone,United took a lead as David Barnes swept a left-foot shot into the left-hand corner of Hans Segers'goal after some defensive confusion. But the equaliser was not far away as Carlton Fairweather netted with an overhead kick from close range after Detzi hit the crossbar with a screaming 25-yard volley.
Just before half-time,Jones was booked for a crude challenge on Blackwell.An amusing sight at half-time was two young children tying a Vinnie mask to the perimeter fencing and chucking rubbish at it!!!
Disaster-struck just into the second half as big John Gayle was sent-off for two bookable offences in quick succesion,both involving Jones and the second of which looked suspiciously as if there was a slight over-reaction on Vinny's part.Both Ray Harford and the majority of the Dons'500-strong contingent thought so,but these controversies were forgotten when John Fashanu,first half substitute for the injured Lawrie Sanchez,lashed in a 25-yarder past Phil Kite to give the Dons three precious points and their second away win of the season.

2.24th November 1990
Everton(home)2-1
Scorers:Barton,Gibson.

A second successive win for the improving Dons,and one which sent shockwaves through Fleet Street.We beat Everton playing some really attractive football.This even moved Elton Welsby,an Everton supporter,to say:"Wimbledon played some good football and outplayed Everton" which was a very sweet moment. But the best thing was seeing

no comments by Howard Kendall,who the Dons had made eat his words after his scathing criticism of them earlier in the season,when manager of Manchester City.
The Dons scored their first on 21 minutes when John Fashanu's curling left-foot cross invited Warren Barton to head his first goal for the club.
An absolutely superb second was scored on 55 minutes.Barton's terrific 40 yard pass found Paul McGee on the left wing.He neatly chested down before taking out the defence with a superb pass which prompted Terry Gibson to net his second in two games,beating Neville Southall with ease.
Kevin Sheedy pulled one back for the visitors with about ten minutes to go,firing home a disputed penalty after Roger Joseph alledgedly fouled Raymond Atteveld. But the Dons held on,ensuring the hard-core contingent could travel to East Anglia the following week in fairly optimistic mood.

3.1st December 1990
Norwich City(away)4-0
Scorers:Fashanu 2,Barton,Scales.

A truly amazing match which warmed the hearts of the 200-strong Wombles who made the trek to Carrow Road on this cold December Saturday.
After a stop in Newmarket on the way,we proceeded to the ground.The entrance fee was only 5 pounds,but the difference was made up by paying a pound for a burger which was,to say the least,a bit David Platt(i.e.ugly and stomach churning!).
So,to the match,and Fash set the tone for the afternoon,when he scored a tremendous individual goal after just 26 seconds.John Scales went close before Warren Barton

capitalised on a mix-up between Butterworth and 'keeper Gunn to fire into an empty net on 19 minutes.
Two old codgers were sent around a lap of the pitch with a blackboard carrying the golden goal time after Warren's goal,and they were only half way round when,on 21 minutes,Barton crossed,McGee's

shot was blocked,and Scalesey confidently rammed the third into, the bottom corner to ensure another lung-busting lap for them!
Amazingly,there was still a minute to go to the half-hour mark when Gibbo's defence-splitting pass put Fash away to round a defender before hitting a low shot into the net.
Wimbledon closed the game down in the second half,notable only for two efforts from Detzi;a shot blasted wide after a good run,and a close-range header which hit the post.So a happy journey home for all Dons,excited by a bright young team which promises much for the future.

4.23rd February 1991
Tottenham Hotspur(home)5-1
Scorers:McGee,Curle,Gibson,Fashanu, Cork.

An outstanding result which really emphasized the claim that the present side is the best ever to represent Wimbledon.Who would argue after this?I take some of the credit for this result,having predicted to Stuart and Russell the previous Thursday that Spurs would be narrow winners.We were at the training ground,as striker Andy Clarke completed his transfer from non-league Barnet,and was introduced to the other players.Ray Harford quite rightly pointed out that his arrival had heightened competition for places,and it showed.come 3.00 Saturday afternoon.
Many whinging Spurs "fans"complained of the absence of Gazza and Stewart,but no-one could convince me that Vinny Samways isn't twice as good as Stewart,and if they collapse without Gazza,they are really a one man team.Besides,every Spurs player had experience of First Division football,and the Dons steamrollered them with some terrific football of their own.

brilliant goal(predictably left out of The Match's Goal of the Day competition-why were only five of the 36 First Division goals that weekend shown?). Andy Clarke replaced Corky on 65 minutes,and within 60 seconds,and coming on,scored.Wazza split the Forest defence with another vintage pass,and Andy gobbled up his first first-team goal via a left-foot shot from a tight angle,with the relish and aplomb of a natural goal-scorer.

Before the end,the other substitute,Micky Bennett hit the post after a jinking run,as the Wombles extended their unbeaten league run to 10 matches.

deflection to sidefoot home.But there was to be no Tottenham renaissance.With 11 minutes to go, Wazza,having a sterling match in midfield,curled in a beautiful cross to pick out Gibbo,and he added a perfect header from 8 yards for his fifth of the season against the club that rejected him as a youngster.Then another tremendous Wazza break down the left saw him put in a low centre for Fash to net from close range,albeit at the third attempt.

With just two minutes left,another exquisite Wazza pass sent Scalesey through,and he rounded Thorstvedt and crossed for Corky to bravely head in the fifth,as he collided with the post.Scalesey went close to a sixth with an injury-time header,but an excellent afternoon's work had already been completed.

5.30th March 1991
Nottingham Forest(home)3-1
Scorers:Fashanu,McGee,Clarke.

Another stylish performance against a Forest side overcome by Wimbledon's overpowering approach. But Forest got off to a flying start when debutant Tony Loughlan marked his big day with a goal after just 34 seconds.He capitalised on a weak back-pass by Lawrie Sanchez to beat Hans with a neatly-placed lob.

But from then on,it was all Wimbledon.Both Corky and Scalesey went close,and then came the inevitable leveller.As the ball went up the Wimbledon right to Geoff,standing next to me,said:"Watch this,this is a goal; McGee cross and a Fashanu header." I was pessimistic,but sure enough,Maggot lifted the ball into the box,and Fash headed home his 16th of the season despite Clough's attempt to hack it away.The Dons

were back on course,although at the time I was more worried about whether the header had gone far enough over to the left of the goal to capture me on camera for the end of season video(I've been on both so far).

Into the second half and Gary Elkins,having a splendid match, played a brilliant long pass to Maggot,who controlled it and fired past Crossley for another

SHEFFIELD UNITED.F.C CARICATURES :

NO.1
VINNIE JONES

We took a lead as early as the 9th minute,when Wazza(the thinking man's midfielder)set Fash away down the right flank. He burst past Sedgeley and hit a low cross to the far post,and Maggot slid in to finish from close range.Maggot had to go off as the effect on his knee of colliding with the post when scoring(and falling off Fash's shoulder afterwards)took its toll.

On the hour mark,that lead was extended.Moncur hauled down Detzi about 20 yards from goal, and Curley stepped up to bend the ensuing free-kick around the wall and past Thorstvedt into the top corner.Such a mesmerisingly brilliant goal that even Andrew Fleming nearly said something complimentary about Curle!

Spurs pulled one back with 20 minutes to go when Bergsson took advantage of a lucky

'IF ONLY' BY RORY ARNOLD. 'EAMONN BANNON...' BY IAIN ROSS

EAMONN BANNON and the search for Hair!

Now EAMONN hated being bald,

Professor Kevin mad has invented a new hair restorer Lotion.

Now when EAMONN heard of the lotion he nearly flipped and Prof. Lab, as fast as his wing sprints down the wing (wisn't fast)

"use this once a day" said Prof. Kevin mad. "I'll drink it now" said EAMONN.

"no, no" singt Kevin said the Prof. "your supposed to rub it in not drink it"

If only...

What will Hibs be like in 10 years time? We sent Prof Hibs Supporter in a time machine and this is his report –

"I walk along Easter road and quickly purchase a copy of Hibs O.K? which is in full-colour and it only costs an amazing £2!(programes were abolished) I soon arrive at the100,000 capacity stadium and fish out a £20 note.Its mid season and Hibs are sitting at the top 12points clear. It looks like we're heading for ourthird championship in a row under our great manager,Gordon Strachan. I soon find a standing place (there are no seats) as the attendance is only 60,000. Hibs are expected to win easily against Hearts as the jambos are battling to stay up along with Rangers. There is great roar as the Hibs team runs on. They are wearing their new strip with a goalden harp in the middle (The saturn badge was done away with in 1994.) There is still time to buy something to eat. The facilities are of the usual high-standard and I buy a piping-hot bovril and a greaseless-pie. The game has just kicked off and Hibs score in the first minute. A close-up replay is then shown on the huge screen. I plug in my earphone and listen to the match comentary and by half-time were winning 5-0. No more late half-time results. As soon as the half time whistle goes match reports are flicked on to the huge screen. The game is quickly restarted and Hibs bang in another four goals. The huge roof is pulled over the stadium as it starts to rain. The huge solar lights are also turned on. The full time hooter goes and the Hibs fans rush out dissapointed that we only won 9-0. I turn on my portable-T.V. and find out that top of the table challengers East Fife have beaten third place Stirling Albion. The ancient Firm have drawn a boring 3-3. So its good things to come but we'll have to wait until1 1995 before Mercer is assasinated.1998 before Scotland win the world cup and 1999 before Hibs play in the first 'Space friendly' against Dynamo Mars."

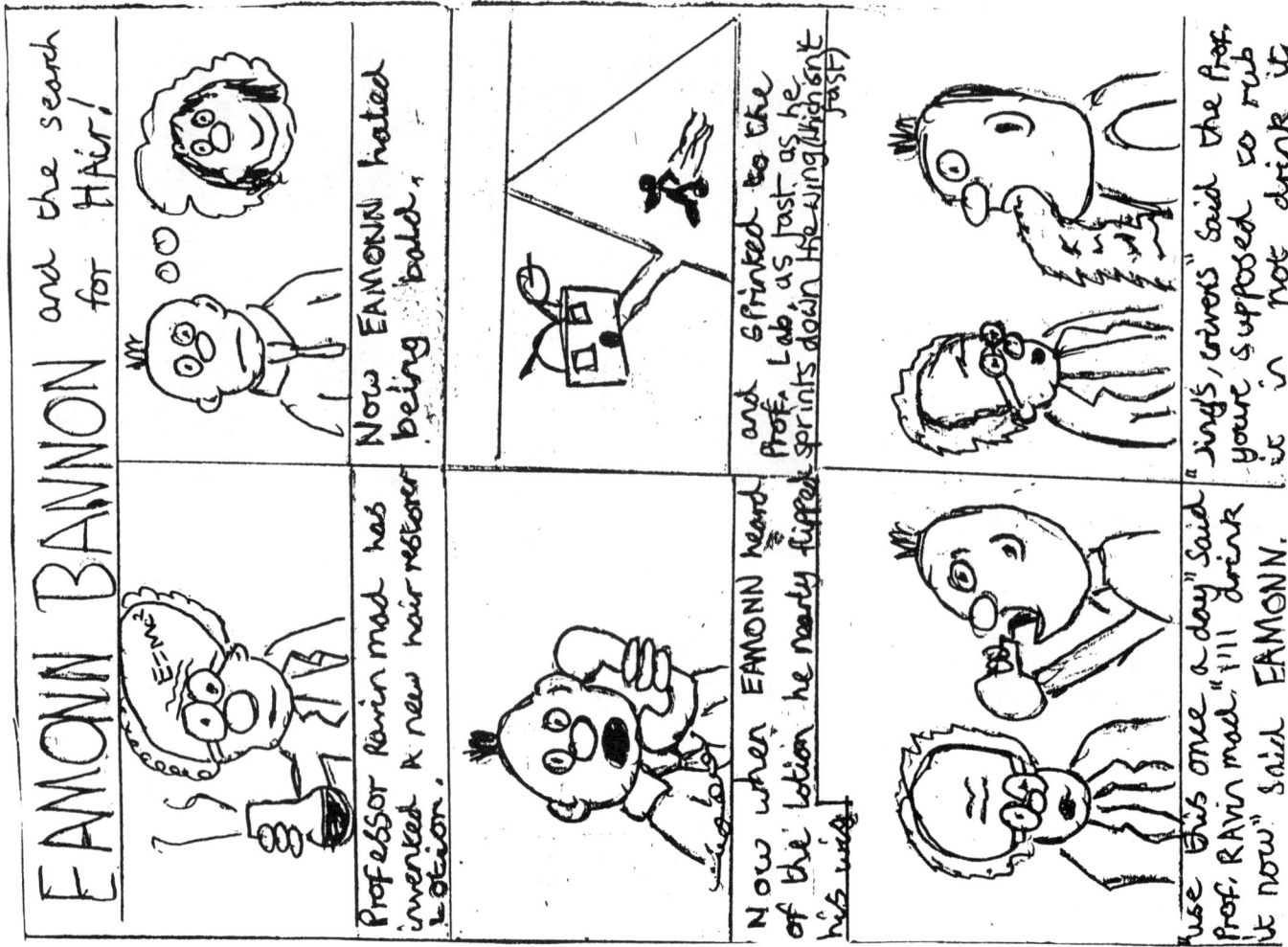

Que sera, sera

They say that every dog has its day. TONY MATTHEWS of Eagle Eye recalls when the underdogs of Crystal Palace had theirs.

'D been playing Sunday football and got home shortly before the end of QPR's FA Cup quarter final with Liverpool which was being shown live on BBC1's *Match of the Day*.

The day before, Palace had scraped their way past Cambridge United, with a Geoff Thomas grass cutter, and into the semi-finals.

The draw was to be made after Rangers had, I hoped, disposed of Kenny Dalglish's boys. But The Rs didn't quite have enough and so it was back to Anfield for a replay.

The draw for the semis followed, and I didn't realise what the agonising possibilities were until it was too late. After all Palace had rarely been in a semi-final draw and I wasn't used to such an event. Man United's pairing with Oldham didn't concern me. Until it dawned that we were going to face, in all probability, Liverpool.

My heart sank. Not another semi-final defeat. We couldn't beat them. It was impossible. We were a rubbishy collection of first division strugglers missing out best player, Ian Wright, because of a broken leg, and they were...well, they were Liverpool. We were out of the Cup. So near yet so far.

Our only hope was for Rangers to pull off a shock at Anfield in the replay. What were the chances? None, I thought. And I was right.

So we prepared to face a team that, as everybody took great pleasure in pointing out, had beaten us 9-0 not six months before.

At *Eagle Eye* we decided to get our "sour grapes" in before the inevitable defeat. We filled the special semi-final magazine with infantile anti-Liverpool bias and decided that, if nothing else, we were going to show the nation who had the best support in England.

We queued for tickets at Selhurst Park, and relished the moment, as streams of fans wound slowly round the car park outside the ground and down Whitehorse Lane. 15,000 tickets were available to members only. But we barely had 15,000 members.

We spent the weekend before the big match at the The Den, where we effectively sealed Millwall's relegation with a 2-1 win. I didn't want the following Sunday to arrive. Better to be in the semi-finals for evermore than to actually have to play the match and face being knocked out.

We were beginning to get the taste for being in the news. Make the most of this new found interest in Palace we thought. Next Monday we'll be forgotten again.

In midweek we went to Carrow Road and played dismally to lose to Norwich. The highlight was when we started singing *No Scouse at Wembley* and the Norwich supporters joined in. Deep down we all felt it was hopelessly optimistic. We knew that if we played like that again we'd be buried on the following Sunday.

Fiddling

The Saturday seemed to last about six weeks, which was strange because Saturdays usually flew by. My friends and I had agreed that the chances of getting a good night's sleep were effectively none. So, rather than pace up and down our bedrooms fiddling with rosary beads, we decided to have an all night party and set off for the game directly from Finsbury Park.

At about 7am on Sunday, April 8, 1990 we departed, shivering with cold which was liberally mixed with fear. Occasionally we dared to shout *Eagles* into the freezing morning air of North London. If we disturbed anybody's sleep we concluded, they would be Arsenal supporters and deserved no better.

First problem. No tubes to Euston. It was too early. We got a cab — a nice expensive start to the day. We were laden down with bags of *Eagle Eyes*, all newly printed, and thousands of red and blue balloons. There was a steely determination from all concerned to enjoy the day and to show what brilliant support we had. But there was no confidence

that we would enjoy the outcome of our endeavours.

On the trains to Birmingham nobody mentioned the possibility of a Palace victory. No-one spoke of Wembley.

We knew what it was to lose, to be disappointed, to feel anguish. But we had never known the joy of such an important victory. Cup Finals were for other people.

On the train, we sold the fanzines and distributed the balloons, telling everyone to keep them until the team came out and to sing their hearts out.

As we approached our destination, lumps began to appear in throats and knots tied themselves in stomachs. The train pulled in. Silence. This was it. We got our coats.

We walked through sunny but cold streets. No Liverpool fans around. They approached from a different direction. I checked my ticket a dozen times, making sure it was still there.

Inside, on the Holte End at Villa Park, thousands were already singing. It was a minute past eleven. The game kicked off at noon. High noon.

An hour of singing and shouting and nervous anticipation lay before us.

For the first time the matches were to be shown on live television, and up in the commentary box, QPR's Ray Wilkins was being asked to explain to the nation, on behalf of the BBC, how it was possible for Palace to win, and why it really was worth anyone's bother to tune-in. Aside from telling everyone: "it's a semi final and anything can happen", he could give no valid answer.

Back home thousands of Palace video recorders had timers set — the videos waiting to be erased upon our return without even being watched.

The singing was unbelievable. The rival supporters had half the Holte each. But it was all *Eagles, Eagles, Eagles*.

We took up a position just in front of one of the roof supports. It was a great view but it was already occupied by a discarded Mr Kipling apple pie. I stepped in it and spent the rest of the day with sticky trainers.

Everywhere people were blowing up balloons. Many had two in each hand. We stood there squeezed against inflated pieces of

The man they call 'Not the famous Andy Gray' levels the scores.

rubber. Occasionally one would burst and those in the vicinity would be covered in spittle. Now and then the cry would go up "balloons" and everybody would bash their neighbour on the head with them.

The Liverpool fans thought they'd have a go at this singing nonsense. 9-0, 9-0, 9-0 drifted across the fence towards us. We joined in, louder. *NINE-NIL, NINE-NIL*, we spat it back at them with ferocious defiance. That defeat was the Crystal Palace equivalent of Dunkirk, a horrendous defeat turned into a moral victory. The non-plussed Liverpool fans, outnumbering us by very nearly two to one, gave up with that one. Now they know.

The time ticked on. Then came the teams. The noise was deafening as every throat roared its approval. Balloons filled the air. It was a blessed relief to let them go. The tension seemed to drain from us as at last the boys in red and blue stripes came running towards us. But the tension would be back. With a vengeance.

The first half did nothing to ease our worries. Liverpool took the lead through Ian Rush. "The ace goalscorer, makes it look so easy," crowed John Motson from the commentary position. We sang again, trying to lift our team but it was a relief to get to half time with no further damage.

Despite Liverpool's admitted superiority, the later stages of the first 45 minutes had given us cause for hope. At half time, as an RAF dog display team tried vainly to keep us amused, we had that funny feeling. "Palace can do this," we agreed. Down in the tunnel, a former manager and the last man to take us to an FA Cup semi, Malcolm Allison, had the

same idea. Ray Wilkins "couldn't agree with that, Bob". Instead, he thought, Alan Hansen was having a "majestic" game.

The teams returned and what happened next is engraved on my mind forever. John Pemberton, an erratic right back if ever there was one, took off on a blistering run towards the Holte End. "Go on John, go on John, go on John." He crossed.

For the next few seconds all you could hear was OOOOOHHH! AAAHHH! and finally, emphatically a roaring YESSSSSSSSSS!

Experience

Palace had peppered Bruce Grobbelaar's goal with shots and headers, but it was Mark Bright who had finally fired the ball into the roof of the net. We were level. The Palace half erupted into a maelstrom of joy. Fists punching the air. My mate Martin's extra strong mint went down the wrong hole and nearly choked him to death.

Then it was a sea of arms and legs flailing. Bodies smacked into each other. Everybody grabbed their neighbour by the throat in sheer joy.

I'm sure my eyes didn't deceive me when, at one point, I saw a pair of feet emerge above the heads of those in front of me. That bloke must have been completely upside down. It was a truly orgasmic experience.

How we sang! Every song we could think of and, for the first time, we dared *Que Sera, Sera. Whatever will be, will be. We're going to Wember—leeee. Que sera, sera.* Louder and louder, till we couldn't sing anymore. Arms were raised in salute to our boys. *We're on the MARCH with Stevie's army, we're all*

going to Wemberleee....

Palace launched forward seeking to take advantage of Liverpool's indecision. From the other side of the fence there was silence. But our voices felt like they were cracking into thousands of pieces.

Thomas nearly finished a sweeping move with a shot that Grobbelaar stopped literally on the goal-line. Then from a corner, central defender Gary O'Reilly who wouldn't have been picked if manager Steve Coppell had had a choice smacked in the second.

There was no time for stunned disbelief. The place was chaos again, absolute bedlam. I must have moved twenty yards down the Holte from my original position and then been swept back up again, like a shrimp in the tide.

2-1, 2-1, 2-1. We roared our delight, our arms pointing to the Liverpool fans alongside. There were plaintive cries for referee George Courtney to "blow his f***ing whistle", fully half an hour before the end.

The scoreboard faced us. The time on it had stuck. It was just like that film, *The Day The Earth Stood Still.* Wouldn't you bloody know it, some Alien had come down and turned the planet off, just as we were winning.

We wished the seconds away, every minute hurting us. Palace were giving as good as they got, but Liverpool were serious now. This wasn't a nine-nil mickey-take, this was the real thing.

I tried to keep my eyes averted from the scoreboard. Maybe then the minutes would start to tick away at the proper rate.

Six minutes to go. John Salako and Peter

Que sera, sera.....

Beardsley tussled for a ball and the Liverpool man fouled our boy. But Courtney gave it the other way. No, you tart, no!

Looking back now, I have to admit it was a great free kick. Quickly taken to by-pass the defensive wall and fired across the box to where McMahon was waiting to unleash a rocket shot past Martyn and into the net.

Behind Palace's goal the Liverpool supporters went mad. We were stunned. Six minutes to go. Only six minutes. Why, why, why?

Before we could draw breath and start singing again, we were hit once more. Steve Staunton raced onto a through ball and was bundled over by Pemberton. Penalty.

The air was blue with swearing, quickly followed by a concerted attempt to will Martyn to save it. Whatever happened to extra sensory perception? He'd never saved a penalty for us before (and still hasn't, come to think of it), so surely this was the time to start. He dived the right way, but Barnes shot was just about as perfectly placed as you'd ever get. From 2-1 up to 3-2 down in a minute.

Scarves

We stood there, powerless, cursing our luck. B*****ds! Liverpool were cheats (they weren't, but we were clutching at straws) they deserved nothing. Why did God hate us so much? Why us? Why?

Behind me a voice roared out. "Sing you b*****s, Sing!" We tried but we hadn't the heart this time.

All around us were red and white scarves, and *You'll never walk alone, you'll NE-E-VER walk alone. Walk on. Walk on.With hope in your heart.....*It echoed round the ground piercing our hearts like a dagger.

All through the match, Palace's smaller numbers had sung, chanted and cheered their team. Liverpool's fans had packed up trying to match us. Villa Park was ours. Now this.

On those videos which hold pride of place in Palace homes everywhere, there is a very worn out piece of footage. It shows thousands of Koppite scarves high in the air.

Then Palace launched one last effort. There was another almighty scramble and the ball bounced invitingly for Andy Gray to nod it over the line. 3-3, with three minutes left and once more we went stark staring potty.

On the video you can clearly see the Liverpool scarves drop like stones as the third Palace goal went in.

It was followed by another sweet moment, Gray shoved a policeman out of the way as he jumped toward the ecstatic Palace fans.

We were back from the dead and every last reserve of energy was used to roar them on.

Still we weren't finished. Andy Thorn rattled the crossbar with a header and once again we were jumping. God, that would have won it.

It still felt like we had won when the final whistle blew. But we had achieved nothing yet. Everyone was gasping for drinks. The players were getting them. We weren't.

And it's Crystal Palace, CRYSTAL PALACE FC. We're by F-aaa-rrrr the greatest team, the world has ever seen....

Extra time, predictably enough, was an anti-climax after all the excitement that had gone before. You can't stage matches like that and expect players and supporters to keep haring about like there's no tomorrow.

But extra time did contain the one moment all Palace fans will take to their graves. Alan Pardew, whose contribution as usual had been less than emphatic, suddenly arrived to head home the decisive goal.

Even Liverpool, "with all their experience of the big occasion", and other famous cliches, had nothing more to offer. The fourth goal, the winner, brought nothing like the celebrations of the first three, simply because everyone was so exhausted.

We were nearly there, the final seconds ticked away. And we pushed ourselves for one last song, *We're proud of you, we're proud of you, we're PROUD.*

At the end we raised ourselves again to celebrate our greatest day. Hugs and kisses, and handshakes all round. All with total strangers. It didn't seem real. But we were so happy.

Sunshine

There must have been a hundred different groups, singing a hundred different songs. For some there were tears.

I didn't cry although I've had a tear in my eye when I've thought back subsequently, including when I wrote this. When we emerged from the gates into bright sunshine, I looked up and saw red and blue balloons lodged in the trees opposite the ground.

We walked along, past stony faced policemen, and met Palace fans we'd known for years. People who had been there when

we'd had four put past us by Grimsby, who had been there when Blackburn got five at Ewood Park and who were there when we'd lost time and time again to Shrewsbury Town. This really was our moment.

The queues for the trains home were enormous. There was no organisation, we just took any train we could find. Nothing mattered anymore. We would have happily stood there enjoying those moments for the rest of our lives.

Pleased

Other fans have said how quiet the journey home was, with people too tired to celebrate. But not in our carriage we weren't. We sang our way home, waving at any people we could see standing on the station platforms that we passed through.

Two railway engineers gave us the thumbs up and we felt the whole country was pleased for us and, with all respect to Liverpool, was pleased that someone else was going to Wembley instead of them. Just for a change.

We had a "Big Mac" in Trafalgar Square and made our way back to Croydon to celebrate.

The 36 or more hours without sleep hit us hard, but we roused ourselves for the celebrations to come. In The Cherry Trees by Norwood Junction station you could hear *La Bamba* blaring out and see the heads of people jumping up and down.

In the Portmanor, our shattered throats lubricated with lager, we sang *Que sera, sera whatever will be, will be, we're going to WEMBLEY*. And at last we were.

---

merseybeat ch
The Beatles

1. Kenny Lam
2. Lady Made
3. Revolution
4. A Pard Gray's Bright
5. Roll Over Ray Houghton
6. Nowhere McMahon
7. Red Submarine
8. Gray Tripper
9. Ian The Walrush
10. While Grobbelaar
    Gently Weeps.

What do Liverpool and a commuter at Stonebridge Park tube have in common?

Both get off one stop from Wembley!

...of your friends ...ifelong Palace ...e these ...the same peo- ...o have been ...d the piss con- ...ly for ...20

Buckingham Palace

At Buckingham Palace, the Royal Standard fluttered gently at half mast. The BBC commentator, John Motson, 86, was last night under sedation and being comforted by friends and relatives.

...us to ...free rein in the first half, so he'd be knackered in the second. If a Liverpool player runs across you and then falls over and wit?...

What's the difference between Liverpool F.C and Dennis Thatcher?

There's no way Dennis would miss out on three doubles!

AN ALTERNATIVE VIEW OF DARLINGTON F.C.

MISSION IMPOSSIBLE

Blackpool Illuminations September 4th 1990

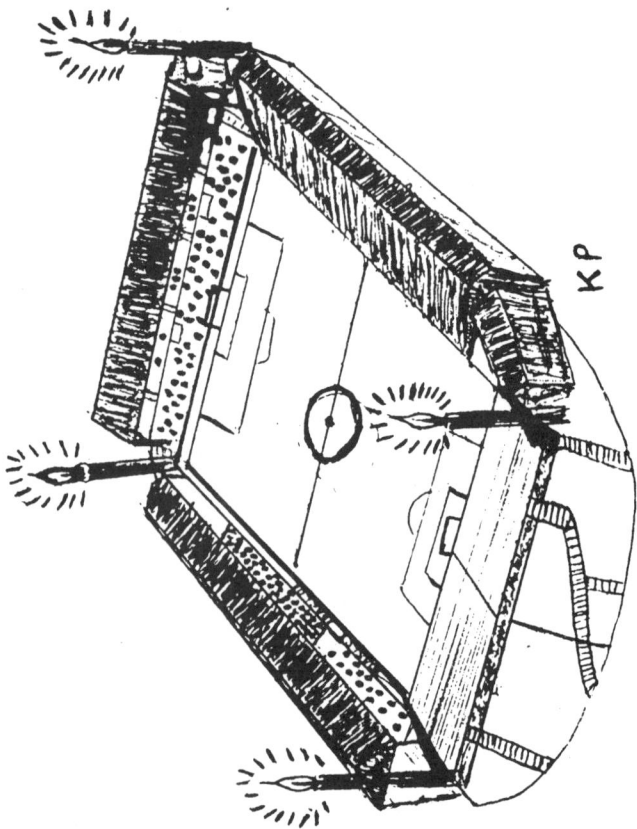

KP

NOT SO SWEET F.A.

THE recent moves by the Football Association to form their own 'Super-League' are potentially disastrous for smaller clubs such as Darlington, and should be totally opposed by all fans. As well as trying to scrap the Third Division before we even get into it, the FA, with the collaboration of the so-called top clubs are trying to create an artificial elite of football in this country.

Not only do the FA ignore the basic premise of football, that it is possible for teams to progress, by merit, from a non-League origin to the success of the First Division and the winning(in Wimbledon's case)of the FA's own competition ,but it also ignores the fact that top-class players are developed by lower-division teams and their youth development policies,(to take David Platt as purely one example).

The reason behind their decision of course, is money — and lots of it. The so-called 'top' teams will cream off the best sponsorship/TV deals, leaving the luckless other 75 clubs to fight for the pathetic amounts that would arise from a credibility-reduced League.

The most exclusive club in the world would become even more exclusive..Really, the Football League as a management body — those wonderful people who demanded a £100,000 bond from the Quakers before this season — have brought the situation upon themselves. They have never truly defended the rights of lower-division clubs and have probably never adapted to the brave new world of football economics. Insisting upon a 22 club First Division, plus ridiculous competitions like the ZDS Cup show little regard for sanity.

Nevertheless, the fans are not responsible for the stupidity of those who administer the game and they should also not be pen-alised by their ridiculous decisions. Boycotts of the FA Cup have been mentioned, in retaliation for these pro-posals. It might be better if clubs in the so-called Super League were banned from signing players from lower League sides. The least you can do is to wr-ite to the FA expressing your disgust.

Steve Raine

From Behind Your Fences

The Independent Boston United Fanzine

MAIN STAND, CANAL STREET.

HOME AWAY HOME AWAY HOME AWAY

A MEXICAN WAVE AT RUNCORN.

THIS GAME'S GOT 'NIL-NIL' WRITTEN ALL OVER IT!

THE MAN with NO PARENTS

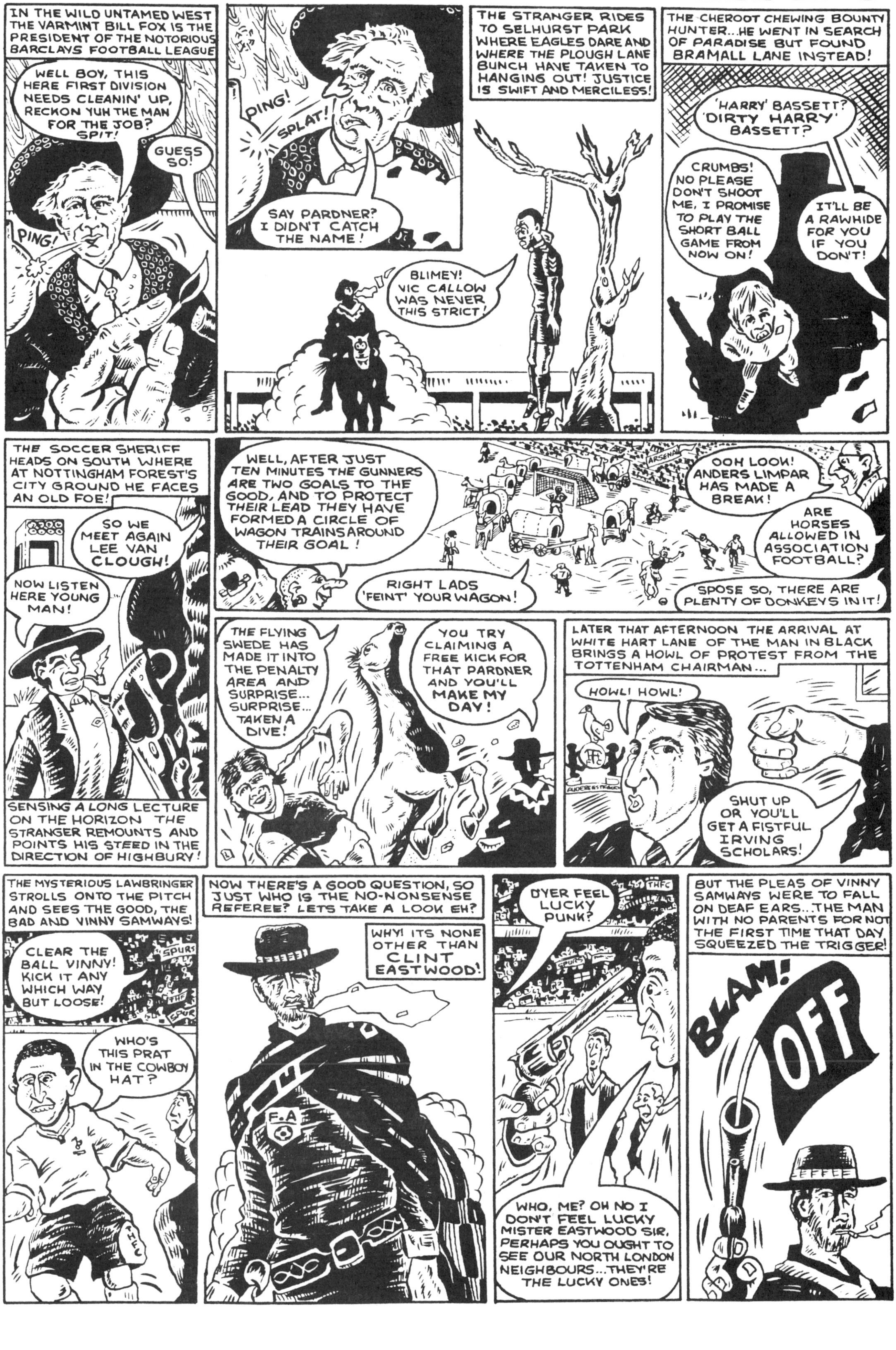

A WOLVERHAMPTON WANDERER

Anyone who follows a Midland team learns to be stoical about defeat and, indeed, about most other things. Our milkman shed a tear when Villa slid into Division Three in 1970 - but he carried on with his round. And when Liverpool put six past Wolves at Molineux, my brother was speechless for hours, but still managed to get up next morning to sing in the church choir. Life goes on.

1976 was a vintage year for stoicism. It was there on the Ipswich keeper's face as he retrieved the ball from his net; a high, sweetly curving free kick from the half-way line, and Bobby Gould had put Ipswich out of the Cup.

A few rounds later that look was there again, on John Richards' face. He'd scored one of his characteristically stylish goals early in the replay against Manchester United, but they got a winner in the dying moments of extra time.

Lastly I saw it in the shaving mirror on 5th May; the morning after we were relegated. That game was_the_ finish to the season. Never mind the Cup Final which preceded it. Liverpool had to win to nick the title from QPR; Wolves had to win to avoid the drop.

An Everton supporter with as much interest in a Wolves win as me came along too. We arrived hours before kick-off only to find the gates closing faster than we'd been letting in goals all season.

We found ourselves jammed against the back of the South Bank, yards from the turnstiles in a solid block of sweating humanity. Even the Scousers, more used to this sort of crush, gasped for breath.

Cullis
- He's got the look

Every few minutes a mounted policeman rode into the back of the crowd; clearly an early experiment in sympathetic policing.

There was a curious tearing noise in my ears; the match had started. God knows what it sounded like inside the ground.

But by now my over-powering interest was to have my feet on the floor again.

After fourteen minutes, Wolves scored. The entire town moved sideways a foot or so, facilitating our escape. We shot from the crowd like melon pips between wet fingers.

Liverpool won 3-1 and down we went. But, it being the year for stoicism, we sat smoking our Players, squashed to the shape of a Sullivan and Powell Turkish, discussing next season.

Next day we met up with a very short friend who had actually got in - pushed backwards through a turnstile as it happens.

"How was the game then?"

"Saw Keegan's shorts once, just before half-time!"

Stoicism.

Crazily, it was to be another eleven years before I was inside the ground again. I moved a long way from the Midlands, and the passion lost its edge, not least because I found a true love away from John Richards.

The woman I married was from one of those strange southern towns never blessed by the lips of James Alexander Gordon's classified results. A town without a football team.

Having married Anne, for better, for worse, I felt sure that even God's conception of 'worse' wouldn't embrace football in the Midlands. So for eleven seasons it was just the occasional away game; a rather blurred period, in football terms, but I remember watching defeats at all sorts of venues, from Bootham Crescent to the City Ground.

Two events changed everything; relegation to Division Four (more stoicism here) and a train crash in Czechoslovakia (she wasn't hurt). It was possible to neglect a team that threw money around so pointlessly, that sacked Graham Hawkins, that employed Tommy Docherty, that sent John Richards to Spain swearing never to play in Wolves' colours again.

But it is alien to my nature to neglect a side that had plummeted to the Fourth Division and showed no signs of stopping; a side without money, friends or a team. When the 1986/87 season began and 'The Guardian' gloated "The Wolves will never rise again," I knew what I had to do. Start being a real supporter again, and stop reading that bloody newspaper.

A few months earlier, Anne was in Czechoslovakia with a Sheffield Wednesday supporter. Near Brno, their train was derailed. They were rescued from the confusion by a Trnava fan who spoke good English. What could have been more natural than that they should all end up at a football match together a few days later.

And so Anne watched her first football match in bright May sunshine in the Spartak stadium. Trnava lost to Sparta Prague, and they drowned their sorrows in Chicken Paprika and rice. She returned to England interested in a sport we had never even discussed.

We began going to matches together. It was bound to lead to Molineux. On an overcast Bank Holiday Monday we drove through Herefordshire and Worcestershire to Wolverhampton, passing as we did so, into brilliant sunshine. We arrived with an appetite.

Wolverhampton has never gone much on lunch, but Woolworth's cafeteria was open, still turquoise, orange, and irredeemably 1963. The food was good and there was time to read the Express and Star's account of Saturday's 2-1 win at Hereford. Ticket restrictions had kept us out of Edgar Street for that victory, and the same nonsense kept us out of the stunning main stand at Molineux. Instead we paid the club less money and stood high on the South Bank.

It was an emotional moment stepping out onto the terracing. In eleven years the pitch had sidled steadily towards the new stand. I had never seen a playing turf look so green and rich. But the North Bank was closed, the Cowshed choir grown old and homeless. The Waterloo stand where the great Stan Cullis once sat was closed, it's yellow paint rubbed and worn. The Paddock in front of it contained only a few ambulance men; no lucky beggar would stand six feet from Bobby Gould as he scored...

But it still looked beautiful.

Out across the roof of the old stand, across the roofs of Whitmore Reans and Aldersley, across the whole blue afternoon of sunlight and trees - I'd forgotten all the trees - we could see clear to the edge of town and off into Staffs and Salop. For a moment I could see even further, back to the Fifties when a little boy knelt on his bedroom chair and looked out through the window at the floodlights glowing in the distance. The window was open a crack so he could hear across the winter afternoon the vast punch of sound that meant a goal, another goal.

Back in 1987 we were looking to wrest three points from Scunthorpe. Their centre-forward laboured under the name Flounder; he did no such thing of course, scoring in most games.

Old Gould

The teams trotted out. Someone forgot to play the brass band record of the Wandering Song; a horrible oversight, it being inconceivable that this ritual could have been abandoned.

It was a curious game. Our best midfield player was not fit and didn't play. Scunthorpe closed down his patch. We still managed to win 4-1, the goals shared - inevitably these days - by Steve Bull and Andy Mutch. They were four splendidly old-fashioned, individualist goals with long runs, dribbling and stuff. Their goalie, an ex-Walsall player, was fairly stoical about it all.

But the result somehow mattered less than usual. Home again.

Peter Wakefield

RIVER DAMNED

"In 1983/84 Buckingham Town reached the first round proper of the F.A. Cup and were unlucky to lose at home to Orient in front of a record crowd of 2,500. The previous highest crowd had been for an F.A. Vase tie with Barton Rovers which was hit by an unusual postponement. The Barton Rovers' coach driver took a wrong turn on entering the ground and drove the coach into the River Ouse, which runs alongside the Buckingham ground. The coach dammed the river, causing the floodwater to run onto the pitch and consequently the game had to be postponed because of a waterlogged pitch!"

Culled from PHEEP, magazine of the Hounslow Referees' Association, who culled it from the Southern League Referees and Linesmens' Association Newsletter.

Fly Me To The Moon - Middlesboro

It is a little known fact

Intellectual Gigantus Alan Morley © 1991.

The storming of the Bastille was inspired by Boro's 1780's 5-3-2 formation!

Boro were engaged in the Mediterranean and Baltic Sovereign States Championship at the time a revolution was going on in France. French peasants were rioting against the aristocracy of the country who were financially ruining it.

Meanwhile, Boro had a system that relied heavily on massive goal scoring. It had a weak midfield and defence arrangement and was vulnerable to attack, often having loads of goals put passed it. But, the five striker set-up throughout the 1780's snatched victories cos of its ability to notch-up school-boy type goal tallies. We beat Dortmund Rhinelanders 11-9 in the quarter finals and C.F. Athens 10-7 in the semi's. The final was with Athlete Belgrade at the new Louis XVI Stadium in Paris. The game almost postponed cos of the trouble in the town, was played in front of 95,000 whacko Parisians thirsty for inspiration and a motive to get nasty. Boro and Belgrade scrapped hard in a messy match with the ref' spoiling it with his, for some reason, biassed decisions in Belgrade's favour. The crowd sensed the injustice and got behind the lion hearted Boro. We climbed back on the cheering of the French from 0-3 down to scrape an 8-7 victory. The battling Boro had fired the French spirit and the hordes spilled out of the stadium and along to the hated symbol of their government, the prison Bastille. They organized themselves so that half the crowd made a direct attack on the building, while one third formed into a back-up wave to support the first assault; the remaining fraction hanging a little-way back in a medical roll.

On their return across the Channel the Boro team were questioned by Kent C.I.D. about their involvement in the French Revolution. Loftus born, Outside-Inside Right, Tommy Beddlow told them: "We only stayed behind in Paris after the match to make sure no-one got hurt!"

In excess of 500 people died in the storming of the Bastille and over 2,000 bonces bounced from the blade of the guillotine, in the name of: LIBERTY, EQUALITY, FRATERNITY!

Resign Roberts Re-Sign !

A Northwich Victoria Fanzine

Exclusive Photo of Albion Training

*** FREE GIFT INSIDE ***

Thieves in the Temple

Following the visit of the Fifth Horseman some of the temple money lenders, or as they were also known money losers, fled like the rats they were, others stayed and a few were rewarded for their long service. Once a week the local Prophet of Doom would try to convince the few remaining followers that the end was nigh and that they should follow another local, but much lesser religion. For it would be written every Wednesday that the sun shone out of the lesser religions leaders nether regions but the true believers knew it was just the Prophet talking out his.

They knew that the second coming would soon happen, for they had seen the signs. Many of them saw Bill King turn beer into water and most had seen the glow from the fires to the North and to the East, and most other directions as well. Many had marvelled at the feeding of the 500, although some were unhappy that there were no chip and burger batches left at half-time.

Then came the final sign - the Pixies hit the charts.

And so it came to be that a giant of a man came from a strange land and the believers saw him to be the new Messiah. And like a true chosen one he denied that he was the son of god but the book of Revelations showed his true identity.

"And so it came to pass that the beast was slain. And it is written that the Messiah shall follow the beast, and that the Messiah shall have a name. For it is a human name, the name is Martin Dobson."
Revelation XI 26

What was not written was that the bastard would do a runner to Bristol Rovers before any miracles were performed. And so it came to pass that the followers were left with a bitter taste in their mouths and, more angry and cynical than before, they awaited the next arrival.

The Prophet on Mount Sinai

And it came to pass that the prophet climbed the mountain and at the top the Guardian gave him a tabloid with the following five commandments on it.

1:Thou shalt tell the truth, the whole truth or nothing like the truth
2:Thou shalt not praise Malcolm O'Connor
3:Thou must worship the false idol known as Witton Albion
4:Thou must adulerate thy match reports with thine opinions
5:Thou must covert thy neighbours manager
Alas just 5 didn't fill the paper so using no.1 he invented 5 more!

KING OF THE KIPPAX

On top of a full time demanding job (i.e.not 9 to 5),a larger than average family,with a larger than average age span and what with reading, writing, cartooning, prit-sticking, editing, dealing with correspondence, parcelling up, licking and sticking stamps, servicing outlets, telephoning, interviewing, reading the papers, watching T.V., bagging up, checking every single zine for print quality, listening to the radio, watching the 1st., 2nd., & 3rd. teams home & away, attending functions, going to F.S.A. meetings,being on the radio & T.V.(sometimes!) plus selling & chatting to fans in all weathers, and, as the paintwork peels & the garden grows & grows,there is precious little time left to devote elsewhere......no matter how appealing a cause may be.

However,having lost a cousin through M.S.(rest peacefully Ian) & having certainly one subscriber to K.K.,Brian Rooney,who suffers,the least we can do is contribute to and support this worthy cause.So this 'Wallace Wish'is to do whatever we can in the time available.

King of the Kippax is a Man. City fanzine which derives it's name from City's equivalent of the Kop which runs the full length of the pitch opposite the main stand.The King was, of course, Colin Bell,but to us all Blues are 'King'.

We've been on the go now as a fanzine for 3 years,starting at Barnsley in Sept.1988, when City were in division 2 & striving to get back up.Maggie was in 'power',the I.D. cards were the major football issue,English teams were banned from Europe,away fans were banned from Luton,& the reporting in the tabloids on the Euro. championships was reactionary & bobbins as we say oop norf!

We're a man & wife editorial team with all the family chipping in & we've now got an extended family of sellers, contributors, subscribers, and morale boosters which keeps us going.

KK we feel,is in keeping with the best traditions of fanzines, with views from fans on the terraces, in the seats, in the Pub., & from far afield. Apart from providing a platform for fans views we aim to be humourous(!!??) & promote a friendly rivalry between supporters.Here's some snippets from the most recent KK's which should give a flavour of the mag. bearing in mind the purpose of '12 INCHES HIGH'..........

DAVE & SUE WALLACE

KENDALL BLOWS K.K's COVER

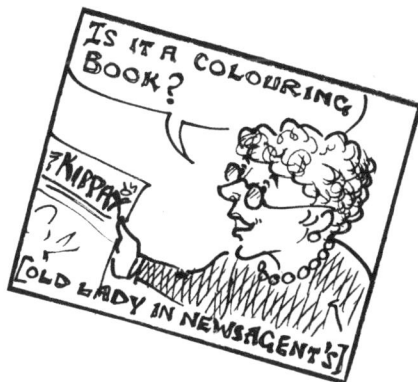

Most traumatic KK was, ironically,number 13,of November last year....it was at the printers when news of Kendalls departure was announced,causing the midnight oil to be burnt well into the early hours,and the front page to be held whilst an an extra cover was grafted on at great expense.

The best thing about City now is the fans, to the point where two or three seasons ago they were prepared to make their own entertainment on the terraces 'cos it was better than what was going on on the field and they gained a reputation all over the country as well- almost like 'the Acid Housers' of football, and a lot of that has had to do with their incredible loyalty, like when El Cid rode back into Castille - the skill will come back 'cos it's the natural game.

THAT'S IT! — NEXT SEASON WE'LL PLAY IN TURQUOISE!!!

TURQUOISE MOON? SINGIN' THE TURQUOISE? SUMMERTIME TURQUOISE?

DAILY PULP — ICKE TO SAVE WORLD IN TURQUOISE — DAVID ICKE 'GROUNDING EX-TURQUOISE ANNOUNCED HERE NEXT...'

IS THAT THE SAME 'ICKE' WHO USED TO SING WITH TINA TURNER?

HOW WAS IT ...FOR YOU?

STARDOM!

IT'S A FIX!

ALL TICKET AWAY GAMES! GRRR!!! —.ENDLESS TRIPS TO THE TICKET OFFICE— AND QUEUEING, QUEUEING, QUEUEING ------------!

HAVE I GOT THIS ONE?

KING OF THE KIPPAX

IS IT THE PROGRAMME?

KING OF THE KIPPAX

EURO CONFESSIONS OF A BLUE VICAR

PART THREE

IS THIS THE ONE ME MATE'S GOT?

KIPPAX

CEP SOUNDS OFF

AND ANOTHER THING....

THE KIPPAX KING

OH, S**T — IT WAS IN!

IT WAS OUT!

iT Was IN!

CITY'S BEAT US TWICE!

CLOUGHIE WENT ON TO WEMBLEY AND AN O.B.E. (OH BLUDDY'ELL) BUT DID IT BRING A SMILE?

NO, NOT EVEN HEINEKEN CAN DO THIS

Wednesday 21st August 1991, the shock waves were felt throughout the region. The whole of the North West was shaken to its very foundations and divided, nay, rent asunder by the cataclysmic event which occurred on that fateful night.

Out of the early evening cathode ray tube galloped GRANADA TONIGHT in a quest for peace, harmony and larger viewing figures. Once and for all, they would finish the endless speculation on David White's second goal against Liverpool and deliver the verdict to an expectant public.

Later that week.... (Scene — busy TV studio with tasteful pastel background. Lucy Meacock has just closed an informative peice on Norwegian buttock welding in Eccles)

SAY IT AIN'T SO JOE

BLUE on BLUE

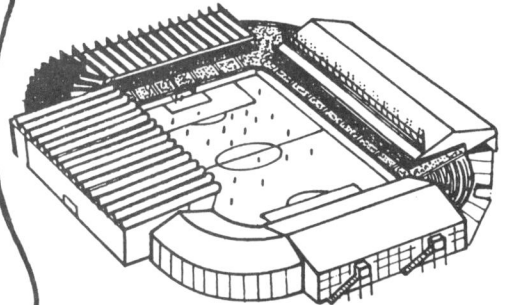

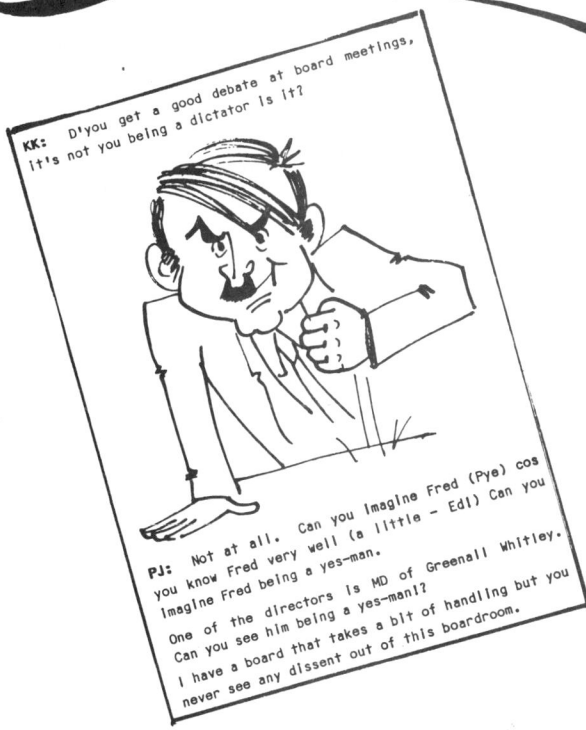

KK: D'you get a good debate at board meetings, it's not you being a dictator is it?

PJ: Not at all. Can you imagine Fred (Pye) cos you know Fred very well (a little — Ed) Can you imagine Fred being a yes-man.
One of the directors is MD of Greenall Whitley. Can you see him being a yes-man? I have a board that takes a bit of handling but you never see any dissent out of this boardroom.

K.K. AND M.S.

What about football fans raising funds for M.S. Research? Answer: 'I don't believe in charities, the government should provide'. Agreed. However, the dilemma is that people are suffering and dying NOW, and who are we to with-hold help for the sake of a political dogma?

We marvel at the selflessness of those who, knowing that their own case is hopeless, nevertheless campaign tirelessly for others (remember Mandy Turner? Who could forget?!). We ache as we read the plaintive messages in the newspaper columns 'No flowers please, donations to.....'.

Faced with personal tragedy, families are invariably overwhelmed with compassion for others. So why, then, when we, and ours, are fit and well, do we look the other way?

Only when we too are suffering, do we have the right to say "I don't believe in charity". So let's keep our political opinions for the ballot box and dig deep for M.S. Research, because the sick can't wait for the political will to render charity unnecessary.

Frattonise - Portsmouth

THE REAL NORTH STAND CRITIC

YOU'RE CR*P! ERNIE BUTLER'S HANDLING WAS LEGENDARY

FRANK

The Frank Burrows Player Assessment Guide

Our Fratton mole has exclusively revealed the secrets of Frank's patented method of judging the worth of any player under consideration for the club. We reproduce here the very document (as issued to Pompey Scouts) for you to do your own marking during the close season transfer rumours.

PERFORMANCE FACTORS	FAR EXCEEDS JOB REQUIREMENTS	EXCEEDS JOB REQUIREMENTS	MEETS JOB REQUIREMENTS	NEEDS SOME IMPROVEMENT	DOES NOT MEET MINIMUM REQUIREMENTS
QUALITY	Leaps tall buildings with a single bound	Must take running start to leap over tall buildings	Can only leap over a short building, or medium with no spires	Crashes into buildings when attempting to jump over them	Cannot recognise buildings at all, much less jump them
PACE	Is faster than a speeding bullet	Is as fast as a speeding bullet	Not quite as fast as a speeding bullet	Would you believe a slow bullet? DUM DUM	Wounds self with bullets when he attempts to shoot gun
STRENGTH	Is stronger than a locomotive	Is stronger than a bull elephant	Is stronger than a bull	Shoots the bull	Smells like a bull
ADAPTABILITY	Walks on water consistently	Walks on water in emergencies	Washes with water	Drinks water	Passes water in emergencies
COMMUNICATION	Talks with God	Talks with the angels	Talks to himself I'M THE GREATEST	Argues with himself OH NO I'M NOT!	Argues with himself and loses OKAY YOU WIN

:::: TICK WHERE APPROPRIATE ::::

GIVE 'EM BEANS!

ADVERTISEMENT

COMING SOON TO A VIDEO SHOP NEAR YOU!

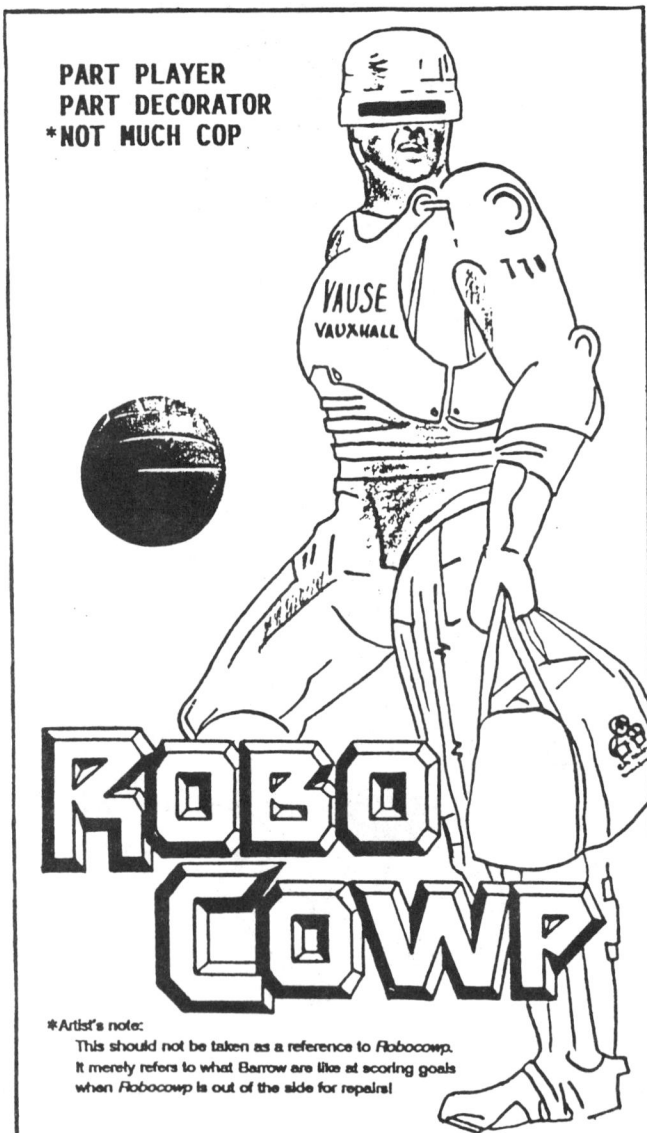

OTHER GREAT TITLES CURRENTLY AVAILABLE

PLANES, TRAINS AND AUTOMOBILES
Documentary on the various means of transport used by Barrow fans to get to matches in Yeovil, Bath, Colchester and other out-of-the-way places down south.

THE RUNNING MAN
Not the one with Arnold Schwarzenegger and the chainsaw; this features a bald linesman in the Bass North-West Counties League Division Two. A classic.

THE COLOR OF MONEY
As it's been so long since they had any, the directors of Barrow FC should borrow this one, just to remind themselves what it looks like!

THE TALL GUY
Featuring a stunning performance from Stuart Todhunter in the title role!

THE WAY WE WERE
Horror movie about the days when Barrow played in light and dark blue checks. Not for the squeamish!

BOB AND CAROL AND TED AND ALICE
A personal introduction to the fans at one of Fisher Athletic's home matches.

RISKY BUSINESS
Instruction video on defending introduced by Tony Chilton.

Life with Ray

LAST SEASON AT HOLKER ST...

AH, COME IN, — *, NOW WHAT WAS IT YOU WANTED TO SEE ME ABOUT?

WELL BOSS, IT'S LIKE THIS. WHY IS IT I'M ALWAYS ON THE SUBS' BENCH?

OH, THAT'S SIMPLE, IT'S BECAUSE WE DON'T HAVE ANY RESERVES TO PUT YOU IN!

*ANY NAME AT ALL WILL DO, BUT HERE ARE A FEW YOU MAY LIKE TO CONSIDER - BIRDY, BARRY, PETER etc.

MONKEY NUTS

One of the most obscene sounds when you're trying to watch a game of football is when a bunch of inadequates pretending to be football fans start making monkey noises if a black player has the cheek to get the ball.

It's also no coincidence that this only occurs at big games like Bolton or Kettering. Most Barrow fans are decent people who judge players on their skills not the colour of their skins. But the big match brings out all the dregs. All the 'did you spill my pint?' clowns and their pathetic hanger on mates who know nothing about football and use the greatest game in the world as a platform for their racism.

I felt ashamed at Bolton as these morons chanted 'Barrow are white'. Ashamed because the people of multi racial Bolton might think all Barrow fans are mindless racists.

Regular Barrow fans are not rent-a-bigots. The response to our anti nazi campaign was very positive and week in, week out there is no monkey noises or racist chanting as Barrow fans watch the game and judge players as they see them. Who could fail to appreciate the skill of Barnet's Andy Clarke last season when he wrecked us up here. Clarke is not a great, black footballer he is just a great footballer.

I don't suppose many of the thugs and hangers on will read this but if anyone of our readers know any of these morons perhaps you could show them. Because our message is simple, WE DON'T WANT YOU AT OUR GROUND AND WE DON'T NEED YOUR SORT OF SUPPORT. GET A LIFE.

A MATTER OF SOME WEIGHT !

Well, it does say that Eammon Collins has the nack (sic) of making news, but isn't this taking it all a bit far?

Look beside the heading *WEIGHT* and you'll see that lucky Eammon has slimmed down by three pounds. But then, perhaps Colchester United have fans so demanding and a programme editor so dedicated, they felt they just couldn't leave out even such a minor detail as this.

Just imagine if the idea was adopted for the programme at Holker St., or if the Soccerline got hold of it.....

Player Profile Number Six

- MEET EAMMON COLLINS -

HEIGHT - 5 foot 6 inches

WEIGHT - lost 3 pounds

PREVIOUS CLUBS - Blackpool, Southampton and Portsmouth

———:———

Ball players of quality are a rarity these days - certainly in the G.M. Vauxhall Conference. But Colchester United have one in Eammon Collins who, say what you will, is a character and a footballer with a nack of making news.

"Welcome to the Barrow AFC Soccerline, and while there have been no games in the GMVC this week, our friends at WeightWatchers report that Barrie Stimpson has lost over half a stone in the last few days. They say that if success continues at the present rate then he can have his jaws unwired within the month. Meanwhile, Ian Burgess has gone on a diet of high protein foods and gamma rays to build his frame up to the Hulk-like proportions needed to face the average Conference full-back. That's all from us for now, but there'll be more from I Speak Their Weight on the next Soccerline!"

(Cutting from Colchester United v. Barrow programme 27.10.90.)

WHEN SATURDAY

CAME TO ALBANIA

BY CRAIG BREWIN

In March 1989 "When Saturday Comes", the half-decent football magazine, organised a coach trip to the Albania v England World Cup qualifier in Tirana. For someone like me, who has always fancied watching England play abroad, and was in desperate need of a holiday, it was a chance not to be missed. I expected the journey of a lifetime, but even I wasn't prepared for the adventure it turned out to be.

"When Saturday Comes" is a magazine, not a travel agency, and this event was a one-off, organised for specific purposes. The WSC editors figured that there was unlikely to be a large number of England fans out there, and if they took a party of their readers over it would provide an excellent opportunity to show one country at least that football supporters are, on the whole, not (as the press would have it) violent invaders set on destruction, but people just out to enjoy themselves at no-one else's expense. The publicity value back home would also give us the chance to promote the magazine and the FSA's "Say No to I.D. Cards" campaign.

We arrived in Albania a day late, just a few hours before the under-21 game kicked off in Shkoder. Getting there for this match appeared to be most people's main concern as we sped along the Yugoslavian coast road. Fortunately the game was to be played in the north of the country, so we knew that if we made it to the border by mid-morning, we would make the match. Our late arrival was due in the main to a D-registration Daf coach which broke down in both England and Yugoslavia. A lost passport lost us three hours, but this was made up for by some maniac driving by the Yugoslavian drivers of our replacement coach. Our grateful thanks were expressed in the form of a wad of notes, the size of which would have made even Harry Enfield turn green with envy (until he realised how little it was worth in sterling).

A passport wasn't the only thing left in our abandoned coach. We also left our football. We'd managed to play one game with it, against some Yugoslavs who beat us 2-1, despite the England banners draped around the small concrete pitch and the presence of an enthusiastic English crowd/substitute's bench, but what we really wanted was a game with the Albanians. It was Graham Kelly, the FA's new Chief Executive, who came to our rescue. Finding myself in a lift with him at the Hotel Tirana, I took the opportunity of asking him if he would lend us a ball. "Why are you asking me?" he said. "I believe in starting at the top," I told him. "Ask me again in the morning," he replied. I spotted Graham Kelly again after breakfast the following day, and after only the briefest of grovelling he gave me the key to his room. On his bed, atop the pennant that I assumed had been presented to England before the under-21 game, was one of the England training balls.

In the end, a game with the Albanians proved impossible, due to the celebrity status to which we were subject. Wherever we went we were waved at, and the people crowded our coach as we embarked or disembarked outside our hotel. One of my most memorable incidents, however, was the reception we received immediately after crossing the border. The last few miles of the journey to Albania involved a drive across the mountains, and along a narrow road with more twists and turns than a Peter Beardsley run at goal. On reaching the Yugoslav border we left our coach and walked to Albania, luggage in hand, like a party of refugees. After a surprisingly straightforward immigration check, it was onto our third coach (we used four in all) for the short ride to Shkoder.

As we began our first ride through the country I couldn't help feeling that the place had a South East Asian feel to it. The countryside was flat in the immediate vicinity but with a row of hills across the horizon of such even proportion that they looked as if they had been drawn by schoolchildren. Many of the fields had been flooded by the nearby lake, giving them the appearance of a paddy field, and the Asian feel was completed by the large number of bicycles, particularly in the main square of the town. It was during this part of the journey that we first encountered the warm hospitality of the Albanian people, who lined the streets as we passed by and applauded the WSC T-shirt, emblazoned with a friendly slogan translated into Albanian, which we had sellotaped to the coach window.

We did get a couple of games of football in, one on the beach, where we discovered that Earnest, one of our Albanian guides, could probably get into any team that any of us played for, and one in the Dinamo Tirana Stadium. Imagine doing what we did in London. You're on a guided sightseeing tour of the city and you pass by a major first division football ground. You demand that the coach be stopped, grab the football that you had borrowed from the England squad earlier in the day, find a way in and promptly play an impromptu match in front of a crowd of local people that seemed to be ever-increasing as the game went on.

The trip wasn't all fun and games, however, and we were reminded of the reason why there was a need for us to make this fairly well-publicised trip, after meeting a few people with IQs as low as Gary Lineker's recent England strike rate [!!! - Eds.] Albania is a fairly closed society and the Albanian authorities are fairly choosy about who they let in. Only about 12,000 visitors are allowed each year in order to prevent Albanian society being contaminated by the decadence of the west, and after meeting some of the England supporters I would not be surprised if they retained this policy a little longer.

Despite the restrictions, and despite about 20 visa applications being refused, there were about 200 England fans in Tirana for the game. Our problems were with a small group of people who described themselves as "fascists". I was told by one of them that they had "a firm" of 13 and they were going to do our lot "easy". Many of our party were given a Nazi salute every time they walked into the hotel restaurant, and others were simply abused as they walked around the hotel.

The reasons for this venom were varied, but I think that at the bottom of it lay the fact that they resented our friendly intentions towards the locals. These people follow England to cause trouble, and with the Albanians being amongst the most hospitable people on earth, we provided a more easily identifiable target. Also, it has to be said, we antagonised them. Many of our party dissociated themselves from the Nazi salutes at the under-21 match by refusing to stand for the National Anthem. Others went further by shouting them down.

The problems began with a ferocious argument in the car park at Shkoder. We met the "sieg heilers" by their coach and a small group began shouting at John Duncan, the organiser of our trip. Just because there was a difference of opinion we should not have disturbed their singing of the National Anthem, they yelled, before the sheer number of obscenities made the conversation difficult to follow. "We're fascists and you're dead, you're all dead" was the final contribution to the debate before their coach took them off to their hotel in Durres.

Things almost came to a head after all the England fans in Albania were placed in the same hotel in Tirana, the England squad conveniently making room for them by flying home. In order to avoid trouble, those of us who had decided not to spend the night in our rooms went to Tirana's other hotel for the evening. On the way in we met some of the more neanderthal elements leaving after they had forced the bar to close following a disturbance. Our party, faced with a torrent of abuse, turned and walked out. I remember one of them shouting, "we get all this from the Sun and then you people come along". Those who ran were chased, although given the size of these people it turned out to be an extremely slow chase. Curiously, those who just stood their ground were ignored as the thugs went lumbering by.

By the time the police arrived, the two groups had separated themselves and we were advised to stay in the hotel while the others were put under plainclothes observation in the Hotel Tirana Tavern. We have a lot to thank the police for, as the remainder of the evening turned into one of the most enjoyable nights I've had for ages and one that exploded a few myths about Albania. The bar, which apart from us was filled with a number of comparatively affluent Albanians, contained a band which played Albanian folk music, a peculiar type of contemporary jazz, and, after heavy pressure from the English, rock'n'roll. "Jailhouse Rock", sung in Albanian, is something that has to be experienced to be believed. The crowd went wild, as they say.

We went to the same bar the following evening, but this time Attila the Stockbroker took over the bass guitar to give the Albanians the same sort of culture shock the English had experienced the night before. We later tried translating a few Attila the Stockbroker poems into Albanian, but if you have ever heard then you will appreciate the difficulty in getting them to scan, even when translated into everyday English. This was a good night too, as the fascist element had gone home to England by then, and the remaining England fans, from all the different parties, were mixing quite freely.

Needless to say, the people under police observation the previous evening were eventually ejected from the Hotel Tirana Tavern. The incident that led to it involved one of them stripping naked in the bar. However, that may not have been the end of their activities, as I was told the next day by people who had stayed in their rooms that evening and had been disturbed by regular knocks on their hotel room doors accompanied by shouts of "Kill, kill, kill" and "we're coming in".

The attitude of the Albanian police was incredibly low-key. We discovered that we were under regular observation by plainclothes police after only a short time in the country simply by bumping into the same people at different times. I was quite surprised when, at the end of the under-21 match, an Albanian sitting among us, wearing sunglasses and a shirt and tie rather than the more uniform polo-neck sweater, politely rose and said, "I think you'll find the most convenient way out is down to the front and turn left". I did not realise the significance of this until the full international match the following day, when, having said that I didn't want any England fans I didn't know in the seats behind me, another man wearing a shirt and tie tapped me on the shoulder and said, "it's all right, we're the police". I later discovered that a plainclothes officer had been specifically placed with John Duncan for the game.

There was no trouble at the match, probably due to the overcrowding in the stadium, an early goal from England, and the fact that we had agreed to ignore the Nazi salutes. Many of the people that we had problems with did not even stay for the match. They sang the National Anthem, shouted their political slogans and then left to find a bar. The match to them was merely an opportunity to abuse the National Anthem. Given the number of visa applications refused, there must have been some form of vetting procedure, and as these people obtained visas it is not unreasonable to assume that they are not on any blacklist anywhere, nor that they have any criminal convictions. So much for Part Two of the Football Spectators Bill.

We all agreed that the FA policy of discouraging people from following England abroad is wrong. We annoyed the nutters by diluting their influence and not following their lead. When shouting down their salutes we noticed that many other people, not in our party, joined in. Even more encouraging was the fact that the fascists stopped immediately, though I think that this was as much due to surprise as anything else.

When we left the country Ari, our other guide, thanked us for visiting Albania. "You have shown us that not all English football supporters are like the nasty people," he said. It was a statement that we appreciated greatly, given the provocation that we had faced, but as Enver Hoxha, Albania's late president, once said in a book that we managed to hide from the Yugoslavs as we went through immigration: "They may intimidate us, but we frighten them".

My lasting impression of Albania is of a poor but beautiful country whose people are so friendly that it almost becomes embarrassing. Not surprisingly, we found most of the stories that we had read about Albania to be hopelessly inaccurate, although whether this was due to malice or ignorance is difficult to know. One thing that did become apparent to me, as we were shown Albania's spectacular scenery, its history and economic achievements, was the extent to which the Albanian people are, despite its poverty and anachronistic politics, proud of their country. Unlike some Englishmen, however, they didn't feel the need to beat anyone up to prove it.

CRAIG BREWIN

[Eds' note: When Graham Kelly spoke at a meeting of the London Branch of the FSA in 1990, his first words to Craig Brewin were: "Can we have our ball back?"]

Statue of the 'When Saturday Comes' mascot outside the Dinamo Stadium

Sight seeing before the big match

VIVA ALBANIA!

'I've found a way in lads'. When Saturday Comes descends on the Dinamo Stadium

The Fanzines...

Fanzine	Club	Address
The Northern Light	Aberdeen	PO Box 269, Aberdeen, AB9 8EN
Tomato Soup and Lentils	Arbroath	33 John Street, Arbroath, Tayside, DD11 1BT
The Gooner	Arsenal	BCMM Box 7499, London, WC1N 3XX
Give 'Em Beans	Barrow AFC	276A The Broadway, West Hendon, London, NW9 6AE
Cross Rhodes	Bishops Stortford	36 Wetherfield, Stanstead, Essex, CM24 8JB
From Behind Your Fences	Boston United	4 Court Farm Road, Rosehill, Oxford, OX4 4UL
Seasons Of Missed Opportunities...	Brighton	27 Brattle, Woodchurch, Nr Ashford, TN26 3SW
The Abbey Rabbit	Cambridge United	6 Harston Road, Newton, Cambs, CB2 5PA
The Cumberland Sausage	Carlisle	53 Yewdale Road, Carlisle, Cumbria, CA2 7SN
Chelsea Independent	Chelsea	PO Box 161, Harrow, Middlesex, HA2 6NZ
The Wee Red	Cliftonville	PO Box 429, Belfast, BT9 6PT
Clyde-O-Scope	Clyde	3 Station Road, Hounslow, Middlesex, TW3 2AL
So Glad You're Mine	Crystal Palace	368 Seaside, Eastbourne, East Sussex, BN22 7RY
Eagle Eye	Crystal Palace	30 Manor Court, York Way, Whetstone, N20 0DR
Come On Dagenham - Use Yer Forwards	Dagenham	10 King Edward Road, Romford, Essex, RM1 2DH
Mission Impossible	Darlington	8 Bramley Parade, Bowesfield Lane, Stockton-on-Tess, TS18 3JG
Raise The Roof	Doncaster Rovers	28 Wykegate Road, Thorne, Doncaster, DN5 6QL
Dens-Scene	Dundee	47 Malcolms Mount, Stonehaven, Kincardineshire, AB3 2S
It's Half Past Four And We're 2-0 Down	Dundee	Eassie House, Glamis, Forfar, DD8 1SG
When the Hoodoo Comes	Dundee United	29 Philips Street, Bainsford, Falkirk, FK2 7JE
The Final Hurdle	Dundee United	PO Box 91, Dundee, DD1 9DW
Away From The Numbers	East Fife	60 Rothes Road, Glenrothes, Fife, KY6 1BN
Speke From The Harbour	Everton	8 Inglewood Court, Belfast, BT41 1RY
There's Only One F in Fulham	Fulham	PO Box 154, Epsom, Surrey , KT19 9TB
Brian Moore's Head	Gillingham	11 Watts Avenue, Rochester, Kent, ME1 1RX
Follow Follow	Glasgow Rangers	PO Box 539, Glasgow, G11 7LT
Follow Your Instinct	Halesowen Town	6 Queen's Gate, Lipson, Plymouth, PL4 7PW
Crying Time Again	Hamilton	c/o The Bay Horse, 39 Bothwell Road, Hamilton, Lanarkshire
No Idle Talk	Hearts	71 Deanburn Park, Linlithgow, West Lothian, EH49 6HA
Still Musn't Grumble	Hearts	PO Box 310, Edinburgh, EH9 1BU
Hibs OK?	Hibernian	1/L 68 Kelvin Drive, Maryhill, Glasgow, G20 8QN
From Hull To Eternity	Hull City	Spring House, Seaside Road, Easington, HU12 OTY
Dribble!	Ipswich	63 Woodbridge Road, Ipswich, Suffolk,
Those Were The Days	Ipswich	46 Smarts Green, Cheshunt, Herts, EN7 6BA
The Mad Axeman	Lancaster City	10 Yealand Drive, Lancaster, LA1 4EW
Just A Quick Word Lads Please	Leeds	67 Selly Hill Road, Selly Oak, Birmingham, B29 7DL
The Hanging Sheep	Leeds	41 Woodhall Terrace, Thornbury, Bradford, BD3 7BZ
Deranged Ferret	Lincoln City	30 Church Meadow, Alpington, Norwich, NR14 7NY
One Minute To Go	Liverpool	89 Buckingham Road, Maghull, Liverpool, L31 7DW
When Sunday Comes	Liverpool	2 Maybury Court, Shaftesbury Road, Woking, GU22 7DT
Mad As A Hatter	Luton	30 Linden Road, Dunstable, Beds, LU6 4NZ
Electric Blue	Manchester City	8 Pentwyn Grove, Wythenshawe, Manchester , M23
King Of The Kippax	Manchester City	26 Holdenbrook Close, Leigh, Greater Manchester, WN7 2HL
United We Stand	Manchester United	8 Hartland Avenue, Urmston, Manchester, M31 1PG
Size 10 ½ Boots	Mansfield	10 Dollis Avenue, Finchley, London, N3 1TX
Follow The Yellow Brick Road	Mansfield	73 Rowan Drive, Kirkby-in-Ashfield, Notts, NG17 8FP
Alternative Mansfield Matters	Mansfield	29 Ladybank Road, Mickleover, Derbyshire, DB3 5PF
John Wickens - On the Wagon	Margate	30 Stirling Way, Ramsgate, Kent, CT12 6NA
Roll On 4.40	Meadowbank	63 Ambrose Drive, Dedridge, Livingston, EH54 6JT
Fly Me To The Moon	Middlesborough	14 Selkirk Close, Saltersgill, Middlesborough
Treble Chance	Morton	6 Dunrobin Drive, Gourock, PA19 1EB
Never Say Dai	Newport AFC	11 Augustan Drive, Caerleon, Gwent, NP6 1DD
Resign Roberts Re-sign	Northwich	488 London Road, Davenham, Northwich, CW9 8HW
Spud International	Norwich	17 St Mary's Close, Attleborough, Norfolk , NR17 2ED
Never Mind The Danger	Norwich	4 Cecil Gowing Court , Sprowston, Norwich, NR7 8NA
The Tricky Tree	Nottingham Forest	149 Blake Road, West Bridgford, Nottingham, NG2 5LA
The Thin Yellow Stripe	Notts County	2 Norbett Road, Arnold, Notts, NG5 8EB
Flickin' 'n' Kickin'	Notts County	7 Loughborough Road, Burton-on-the-Wolds, Loughborough, LE12 5AF
The Johnny Flood Experience	Partick Thistle	48 Windyedge Crescent, Glasgow, G13 1YF
Fulton 1-0	Pollok	PO Box 575, Glasgow, G11 7HQ
Frattonise	Portsmouth	PO Box 122, Southsea, PO4 9UL
In The Loft	QPR	24 Woodham Road, Catford, London, SE6 2SD
Windy And Dusty	Rotherham	16 South Way, North Harrow, Middlesex
Scarborough Warning	Scarborough	'Lagniappe', 1B Stepney Drive, Scarborough, YO12 5DP
Southender	South Liverpool	1 Adstone Road, Bellvale, Liverpool, L25
On The March	Southampton	Flat 10B Godfrey Olson House, Yonge Close, Eastleigh, SO5 4ST
Jackmail	Swansea	PO Box 24, Port Talbot, West Glamorgan, SA12 1QN
Nobody Will Ever Know	Swansea	219 Portland Place, South Tottenham, London, N16 4SZ
My Eyes Have Seen The Glory	Tottenham	PO Box 844, London , E164HE
Three Men In A Boat	Tranmere Rovers	PO Box 6 , Hoylake, Wirral, L47 0NP
Mud Sweat And Beers	Watford	PO Box 436, Hemel Hempstead, Herts, HP3 8UF
Grorty Dick	WBA	7 Ruth Close, Tipton, Staffs, DY4 0AR
There's Only One Mark Dziadulewicz	Wimbledon	58 Foxborough Gardens, Crofton Park, London, SE4 1HX
Go Joe Go!	Wimbledon	Flat 3 , 43 Gwendolen Avenue, Putney, SW15 6EP
Yidaho!	Wimbledon	29 Coniston Drive, Reading, Berks, RG3 6XS
A Load Of Bull	Wolves	PO Box 277, 52 Call Lane, Leeds, LS1 6DT
The Sheeping Giant	Wrexham	'Tarren', Llangedwyn, Nr Oswestry, SY10 9LT
Football Utopia	General	Spring Place, St Aubyns Close, Orpington, BR6 0SN
The Expression She Pulled	General	120 Greenhill Road, Bramley , Leeds
Each Game As It Comes	General	79 Harlow Crescent, Harrogate, North Yorks, HG2 0AL
The Absolute Game	General	PO Box 303, Southern D.O., Edinburgh, EH9 1NE
The Jolly Green Giant...	General	4 Greylag Close, Beechwood, Runcorn, WA7 3JS
Five To Three	General	PO Box 10, Pwllheli, Gwynedd, LL53 5BE
Start!	General	36 Hazelmere Road, St Albans, Herts, AL4 9RN
Elfmeter	General	16 Mallory Road, Perton, Staffs, WV6 7XN
Let's Get Talking	General	41 Lockington Avenue, Hartley, Plymouth, PL3 5QG
The Globe	General	PO Box 395, Cambridge, CB1 3LT
From Home To Home		

Also
Maybe It's Because, Off The Ball, From Casuals To Cup Winners, The Lad Done Brilliant

Whoever You Support
We Support You

The Football Supporters Association (FSA) was established in the mid 1980's in order to campaign for more supporter involvement in the running of football.

It now has many branches throughout England, Scotland and Wales and has had considerable success in changing the relationship between football supporters and the authorities.

Major successes include the Taylor Inquiry, which after being persauded to allow the FSA to become the first supporters organisation to be represented at a major inquiry into football, condemned 'squalid' football grounds and recommended a massive investment in facilities.

The FSA also gave evidence to Parliaments Home Affairs Committee which then produced a report stating that supporters should no longer be treated as 'fodder for exploitation'.

During the last World Cup in Italy the FSA organised an 'embassy' which sought to enhance the image of British Football Supporters abroad and provide travel and accommodation services. Two thirds of English supporters used this service.

The FSA has also organised a whole series of campaigns around issues large and small. The most prominent of these was the campaign against compulsory identity card which involved the collection of 250,000 signatures.

There is still much to do. The FSA meets regularly with Police, the FA's and Leagues, the Government and the two bodies doing most to change the way in which we watch football - The Football Licensing Authority and The Football Stadia Advisory Council.

The FSA is an entirely voluntary organisation. Members get an irregular magazine - The Football Supporter - posted free every now and then, local newsletters and access to branch meetings where you get to influence our policy and question some of the more influential figures in the game.

Unlike the traditional supporters club, membership of the FSA is based on where you live rather than who you support. Therefore each branch comprises fans of many clubs, a structure ensuring that parochial loyalties do not undermine the organisation's effectiveness and credibility.

Annual membership is £6 (£3 for OAP's and under 16's, unemployed and students). Also available for an extra £2.50 (inc P+P) is a 1992 Supporters Diary which includes all league fixture lists for 91/92 season.

If you are concerned about all-seater stadia and the super league then you should join the FSA now.

Just complete the form below and send to FSA, PO Box 11, Liverpool, L26 1XP.

FSA MEMBERSHIP APPLICATION	TEAM SUPPORTED		
	AGE : UNDER 16	16-21	Over 21
(If renewal quote membership number)	SEX : MALE/FEMALE		
Please print clearly	DISABLED: NO/YES (sight,hearing,physical)		
SURNAME	Membership (12 months) - £6.00		
FORENAME(S)	Under 16, Students, Unwaged £3.00		
ADDRESS	Europe - £7.00 Overseas - £12		
	Enclose cheque/postal order, send to :		
POSTCODE	FSA, PO BOX 11		
TEL: (inc STD)	LIVERPOOL, L26 1XP		

Acknowledgements

Tony, Perry, Brian and Sue would like to extend their warmest thanks to the following people :

Tim Barnett of Fleetway Publications (Roy of the Rovers)
Chris Donald of House of Viz (Billy the Fish)
Tom Pendry MP
Colorsport
Bromley Clarke and everyone from ARMS
Martin Lacey of Juma
Peter Creasy, Roberta Pearce, Craig Brewin,
Bill McComish, Steve Beauchampe, Debbie Smith
Jackie Mayes, Michelle and David Melkman
Dick and Margaret Baughen,
and finally,
Bill the SW19 Postman.

Most of all we would like to thank all the fanzine editors
and contributors who supplied material for this
compilation, without whom nothing would have been
possible.

Printed by : Juma, Trafalgar Works, 44 Wellington Street, Sheffield

Football Against Multiple Sclerosis

The footballing world is joining forces for the biggest charity initiative in the history of the game. "Football Against MS", aims to raise £3.5 Million in support for Action and Research for Multiple Sclerosis and will involve everybody at all levels within the game.

Football Against MS already has the support of League clubs in England, Scotland and Wales, the governing bodies, and supporters groups within the game. It will encompass numerous events taking place between September 1991 and May 1992.

The focal point will be three simultaneous walks visiting every League club, plus some non-league clubs along the way in England, Scotland and Wales Players, staff and celebrities will walk between each club ground and supporters will be encouraged to raise money and walk with them.

Starting on 12th January, two of the walks will finish at Wembley Stadium during half time of the FA Cup Final, and the third will finish in Glasgow on Scottish FA Cup Final day.

The week 25th April to 2nd May has been designated "Football Against MS Week" when football orientated events will take place all over the country to raise funds for the cause.

Amongst the many things being done for FAMS are : A Balloon Race Competition attempt at the World record of 2.17 Million balloons released, National under 14 5-a-side competition with the finals at Wembley before the FA Cup Final, a woman's 5-a-side tournament, Two books - "The Match Of My Life" and a fanzine compilation by the Football Supporters Association called "It's Twelve Inches High... And It's Made of Solid Gold", Veteran matches where supporters will have the chance to play the "old" team of the club they support, collections, competitions and auctions of football memorabilia.

As well as helping ARMS the event will also put a substantial amount of money back into the game at all levels.

Multiple Sclerosis affects an estimated 100,000 people in Britain. It is a progressive disease with no known cause or cure.

Action and Research for Multiple Sclerosis (ARMS) will use the money raised from "Football Against MS" to further research and assist with the practical management of the condition.

The FSA urge you to support this event and to get involved as much as you can.

Multiple Sclerosis can affect anybody - it is not hereditary. It can strike at anytime. It could affect someone you know - tomorrow

For further information contact ARMS at 4a Chapel Hill, Stansted, Essex or watch out for details that will appear just about everywhere.

ARMS Registered Charity number 268899   **Registered Company number 1196338**